# THE CATHARS

# THE MEDIEVAL WORLD

*Editor: David Bates*

# THE CATHARS

## Dualist Heretics in Languedoc in the High Middle Ages

### MALCOLM BARBER

*An imprint of* **Pearson Education**

Harlow, England · London · New York · Reading, Massachusetts · San Francisco
Toronto · Don Mills, Ontario · Sydney · Tokyo · Singapore · Hong Kong · Seoul
Taipei · Cape Town · Madrid · Mexico City · Amsterdam · Munich · Paris · Milan

**Pearson Education Limited**
Edinburgh Gate
Harlow
Essex CM20 2JE
England

and Associated Companies throughout the world

*Visit us on the world wide web at:*
http://www.pearsoneduc.com

First published 2000

© Pearson Education Limited 2000

ISBN 0 582 25662 3 (CSD)
ISBN 0 582 25661 5 (PPR)

**British Library Cataloguing in Publication Data**
A catalogue record for this book is available from the British Library

**Library of Congress Cataloging-in-Publication Data**
Barber, Malcolm.
    The Cathars / Malcolm Barber.
      p.  cm. — (The medieval world)
    Includes bibliographical references and index.
    ISBN 0-582-25662-3 (hardcover : alk. paper) — ISBN 0-582-25661-5 (pbk. : alk. paper)
    1. Albigenses—France—Languedoc—History.   2. Languedoc (France)—Church
history.  I. Title.  II. Series.

BX4891.2.B37   2000
273′.6—dc21                                  00-022125

Typeset by 35 in 11/13pt Baskerville MT
Produced by Pearson Education Asia Pte Ltd.
Printed in Singapore (MPM)

10 9 8 7 6 5
05 04 03 02

To Paddy McNulty and Jim Holt

# CONTENTS

# TABLES, MAPS AND ILLUSTRATIONS

# EDITOR'S PREFACE

The spread of Catharism in Western Europe in the twelfth century is one of the most fascinating and significant episodes in the history of medieval Europe. Although heresies of various kinds were a consistent feature of the history of the Byzantine Empire throughout the Middle Ages, Catharism was the first organised and theologically coherent heresy to develop in Western Europe since the time of the Late Roman Empire. The seemingly monolithic Catholic Church, the papacy and its priesthood, were challenged in ways which were novel and very threatening. After initial attempts at debate and persuasion, their reaction ultimately took the forms of violence and persecution. The development of techniques of institutionalised repression associated with the Inquisition shaped many aspects of the history of the succeeding centuries.

Although the heretical movements of the twelfth and thirteenth centuries were geographically widespread – there was even an outbreak in England – they became most deeply entrenched in northern Italy and south-western France. In the midst of the extensive literature on medieval heresy published since the great upsurge of interest in the 1960s, no accessible book for the student and general reader has ever been devoted specifically to Languedoc, the region where Catharism undoubtedly left its deepest imprint, and which is to this day most closely associated with it. This book is therefore a very welcome addition to *The Medieval World* series. The history of Catharism is a complex phenomenon, whose development and decline requires familiarity with, among other things, Catholic and Cathar theology, the peculiarities of Occitan society, the Crusades and the procedures of the Inquisition. Professor Barber's book covers all these themes, moving forward from a thorough analysis of the relationship between Languedocian Catharism to eastern European heresies to the place of Catharism in south-western French society and the organisation of the Cathar Church. Extensive quotations from contemporary sources are inserted at key moments in the text. While the book's core is beyond doubt the central chapters devoted to the Cathar Church, the Catholic reaction and Catharism's decline, Professor Barber adds a very illuminating final chapter on the twentieth-century idealisation of the Cathars and their exploitation by the tourist industry.

Malcolm Barber is not only a scholar who has written extensively on the Cathars and Catharism, but also one with an exceptionally wide interest in many aspects of the medieval Church and its institutions as well as the general history of medieval Europe. As a result, he writes with vigour and authority, not just about Catharism and the society of south-western France, but about matters such as the canon law background to persecution, evolving papal authority, the violence and strategy of the Albigensian Crusade and the rigour of the Inquisition. This is another excellent addition to *The Medieval World* series.

David Bates

# AUTHOR'S PREFACE

I came to the Cathars through the study of the Templars. Both were brought before papal inquisitors, and both disappeared, at least partially through inquisitorial efforts, although it took a great deal longer to suppress the former than the latter. The major difference was that many of those accused of the various forms of dualist heresy known as Catharism were prepared to die for their beliefs, whereas the Templars were quite horrified by the charges laid against them and made every effort to avoid going to the stake. Romantics like to see connections between the two, but there were none: no fabulous treasure passed on to the Templars after the fall of the Cathar fortress of Montségur in 1244, no shared anti-Christian beliefs pervaded by esoteric eastern cults, no Grail hidden in a mountain cave on behalf of a secret alliance. Inevitably, some of the accusations against the Templars derive from those against the Cathars – they were, after all, embedded in the minds of those who pursued dissent – but the interest lies not in a fruitless search for a non-existent conspiracy, but in comparison between the ways these two central elements of thirteenth-century life both succumbed to the power of an establishment determined to put an end to them.

I am deeply indebted to many friends and colleagues for their help and advice. This generosity remains an integral part of the academic world, and I doubt if there has been a single decent historical work published which has not benefited in this way. Two long-standing friends, Bernard Hamilton and Paddy McNulty, read the typescript; Claire Dutton, Ann Peal, Mark Pegg, and Andrew Roach allowed me to plunder their excellent theses; Michael and William Sibly provided me with a copy of their translation of the chronicle of Peter of Les Vaux-de-Cernay long before it was published; Karen Carroll of the National Humanities Center, North Carolina, edited the typescript and deciphered my degenerate handwriting. Many others helped in a wide variety of ways, including Tom Asbridge, Craig Atwood, Elizabeth Barber, David Bates, Anne Curry, Peter Kaufman, Bob Kendrick, Linda Paterson, Walter Wakefield, and Joe Wittig. I owe particular thanks to the Library staff of Reading University and the National Humanities Center. The final result, however, with all its imperfections, is the author's responsibility, but would not have been possible without the time to pursue research. I am therefore very grateful to the Leverhulme Trust, the National Humanities Center, and the Lilly Foundation, the first for a grant to help cover teaching costs, the second and third for the award of a Fellowship which allowed me to spend the academic year, 1998–99, in the privileged environment of the NHC, a truly civilised institution.

Malcolm Barber

# Acknowledgements

We are grateful to the following for permission to reproduce copyright material:

Ashgate Publishing Ltd for extracts from *The Song of the Cathar Wars, A History of the Albigensian Crusade, William of Tuleda and an Anonymous Successor* by J. Shirley (1996); Boydell and Brewer Ltd for extracts from *Peter of Les-Vaux-de-Cernay, The History of the Albigensian Crusade* by W. A. Sibly and M. D. Sibly (1998); Centre d'Etudes Historiques de Fanjeaux for Plate 3 and Plate 8 from 'Vulgarisation et Récupération: Le Catharisme à Travers les Mass-Media' by C.-O. Carbonell, *Cahiers de Fanjeaux*, 14 (1979); Columbia University Press for extracts from *Heretics of the High Middle Ages* by W. Wakefield and A. Evans; Manchester University Press for extracts from *Christian Dualist Heresies in the Byzantine World* by J. Hamilton and B. Hamilton (1998), reproduced by permission.

While every effort has been made to trace the owners of copyright material, in a few cases this has proved impossible and we take this opportunity to offer our apologies to any copyright holders whose rights we have unwittingly infringed.

# ABBREVIATIONS

*CEI* J. Berlioz and J.-C. Hélas, eds, *Catharisme: l'édifice imaginaire.*
*Actes du 7e colloque du Centre d'Études Cathares/René Nelli,*
*Carcassonne, 29 août–2 septembre 1994* (Carcassonne, 1998).

*CF* *Cahiers de Fanjeaux.*

*Chanson* *La Chanson de la croisade contre les Albigeois*, ed. and trans.,
E. Martin-Chabot, 3 vols (Les Classiques de l'Histoire de
France au Moyen Age) (Paris, 1931, 1957, 1961). English
trans. J. Shirley, *The Song of the Cathar Wars. A History of the
Albigensian Crusade. William of Tudela and an Anonymous Successor*
(Aldershot, 1996).

Doat Paris, Bibliothèque Nationale, *Fonds Doat*, vols 21–7.

*Heresis* *Heresis. Revue d'hérésologie médiévale. Centre d'Études Cathares/René
Nelli.* Since 1983.

*HGL* C. Devic and J. Vaissète, eds, *Histoire générale de Languedoc*,
ed. A. Molinier, vol. 8 (Toulouse, 1879) (reprint Osnabruck,
1973).

HH J. Hamilton and B. Hamilton, ed. and trans., *Christian
Dualist Heresies in the Byzantine World c. 650–c. 1450*, with the
assistance of Y. Stoyanov (Manchester Medieval Sources)
(Manchester, 1998).

*MGH* *Monumenta Germanica Historica. Scriptores.*

Pelhisson *Chronique de Guillaume Pelhisson (1229–1244), suivie du récit des
troubles d'Albi (1234)*, ed. and trans., J. Duvernoy (Paris, 1994).
English trans. W. L. Wakefield, *Heresy, Crusade and Inquisition
in Southern France, 1100–1250* (London, 1974).

*PL* J. P. Migne, ed., *Patrologiae cursus completus. Series Latina*,
vols 181, 182, 185, 189, 195, 204, 210, 211, 214, 215, 216.

PVC P. Guébin and E. Lyon, eds, *Petri Vallium Sarnaci Monachi
Hystoria Albigensis*, 3 vols (Paris, 1926, 1930, 1939). French
trans. P. Guébin and H. Maisonneuve, *Histoire albigeoise*
(Paris, 1951). English trans. W. A. Sibly and M. D. Sibly,
Peter of Les Vaux-de-Cernay, *The History of the Albigensian
Crusade* (Woodbridge, 1998).

| | |
|---|---|
| *RF* | J. Duvernoy, ed., *Le Registre d'inquisition de Jacques Fournier, évêque de Pamiers (1318–1325)*, 3 vols (Toulouse, 1965). French trans. J. Duvernoy, 3 vols (Paris, 1977–78). |
| *RHG* | *Recueil des Historiens de Gaul et de France.* |
| *RIS* | *Rerum Italicarum Scriptores.* |
| WE | W. L. Wakefield and A. P. Evans, trans., *Heresies of the High Middle Ages. Selected Sources* (New York and London, 1969). |
| WP | J. Duvernoy, ed. and trans., *Chronica Magistri Guillelmi de Podio Laurentii* (Paris, 1976). |
| WT | William of Tudela (see *Chanson*, of which William is the author of the first part). |

# INTRODUCTION

Catharism was the greatest heretical challenge faced by the Catholic Church in the twelfth and thirteenth centuries. The attempt by the Cathars to find an answer to the fundamental religious and philosophical problems posed by the existence of evil, combined with their success in persuading large numbers of Christians in the West that they had solved these problems, shook the Catholic hierarchy to its very core, and provoked a series of reactions more extreme than any previously contemplated.

The Cathars would not accept that an omnipotent and eternal God could have been responsible for the material world; for them, this world was the work of an evil creator. Such a creator was either a being fallen from the perfection of Heaven who had seduced a proportion of the angelic souls there and then entrapped them in matter, or he was a co-eternal power, quite independent of the Good God of the Spirit. The only release for those souls encased in the material prison of the body was through the Cathar ceremony of the *consolamentum*, which was the means by which they could return to their guardian spirits in Heaven. The Cathar Church was organised into dioceses, whose bishops presided over an order of succession consisting of elder and younger 'sons', deacons, and *perfecti* and *perfectae*, equivalent to ministers of the Church. Most of the lay supporters of the Cathar Church, known as *credentes*, took the *consolamentum* when near death, for the ascetic rigours of the life of the *perfecti* were too great for most people to be able to sustain. There would be no arbitrary Last Judgement; the world would end when the last of the angelic souls had been released, thus once more disentangling the spiritual and material worlds. Given the imperfections of most people's lives this process would not necessarily be completed rapidly, for some souls would need to transmigrate through a variety of material vessels (including animals) before entering the body of a person who understood the importance of the *consolamentum*.

Catharism represented total opposition to the Catholic Church, which was viewed by the Cathars as a false and fraudulent organisation which had prostituted itself for power and ill-gotten wealth. The sacraments through which the Catholic Church claimed to open the way to salvation were quite valueless, since they were founded upon the claim that Christ really had lived

1

on earth, had been crucified, and then resurrected, events clearly impossible, since God could not have taken on material form in the first place. For Catholics therefore, there could be no compromise with the Cathars, manifestly working to subvert the faithful at the behest of the Devil; it was the responsibility of all Catholic leaders, ecclesiastical and lay, to strive to overcome this heresy with all the strength at their command. This would have been true at any point in the history of the Latin Church, but it was particularly pertinent to the reformed papacy which, since the 1050s, had been working to reassert its leadership of the universal Church. By this means it was attempting to infuse both clergy and laity with a new set of moral values. Repression of Catharism was not therefore a question of choice, nor was there any option of toleration, for it was a positive obligation upon those charged by God to lead His Church on earth. The principal weight of this obligation naturally fell upon the pope, as the holder of the see of Saint Peter, first of the Apostles and the rock upon which Christ's Church had been founded.

The origins of Catharism remain controversial. Most historians accept that the dualist Bogomil Church, established in parts of Macedonia and Bulgaria from at least the 930s, played a role in the formation of western Catharism, although tracing possible links with earlier dualistic religions such as Paulicianism, and beyond that to the Manicheans and the Gnostics, remains a virtually impossible task. The most important means of transmission to the West seems to have been through Thrace and Constantinople, although it is unlikely that this was the work of any single individual or group or that dualistic belief spread to the West by only one route. Indeed, by the mid-twelfth century there are signs of this heresy in several areas, in particular the Rhine Valley, the Champagne region, the plains of Lombardy, and the mountains, hills and river valleys of western Languedoc. There is, though, little agreement on the extent and importance of Bogomil influence, and still less on the chronology of its spread. Evidence for the presence of Cathar adherents in the Rhineland can certainly be found in the 1140s, but some historians remain convinced that forms of proto-Catharism can be discerned possibly as early as the first half of the eleventh century. Whatever its origin, initially the predominant manifestation of this belief in the West took the form of mitigated or moderate dualism, which is based on the idea of some kind of fall from grace by the Devil, rather than absolute dualism, which claimed the existence of two quite independent and co-eternal powers. However, by the late twelfth century, most of the Cathars of Languedoc and some of those of northern Italy had been converted to absolute dualism, probably by the Greek Nicetas, who reorganised the Cathar Church at St Félix-de-Caraman, a bourg situated about half-way between Toulouse and Carcassonne, where the Cathars held a council either in 1167 or in the mid-1170s.

By this time the papacy and many leading members of the Catholic hierarchy had become convinced that Catharism represented a dire threat to orthodoxy. Their fears were not allayed by the failure of missions sent to convince the Cathars of their errors, and by the evident futility of condemnations at Church councils like that of the Third Lateran in 1179. The accession of the dynamic Pope Innocent III in 1198 brought matters to a head. Although he never entirely lost faith in the power of persuasion, he became convinced that he would have to use force in the form of a crusade if the problem was not to become insoluble. In 1208, following the murder of the papal legate, Peter of Castelnau, by a vassal of Count Raymond VI of Toulouse, he called upon the faithful to assemble in order to crush the heresy in Languedoc, offering full remission of sins to those who would take part. Although he was unable to convince King Philip II of France that participation was in his best interests, for this most pragmatic of Capetian rulers remained deeply involved in his uncompromising conflict with the Angevin, King John of England, he did inspire two powerful northern armies to descend upon Languedoc in 1209. The more important of these attacked Béziers from the east, having travelled down the Rhône valley and, following the capture of the city and the massacre of a large proportion of its population, went on to force the submission of Carcassonne and its lord, Raymond Roger Trencavel. The leading lay power of the region, Raymond VI of Toulouse (died 1222), had temporarily avoided the consequences of the previous laxity of his father and himself towards heresy by joining the crusade at the last moment. It was a short respite. In late August 1209, Simon of Montfort, an important baron from the western region of the Ile-de-France, was chosen as the leader of the crusade, and from then until his death in June 1218, while besieging Toulouse, he waged a relentless war on the heretics and those whom he perceived to be *fautors* or protectors of heresy. During that time he came into conflict with all those lay powers with interests in western Languedoc, most spectacularly with Peter II, King of Aragon, whom he defeated and killed at the battle of Muret (south-west of Toulouse) in September 1213.

Papal control over these events was quite limited. Assailed by special interests, which included his own legates on the one hand and the secular powers of Languedoc on the other, Innocent III became increasingly uneasy about the course of the crusade. At the Fourth Lateran Council, held in November 1215, he determined to protect the interests of Raymond VI's son, the future Raymond VII, on the grounds that he bore no responsibility for the situation, and he therefore reserved to him the Provençal lands of the house of Toulouse. This proved to be the catalyst for a southern revival for, while the younger Raymond attacked Beaucaire, his father re-invaded his Toulousan lands, inciting revolt in his principal city at the same time.

This resistance gathered strength after Simon of Montfort's death and was only finally extinguished by the crusade of King Louis VIII (1223–26) and the occupation of royal troops which followed. In April 1229, Raymond VII had no alternative but to accept the harsh terms of the Treaty of Paris under which he was left with only a small proportion of his Toulousan lands. Most importantly, his daughter, Jeanne, was to marry one of King Louis IX's brothers, and their offspring would succeed to the inheritance of the house of Toulouse.

Despite the reluctance of Philip II to become involved, the chief beneficiary of the Albigensian Crusades had evidently been the Capetian monarchy, now politically dominant in Languedoc in a manner quite unthinkable only a generation before. Yet the problem of heresy remained, albeit displayed less overtly than in the days before the crusades. These were the circumstances which led Pope Gregory IX to designate specialist inquisitors, whose sole purpose was to investigate heresy on a systematic basis, probing the façade of opposition in community after community until fissures were opened up to reveal the heretics and those who had helped them. From the early 1230s until the demise of Catharism in Languedoc a century later, the persistence, courage and, occasionally, corruption of the inquisitors, played a major role in uncovering and eliminating the followers of Catharism. During this time they suffered many vicissitudes – in May 1242, for example, two inquisitors and their staff were murdered while they were staying overnight at the village of Avignonet – but in general they operated in a far more favourable political environment than those clergy who had tried to combat heresy in the pre-crusade days. Ultimately, a combination of political change and inquisitorial determination, helped by a developing economy, ground down the Cathar Church in Languedoc. It was no longer possible for the Cathar leadership either to organise itself effectively or maintain its ideological coherence when survival became the chief priority; when their last important refuge in the Pyrenees, the castle of Montségur, fell to royal forces in March 1244, the elimination of the Cathar Church as a coherent force was no longer in doubt. In the second half of the thirteenth century, isolated *perfecti* continued to operate but, after Montségur, adherents of the Cathars usually had to look towards northern Italy, where many of the heretical leaders had taken refuge, if they were to find spiritual comfort or receive the *consolamentum*.

Catharism was not easily overcome. Even after the defeats of the thirteenth century, it was still possible for two notaries from Ax on the western edge of the Sault Plateau in the central Pyrenees to organise a limited revival in the early 1300s. Peter and William Autier spent at least two years in Lombardy studying with the Italian Cathars as well as with their own compatriots in exile, before returning home and, at great personal risk, attempting to spread the Cathar belief once again. Although restricted in geographical extent, this revival was sufficiently strong for the inquisitors (now better organised and more institutionally consistent than ever before) to feel it necessary to engage in an all-out drive to bring it to an end. Peter Autier himself was executed in April 1310, although the traces of his influence can still be found in the 1320s. William Belibaste, the last surviving *perfectus* from the Autier period, was eventually caught and burnt to death in 1321.

No longer a living force in the Latin West after *c.* 1330, nevertheless, the resonances of the Cathar era can still be felt today. Catharism was no minor deviation from orthodoxy; on the contrary, it presented itself as the only true Christian community in a corrupt world dominated by a mendacious Catholic Church. Even the most cautious historians accept that it had a continuous impact in the Latin West for nearly two centuries between the 1140s and the 1320s, while some argue that its effects were felt well before this time, possibly as early as *c.* 1000. Not surprisingly, others have been attracted to it since, all with different motives. Among these have been Protestants seeking a provenance with which to counter the Catholic charge of innovation; southern patriots railing against north French domination; romantics lamenting the loss of a cultured civilisation; and commercial interests from local *maires* to exploitative publishers and authors who see the opportunity to profit from the religion of anti-materialism. Even more than most historical subjects, the Cathars are viewed today through the many-layered filters of the more recent past.

CHAPTER ONE

# The Spread of Catharism

## Dualism

Of course you all know how this heresy – God send his curse on it! –
became so strong that it gained control of the whole of the Albigeois, of
the Carcassès and most of the Lauragais. All the way from Béziers to
Bordeaux many, or indeed, most people believed in or supported it. When
the lord pope and the other clergy saw this lunacy spreading so much
faster than before and tightening its grip every day, each of them in his
own jurisdiction sent out preachers. The Cistercian order led the campaign
and time and again it sent out its own men. Next the bishop of Osma
arranged a meeting between himself and other legates with these Bulgars
at Carcassonne. This was very well attended, and the king of Aragon and
his nobles were present. Once the king had heard the speakers and
discovered how heretical they were, he withdrew, and sent a letter
about this to Rome in Lombardy.

God grant me his blessing, what shall I say? They think more of a
rotten apple than of sermons, and went on just the same for about five
years. These lost fools refused to repent, so that many were killed, many
people perished, and still more will die before the fighting ends. It cannot
be otherwise.[1]

This is part of the introduction of an extended poem, written in Provençal,
the first third of which is by William of Tudela, who describes himself as a
'clerk in holy orders'. He was originally from Tudela in Navarre, and the
poem covers the period just before and during the Albigensian Crusade,

---

1 *Chanson*, vol. 1, laisse 2, pp.8–11; trans., Shirley, pp.11–12.

between 1204 and 1218. He is a generally reliable source, pro-crusader in approach, but with an awareness of the suffering of the victims of the crusade as well.

The cursed heresy is Catharism and the early thirteenth-century followers in the region to which William refers believed in a version of it known as absolute dualism. According to the *De heresi catharorum*, written by an anonymous but knowledgeable Lombard, perhaps towards the end of the twelfth century, this party of Cathars 'believe and preach that there are two gods or lords without beginning and without end, one good, the other wholly evil. And they say that each created angels: the good God good angels and the evil one evil ones, and that the good God is almighty in the heavenly home, and the evil one rules in all this worldly structure'. Lucifer is the son of this god of darkness and he ascended to heaven, where 'he transfigured himself into an angel of light', and persuaded the angels to intercede with God on his behalf and have him appointed steward of the angels. In this capacity he seduced some of the angels and, in the great battle which followed, they were expelled from Heaven with Lucifer. The angels were made up of body, soul, and spirit and 'the souls were seized by Lucifer and were put into the bodies in this world'. Christ, the Son of God, 'came to save only these souls'. 'They explain that human bodies are in part animated by those evil spirits whom the devil created and in part by those souls that fell. Those souls do penance in these bodies and, if not saved in one body, a soul goes into another body and does penance.'[2]

The Cathars of Languedoc had followed these doctrines since the assembly of a council at the village of St Félix-de-Caraman, situated about halfway between Toulouse and Carcassonne, which was held either in 1167 or a few years later, sometime between 1174 and 1177.[3] It had been attended

---

2  *De heresi catharorum in Lombardia*, in A. Dondaine, 'La Hiérarchie cathare en Italie', I,
   *Archivum fratrum praedicatorum* 19 (1949), pp.309–10; trans. WE, no. 23, pp.164–5.

3  The dating, purpose, and even the existence of this council remain the subject of intense
   debate among historians. The date is traditionally given as 1167, derived from documents
   describing the assembly published by Guillaume Besse in 1660, documents which
   themselves have sometimes been challenged as forgeries, since Besse's original manuscript
   has not been found. There are two fundamental articles on the subject: A. Dondaine,
   'Les Actes du concile albigeois de Saint-Félix de Caraman. Essai de critique d'authenticité
   d'un document médiéval', in *Miscellanea Giovanni Mercati*, vol. 5 (Studi e testi, 125) (Città
   del Vaticano, 1946), pp.324–55, and B. Hamilton, 'The Cathar Council of Saint-Félix
   reconsidered', *Archivum Fratrum Praedicatorum* 48 (1978), pp.23–53. Dondaine persuaded
   most historians that the documents were genuine, while Hamilton argues that the council
   probably took place between 1174 and 1177. Integral to both articles is the view that
   Nicetas's mission was threefold: to reconsecrate the leading Cathars in the West, to establish
   a set of bishoprics through which the message of the Cathar Church could best be conveyed,
   and to convert the westerners from mitigated to absolute dualism. However, as Hamilton
   admits, the last of these matters is 'nowhere explicitly stated in the document' (p.29) and,

by leading Cathars from both 'France', that is the lands north of the Loire, and Languedoc, who had been converted by Nicetas, bishop of the Bogomil Church of Constantinople, from their belief in moderate or mitigated dualism. These moderate dualist Cathars, says the author of *De heresi catharorum*,

> believe in and preach one only good God, almighty, without beginning, who created angels and the four elements. They assert that Lucifer and his accomplices sinned in heaven, but some among them are uncertain as to how their sin arose. Some, indeed, hold – but it is a secret – that there was a certain evil spirit having four faces: one of a man, the second of a bird, the third of a fish, and the fourth of a beast. It had no beginning and remained in this chaos, having no power of creation.

Lucifer came down and was led astray by this evil spirit and when he returned to heaven seduced others.

> They were cast out of heaven but did not lose the natural abilities which they possessed. These heretics assert that Lucifer and the other evil spirit wished to separate the elements, but could not. Thereupon, they begged from God a good angel as an assistant, and thus with God's acquiescence, with the aid of this good angel, and by his strength and wisdom, they separated the elements. And, they say, Lucifer is the God who, in Genesis, is said to have created heaven and earth and to have accomplished this work in six days.[4]

---

for this reason, two leading French Cathar historians, Jean Duvernoy, *Le Catharisme*, vol. 1, *La Religion des Cathares* (Toulouse, 1976), pp.105–7, and Anne Brenon, *Le Vrai Visage du Catharisme*, 2nd edn (Portet-sur-Garonne, 1995), pp.109, 122–28, supported by the English historian, Janet Nelson, 'Religion in "*Histoire Totale*": some recent works on medieval heresy and popular religion', *Religion* 10 (1980), pp.68–9, have insisted that Nicetas was concerned solely with organisational matters and not with belief. Subsequent disputes among the Cathars in the West, especially in Italy, arose from doubts about the probity of some of those responsible for the consecrations of bishops, not from any division between mitigated and absolute dualists. However, having said this, Brenon accepts the presence of absolute dualism in Lombardy by 1190 at the latest, basing her view on the testimony of Bonacursus, a Cathar converted sometime between 1176 and 1190, *Manifestatio haeresis catharorum quam fecit Bonacursus*, in WE, no. 25, pp.170–3 (where the different texts are collated). This she sees as an element of internal development in western Catharism, owing nothing to outside influence. Given that the author of the *De heresi catharorum*, writing about this period in the early thirteenth century, states both that Nicetas was from the sect of Drugunthia and that the Drugunthians were absolute dualists, it seems perverse to argue, as Brenon does, that there is no proof that the Drugunthian Church had been absolute before the Churches in the West and that Nicetas was not therefore a believer in absolute dualism. Even more radical is the recent view of M. G. Pegg, *The Corruption of Angels: The Great Inquisition of 1245–46* (Ph.D. diss., Princeton University, NJ, 1997), pp.149–53, who does not accept that there was any Bogomil influence. He thinks that it is likely that the documents were forged in the thirteenth century; see his book, *The Corruption of Angels: The Great Inquisition of 1245–1246* (Princeton, NJ, 2001). For a balanced summary of the arguments, see M. D. Lambert, *The Cathars* (Oxford, 1998), pp.54–8.

4 *De heresi catharorum*, p.310; trans. WE, p.165.

Ultimately this change was very significant for Languedoc, for moderate dualism has recognisable similarities to the Catholic version of the Fall, but absolute dualism has no common ground with the Catholics at all. By 1209, having failed to make any inroads against the absolute dualists of the region, Pope Innocent III saw no feasible alternative to the use of force. For him, drawing on the ideology of the just war worked out by St Augustine in the early fifth century, this was a legitimate weapon in the face of unbending obstinacy.[5]

William of Tudela claims that this heresy was rife all the way from Béziers to Bordeaux, but he only hints at how it might have arrived there in the first place when he refers to a meeting at Carcassonne between the bishop of Osma and those he calls 'Bulgars'. The name Bulgar derives from the Bogomil heretics of the Balkans, in particular those of Thrace, Macedonia, and Bosnia, but by William's time it was extensively used to describe western heretics, reflecting a widespread perception that their beliefs and organisation had originally derived from these regions. However, while historians have shown that this perception was quite correct, the process by which it occurred is by no means self-evident. The Bogomils did share some characteristics with two earlier eastern heresies – Paulicianism and Messalianism – both of which were present in the Balkans as a result of Byzantine policy which aimed to break up opposition in the imperial heartland of Asia Minor by the physical removal of disaffected populations to other regions. The Paulicians were strengthened in the eighth century when the Isaurian dynasty – the so-called 'iconoclast emperors' – attempted to suppress the use of icons, an attitude which, from the 730s, persuaded them to tolerate those equally unsympathetic towards the externals of Christian worship. Moreover, when the Emperor Constantine V reconquered Armenia from the Muslims in the 750s, Paulicians from the region were among those resettled in Thrace, depopulated by plague a few years before. With the ending of the Iconoclast regime in the mid-ninth century, Paulicians were persecuted once again, suffering serious military defeat when their fortress at Tefrice in the theme of Armeniakon in eastern Anatolia fell to Basil I in 878; even so, they were not eliminated, for some were recruited into imperial armies, where their presence was regularly reported down to the twelfth century, while the removal by the Emperor John Tzimisces of further communities from the eastern frontier to Philippopolis in Thrace during the 970s added to their presence in the Balkans.[6]

---

5   See below, ch. 4, pp.107–8.
6   For a concise summary of the Paulician heresy, see HH, pp.5–25.

Both sects found their origins in the East, the Messalians in fourth-century Edessa, the Paulicians in Mesopotamia in the mid-seventh century. Both gained adherents throughout the Byzantine Empire, for during the fifth century Messalians could be found in Syria, Cappadocia, and Asia Minor, while by the early ninth century the Paulicians claimed to have seven churches extending from the Euphrates in the east to Corinth in the west.[7] Neither accepted the Judeo-Christian belief in the creation of the world by God; both sought an explanation for evil in the existence of matter, a key component of which was the human body. However, while the Messalians thought that a demon inside each body needed to be expelled by intense prayer, the Paulicians were part of the dualistic tradition, in that they believed in the eternal separation of God and Matter. These are the 'Two Principles' which ultimately came to characterise the absolute dualists of Languedoc and northern Italy from the 1170s onwards.

The origins of Paulician belief are therefore a matter of importance to historians seeking the inspiration of medieval heresy in the West. Byzantine writers almost invariably called them 'Manichaeans'. Manichaeism was the work of a Persian called Mani, put to death by the Zoroastrian establishment in 276 AD. Systematic dualism originated with the Gnostics of the first century for whom matter was intrinsically evil, but Mani himself seems to have been subject to a variety of ideas drawn from Zoroastrianism, Christianity, Buddhism, and Babylonian Mandaeism (in which he had been brought up). Among the identifiable elements is the influence of Marcion, the son of the bishop of Sinope, who died in 160 AD. Marcion's dualism took the form of rejecting the God of the Old Testament, since he was responsible for the evil in the world, so that this God therefore had no connection with the New Testament at all. In Mani's cosmology, Darkness and Light were quite separate in origin, but the capture of some particles of Light by the aggressive forces of Darkness (which took the form of a composite creature with a lion's head, dragon's body, bird's wings, fish's tail, and beast's feet) meant that God had been obliged to undertake a series of actions to undo this catastrophe. The consequence was a long and, as yet, unresolved conflict, in which God sent a series of 'evocations' to create a material world in which to imprison the forces of Darkness. In reaction to this the power of Darkness invented man, self-propagating like the demons, in order to ensure that the particles of Light remained imprisoned, in this case in the human body. Jesus Christ was one of these divine 'evocations',

---

7   See B. Hamilton, 'The Cathars and the seven churches of Asia', in J. D. Howard-Johnston, ed., *Byzantium and the West c. 850–c. 1200. Proceedings of the XVIII Spring Symposium of Byzantine Studies, Oxford* (Amsterdam, 1988), pp.284–6. Also D. Obolensky, *The Bogomils* (Cambridge, 1948), pp.28–58, and M. Loos, *Dualist Heresy in the Middle Ages* (Prague, 1974), pp.32–8.

sent to bring the message of dualism. Mani himself was the last of these, possessed of the final revelation which was intended to make these beliefs universally accepted. The ultimate goal was a return to the complete separation of Light and Darkness.[8] Like their counterparts in the Orthodox Church, for many Latin clerics these ideas were not lost in the obscurity which the passing of ten centuries might have brought. St Augustine had, for about nine years, been an 'auditor' among the Manichaeans, which meant that the word was deeply embedded in the vocabulary of all literate men in the medieval West.[9] Many ecclesiastical writers were therefore ever ready to see 'Manichees' at the root of all 'heretical depravity' without feeling the need for further investigation.

Not surprisingly modern historians have neither been so easily convinced nor have they found such ready unanimity. It is notoriously difficult to trace the path of ideas over centuries, especially when those ideas run counter to prevailing orthodoxy and are therefore subject to vilification, distortion, and suppression. Some historians – among them Dmitri Obolensky, Steven Runciman, and Hans Söderberg and, more recently and tentatively, Yuri Stoyanov – while fully aware of the propaganda value of the Manichaean label to the orthodox, have been prepared to accept the essential continuity of dualism, tracing it from Gnosticism and Manichaeism to the Paulicians and thence to the Bogomils and the Cathars.[10] Söderberg's view is especially clear-cut: absolute dualists derived from Persian Manichaeism, and mitigated dualists were influenced by Egyptian and Syrian Gnosticism. For him the Cathars gave 'a Christian clothing to the myth of the combat between the two powers'; between them and Gnosticism there existed 'an uninterrupted, traditional chain'. Arno Borst sees this more in terms of context than continuity, pointing to the fundamental nature of the problem of the existence of evil. Thus there is a common element in the religions of the first millennium before Christ seen in both Persian Zoroastrianism and the cults of ancient Greece, which was the inherence of evil in matter which imprisoned the soul. Thereafter Pauline Christianity, heavily influenced by the Greek perspective, emphasised the duality between God and the world, while a range of Christian heretics, including Marcion in the second century

---

8   See Obolensky, *The Bogomils*, pp.2–28; Loos, *Dualist Heresy*, pp.21–39; V. N. Sharenkoff, *A Study of Manichaeism in Bulgaria* (New York, 1927), pp.5–15; Y. P. Stoyanov, *The Hidden Tradition in Europe* (Harmondsworth, 1994), pp.87–103.
9   See P. Brown, *Augustine of Hippo. A Biography* (Berkeley, CA and London, 1967), pp.46–60.
10  Obolensky, *The Bogomils*, pp.109–10; S. Runciman, *The Medieval Manichee. A Study of Christian Dualist Heresy* (Cambridge, 1947) (reprint, 1955), pp.62, 87–8, 171–4; M. Söderberg, *La Religion des Cathares. Etude sur le Gnosticisme de la basse antiquité et du moyen âge* (Uppsala, 1949), pp.82, 265–8.

and the Spaniard Priscillian in the fourth century, threatened the orthodox with their dualistic beliefs. Two heresies – the Messalians and the Paulicians – proved more durable, stamping their presence on the minds of the Byzantine theologians of the early middle ages.[11] It is entirely understandable that medieval churchmen should see contemporary dualists as Manichaeans, but Manichaeism as such disappeared in the Byzantine Empire after the persecution of the Emperor Justinian (527–65), although it persisted further east. Some historians – such as Bernard Hamilton and Yliva Hagman – therefore reject the idea of ultimate Manichaean derivation, pointing out that the Paulicians, the Bogomils, and the Cathars all saw themselves as 'good Christians'.[12] As Hamilton expresses it: 'The Christian dualists were not an alien graft on a Christian stock, but dissenters who had broken away from the Orthodox Church and interpreted the Christian faith in an exceptionally radical way.' In this view the founder of the Paulicians, Constantine of Mananalis, was therefore the first Christian dualist and the originator of a new heretical movement.

# The Bogomils

Neither position, though, solves the problem of the possible links between the Messalians and Paulicians and the Bogomils; to make any progress in this direction it is necessary to find out what is known about the Bogomils themselves. The first detailed description of dualist heresy in Bulgaria is by Cosmas the Priest, whose *Discourse* or *Treatise against the Bogomils* can be dated between 969 and 972. Cosmas may have been a bishop, or at least held a position of authority within the Church; it is evident that he felt a responsibility to protect 'the simple and ignorant' from the hypocrisy of the heretics, while at the same time deploring some of the behaviour of the Orthodox clergy. His account is based on his own observations and owes little or nothing to previous tradition.[13] Cosmas places the appearance of the heresy in the reign of the Tsar Peter (927–69), preached by a priest called

---

11  A. Borst, *Die Katharer* (Schriften der Monumenta Germaniae historica) (Stuttgart, 1953), pp.59–60.

12  HH, pp.2–3; Y. Hagman, 'Les historiens des religions et les constructions des ésotéristes', in *CEI*, pp.131–43.

13  H.-C. Puech and A. Vaillant, eds and trans., *Le Traité contre les Bogomiles de Cosmas le Prêtre* (Paris, 1945), pp.13–47, for the background, and pp.53–128, for the text in French translation. HH, no. 15, pp.114–34, for English translation. All translations are taken from this version.

Bogomil, the first to do so in Bulgaria.[14] A letter of Theophylact Lecapenus, Patriarch of Constantinople, written at Peter's request sometime between 940 and 950, confirms that a heresy based on dualist belief had been troubling the ruler, although its content depends much more upon Theophylact's theological knowledge of Manichaeism and Paulicianism (or that of his staff who probably drafted the letter) than any direct experience, and it is not absolutely certain that he is referring to the Bogomils.[15] Cosmas was fully aware of the persecution of the heretics which this exchange suggests, but he says, 'How can they deserve any compassion, even if a host of them suffer, when they claim the devil as creator of mankind and all the divine creation? And because of their great ignorance some call him a fallen angel, and others call him the "steward of iniquity".' Indeed, they say that 'it is by the devil's will that all exists: the sky, the sun, the stars, the air, mankind, the churches, the cross; all that belongs to God they ascribe to the devil; in short, everything that moves on the earth, whether it has a soul or not, they ascribe to the devil'. The Devil's dominion over the material world was evident in Matthew 4: 9, where he offers Christ, 'All these I will give you, if you will fall down and worship me.' In 'the parable of the two sons' (that is, the Prodigal Son) in Luke 15, the elder is identified as Christ, the younger, 'who deceived his father, the devil'. They call the Devil Mammon, says Cosmas, saying that 'it was he who bade men take wives and eat meat and drink wine'. Those who marry are 'servants of Mammon' and their offspring are 'the children of Mammon'. The corollary of this is the condemnation of the basis of Orthodox belief, together with the symbols of the Christian religion. They could not accept the idea of the redemption of the human race through Christ's death and resurrection, nor the role of the prophets, John the Baptist, or the Virgin Mary. These people rejected the cross, icons, relics, and saints, 'wagging their heads like the Jews when they crucified Christ'. They claimed that 'the Eucharist is not really, as you [the priests] claim, the body of Christ, but a simple food like all others'.

---

14  Bogomil may have been an adopted name meaning 'beloved of God'. Obolensky, *The Bogomils*, p.120, believes that his Christian name was Theophilus. However, recent modern opinion tends to accept that his actual name was Bogomil, which Loos, *Dualist Heresy*, pp.65–6, n.47, argues was 'a common personal name of the time'. The view which has sometimes been expressed that there was no such figure can be dismissed, see D. Anguelou, *Le Bogomilisme en Bulgarie*, trans. L. Pétrova-Boinay (Toulouse, 1972) (originally 1969), p.49, and Puech, *Traité*, pp.283–9, who thinks it very unlikely that a mythical figure would have developed so soon after his alleged death.

15  HH, no. 10, pp.98–102. Greek text in I. Dujčev, 'L'epistola sui Bogomili del patriarca constantinopolitano Teofilatto', in *Melanges Eugène Tisserant*, vol. 2 (Studi e testi, 232) (Città del Vaticano, 1964), pp.88–91.

Cosmas regarded the heretics as hypocrites, especially as they often con-cealed their beliefs by attending church and taking part in the sacraments and the liturgy. Most infuriating to him, though, was what he saw as their deliberate obstinacy in misinterpreting important biblical passages. Their presentation of the accounts of Christ's miracles in the Gospels was a case in point.

> How, indeed, are they not the enemies of God and man, they who do
> not believe in the Lord's miracles? Because they call the devil the creator,
> they do not admit that Christ performed any miracles. Although they hear
> the evangelists proclaim out loud the Lord's miracles, they 'twist them to
> their own destruction' [2 Peter 2: 16], saying, 'Christ did not restore any
> blind person's sight, he cured no cripple, he did not raise the dead; these
> are only parables. The evangelists present sins which were cured as if
> they were diseases.'

Cosmas says nothing about any kind of structured organisation, so prob-ably none existed at this time, although it is clear that there was an elite group of travelling preachers who relied upon the support of sympathisers and converts. 'People who see this great humility of theirs, who think that they are good Christians and able to direct them to salvation, approach them and take their advice about their souls' salvation; while they, like a wolf about to snatch away a lamb, at first pretend to sigh, and answer humbly.' They pray eight times every twenty-four hours, reciting exclusively 'Our Father', but they do no work, instead 'they go from house to house and eat the goods of others, those of the men they have deceived'. They confess and give absolu-tion to each other, women as well as men, an action quite contrary to Paul's command that women were not to teach or have authority over men.

Again, there is no consensus on the derivation of these ideas. For Obolensky the influence of the Messalian and Paulician heresies is evident. Messalians believed in intensive prayer, an ascetic lifestyle, and the enhanced role of women, while Paulician dualism denied the whole basis of Orthodox Christian belief and the formal ecclesiastical structure that went with it.[16] Hamilton rejects Messalian influence since there is no evidence to suggest that this was a living faith after the seventh century, and accords only a relatively small role to the Paulicians since, although both saw the devil as the evil creator, as well as agreeing on some specific points such as their refusal to accept the Eucharist, the Bogomils differed fundamentally in believ-ing in only one God and not in two co-eternal deities. Moreover, there was no ascetic tradition among the Paulicians; for Hamilton this was much

---

16   Obolensky, *The Bogomils*, pp.59–167.

more likely to have been drawn from Orthodox monasticism, although with a quite different motivation. If there was an external influence from eastern dualism, then he suggests it was possibly from Zurvanite Zoroastrianism with which the Bulgars had previously come into contact and which had great similarities to the mitigated dualism of the Bogomils.[17] Nevertheless, although historians differ over influences most agree that this was a new heresy and that Cosmas is describing a set of beliefs quite specific to his time and place. Bogomil was the true founder of an original Church, which by the mid-eleventh century, when contemporaries began to use the term 'Bogomilism' to describe his legacy, had had a profound influence far beyond Macedonia.[18]

However, no completely convincing explanation has ever been put forward for the appearance of the heresy at this particular time. Most historians attribute its success to the prevailing religious, political, and social instability, and there is no doubt that the cultural foundations of 'Bulgaria' were still in the process of formation in the mid-tenth century. Conversion to Christianity was relatively recent and still incomplete, dating from the mid-ninth century, although no systematic missionary work seems to have been undertaken until the entry of Clement, Naum, and Angelarius, in 885, disciples of St Methodius who, together with his brother Cyril, had evangelised the Slavs of Moravia.[19] They may, too, have made an inadvertent contribution for in their concern to ensure the permanence of their efforts, they established a school at Ochrida, where the translation of the New Testament and other texts into Old Slavonic greatly facilitated Bogomil propagation of their own interpretations of these materials.[20]

The situation was complicated by the ambiguities of the links with Byzantium, for the political and military relationship oscillated between subservience and sometimes violent Slav resistance. This turmoil was compounded by the attempt of Khan Boris (852–89) to ally with the Carolingian Louis the German, which would have opened the way for the papacy. The result was forceful Byzantine intervention in 864, compelling the Khan to accept Greek Orthodoxy. It is not surprising to find Paulician missionaries from Tefrice at work in Bulgaria shortly after – probably around 870 – since the conflicting religious currents offered evident opportunities for

---

17   HH, pp.29–31. On the Eucharist, see Cosmas, HH, p.119. See also Puech, *Traité*, pp.292–304, where he reviews the 'genealogy' of heresy. He thinks that direct Manichaean influence was negligible, but ascribes a greater role to elements of Paulicianism and Messalianism.

18   See Obolensky, *The Bogomils*, p.119; Loos, *Dualist Heresy*, p.67; Stoyanov, *Hidden Tradition*, pp.130–1.

19   Obolensky, *The Bogomils*, pp.88–9.

20   Stoyanov, *Hidden Tradition*, pp.132–3; HH, p.31.

proselytisation.[21] As a consequence historians have often taken up positions based on a view derived either from a 'religious' or a 'social' explanation, approaches which have become equally characteristic of the modern presentation of Catharism.[22] For Obolensky, the spread of heresy was essentially a consequence of the inability of the Orthodox Church to establish itself effectively in the face of the religious, social, and economic unrest of mid-tenth-century Bulgaria, a situation which could at least be partly explained by the deficiencies of the ecclesiastical establishment. Cosmas himself is very critical of the contemporary Church, especially its monastic and eremitical strands, although quite unwilling to accept that there was any external justification for the heretics' behaviour.

Cosmas, nevertheless, saw this religious dissent as encompassing incitement to social revolt. 'They teach their followers not to obey their masters; they scorn the rich, they hate the Tsars, they ridicule their superiors, they reproach the boyars, they believe that God looks in horror on those who labour for the Tsar, and advise every serf not to work for his master.'[23] Obolensky's interpretation of this passage is wary: 'one should beware of attributing too much importance to the social anarchism of the Bogomils or of seeing in them Slavonic communists of the Middle Ages.'[24] However, in contrast to Obolensky, Dimitur Anguelou identifies the prevailing socio-political climate as the key to understanding the spread of Bogomilism at this time. 'Although in its form it represents a heresy, at its base it was a social movement, directed against feudal oppression.' For him, Bogomilism was essentially a grass-roots movement, which appealed to an oppressed and overtaxed peasantry and an impoverished urban proletariat, which felt little affinity with a wealthy Church and a boyar class which held almost all the economic and jurisdictional power. Violence, pillage, and torture by soldiers exacerbated their already precarious situation. In Anguelou's view, the hierarchical concept of Orthodoxy simply provided an ideological justification for the existing state of feudal domination.[25] Anguelou's Marxist interpretation seems too schematic to be entirely realistic, but equally Obolensky is too dismissive. The rejection of those who possessed material

---

21  On the Bulgarian situation in the second half of the tenth century, see Stoyanov, *Hidden Tradition*, pp.120–3. The account of the Paulician missionaries derives from the report of the Byzantine envoy to Tefrice, Peter of Sicily, HH, p.67.

22  Janet Nelson in 'Religion in "*Histoire Totale*"', p.60, regards the debate between 'religious' and 'social' factors as 'a dead duck'. She may be right, but much of the fundamental historiography predates this time.

23  HH, p.132.

24  Obolensky, *The Bogomils*, p.137.

25  Anguelou, *Le Bogomilisme*, pp.23–9. See too Vaillant, *Traité*, pp.28–9, who see Bogomilism as a movement of protest and social agitation which found its origins among the lower clergy.

power seems entirely consistent with the other information provided by Cosmas. However, if this is the case, a transformation in the extent of its social acceptance was not the least of the mutations which Bogomilism underwent in the course of its transfer to the West.

Cosmas had hoped that his warnings would alert his contemporaries to the danger and that the heresy would therefore be eliminated before it could make further inroads. But his efforts were in vain. By the early twelfth century Bogomilism was not only common in Bulgaria, but had also been identified by Byzantine writers in Thrace, in western Asia Minor in the theme of Opsikion and, most importantly, in Constantinople itself. Anna Comnena, daughter of the Byzantine emperor, Alexius I (1081–1118), wrote the *Alexiad*, her panegyric of her father, in the 1140s.[26] She was as concerned to emphasise his intellectual gifts as to demonstrate his military prowess; for her, Alexius's debates with heretics made him 'the thirteenth apostle'. She identifies Philippopolis in Thrace and Constantinople as the two major centres of heresy in her father's time. Alexius encountered the heretics of Philippopolis in 1114, when he went there to campaign against the Cumans; in Anna's view, this city was 'a meeting-place … of all polluted waters', for practically all its inhabitants were either Paulicians (whom she identifies with Manichaeans), Armenian monophysites, or 'so-called Bogomils'. According to Anna, despite the obduracy of three of the leaders, Alexius managed to convert many thousands of the 'Manichaeans' and settle them in a new city near Philippopolis called Alexiopolis or Neocastron.[27] The emperor's confrontation with heresy in Constantinople is undated, although internal evidence places it earlier, sometime between 1101 and 1104.[28] Here his main opponents are quite specifically Bogomils, whose heresy Anna believed was previously unknown, although she conceded that it apparently existed before her father's reign, 'but was unperceived (for the Bogomil sect is adept at feigning virtue)'. Their dogma, she says, is

26  Anna Comnena, *Alexiad*, trans. E. Sewter (Harmondsworth, 1969), p.466. Greek text with French translation, Anne Comnène, *Alexiade (Règne de l'Empereur Alexis I Comnène 1081–1118)*, 3 vols (Collection Byzantine publiée sous le patronage de l'Association Guillaume Budé), 2nd edn (Paris, 1967). Anna Comnena's witness is valuable, both because she had been educated in 'the classical-hellenistic tradition' and because her technique was superior to most contemporary western chroniclers. As the events were well-remembered by others, it is likely that her descriptions are grounded upon fact. Moreover, her selectivity suggests that the confrontations with the heretics were regarded as events of major importance in Alexius's reign, see J. Chrysostomides, 'A Byzantine historian: Anna Comnena', in D. O. Morgan, ed., *Medieval Historical Writing in the Christian and Islamic Worlds* (London, 1982), pp.30–46.
27  *Alexiad*, trans. Sewter, pp.463–9.
28  See M. Angold, *Church and Society in Byzantium under the Comneni, 1081–1261* (Cambridge, 1995), p.486. He suggests that Basil's execution may have been some years later, perhaps in 1107.

'an amalgam of Manichaean and Massalian teaching', which had 'deep roots: it had penetrated even the greatest houses and enormous numbers were affected by this terrible thing'. Their leader, Basil, was tricked into confessing his beliefs and publicly burnt to death in the Hippodrome.[29]

However, Anna could not bring herself to describe Bogomil beliefs in detail, but instead refers the reader to the *Panoplia Dogmatica* by the monk Euthymius Zigabenus, commissioned by her father to produce a systematic description of all heresies, together with refutations. His section on the Bogomils seems to have been based directly on Basil's testimony, since he had actually been responsible for interrogating him, so the two writers effectively complement each other.[30] His description is, in essentials, consistent with that taught by Bogomil and his disciples although, as might be expected, doctrinal refinements had taken place. Even so, although in the early 1170s Nicetas brought absolute dualism from Constantinople to the West, at this date the Byzantine Bogomils described by Euthymius Zigabenus still retained the moderate dualism of their founder.[31] 'They say that the demon whom the saviour called Satan himself is also a son of God the Father, called Satanael; he came before the Son, the Word, and is stronger, as befits the first-born.' Satanael was the steward, second only to the Father, and was so carried away by his position that he engineered rebellion, luring some of the angels by offering them 'a lightening of their burdensome services'. When God realised this they were all thrown out of Heaven, but Satanael who 'possessed the power of the Demiurge' used that ability to create the earth, as described in the Book of Genesis. Basil's version of the creation of man is represented by Euthymius as follows:

> Then he moulded the body of Adam from earth mixed with water, and made him stand up, and some moisture ran down to his right foot, and leaking out through his big toe, ran twisting on to the ground and made the shape of a snake. Satanael gathered together the breath that was in him and breathed life into the body which he had moulded, and his breath, running down through the emptiness, ran down to the right foot in the same way, and, leaking through the big toe, ran out into the twisted drop. This instantly became alive, and separating from the toe, crawled away. That is why it is clever and intelligent, because of the breath of Satanael which came into it.

---

29  *Alexiad*, trans. Sewter, pp.496–504.
30  HH, no. 25, pp.180–95. Greek text in J. P. Migne., ed., *Patrologia Cursus Completus, Series Graeca*, vol. 130, cols 1289–1331.
31  Angold, *Church and Society*, pp.471–6, is not convinced that there was any connection between the Bogomils of Bulgaria and Basil's group in Constantinople. He agrees, though, on 'the similarities of outlook and teaching' (p.476).

Satanael realised then how limited his powers were, so

> he sent an embassy to the Good Father, and asked Him to send His
> breath, saying that the man would be shared if he were to be endowed
> with life, and that the places in heaven of the angels who had been thrown
> out should be filled by the man's descendants. Because God is good, He
> agreed, and breathed into what Satanael had moulded the breath of life;
> immediately man became a living soul, splendid in his body and bright
> with many graces.

Satanael, though, reneged on this agreement, making Eve pregnant with
Cain and his sister, Calomena. Abel, Adam's son by Eve, was killed by Cain
'and so brought murder into life'. It was God's pity for the soul that he had
breathed into the body that led him in the year 5000 to send 'the Word,
that is the Son'. According to the Bogomils, this son was the Archangel
Michael, who 'descended from above and crept through the right ear of the
Virgin, and put on a body which seems physical like a human body, but
in reality is immaterial and divine'. Here Euthymius makes explicit what
is implicit in Anna Comnena, who says only that Basil 'looked askance at
our doctrine of the Divine Nature of Christ and wholly misinterpreted His
human nature'.[32] Christ's role was therefore very limited; he was certainly
not part of an eternal Trinity as conceived by the Orthodox. Bogomil's
'wrong construction', which had so angered Cosmas, had now become the
heretics' standard approach to both biblical and apocryphal texts.

Anna Comnena had wrongly claimed that the heresy was completely new,
but even the better-informed Euthymius Zigabenus did not think it was
much older than his own generation, although his belief in its Manichaean
origins shows that he thought it had deeper roots. He did claim that Basil
had been studying and teaching for more than fifty-five years, which suggests
that Byzantine Bogomilism was already established by the mid-eleventh
century.[33] This is confirmed by an earlier witness, Euthymius, a monk of
the monastery of the Periblepton in Constantinople (who had originally
come from the diocese of Acmonia), who describes the heresy in the theme
of Opsikion in _c_. 1045.[34] It is likely therefore that the direct conquest of
Bulgaria by Emperor Basil II in 1018, which began a period of Byzantine
domination which lasted until 1185, created circumstances which enabled
Bogomilism to spread into other parts of the Byzantine Empire, perhaps

---

32  _Alexiad_, trans. Sewter, p.498.
33  HH, p.203.
34  HH, no. 19, pp.142–64. The text survives in fragments. The version in HH is a composite text.

partly through intermarriage. Moreover, its appearance among 'the greatest houses' in Constantinople shows that not only was the heresy diffused over a wide area, but that it was both socially mobile and intellectually evolving, developments of great significance for the history of Catharism in the West. Certainly it had become too well-established for Alexius to eliminate it, despite his best efforts. Michael Angold suggests that the emperor was particularly alarmed because heresy had ceased to be exclusively a provincial problem as in the past and had penetrated the capital, having taken advantage of the political and social turmoil so evident in Constantinople since the 1040s.[35] It was still there in the 1170s. At about the same time as Nicetas was on his mission to the West, Hugh Eteriano, a Pisan living in Constantinople, wrote a treatise condemning Bogomil belief and demanding that such heretics be executed. According to him, they could be found both in the districts around the Hellespont and throughout the whole city of Constantinople itself.[36] (See Map 1.)

It seems therefore that, during the reign of Alexius Comnenus, the Bogomils of Bulgaria and Byzantium adhered to a common set of beliefs and ritual. When asked at the Council of St Félix-de-Caraman, Nicetas said that there were five Churches: Romania (meaning Constantinople), Drugunthia (the valley of Dragovitsa in the region of Philippopolis), Melenguia (possibly the Church of the Slav Milingui, who lived around Mount Taygettus in the southern Peleponnese), Bulgaria, and Dalmatia (which probably meant Bosnia).[37] However, at some time before the council there had been a doctrinal split in which the Bogomils of Thrace and Constantinople became absolute dualists, leaving Bulgaria and Bosnia as the centres of the original moderate belief. This may, as has been argued by Bernard Hamilton, reflect linguistic and cultural divisions between the Slavs and the Greeks,[38] but it does seem nevertheless that the schism was a relatively recent occurrence, for there is no evidence that either Anna Comnena, writing in the late 1140s,

---

35  Angold, *Church and Society*, pp.477–8.

36  HH, no. 36, p.235.

37  Dondaine, 'Les Actes', pp.344–5, for the identification of these Churches. The location of the Church of the Melingui remains uncertain. According to C. Schmidt, *Histoire et doctrine de la secte des Cathares en Albigeois*, vol. 1 (Paris and Geneva, 1848) (reprint Bayonne, 1983), p.57, n.5, it was 'without doubt' Melnik in Macedonia. This view still commands some support (e.g. Angold, *Church and Society*, pp.493–4) on the grounds of its proximity to the other known Churches. Dondaine, 'Les Actes', p.345, evades the issues, and Hamilton, 'Cathar Council', pp.38–9, offers circumstantial evidence for the Peloponnese, but the truth is that nobody really knows. Angold, *Church and Society*, pp.494–5, also suggests that Drugunthia might have been in the theme of Moglena in Macedonia, where Bogomilism was combatted by St Hilarion, bishop there between *c.* 1134 and 1164.

38  B. Hamilton, 'The origins of the dualist church of Drugunthia', *Eastern Churches Review* 6 (1974), p.122.

or contemporary dualist heretics in the West knew of it at that time.[39] There is no solid evidence to explain the appearance of absolute dualism among the Byzantine Bogomils, but exposure to Paulician beliefs was certainly much more likely in Thrace than in Macedonia, especially since the mass deportations to the region by the Emperor John Tzimisces, while Anna Comnena says that Alexius I actually concentrated 'Manichaean' or Paulician heretics in a new city in the vicinity. Perhaps most significant of all was the insistence of Nicetas at the Council of St Félix-de-Caraman on the importance of the Paulician Churches in the history of the beliefs he was transmitting.[40]

## The origins of dualism in the West

According to the anonymous Lombard author of the *De heresi catharorum* Nicetas went first to Lombardy.

> In the early days, when the heresy of the Cathars began to increase in Lombardy, they first had a certain bishop named Mark, under whose rule all the Lombard, Tuscan, and Trevisan [heretics] were governed. Mark was consecrated in the sect of Bulgaria. Then there came to Lombardy from Constantinople a man called Papa Nicheta, who began to declaim against the Bulgarian consecration which Mark had received. This raised doubts in the minds of Bishop Mark and his followers; he gave up the Bulgarian consecration and accepted, at the hands of Nicheta himself, that of Drugunthia, and in this sect of Drugunthia he and all his associates remained for some time.[41]

Nicetas and Mark then travelled on to St Félix-de-Caraman. After convincing the Cathars there that absolute dualism was the correct belief, Nicetas established three further dioceses of Toulouse, Carcassonne, and Agen, adding to the already existing bishoprics of Albi and France.[42] When the Dominican and former Cathar, Rainier Sacconi, reviewed the whole range of Cathar churches in 1250, he counted sixteen in all, concluding with those

---

39  D. Obolensky, 'Papa Nicetas: a Byzantine dualist in the land of the Cathars', in *Okeanos: Essays Presented to Igor Ševčenko* (Harvard Ukrainian Studies, 7) (1983), pp.499–500, thinks that there is evidence of the change in the Old Slavonic *Life of St. Hilarion*, although this is a late source, its author, Euthymius, Bulgarian Patriarch of Trnovo, dying in 1402.

40  Hamilton, 'Seven churches', pp.284–5.

41  *De heresi catharorum*, p.306; trans. WE, pp.160–1.

42  Dondaine, 'Les Actes', pp.326–7.

of Bulgaria and Drugunthia. 'All [the others] sprang from the last two named', he says.[43] As Rainier's summary implies, Nicetas was only partially successful for, soon after his mission, the Bulgarian Bogomils reacted by sending their own man, Petracius (who may have been a bishop), to Lombardy. He claimed that Nicetas had been consecrated by a bishop of Drugunthia called Simon who had subsequently been caught with a woman. If this were true, it would have invalidated all of Nicetas's work in the West, for the Cathars believed that the spiritual powers of their elite depended upon their moral state, in sharp contrast to the Catholic Church which condemned such a view as donatist heresy. The *De heresi catharorum* says that the Italian Cathars were thrown into such confusion by this news that a quarrel arose and they split into two camps. Subsequent attempts to resolve the problem only exacerbated matters, so that 'the whole body of Cathars ... once living in unity was first split in two and then again into six parts'.[44]

However, neither Nicetas nor Petracius actually created Catharism in the West; each was trying to persuade existing adherents that their own cosmology contained the true explanation of the origin of evil. The original consecration of Mark in the Bulgarian *ordo*, as well as the readiness of the westerners to accept the authority of emissaries from Bulgaria and Drugunthia, make clear that there must have been strong contacts before this time but, because of the difficulties of interpreting the evidence, when and how remain matters of great controversy among historians, who have adhered to almost every possible variation on this theme. Some, like Steven Runciman, Hans Söderberg, and Antoine Dondaine have argued that the various heretical groups and individuals which appear quite suddenly in the West in the first half of the eleventh century show such evident similarities to Bogomil practice that there must have been direct connections. More recently, Anne Brenon has assumed that the heresies recorded in the West in the early eleventh century were dualist, but denied their Bogomil filiation; they were 'parallel but different'. Others, like the Italian historian, Raffaello Morghen, draw attention to the fact that there are no explicit references to dualism in these heresies, even though this formed the core of Bogomil teaching and would therefore be expected to be its most characteristic element. On the contrary, some of their beliefs are quite

---

43 Rainerius Sacconi, *Summa de Catharis et Pauperibus de Lugduno*, in A. Dondaine, *Un Traité néo-manichéen du XIIIe siècle: Le Liber du duobus principiis, suivi d'un fragment de rituel cathare* (Rome, 1939), pp.70; trans. WE, no. 51, p.336.

44 *De heresi catharorum*, pp.306, 308; trans. WE, no. 23, pp.161, 163–4. A later source, Anselm of Alessandria, writing probably in the mid-1260s, says that there was a report that Nicetas has met 'a bad end', Anselm of Alessandria, *Tractatus de haereticis*, in A. Dondaine, 'La Hiérarchie cathare en Italie, II', *Archivum Fratrum Praedicatorum* 20 (1950), p.309; trans. WE, no. 24, p.169.

incompatible with those of the Bogomils as expressed in Cosmas's treatise. Morghen argues that all their characteristics can be adequately explained without recourse to outside influence.[45] Moreover, there are dangers in the argument by analogy adopted by Dondaine. As R. I. Moore points out, medieval chroniclers readily mixed contemporary information with material taken from ancient authorities found in the monastic library. References to 'Manichees' were as likely to be taken from reading St Augustine, as they were to come from observation of contemporary sects.[46]

For Moore – as for Morghen – there is no unequivocal evidence of dualistic belief in the West until the report in the letter of Eberwin, Premonstratensian Prior of Steinfeld, near Cologne, to Bernard, Abbot of Clairvaux, written in 1143 or 1144. Eberwin speaks of two different groups of heretics, whose disagreement seems to have contributed to their discovery. Among those who appear to have been influenced by the Bogomils, some were reincorporated into the Church, but two of their leaders, 'their bishop and his assistant' debated before a public assembly for three days until 'the people' took matters into their own hands and threw them on to the fire.

> Anyone among them who is thus baptised [by the imposition of hands] they refer to as 'Elect', and say that he has the power to baptise others who shall be found worthy, and to consecrate the body and blood of Christ at his table. By the imposition of hands one is first received from the ranks of those they call 'auditors' into the number of the 'believers'; thus he gains permission to be present at their prayers until they deem him sufficiently tested to be made an 'Elect'. They give no credence to our baptism. They condemn marriage, but I could not learn from them the reason, either because they dared not reveal it or, more probably, because they did not know.

---

45 Runciman, *Medieval Manichee*, pp.117–22; Söderberg, *La Religion des Cathares*, pp.36–7; A. Dondaine, 'L'Origine de l'hérésie médiévale: à propos d'un livre récent', *Rivista di Storia della Chiesa in Italia* 6 (1952), pp.47–78, is a criticism of the section on heresy in R. Morghen's *Medievo Cristiano* (Bari, 1951), pp.212–49 with the detailed notes, pp.346–65. 'Il Cosidetto neo-manicheismo occidentale del secolo XI', in *Convegno di Scienze Morali Storiche e Filologiche* (Rome, 1957), pp.84–104, and 'Problèmes sur l'origine de l'hérésie au moyen âge', *Revue historique* 336 (1966), pp.1–16, are two characteristic statements of this author's position. For Brenon's variants on all these views, see *Le Vrai Visage*, pp.98–9. For a recent general survey of ideas on the origins of heresy, see H. Fichtenau, *Heretics and Scholars in the High Middle Ages, 1000–1200*, trans. D. A. Kaiser (Philadelphia, PA, 1998) (originally Munich, 1992), pp.105–26. For an analysis of the common features of Bogomilism and Catharism, as well as the differences, see Lambert, *The Cathars*, pp.29–32. While not suggesting that Bogomils were active in the West as early as the first decades of the eleventh century, Lambert nevertheless argues that the Rhineland Cathars of 1143 'had already passed beyond the first missionary phase'.

46 R. I. Moore, trans., *The Birth of Popular Heresy* (Documents of Medieval History, 1) (London, 1975), pp.5–6. See also Moore, *The Origins of European Dissent* (new edn, Oxford, 1985) (originally 1977), pp.8–20, for the problems presented by the sources for heresy.

Those who had returned to the Church

> have told us that these heretics have a very large number of adherents
> scattered throughout the world, among whom are many of our clergy and
> monks. Indeed, those who were banned told us during their defence that
> this heresy has lain concealed from the time of the martyrs even to their
> own day, and has persisted thus in Greece and certain other lands.[47]

Eberwin of Steinfeld's informant may have exaggerated when he claimed
that there were 'very large numbers of adherents scattered throughout the
world'. Nevertheless, the first canon of the provincial council, held by Archbishop Samson at Reims in October 1157, was directed against *Piphiles*,
who rejected marriage, and lived in impure or even incestuous unions,
while the very important Council of Tours of May 1163, presided over by
the pope and attended by seventeen cardinals, included legislation specifically aimed at 'Albigensians' and those who helped them.[48] Moreover, there
are a number of reports of heretics who appear to have held at least some
of the beliefs which characterised the Bogomils. In 1145 the clergy of Liège
described a group at Mont-Aimé (Montwimers) in Champagne, who had
three classes of followers, that is auditors, believers, and Christians, the last
meaning 'its priests, and its other prelates, just as we have'. They did not
believe in baptism, the Eucharist, or marriage, and refused to take oaths
which they said were criminal.[49] It is possible that the 'prelates' referred
to may have been the Cathar bishops of France and Lombardy known to
Nicetas in the early 1170s or their predecessors.[50] Other reports emanate
from the 1160s: at Lombers (south of Albi) 'Good Men' told an assembly of
clergy and people that 'they do not accept the law of Moses, nor the
Prophets, nor the Psalms, nor the Old Testament, but only the Gospels, the
Epistles of Paul, the seven canonical Epistles, the Acts of the Apostles, and

---

47  Eberwin of Steinfeld, *Epistola ad S. Bernardum*, in *PL*, vol. 182, ep. 472; trans. WE, no. 15,
pp.126–32. See Moore, *Origins*, pp.41–2, 164–96. On the importance of this source,
see A. Brenon, 'La Lettre d'Evervin de Steinfeld à Bernard de Clairvaux de 1143: un
document essentiel et méconnu', *Heresis* 25 (1995), pp.7–28. Obolensky, *The Bogomils*,
pp.222–3, draws attention to reports of Bogomilism in Cappadocia and south-eastern
Macedonia from 1143 onwards. This appears to suggest an upsurge in the heresy at
the same time as the Cologne heretics became known, but it looks as if most of the
Byzantine cases were political rather than heretical in nature, HH, pp.40–1.

48  The relevant decrees are conveniently gathered together in J. Fearns, ed., *Ketzer und
Ketzerbekämpfung im Hochmittelalter* (Historische Texte, Mittelalter, 8) (Göttingen, 1968),
pp.59–60. See also C. J. Hefele and H. Leclercq, *Histoire des Conciles*, vol. 5(ii) (Paris, 1913),
pp.913, 963–72.

49  *Epistola ecclesiae Leodiensis ad Lucum papam II*, in E. Martène and V. Durand, eds, *Veterum
scriptorum et monumentorum historicum, dogmaticarum, moralium amplissima collectio*, vol. 1 (Paris,
1724), pp.776–8; trans. WE, no. 17, pp.139–41.

50  See Borst, *Die Katharer*, p.93.

the Apocalypse';[51] at Oxford, at about the same time, a group of Germans identified as 'Publicans' 'scorned holy baptism, the Eucharist, and matrimony';[52] and at Vézelay in Burgundy in 1167, another group of so-called 'Publicans' were judged to have been guilty of rejecting all the sacraments of the Church.[53] According to a reliable contemporary, the Austin canon, William of Newburgh, who is the source for the heretics condemned at Oxford, they had originated in Gascony, but had 'spread the poison of their infidelity' in France, Spain, Italy, and Germany.[54] In all the cases cited it was claimed that the heretics had made efforts to conceal some or all of their true beliefs, often by falsely taking part in Catholic ceremonies.

Most importantly, this period also saw the first detailed polemical response to the perceived threat by Eckbert, a former canon of Bonn and later abbot of Schönau in the diocese of Trier, who wrote his *Sermones contra Catharos* for Rainald of Dassel, the imperial chancellor and Archbishop of Cologne, in 1163. This consists of a short introduction followed by thirteen sermons setting out the origin of the heresy and refuting its major tenets one by one. An excerpt from St Augustine's *De Manichaeis* is added to the end, which suggests that, like earlier commentators, Eckbert too was influenced by Augustine and that such knowledge does not necessarily exclude the writer's own observations. Eckbert says that they were generally called Cathars, which was the name used in his part of the world, but were also identified as *Piphles* in Flanders and *Texerant* in France, from their occupation as weavers. There is an echo of the frustration of Cosmas the Priest when he castigates them for not understanding 'the right meaning which lies in the sacred words', for it appears that when he was at Bonn Eckbert and his friend, Bertolph, had often disputed with them. His reference to the past execution of some of them in the city of Cologne suggests strongly that these were the same heretics described by Eberwin of Steinfeld twenty years before, and confirms the importance of that witness in tracing the history of Catharism, for Eckbert's heretics are the first in the West who can be seen as unambiguously Bogomil in their beliefs. 'Those who have entered their sect as *perfecti* avoid all flesh, not for the reason that monks do, or others living spiritual lives abstain from it, but they say that the consumption of flesh should be avoided because it is all produced as a result of sexual

---

51  *Acta concilii Lumbariensis*, in *RHG*, vol. 14, pp.431–4; trans. WE, no. 28, pp.189–94. See below, ch. 4, p.118.

52  William of Newburgh, *Historia rerum anglicarum*, ed. R. Howlett, in *Chronicles of the Reigns of Stephen, Henry II, and Richard I* (Rolls Series, 82) (London, 1884), pp.131–4, trans. WE, no. 40, pp.245–7.

53  Hugh of Poitiers, *Historia Vizeliacensis monasterii*, in *RHG*, vol. 12, pp.343–4, where they are called *Deonarii* or *Poplicani*; trans. WE, no. 41, pp.248–9.

54  William of Newburgh, *Historia*, p.245.

intercourse; and for this reason they judge it to be unclean.' He goes on to say that this is their public explanation, 'but in secret they say what is worse, namely that all flesh is made by the devil, and that they never touch it even in the greatest necessity'. They rejected marriage, infant baptism, baptism by water, prayers for the dead, masses, and the Eucharist. Christ, they said, 'was not truly born of the Virgin, nor indeed had human flesh, but an imitation of the flesh; nor had he risen from the dead, but, his death and resurrection were a simulation'. For Eckbert this confirmed that they were truly Manichaean, for they did not celebrate Easter, he claimed, but rather 'a certain other feast, on which was killed their heresiarch Manichaeus, to whose heresy they without doubt adhere'. Eckbert describes these Cathars as extremely loquacious, but he, like the other witnesses, claims that they held some of their beliefs in secret.[55]

Moore therefore regards as unsafe any attempt to trace the transmission of Bogomilism to the West before the relatively solid evidence of the early 1140s. It is a view now widely accepted as the most likely to reflect twelfth-century realities. However, there has recently been dissent from Bernard Hamilton.[56] He agrees that there is no evidence of 'fully-fledged Bogomilism' in the West before 1050, but argues that this is because it did not yet exist in the East in that form either. In other words, Bogomilism was continuing to evolve in Macedonia, Thrace, and Constantinople, even while it was spreading elsewhere. He believes that there is a connection between the development of the 'newly appeared' heresy described by Cosmas the Priest, the spread of Bogomil beliefs into Thrace, and, soon after, in the first half of the eleventh century, the reporting of apparently isolated outbreaks of heresy in Italy and France after a long period of quiescence dating back to the decline of the Arian heresy in Spain in the early seventh century. He speculates that visits by Orthodox monks to western shrines might have been one means of transmission. However, he accepts the generally agreed view that there is no sign of western dualist heresy between 1051 and 1114, so that if there were Bogomils in the West in the earlier eleventh century, then their teachings did not at that time flourish. As Hamilton sees it, the Bogomils began the successful spread of their beliefs in the West in the early twelfth century in the period after the First Crusade (1095–1101).

---

55  Eckbert of Schönau, *Sermones contra haereticos*, in *PL*, vol. 195, pp.13–16; re-edited by R. J. Harrison, *Eckbert of Schönau's 'Sermones contra Kataros'*, vol. 1 (Ann Arbor, MI, 1990), pp.1–373; partial trans. in R. I. Moore, *The Birth of Popular Heresy* (Documents of Medieval History, 1) (London, 1975), pp.88–94. Harrison argues, vol. 2, pp.374–693, against those historians who believe that Eckbert's treatise is so pervaded by his knowledge of Augustinian Manichaeism that it is of little value as a source for contemporary heresy.

56  B. Hamilton, 'Wisdom from the East', in P. Biller and A. Hudson, eds, *Heresy and Literacy, 1000–1530* (Cambridge, 1994), pp.38–60.

A key passage in this debate is the account given by Anselm of Alessandria, who was Inquisitor in Milan and Genoa from 1267, and one of the few western writers who attempted to investigate the history of the Cathars.

> Presently, Greeks from Constantinople, who are neighbours to Bulgaria at a distance of about three days' travel, went as merchants to the latter country; and, on return to their homeland, as their numbers grew, they set up there a bishop who is called bishop of the Greeks. Then Frenchmen went to Constantinople, intending to conquer the land, and discovered this sect; increasing in number, they established a bishop who is called bishop of the Latins. Thereafter, certain persons from Sclavonia, that is, from the area called Bosnia, went as merchants to Constantinople. On return to their own land, they preached and, having increased in number, established a bishop who is called the bishop of Sclavonia or of Bosnia. Later on, the French who had gone to Constantinople returned to their homeland and preached and, as their numbers grew, set up a bishop of France. Because the French were originally led astray by the Bulgars, throughout France these persons are called Bulgarian heretics. Also, people of Provence who are neighbours of those of France, hearing the teachings of the French and led astray by them, grew so numerous that they set up four bishops, namely, bishops of Carcassonne, of Albi, of Toulouse, and of Agen.[57]

This passage is clear enough, but provides no dates, so historians are left with the problem of exactly when 'Frenchmen went to Constantinople, intending to conquer the land'. Given the frequency with which crusading armies passed through Constantinople from the late eleventh century onwards, this is not easy to resolve. The phrase is usually taken to mean the Second Crusade of 1147–48, when a belligerent section of Louis VII's army was certainly willing to mount such an attack.[58] Malcolm Lambert, however, has argued forcefully that Anselm can only be referring to the Fourth Crusade of 1204; indeed, for him that is 'the plain meaning' of the words.[59] However, although the Fourth Crusade was the only one actually to conquer Constantinople, Anselm in fact says only 'in order that they might conquer the land',[60] which could in fact apply to almost any of the crusading armies which passed through or by Constantinople. Moreover,

---

57   Anselm of Alessandria, *Tractatus de haereticis*, p.308; trans. WE, no. 24, pp.168–9.

58   See C. Thouzellier, 'Hérésie et croisade au XIIe siècle', *Revue d'Histoire Ecclésiastique* 49 (1954), p.861; Borst, *Die Katharer*, p.90; WE, p.695; Obolensky, 'Papa Nicetas', p.495, among others.

59   M. D. Lambert, *Medieval Heresy. Popular Movements from the Gregorian Reform to the Reformation*, 2nd edn (Oxford, 1992), p.60.

60   *ut subiugarent terram* (subjunctive).

the evidence already discussed shows that the French had already set up a Cathar bishop by the 1160s so, if Anselm is any guide at all to events, he cannot be referring to 1204.[61] Hamilton picks the third option, which is the First Crusade, a date which he sees as according with the apocalyptic visions of St Hildegard of Bingen, whose knowledge may have come from her friendship with St Elizabeth of Schönau, sister of Eckbert, the scourge of the Cathars in 1163. In that same year Hildegard wrote that the devil led people astray 'sixty years and twenty and four months' ago, and that the spread of the error was 'twenty-three years and four months' ago, which would give dates of 1101 (the last of the great armies of the First Crusade) and 1140 (the first appearance of Cathars in the Rhineland) respectively.[62]

These arguments suggest that reports of heresy in Latin Christendom from before 1140 may be relevant, despite the scepticism of many historians. One case – that of a peasant called Leutard, who lived in the village of Vertus, near Châlons-sur-Marne, around the year 1000 – has featured prominently in some recent accounts (notably those of Brenon and Fichtenau), as the first possible instance of dualistic belief in the West. Leutard's activities included sending his wife away, breaking a cross in the local church, and preaching to others in the vicinity. Part of his message was that there was no need to pay tithes. He was eventually shown the error of his ways by the bishop of Châlons, but committed suicide soon afterwards. In the report by the Cluniac monk, Raoul Glaber, he seems an isolated individual, but he does appear to have been part of a group, from which he probably learned some of the ideas he propounded. Brenon, though, does not accept outside influence, whereas Fichtenau suggests an ultimate Balkan source, although through intermediaries. Both historians are influenced not only by the actions described (which are a slim basis for asserting dualistic belief), but the recurrence of reports of heresy in Champagne thereafter, especially centred

---

61  Lambert, *Medieval Heresy*, p.60, calls Anselm's account 'semi-legendary'. This seems a harsh judgement, for much of what he says accords with *De heresi catharorum*, which is much nearer to the actual events, while other statements (such as the establishment of the Cathar bishoprics of Toulouse and Agen) can be corroborated from other sources. Anselm's mistaken idea that Mani actually taught in Drugunthia, Bulgaria, and Philadelphia, does not invalidate the information he had gathered for more recent times. More recently, Lambert, *The Cathars*, pp.35–7, is less dismissive of Anselm's account.

62  Hamilton, 'Wisdom from the East', pp.42–4. There are problems with the first date as the phrase is ambiguous: *sexaginta anni sunt atque viginti et quatuor menses*. It could therefore mean 80 years ago. The use of *atque* might be important as it sometimes indicates a closer connection between words than *et* (Lewis and Short, *Latin Dictionary*, p.189). If so, then Hamilton suggests she is referring to the capture of St Peter's by Emperor Henry IV in 1083, an event of equal apocalyptic significance. Either way the argument for an introduction of Bogomil ideas into the West before *c.* 1140 still stands.

at Mont-Aimé, which is about four kilometres from Vertus. By the 1170s this appears to have been the focus of the 'Church of France', whose bishop, Robert of Spernone, Nicetas reconsoled at St Félix. Moreover, it was the execution of 183 heretics at Mont-Aimé in 1239 which seems to have seen the end of Catharism in the region.[63]

Taken at face value, there are six further reports of heresy between c. 1018 and 1114 which suggest possible Bogomil influence. In chronological order they encompass Aquitaine, Périgord, Toulouse, Orléans, Arras, Montforte (near Turin), Châlons-sur-Marne, and Soissons. Three writers call them Manichaeans: Adhemar of Chabannes, a monk of Angoulême, describing those in Aquitaine and in Périgord, Toulouse and Orléans in 1022; Roger II, Bishop of Châlons, discussing those in the countryside around Châlons-sur-Marne sometime between 1043 and 1048; and Guibert, Abbot of Nogent, speaking of heretics near Soissons, in c. 1114.[64] Adhemar's identification of the heretics in Périgord may possibly be confirmed by the mysterious monk, 'Heribert', who claims 'numerous heresies' in the region, the characteristics of which included a pretence that they were leading an apostolic life, abstention from meat and wine, and a rejection of alms, liturgical chant, the Eucharist, and the cross.[65] Guibert says that he had re-read St Augustine and that this enabled him to say that the heresy he had reported 'resembles none other than that of the Manichaeans' which, if he is telling the truth, suggests that, initially, at any rate, he had received his information from a source other than St Augustine. As the designation of Bogomils does not seem to have been used even in Macedonia and Thrace before the time of Euthymius of the Periblepton in c. 1045, it is difficult to see how either Adhemar or Roger could have described what they believed to be dualist heresy other than as Manichaean. Three reports

---

63   *Rodulfi Glabri Historiarum libri quinque. The Five Books of the Histories*, ed. and trans. J. France (Oxford Medieval Texts) (Oxford, 1989), pp.88–91; Brenon, *Le Vrai Visage*, pp.45–8; Fichtenau, *Heretics and Scholars*, p.17.

64   Adhemar of Chabannes, *Chronique*, ed. J. Chavanon (Collection de textes pour servir à l'étude et à l'enseignement de l'histoire, 20) (Paris, 1897), pp.173, 184–5; trans. WE, no. 2, pp.73–4; *Herigeri et Anselmi Gesta episcoporum Leodiensium*, ed. R. Koepke, in *MGH Scriptores*, vol. 7, pp.226–8, trans. WE, no. 6, pp.89–93; Guibert de Nogent, *Histoire de sa vie (1052–1124)*, ed. G. Bourgin (Collection de textes pour servir à l'étude et à l'enseignement de l'histoire, 9) (Paris, 1907), p.213; trans. WE, no. 9, pp.101–4. See the lists drawn up by Dondaine, 'L'Origine', pp.59–61, for comparison.

65   Heribert's letter on the subject has been redated to the early eleventh century, having previously been thought to belong to the 1140s. However, some historians deny that such a person existed or that the description applies to a real group of heretics at all. See G. Lobrichon, 'The chiaroscuro of heresy: early eleventh-century Aquitaine as seen from Auxerre', in T. Head and R. Lander, eds, *The Peace of God. Social Violence and Religions Response in France around the Year 1000* (Ithaca, NY and London, 1992), pp.80–103 (with English trans.) and 347–50 (Latin versions of the text).

(by Paul, a monk of St Père de Chartres, writing in *c.* 1072 about the Orléans heretics of 1022, Landulf, a cleric of Milan describing the heretics of Montforte in *c.* 1028, and Guibert of Nogent) emphasise the docetic views of the heretics, that is their belief that the human life of Christ was an illusion.[66] Two reports (from the Synod of Cambrai in 1025 which looked at the allegations against the heretics of Arras, and Guibert of Nogent) say that the heretics only believed in the Gospels and the Acts of the Apostles.[67] Roger of Châlons describes the ritual of the laying-on of hands.[68] Guibert says that they rejected food produced by coition.[69] All the cases exhibit strong anti-sacramental opinions, including the denial of the validity of baptism, the Eucharist, penance, and marriage. Chastity and fasting were central to their lifestyle. All these beliefs are consistent with Bogomil teaching, and in three cases there is some hint of outside influence in which Italy is the common factor. According to Raoul Glaber, the heretics at Orléans in 1022 were influenced by a female missionary from Italy, the synod at Cambrai found that the heretics at Arras were followers of an Italian called Gundolfo, and Landulf of Milan said that those at Montforte 'had come into Italy from some unknown part of the world'.[70] By 1139, at the Second Lateran Council, it was thought necessary to issue a general condemnation of those who 'simulating a kind of religiosity' denied the validity of the Eucharist, the baptism of children, and legitimate marriage, as well as denigrated the priesthood.[71]

Most historians accept that there is little or no identifiable heresy in the West in the second half of the eleventh century; its absence is conventionally ascribed to the turmoil created by the papal reform movement, which absorbed most potential dissenters.[72] If this was so, it was only a temporary respite. In the first half of the twelfth century new critics appeared, more strident and populist than their predecessors. The activities of one of these men – Tanchelm of Antwerp (died *c.* 1115) – are known largely through the

---

66  Paul of Saint-Père de Chartres, *Vetus Aganon*, ed. B.-E.-C. Guérard, in *Cartulaire de l'abbaye de Saint-Père de Chartres* (Collection des cartulaires de France, 1) (Paris, 1840), p.111, for docetic views; trans. WE, no. 3(B), pp.76–81; *Landulphi senioris Mediolanensis historiae libri quatuor*, ed. A. Cutolo, in *RIS*, vol. 4, pt. 2 (Bologna, 1900), pp.67–9; trans. WE, no. 5, pp.86–9. Puech points out that Cosmas never calls them Bogomils, but only uses the term heretics, *Traité*, p.280.

67  *Acta synodi Atrebatensi a Gerardo Cameracensi*, in P. Fredericq, ed., *Corpus documentorum inquisitionis haereticae pravitatis Neerlandicae*, vol. 1 (Ghent, 1899), pp.2–5; trans. WE, no. 4, pp.82–6.

68  *Herigeri et Anselmi Gesta episcoporum Leodiensium*, p.226.

69  Guibert of Nogent, *Histoire de sa vie*, p.212.

70  *Rodulfi Glabri Historiarum libri quinque*, pp.138–9.

71  N. J. Tanner, ed., *Decrees of the Ecumenical Councils*, vol. 1, *Nicaea I to Lateran V* (London, 1990), p.202.

72  See Borst, *Die Katharer*, pp.71–80.

account of the canons of Utrecht, whose violent denigration of his character seems to have been more concerned with what they saw as his interference in diocesan affairs than with any coherent presentation of his beliefs.[73] More significant was the preaching of Henry the Monk and Peter of Bruys, both because their careers were longer and, in the case of Henry, affected the Toulousain directly. As with Tanchelm it is necessary to prune the thickets of clerical outrage in order to find the core of their teaching, but in essence it amounted to an attack upon the sacramental functions of the priests and the externals of worship which were associated with them. In Henry's case the basis of his argument was donatist – sacraments administered by sinful priests were worthless – while Peter of Bruys particularly targeted church buildings and crosses, as well as denying the validity of infant baptism, the Eucharist, and prayers and offerings for the dead. Peter was killed at St Gilles sometime after 1131, but Henry remained a persistent and persuasive opponent of the clerical hierarchy, drawing crowds in important cities of the west, including Le Mans, Poitiers, Bordeaux, Cahors, and Périgueux, and then, in the 1140s, in and around Toulouse. In 1145 a preaching tour by Bernard, Abbot of Clairvaux, seems to have undermined him and he was probably captured in the autumn of that year.[74] Elie Griffe believed that 'Arians' in Toulouse were really Cathars and that their existence predated Henry's appearance, but it is difficult to connect Henry with dualistic belief from any of the existing evidence.[75] More pertinent may be St Bernard's pointed question to Count Alfonso-Jordan before he journeyed to Toulouse, when he asked him why it appeared that his lands were the only ones to offer sanctuary to Henry now that he had been driven out of 'France'.[76] The answer may have lain less in the count's neglect, which is

---

73 *Traiectenses Fridericum I archiepiscopum Coloniensem hortantus, quod ceperit Tanchelmum haereticum eiusque socios, Manassen et Everwacherum, ne eos dimittat*, in *Codex Udalrici*, ed. P. Jaffé, in *Monumenta Bambergensis* (Berlin, 1869) (reprint 1964), pp.296–300, and *Sigiberti Gemblacensis chronographia: Continuatio Praemonstratensis*, ed. L. C. Bethmann, in *MGH Scriptores*, vol. 6, p.449; trans. WE. nos 8(A) and (B), pp.97–101.

74 *Actus pontificum Cenomannis in urbe degentium*, ed. G. Busson and A. Ledru (Archives historiques du Maine, 2) (Le Mans, 1901), pp.407–15, 437–8; R. Manselli, 'Il monaco Enrico e la sua eresia', *Bullettino dell'Istituto storico italiano per il medio evo e Archivio Muratoriano* 65 (1953), pp.44–63; Peter the Venerable, *Epistola sive tractatus adversus petrobrusianos haereticos*, in *PL*, vol. 189, cols 719–24; Bernard of Clairvaux, *Epistolae*, in J. Leclercq and H. Rochais, eds, *S. Bernardi Opera*, vol. 8 (Rome, 1977), no. CCXLI, pp.125–7; trans. WE, no. 11–14, pp.107–26.

75 E. Griffe, *Les Débuts de l'aventure cathare en Languedoc (1140–90)* (Paris, 1969), pp.34–7. However, James Fearns argues that the Petrobrusian attitude towards the cross suggests Bogomil influence, see 'Peter von Bruis und die religiöse Bewegung des 12. Jahrhunderts', *Archiv für Kulturgeschichte* 48 (1966), p.325.

76 *Epistolae*, no. CCXLI, p.126. Trans. B. S. James, *The letters of St Bernard of Clairvaux* (reprint Stroud, 1998), p.388.

what St Bernard implies, but in popular resentment at the success of the Church in extending its financial control over so many areas of social life, in particular marriage.[77] Henry's temporary success may show that there were issues which the Cathars could readily exploit.

Moore's belief that dualism in the West cannot be proven before *c.* 1140 rests upon a strict and cautious reading of the sources and, as such, forms a distinct marker-point in the elusive search for evidence of the spread of heretical ideas. For him, the disparate nature of the beliefs reported, their wide geographical spread, and the lack of any evidence of Bogomil activity suggest that these heresies were generated by the circumstances prevailing in western Christendom in the eleventh and early twelfth centuries and owe nothing to outside influence.[78] Nevertheless, given the powerful missionary zeal of the Bogomils, as well as their evident spread east as far as Constantinople, it does seem intrinsically unlikely that Italy (if nowhere else) would have remained hermetically sealed from their ideas for the better part of one and a half centuries. Moreover, if the 1143 date really does represent the first appearance of Bogomilism in the West, then it put down roots remarkably quickly. If Anselm of Alexandria is correct, at some time point before Nicetas's mission in the early 1170s, Catharism not only spread from northern France into Languedoc, but also into Italy, when 'a notary from France' led astray Mark, who was a gravedigger, and his two friends John Judeus and Joseph, a weaver and a smith respectively. They added a fourth man, Aldricus of Bando.

> All these deluded persons took counsel with the aforesaid notary, who sent them to Roccavione – that is a place near Cuneo – where dwelt Cathars who had come from France to settle. The bishop of the heretics was not there, being at Naples. Thither they went and sought him out, staying in that city for a year. Thereafter, having received the imposition of the hand, Mark was made a deacon. The aforesaid bishop sent him back to his native place of Concorezzo, where Mark himself began to preach. As a result of his preaching in Lombardy, then in the March of Treviso, and later in Tuscany, the number of heretics greatly increased.[79]

The passage suggests that the bishop of France had already established a community at Roccavione and that he was continuing his work in southern Italy. Mark's consecration as a bishop 'in the sect of Bulgaria', as described

---

77  Moore, *Origins*, pp.89–95; M. Costen, *The Cathars and the Albigensian Crusade* (Manchester, 1997), pp.95–6.
78  Moore, *Origins*, pp.41–5.
79  Anselm of Alessandria, *Tractatus de haereticis*, pp.308–9; trans. WE, no. 24, p.169.

by the author of the *De heresi catharorum*,[80] could well have followed these events, and it could have been done by either the bishop of France or by Bulgarian Bogomils.

However these sources are interpreted, it is not disputed that missionaries from the Bogomil Church did proselytise in the West at some point, and that cannot have been later than about 1140. There remains the problem of how this was done. As so much must have been transmitted orally, there are strict limits as to what can be discovered, as the matter can only be approached through an analysis of the surviving literature. Bernard Hamilton has shown that the Cathars only obtained a limited amount of their literature from the Bogomils, but that this was mainly from the period before *c.* 1170. Three items were particularly important: the Ritual (from which the Cathars derived their initiation ceremony known as the *consolamentum*), an apocryphal work known as *The Vision of Isaiah* (which dates probably from the first century AD), and probably a collation of the Vulgate text of the New Testament with the text established by the Bogomils. All these, Hamilton argues, must have been translated from Greek into Latin (and later the Ritual and the New Testament were translated into Occitan). This work of translation is unlikely to have been done by merchants, travellers, or crusaders, however much they might demonstrate contact between the Latin and Byzantine worlds, but it must rather have been done by the westerners resident in Constantinople mentioned by Anselm of Alessandria. These were the people who formed the Cathar (that is Latin) Church in Constantinople, which was distinct from the Bogomil Church there, and they must have been responsible for the evangelisation of the West, since they had the capability to do so.[81] It was men such as these who had prepared the ground for Nicetas and Petracius.

80   *De heresi catharorum*, p.306.
81   Hamilton, 'Wisdom from the East', pp.46–60.

# CHAPTER TWO

# The Cathars and Languedocian Society

## The nobility

The most important Catholic chronicler of the Albigensian Crusade is Peter, a Cistercian monk, from the abbey of Les Vaux-de-Cernay, situated about thirty-five kilometres to the south-west of Paris. The abbey had strong connections with the family of Simon of Montfort, who was chosen as leader of the crusade in late August 1209, and Peter accompanied the crusade for much of the time Montfort was in charge, so he was either an eye-witness or gained his information from participants. According to Peter, the fortified town of Lavaur, thirty-seven kilometres to the north-east of Toulouse, was 'the source and origin of every form of heresy'. William of Puylaurens, a cleric from Toulouse who offers an overview of events from a mid-thirteenth-century perspective, even though a much less biased commentator than Peter, was equally provoked. It was a place 'in which through the heretics the Devil had prepared a seat for himself'.[1] In late March 1211, Simon of Montfort, reinforced by a fresh contingent of crusaders from the north, set out from Carcassonne with the intention of conquering this 'synagogue of Satan'. He had originally planned to besiege the fortress of Cabaret in the Black Mountain just to the north of Carcassonne, but its lord, Peter Roger, despite his reputation as a defender of heretics, had decided that the wiser course would be to submit and had handed over his castle to Simon's companion, Bouchard of Marly. The inhabitants of Lavaur, however, determined to resist. 'In Lavaur', says Peter of Les Vaux-de-

---

1   PVC, vol. 1, para. 220, p.219; trans. Sibly, p.113; WP, pp.28–9.

Cernay, 'were the traitor Aimeric, who had been the lord of Montréal, and numerous other knights, enemies of the cross, up to eighty in number, who had entered the place and fortified it against us. The Dame of Lavaur was a widow named Giraude, a heretic of the worst sort and sister to Aimeric.'[2]

Aimery was the son of Sicard II of Laurac and his wife, Blanca, and he had inherited the lordships of two of the most important fortified places in the Carcassès, Laurac and Montréal, when his father died in 1200. Peter of Les Vaux-de-Cernay regarded him as 'the most powerful and noble man in the whole area except for the Counts', while William of Tudela claimed that 'there was not a richer knight in all the Toulousain nor the rest of the county, nor a more generous spender or of higher rank'.[3] Certainly the family was well-connected. Three of Aimery's sisters had married into important noble houses: Guirauda to the lord of Lavaur, Navarra to Stephen of Servian, and Esclarmonda to William of Niort.[4] These marriages placed the lord of Laurac and Montréal at the heart of a network which stretched from Lavaur on the borders of the Albigeois in the north to Niort in the *pays* de Sault in the Pyrenees in the south, and eastwards to Servian in the Biterrois, just north of Béziers itself.

There is no doubt that this was a heretical network, which the female members of the family played a key role in sustaining. After Sicard's death, Blanca became a Cathar *perfecta* at Laurac, where she set up a home for Cathar women, one of whom was another daughter, Mabilla. There were regular meetings of Cathars and their supporters at Laurac and Montréal, as well as public debates on matters of belief, including confrontations at Montréal in 1207 between Catholics led by Diego, Bishop of Osma, and Cathars led by Arnaud Oth, a deacon from Laurac, and at Laurac, the next year, between Isarn of Castres, Cathar deacon of nearby Mas-Saintes-Puelles, and the Waldensian, Bernard Prim.[5] A good idea of the religious milieu of the area in the late twelfth and early thirteenth centuries can be gained from the memories of Hélis of Mazerolles, wife of Arnaud, a knight from Montréal. She deposed before the inquisitors in 1243 and recalled gatherings of up to fifty years before. Her grandmother, Guillelma of Tonneins, had presided over a house of *perfectae* at Fanjeaux, which is about half-way

---

2  PVC, vol. 1, para. 215, pp.214–15; trans. Sibly, p.111.

3  PVC, vol. 1, para. 135, p.138; trans. Sibly, p.73; *Chanson*, vol. 1, laisse 68, pp.164–5; trans. Shirley, p.41.

4  See W. L. Wakefield, 'The family of Niort in the Albigensian Crusade and before the Inquisition', *Names. The Journal of the American Name Society* 18 (1970), pp.98–100.

5  PVC, vol. 1, para. 26, pp.28–9; trans. Sibly, p.20; WP, pp.50–1 (Montréal); Bibliothèque municipale, Toulouse, *Manuscrit 609* (hereafter *Ms. 609*), f.109a (Laurac).

between Laurac and Montréal and, as a young girl, Hélis had visited her there. In turn, her mother, Auda, became a *perfecta* in the house as well. Guilhabert of Castres, who took part in the debate with Bishop Diego in 1207 and who later became Cathar bishop of Toulouse, lived in Fanjeaux at this time. Among the many meetings she had attended Hélis recalled one at Montréal in 1203 at which two *perfecti*, Bernard Coldefy and Arnaud Guiraud, had preached to a group of ten women, several of whom were wives of knights of Montréal. Her sister, Braida, and her sister-in-law, Fabrissa, had houses at Montréal and Gaja-la-Selve (just to the west of Fanjeaux) and she had visited them many times. Among the many others she had seen at the house at Montréal were Aimery of Montréal and two of her husband's brothers, Raines and Peter.[6]

Although the chroniclers never actually describe Aimery himself as a heretic, the Cathars clearly lived openly at Laurac and Montréal and were in regular contact with neighbouring places in which heretics were established. Many, perhaps most, of his knights and their families respected the *perfecti* and their teaching. William of Tudela lamented the day that Aimery had met the 'heretics and clog-wearers' (meaning Waldensians), for he saw them as the reason for his downfall.[7] In one sense this was correct, for the Cathar penetration of the lordships of the viscounties of Béziers and Carcassonne held by the Trencavel family was the immediate reason for the crusader invasion. However, William of Tudela's view is only a partial explanation of Aimery's situation, for his patronage of the Cathars stemmed from a fundamental perception of his own social and political position which he shared with other similar lords of the region. Peter of Les Vaux-de-Cernay calls him 'a traitor of the worst sort' because he twice reneged on his promises to Simon of Montfort, once at the time of the fall of Carcassonne in August 1209, when he had abandoned Montréal and joined the crusaders, only to take over the castle again when Montfort's represent-ative handed it over to him, and again a year later, when he had agreed peace in exchange for what Peter calls an equivalent territory which was in open country and unfortified.[8] Between times he had tried to negotiate an agreement with Peter II, King of Aragon who, early in 1211, had reluct-antly accepted Montfort's homage for the Trencavel lands in place of the former viscount Raymond Roger, who had died in prison in November 1209. In May or June 1210, Raymond of Termes, Peter Roger of Cabaret, and Aimery of Montréal had offered their homage directly to the king, but

---

6   Doat, vol. 23, ff.162–80.
7   *Chanson*, vol. 1, laisse 68, pp.164–5; trans. Shirley, p.41.
8   PVC, vol. 1, para. 135, pp.138–9, para. 167, p.170; trans. Sibly, pp.73, 90.

Peter II would only accede to this if they accepted the principle of rendability, which meant the king would be allowed, as a matter of right, to take over their castles whenever he wished, although this would in no way abrogate his vassals' prerogatives.[9] This appears to have been a step too far for these lords and negotiations broke down.[10] Aimery of Montréal's manoeuvres and his final defiance at Lavaur grew out of the nature of these lordships. These lords had never been accustomed to the close control over their actions which the Capetians in northern France or the Angevins in England had been imposing upon their vassals during the twelfth century. Although they accepted the overlordship of the viscount of Béziers – and indeed they seem to have attended his court[11] – they were not prepared to allow him to curtail their political or economic independence to any great degree. It is not difficult to see how a set of religious beliefs which, for Cathar believers, demanded nothing of the increasingly burdensome penitential system of the Catholic Church, could fit into this world.[12] In these circumstances, Aimery's defence of Lavaur is easy to understand. According to William of Tudela, 'he had lost Montréal, Laurac and all his other lands to the crusaders; they had reduced his fief by 200 knights, and he was angry'.[13]

The regional power of such lords had been consolidated by dynastic alliances, as the marriages of Aimery's sisters demonstrate. However, because of their geographical positions in relation to crusader activity the histories of the lordships of Servian, Niort, and Lavaur are quite different. Servian was abandoned even before the fall of Béziers on 22 July 1209, for the crusaders took possession of the empty castle the day before they reached the city.[14] Like Montréal, in 1206 it had been the setting for a debate between Catholic preachers and heretic leaders, to whom Stephen of Servian had given his protection. Stephen admitted this in February 1210, when, at the abbey of St Thierry in the presence of the papal legate, Arnald Amalric, he abjured his heresy. 'I have received in my castles heretics and even heresiarchs, namely Theoderic, Baldwin, Bernard of Simorre, and others who wished to come, and I have protected and maintained them, and allowed them to

---

9   See C. Coulson, 'Fortress policy in Capetian tradition and Angevin practice: aspects of the conquest of Normandy by Philip II', in R. A. Brown, ed., *Anglo-Norman Studies VI, Proceedings of the Battle Conference 1983* (Woodbridge, 1984), pp.13–38, for a discussion of rendability.

10  PVC, vol. 1, paras 148–9, pp.152–3; trans. Sibly, p.81.

11  F. L. Cheyette, review of J. Strayer, *The Albigensian Crusades, Speculum* 48 (1973), pp.411–15.

12  J. H. Mundy, *Men and Women at Toulouse in the Age of the Cathars* (Studies and Texts, 101) (Toronto, 1990), pp.1–4, for a discussion of the various theories put forward by historians about the possible attractions of Catharism.

13  *Chanson*, vol. 1, laisse 68, pp.164–5; trans. Shirley, p.41.

14  *Innocentii III Registrorum sive Epistolarum*, in *PL*, vol. 216, col. 139. Letter of the legates Arnald Amalric and Milo to Innocent III.

hold schools of heresy, and to preach and dispute publicly.'[15] While Navarra's husband was affected by the crusade almost instantly, Esclarmonda was married to William of Niort, whose family was only gradually drawn into the conflict. In contrast to Servian, the core of the Niort lands, which were situated in the mountains in the Rebenty gorge west of the upper Aude river, was remote from the operations of the crusade. Nevertheless, the family was an integral part of the Cathar world: Bernard Oth, Esclarmonda's eldest son, was partly brought up by his grandmother, Blanca, in her house at Laurac in the early years of the thirteenth century. Such early influences were reflected in adulthood, for both Bernard Oth and his brother Raymond were actively involved in protecting heretics in the 1220s and, indeed, the latter died hereticated sometime between 1223 and 1227. Bernard Oth himself was married to Nova, a daughter of another heretical lord and a former associate of his uncle, Peter Roger of Cabaret. In the early 1220s, taking advantage of the southern revival under the new Count of Toulouse, Raymond VII, he had regained possession of Laurac and Montréal. Although Bernard Oth did attempt a reconciliation with King Louis VIII in 1226, for most of his career he was in conflict with the prelates and inquisitors of the region, none of whom saw any redeeming features in the beliefs of his entire family. In fact, individuals within the Niort clan did show varying degrees of enthusiasm for the Cathars, but it is unlikely that the lords of Laurac would have married Esclarmonda into the family if they had been unsure of its commitment to their beliefs. Their activities continued until, following their involvement in the failed Trencavel rising of 1240, their castles were confiscated by the king. Despite several attempts, they never regained their previous position.[16]

Lavaur stands on the west bank of the Agout, at a point where the river has cut a steep cliff as it swings across the valley, before bending back into a relatively narrow defile. Aimery seems to have decided that it was a more formidable place than his castle at Montréal, despite the latter's hilltop situation. William of Tudela says that no stronger town was ever seen outside the mountain *castra*, for it was protected by ramparts and deep ditches.[17] Peter of Les Vaux-de-Cernay calls it 'very noteworthy and extensive'; during the siege fully-armed knights rode along the walls 'to show their contempt for our side and demonstrate that the walls were substantial and well fortified'.[18] This fits the pattern of fortified towns and villages, which

---

15  *HGL*, vol. 8, no. 150, col. 584. See also PVC, vol. 1, para. 23, p.26; trans. Sibly, pp.18–19.
16  See Wakefield, 'Family of Niort', pp.97–117, 286–303, and revised version, privately circulated in typescript, 1989, for a thorough survey.
17  *Chanson*, vol. 1, laisse 68, pp.164–5; trans. Shirley, p.41.
18  PVC, vol. 1, para. 215, p.214, para. 222, pp.222–3; trans. Sibly, pp.111, 115.

Anne Brenon has called *bourgades*, found from at least the eleventh century in Italy, Provence, and Gascony as well.[19] Such places were not simply military garrisons, but had a strong community life, often centred upon an important public open space within the walls. Lavaur was a civilised place to live; when it fell to the crusaders the booty included bay and sorrel warhorses, good iron armour, ample supplies of corn and wine, and cloth and rich clothing,[20] and when Simon of Montfort moved on in his military campaigning, this was the place he chose to leave his wife. Before the crusade the matriarchal figures who seem to have been so influential in maintaining the heretical networks flourished in this setting. From the twelfth century onwards female life expectancy was greater than that of men and the general health of women improved. At the same time age gaps within marriage seem to have become more common with many women at least twenty years younger than their husbands, so that not only was there a considerable likelihood that they would become widows but also that they would be better placed to mould the outlook of their children.[21] By 1211 Guiraude had already lost her husband, but she continued to reside at Lavaur, where she had gained a considerable reputation as a generous hostess.[22] While Lavaur was hardly the source of the whole Cathar movement – Peter of Les Vaux-de-Cernay's hyperbole may well have been a means of justifying what contemporaries saw as the exceptional bloodshed which followed the fall of the town – it was nevertheless a key Cathar centre. A generation before it had been singled out for attack by Henry of Marcy, Abbot of Clairvaux, who, in 1181 had besieged it with the help of forces supplied by Raymond V, Count of Toulouse. Henry probably chose it because, three years before, he had confronted two heretics from Castres, Raymond of Baimire and Bernard Raymond, at Toulouse, and they had since settled in Lavaur. Bernard Raymond had been Cathar bishop of Toulouse since the Council of St Félix-de-Caraman in the mid-1170s. On this occasion the inhabitants were persuaded to submit by Adelaide, wife of Roger II of

---

19  A. Brenon, *Les Femmes Cathares* (Paris, 1992), pp.117–19. On the nature of his 'castle-villages', see F. L. Cheyette, 'The castles of the Trencavels: a preliminary aerial survey', in W. C. Jordan, R. McNab and T. F. Ruiz, eds, *Order and Innovation in the Middle Ages. Essays in Honor of Joseph R. Strayer* (Princeton, NJ, 1976), pp.255–72.

20  *Chanson*, vol. 1, laisse 71, pp.174–5; trans. Shirley, p.43.

21  D. Herlihy, 'The generation in medieval history', *Viator* 5 (1974), pp.347–64, and 'Life expectancies for women in medieval society', in R. T. Morewedge, ed., *The Role of Women in the Middle Ages* (Albany, NY, 1975), pp.1–22; V. Bullough and C. Campbell, 'Female longevity and diet in the Middle Ages', *Speculum* 55 (1980), pp.317–25; Mundy, *Men and Women at Toulouse*, pp.81–5. In the testaments studied by Mundy, 'nearly 95 percent of the males left female relicts when they died', p.84.

22  *Chanson*, vol. 1, laisse 68, pp.166–7; trans. Shirley, p.41.

Trencavel, and the two men were handed over.[23] According to William of
Puylaurens, they were converted to Catholicism and spent the rest of their
lives as canons in Toulouse.[24] Henry's efforts, however, bore no other fruit
for the Catholic Church, for Lavaur remained the seat of a Cathar bishopric
and the heretics continued to maintain houses there.[25] 'The fever of heresy
did not abate', says William of Puylaurens.[26]

Just like Laurac and Montréal, Lavaur was surrounded by places in
which there is evidence of heretical presence and, before 1209, the heretics
moved quite freely between them. The river was an important means of
communication: up-river at fourteen, twenty-four, and thirty-six kilometres
respectively were Saint-Paul-Cap-de-Joux, Vielmur, and Castres. Not on
the Agout, but within a radius of less than thirty kilometres, were Rabastens
(on the River Tarn), les Touelles (the present Briatexte), Lombers, and
Lautrec to the north, and Verfeil, Puylaurens, and Lanta to the south.[27]
Both Saint-Paul and Lombers were seats of Cathar bishoprics and Lautrec,
Verfeil, Lanta, Vielmur, and Puylaurens all had Cathar deacons.[28] In April
1211, when the crusaders began the siege of Lavaur, the town's population
had been swollen by Cathars from other towns in the vicinity. One such
town was Villemur, situated thirty-six kilometres downstream from Lavaur,
beyond the point where the Agout flows into the Tarn. In June 1209, this
town had been destroyed by its own inhabitants, who had heard that
a crusading army had entered the region from the Agenais.[29] Arnauda of
Lamothe, a *perfecta* who deposed before the inquisitors in 1244, was there
at the time. Arnauda had been brought up in Montauban, the daughter
of Austorga, a believer of heretics. In about 1206 Arnauda and her sister,
Peirona, had been sent to live in a house of female heretics at nearby

23 See E. Griffe, *Les Débuts de l'aventure Cathare en Languedoc (1140–90)* (Paris, 1969), pp.127–30,
   for these events. On the 1178 mission, see Roger of Howden, *Chronica*, ed. W. Stubbs,
   vol. 2 (Rolls Series, 51) (London, 1868), pp.150–5, and for the submission of 1181,
   Geoffrey of Vigeois, *Ex Chronico Coenobitae Monasterii S. Martialis Lemovicensis ac Prioris Vosiensis
   Coenobii*, in *RHG*, vol. 12, pp.448–9. Trans. of Howden, in WE, no. 29, pp.194–200.
24 WP, pp.28–9.
25 Doat, vol. 24, f.24r. See E. Griffe, *Le Languedoc Cathare de 1190 à 1210* (Paris, 1971), pp.25–6.
26 WP, pp.30–1.
27 See M. Roquebert, *L'Épopée cathare*, vol. 1, *1198–1212: L'Invasion* (Toulouse, 1970),
   appendix, pp.525–37, for places with known Cathar sympathisers.
28 See J. Duvernoy, *Le Catharisme*, vol. 2, *L'Histoire des Cathares* (Toulouse, 1979), appendix II,
   pp.347–51, for Cathar bishops and deacons. A. Brenon, *Le Vrai visage du Catharisme*, 2nd
   edn (Portet-sur-Garonne, 1995), p.119, for map.
29 *Chanson*, vol. 1, laisse 14, pp.42–5; trans. Shirley, pp.17–18. This was a different army
   from that which attacked Béziers in the east in the following month, and it had little
   impact on the crusade as a whole. It consisted largely of forces from the Auvergne and
   from Quercy and its most important noble seems to have been Guy II, Count of
   Clermont and the Auvergne.

Villemur, and three years later they had been consoled. Here, they were in the midst of a thriving Cathar community, which had at least two houses of heretics, and was frequently visited by Cathar leaders. All this, though, was thrown into confusion within months when all the heretics fled from the town because 'the crusaders came into the region'. From then onwards Arnauda was unable to settle anywhere. Under the care of Raymond Aimeric, a Cathar deacon, they went first to Roquemaure and Giraussens, and then to Lavaur, where she and her companion stayed for a year at the house of Alzalais, a *perfecta* resident there. The threat of Montfort's army in the spring of 1211 led to another departure, this time to Rabastens.[30]

As she explained, Arnauda was still young at the time and this may have been the reason for taking her to safety. Many other adult heretics stayed – perhaps as many as 400 – either because it was impractical to escape in such numbers or because they were confident that the powerful defences of the town could be maintained. If this was what they believed, they were wrong. At first the crusaders did not have sufficient men to surround the town and the defenders felt strong enough to make a sortie. Indeed, Peter of Les Vaux-de-Cernay claimed that the town contained 'a huge force' which outnumbered the crusaders and that it had been secretly reinforced by the Count of Toulouse despite his previous enmity for Lavaur. However, once joined by members of the 'White Brotherhood', an orthodox militia formed to defend the faith by Bishop Fulk of Toulouse, the crusaders were able to press the attack more vigorously and, after a siege of over a month, the town fell on 3 May.

Retribution was enacted on a scale hitherto unprecedented in the Albigensian Crusade. In July the previous year the crusaders had taken Minerve, a fortified village to the north-east of Carcassonne. Like Lavaur, it was set on river cliffs, although here the confluence of the Rivers Cesse and Brian had cut steep ravines on either side of it. It had two houses of heretics, one male and one female; all but three women remained obdurate and 140 were burnt to death. The other inhabitants had renounced heresy and had been spared, and William, the lord of Minerve, had been granted the revenues of some lands near Béziers.[31] However, according to Peter of Les Vaux-de-Cernay, each winter when the bulk of the crusaders departed, there were defections among the secular lords on a massive scale, more than forty in 1209–10.[32] At Lavaur therefore Simon of Montfort adopted a different policy. Aimery of Montréal and over eighty of his knights were

---

30   Doat, vol. 23, ff.2v–6v.
31   PVC, vol. 1, paras 156–7, pp.160–1; trans. Sibly, p.85.
32   PVC, vol. 1, para. 136, pp.139–40; trans. Sibly, p.74.

**Plate 1**
The fortified village of Minerve, south walls overlooking the confluence of the
rivers Cesse and Brian

either hanged or slaughtered; between 300 and 400 heretics were burnt to death; and Guirauda, screaming and shouting, was dropped into a well and rocks piled on top of her, apparently on Montfort's orders.[33] The killing of Aimery of Montréal and his vassals, as well as that of Guirauda of Lavaur, seems to have a conscious policy aimed not only at eliminating the *perfecti*, but also at terrorising the leaders of the local nobility who had for so long tolerated and protected the heretics.[34] Indeed, William of Tudela had never previously heard of the hanging of a noble of the status of Aimery of Montréal. There is some limited evidence that the killing was not indiscriminate. The knights who were hanged seem to have been from the viscounties of Béziers and Carcassonne and were therefore traitors in Montfort's eyes. Others involved, who came from the county of Toulouse, were probably ransomed.[35] The policy had immediate effect: 'On hearing that Lavaur had been taken, Sicard, lord of Puylaurens, who had at one time sided with our Count but later deserted him, was seized with fear; he left Puylaurens and hurried off to Toulouse with his knights. Puylaurens was a notable *castrum* about three leagues from Lavaur in the diocese of Toulouse.'[36]

## The territorial lords

Both contemporary chroniclers and later inquisitorial records demonstrate that the real strength of Catharism lay in this network of interrelated lordships, particularly but not exclusively in the Toulousain, the Albigeois, and the Carcassès. In the eyes of the Catholic authorities, however, the ultimate responsibility for the spread of heresy lay with the main secular powers of the region: the counts of Toulouse, Foix, and Comminges, and the viscounts of Béziers and Carcassonne. By 1213, when events had forced Peter II, King of Aragon, to take a stand to defend rights which he saw as threatened by the crusaders under Simon of Montfort, the king, too, was added to the list of *fautors* (or protectors) of heresy, despite his crusading feats in the Iberian peninsula. Raymond VI, Count of Toulouse, was seen as prime defender of heretical wickedness. In a letter of March 1208, two months after the murder of Peter of Castelnau, the papal legate in Languedoc, by a vassal of the count, Innocent III held Raymond to be directly responsible.

---

33  PVC, vol. 1, para. 227, pp.227–8; trans. Sibly, p.117; *Chanson*, vol. 1, laisses 68, 71, pp.164–7, 172–3; trans. Shirley, pp.41–2, 42–3. WP, pp.70–1.
34  See, too, the comments of Roquebert, *L'Épopée cathare*, vol. 1, pp.378 and 406.
35  Ibid., p.397.
36  PVC, vol. 1, para. 230, p.230; trans. Sibly, p.118.

43

Against him [the legate] the Devil roused his minister, the Count of Toulouse. This man had often incurred the censure of the Church for the many grave outrages he had committed against her, and often – as might be expected of a person who was crafty and cunning, slippery and unreliable – had received absolution under the guise of feigned penitence. At last he could not hold back the hatred he had conceived against Peter – since indeed in Peter's mouth the word of God was not restrained from executing vengeance upon the nations and punishments upon the people; hatred the stronger because the Count himself was so richly deserving of punishment for his great crimes.[37]

This letter, incorporated in full in Peter of Les Vaux-de-Cernay's chronicle, was in fact composed in the highly-charged atmosphere of the papal curia at that time and, indeed, although not convinced of the count's sincerity, a little over three months later, the pope allowed Raymond to be reconciled to the Church. The new papal legate, Master Milo, who had been appointed on 1 March, took the precaution of acquiring seven of Raymond's Provençal castles as security for his conduct.[38] Peter of Les Vaux-de-Cernay himself had no doubt about Raymond's beliefs. 'The most convincing proof that he always cherished heretics is that none of the papal legates could ever persuade him to drive the heretics from his domain, even though the legates did very often compel him to denounce them.' Peter claimed that Raymond kept heretics in his entourage (although disguised in ordinary clothes) so that, should he find himself close to death, they would always be on hand to administer the *consolamentum* (the rite by which Cathar believers entered the ranks of the *perfecti* or *bonhommes*) and thus admit him into the Cathar Church.[39] Peter's hatred of the count is well-known, but it is interesting to see that William of Puylaurens, who was not an outsider like Peter but brought up in a town little more than a day's journey to the east of Toulouse, and who was writing from the perspective of the mid-thirteenth century, also thought that, as the most powerful lords of the region, the blame must be laid at the door of the counts of Toulouse, 'through whose negligence and failure the evil increased in these parts'.[40]

William seems to be talking about those counts within living memory, that is Raymond VI (1194–1222) and his son, Raymond VII (1222–49). The crucial period, however, was that under the rule of Raymond V, who succeeded to the county at the age of fourteen, when his father,

---

37  PVC, vol. 1, para. 57, pp.52–4; trans. Sibly, p.32.
38  PVC, vol. 1, paras 75–8, pp.75–9; trans. Sibly, pp.43–5.
39  PVC, vol. 1, paras 37, 28, pp.35, 31–3; trans. Sibly, pp.23, 22.
40  WP, pp.30–1.

Alfonso-Jordan, died while on the Second Crusade in 1148. At that time he entered into an impressive inheritance, extending across the south from the borders of Gascony to the Alps, and from Périgord and the Auvergne in the north to the Mediterranean. The origins of this agglomeration went back to the early tenth century when the empire built up by Charlemagne in the late eighth and early ninth centuries was disintegrating in almost every part. In 778 Charlemagne had campaigned in Iberia and, although this cannot be seen as his most successful military exploit, he did establish marcher lordships in Gascony and Catalonia, as well as a comital administrative system in Languedoc itself. The counts of Toulouse emerged from this structure as the Carolingian system broke up in the course of the ninth century. In 924 Count Raymond III gained 'Gothia', which included Narbonne, Montpellier, and Nîmes and, in 990, the marriage of Count William III to Emma of Provence extended the dynasty's power east of the River Rhône. This was not always a steady expansionist progress since the counts suffered several setbacks in the eleventh century, but by 1096 Raymond IV felt confident enough to leave the territories he had reassembled to set off on crusade to the East. The tie with the ruling dynasty in Francia remained; at times it could be useful as when, in 1159, the Capetian king, Louis VII, who was also his brother-in-law, helped Raymond V to protect himself from the combined threat of the Angevin, Henry II, and Raymond Berengar IV, Count of Barcelona.[41] However, such interventions were usually as impractical as they were infrequent, for the Capetian kings had no long-term influence in Languedoc. Indeed, the counts were just as ready to seek an Angevin alliance when it suited them. In 1173, having repudiated his wife, Constance of France, Raymond V accepted Henry as his liege lord; twenty years later, Raymond VI took Joan, sister of Richard I, as his fourth wife, and received the fief of Agenais and the restoration of Quercy, thus extending his power along the right bank of the Garonne beyond Marmande. Not surprisingly, the French king, Philip II, received no help from Toulouse in his conflict with Richard's successor, John, over Normandy between 1202 and 1204.[42]

The counts of Toulouse had therefore expanded their territories in much the same way as other powerful contemporaries in the twelfth century: by military strength, marriage alliances, and opportunistic changes of loyalty. The result has been described as having a 'federal character' in which the various elements each preserved their own local institutions, 'to the detriment of central government'.[43] The counts did have local officials: *viguiers* in the

---

41  See E. Hallam, *Capetian France, 987–1328* (London, 1980), pp.54–62, for an overview.

42  See Y. Dossat, 'Le Comté de Toulouse et la féodalité languedocienne à la veille de la croisade albigeoise', *Revue du Tarn* 9 (1943), pp.78–9.

43  Ibid., p.83.

more important towns, who usually shared power with the local consulate, not always harmoniously, and *bayles* in the countryside. Under Raymond VI *sénéchaux* were introduced with the aim of governing whole regions, but they were not fully established by 1209 when the crusade began and did not develop properly until after the peace of 1229. Even so, this lack of 'centralised' institutions was not untypical. The mighty assemblage of fiefs brought under the rule of Henry II had no more administrative consistency than Raymond's territories.[44] Ambitious rulers looked to gain what they could and to govern what they acquired by whatever means presented themselves.

Nevertheless, Raymond V's inheritance was not as formidable as a map of his domains might suggest, not so much because of its administrative deficiencies but because of political rivalries. Other lords, too, had taken advantage of the decline of Carolingian power, both lay and ecclesiastical. To the counts of Toulouse the most important were the viscounts of Béziers and Carcassonne, whose lands, although subordinate to the counts, stretched from the territory between the Aveyron and the Tarn north of Albi to the Pyrenees in the south, and encompassed Hérault to the east, forming a large wedge of territory cutting right across the main roads connecting Toulouse with Nîmes and the Rhône Valley. Within the Trencavel lands were over fifty *castra* and fortified towns. Friction was inevitable, despite marriage links. In 1150, shortly after Raymond V's accession, Raymond Trencavel, already viscount of Béziers since 1129, added the viscounty of Carcassonne, Albi, and the Razès, to his titles when his older brother, Roger, died. Not only did this consolidate Trencavel power (which thereafter was not subdivided), but it also enabled the rulers of Aragon to insert themselves into the relationship since the viscounty of Carcassonne and the Razès was held from them and not from Toulouse.[45] Moreover, these rulers were always alert to exploit any conflicts within the Toulousan lands. Raymond Berengar IV, Count of Barcelona and ruler of Aragon through his wife, had successfully expanded his power against the Moors, and looked to pursue an equally vigorous policy north of the Pyrenees. Therefore, Raymond Berengar and, when he came of age in 1174, his successor, Alfonso II (1162–96), worked to draw the Pyrenean powers into their orbit, particularly the counts of Foix and the viscounts of Béarn. To this end Raymond Berengar acquired the fealty of the Trencavel viscount in 1150 and, although this was lost by Alfonso II in 1176, Roger II, the new viscount, returned to the Aragonese

---

44   See J. C. Holt, 'The end of the Anglo-Norman realm', *Proceedings of the British Academy* 61 (1975), pp.223–65, and J. Gillingham, *The Angevin Empire* (London, 1984).

45   Dossat, 'Le Comté de Toulouse', pp.88–9.

**Plate 2**
Carcassonne from the south as restored by Viollet-le-Duc between 1852 and 1879

**Plate 3**

Carcassonne, Château comtal

side three years later. Roger's marriage to Adelaide, Raymond V's daughter, in 1171, therefore provided no long-term solution to this instability.[46] Equally sensitive was Provence, where Raymond V inherited the conflicts with Raymond Berengar that his father had pursued. For Raymond V this was particularly important for the evidence of his charters suggests that he was more interested in his eastern domains than the Toulousain.[47] Some ecclesiastical lords had also established their own enclaves, notably the archbishops of Narbonne and Montpellier. Significantly, the dioceses of Toulouse and Carcassonne lay within the province of Narbonne.[48] (See Map 2.)

Raymond V's relative inaction on the matter of heresy may therefore be explained both by his youth at the time of his accession and by his preoccupation with the long-term political and military problems presented by the vast collection of territories to which the counts laid claim. When he did eventually appeal for help to King Louis VII – in a letter to Alexander, Abbot of Cîteaux, in 1177 – he had already been count for nearly thirty years. By this time there is good reason for believing his claim that 'the most noble of my lords, already overcome by the plague of infidelity, have become corrupt and with them a very great multitude of men have been led from the faith'.[49] Evidence of the existence of heretical belief in the territories of the count of Toulouse is strong in the 1140s and, although St Bernard had successfully combatted the preaching of Henry the Monk in Toulouse in 1145, Bernard himself appears to have believed he had not really tackled the root of the problem of heresy in the region.[50] In 1165 there had been the public debate between orthodox bishops and abbots and heretical leaders in the town of Lombers, south of Albi, and in the mid-1170s the Council of St-Félix-de-Caraman had received Bogomil missionaries who had reorganised the Cathar Church.[51] Raymond V's letter may well have been a reaction to the assembly at St-Félix, which, unlike Lombers in the Trencavel territories, was situated in the county of Toulouse itself, but even here his policy is ambiguous, for historians argue that he was at least as concerned to use outside intervention to undermine political enemies like the *consuls* of Toulouse or Roger Trencavel as he was to stamp

46  See T. Bisson, *The Medieval Crown of Aragon. A Short History* (Oxford, 1986), pp.32–8, and Hallam, *Capetian France*, pp.60–2.
47  Dossat, 'Le Comté de Toulouse', pp.78–9.
48  Ibid., p.88; Griffe, *Les Débuts*, p.8.
49  Gervase of Canterbury, *The Historical Works of Gervase of Canterbury*, vol. 1, in *The Chronicles of the Reigns of Stephen, Henry II and Richard I*, ed. W. Stubbs (Rolls Series, 73) (London, 1879), pp.270–1.
50  See above, ch. 1, pp.31–2.
51  See above, ch. 1, pp.7–8, for the Council of St Félix-de-Caraman, and below, ch. 4, p.118, for the Council of Lombers.

out heresy.[52] It is noticeable that when an armed expedition did finally materialise, under Henry of Marcy, Abbot of Clairvaux, in 1181, it was actually aimed at Lavaur in the Trencavel lands.[53] It is ironic that, when he succeeded in 1194, Raymond VI, whose grandfather and great-grandfather had both died while crusading in the East, was already presiding over a society in which religious beliefs were accepted that were at least as shocking to the orthodox as those of the Muslims. Indeed, by the 1180s, Raymond IV, who had died while besieging Tripoli in 1105, was revered as a hero of the First Crusade, a reputation he never held during his lifetime. William, Archbishop of Tyre, whose history of the Latins in Outremer was becoming well-known in the West, greatly admired his determination to stay in the East and offer himself as 'a holocaust to the Lord', despite the fact that he was 'an illustrious and powerful man who, as he had the most ample patrimony, could have in abundance every good thing he wanted'.[54] Any assessment of Raymond VI needs to be seen in this context. Although Peter of Les Vaux-de-Cernay was correct in his belief that there were heretics associated with Raymond's court, it was not the *consolamentum* that the count desired when he died, but the habit of the Hospitallers and burial in the cemetery of their commandery in Toulouse.[55] In this, at least, his attitude is strikingly similar to that of his direct contemporary, William Marshal, Earl of Pembroke, who had a special mantle prepared for his eventual burial in the Templar church in London.[56]

If, for Peter of Les Vaux-de-Cernay, Raymond VI was the arch-villain, the exact counterpoint to Simon of Montfort, he was nevertheless only the most prominent member of a cast which the chronicler saw as equally wicked and perverse. Raymond Roger Trencavel, who succeeded to the viscounties in 1194, the same year as Raymond VI, was the son of Adelaide, daughter of Raymond V, and 'was following his uncle's evil example and was doing nothing to restrain the heretics'. Their contemporary, Raymond

52  For example, W. L. Wakefield, *Heresy, Crusade and Inquisition in Southern France, 1100–1250* (London, 1974), p.83.
53  On this expedition, see below ch. 4, p.114.
54  Guillaume de Tyr, *Chronique*, ed. R. B. C. Huygens, vol. 1 (Corpus Christianorum. Continuatio Medievalis, 63) (Turnhout, 1986), 11.2, p.497. It has been suggested that the political instability of the lands of the counts of Toulouse was a consequence of Raymond IV's absence on crusade between 1096 and 1105, Y. P. Stoyanov, *The Hidden Tradition in Europe* (Harmondsworth, 1994), p.159. It is interesting to note that it was precisely during the following period that King Louis VI (1108–35) established royal authority in the Ile-de-France.
55  J. Delaville Le Roux, ed., *Cartulaire général de l'Ordre des Hospitaliers de Saint-Jean de Jérusalem, 1100–1310*, vol. 2 (Paris, 1894), no. 1617, p.246; WP, pp.112–13.
56  See S. Painter, *William Marshal* (Baltimore, MD, 1933), pp.284–5. William died in 1219, three years before Raymond VI.

Roger, Count of Foix between 1188 and 1223, 'allowed heretics and their supporters to stay in his territories, and helped and encouraged them as much as he could', while his son, Roger Bernard, was a man 'whose depravity in no way fell short of his father's', a mantra which Peter repeats on three further occasions in the course of his chronicle. In Pamiers, Raymond Roger 'kept his wife and her two sisters (who were heretics), along with a crowd of other heretics', in a house he had built for them on the property of the canons of St Antonin. Indeed, Peter devotes a long section to 'the barbarity and malignity of the Count of Foix', which develops an increasingly hysterical tone as he piles up stories of the count's outrages. 'His wickedness exceeded all bounds. He pillaged monasteries, destroyed churches, excelled all others in cruelty.' The real problem, however, lay in the conflicts with the canons of St Antonin arising from shared jurisdiction over the town of Pamiers, rather than disputes over 'the two principles'. Peter of Les Vaux-de-Cernay appears to have been an uncritical listener to the version told him by the abbot.[57] There were three other great Pyrenean lords who came into conflict with the crusaders: Bernard IV, Count of Comminges (1181–1225), his nephew, Roger II of Comminges, Viscount of Couserans and Count of Pallars by marriage, whose lands lay between the counties of Foix and Comminges, and Gaston VI, Viscount of Béarn (1170–1215) and Count of Bigorre, again through marriage. Peter of Les Vaux-de-Cernay knew less about these and bracketed the count of Comminges and the viscount of Béarn with Raymond Roger of Foix as 'that villainous and damned trio'. He clearly agreed with the Catholic prelates at the Council of Lavaur who, in 1213, claimed that Bernard of Comminges had 'allied himself with the heretics and their supporters and joined with these pestilential men in attacking the Church'. Roger of Comminges, who did homage to Montfort during the siege of Lavaur, but later reneged on it, he calls 'a wretched and faithless man', for in Peter's world there could be no ambiguity; men were either on the side of the Lord or in the grip of the devil.[58]

Although Peter of Les Vaux-de-Cernay's language is intemperate and his moral judgements immutable, his view that the great territorial lords of the region tolerated and even protected heretics is nevertheless confirmed by other chroniclers and by witnesses before the inquisitors. William of Puylaurens says that the *milites* adhered to one or other of the heretics and held them 'in such great reverence that they had cemeteries in which those who had been hereticated were publicly buried, from whom they

---

57   PVC, vol. 1, paras 88, 197–209, 219, pp.89–90, 199–208, 218–19; trans. Sibly, pp.49, 103–7, 113.
58   PVC, vol. 2, paras 439, 380, pp.129, 75, vol. 1, para. 228, pp.228–9, vol. 2, para. 358, p.56; trans. Sibly, pp.199, 177, 117, 168.

received complete beds and clothes'.[59] William of Tudela's portrait of Raymond Roger Trencavel is that of a young man, 'generous and open-handed', who laughed and joked with his vassals on an equal basis. However, while he was not himself a heretic, 'all his knights and vavasours maintained the heretics in their towers and castles, and so they caused their own ruin and shameful deaths'.[60] He had been brought up in an environment in which the presence of Cathars was commonplace. When his father, Roger II, died in 1194, he left the protection of the nine-year-old Raymond Roger to one of his senior vassals, Bertrand, lord of Saissac, who was himself a protector of Cathar *perfecti*.[61] The milieu of the count of Foix was little different. William of Puylaurens says that, in 1207, heretics at Pamiers, where Raymond Roger normally resided, were openly protected by his sister, Esclarmonda, who, according to inquisitorial witnesses had become a Cathar *perfecta* in 1204 in the presence of her brother. His wife, Philippa, also became a *perfecta* with a house for Cathars at Dun, about twenty kilometres to the south-east of Pamiers, while the appearance of his aunt, Fais of Durfort, another *perfecta*, in Pamiers, was the occasion of a major altercation between some of the count's knights and the canons of St Antonin.[62] As well as members of his immediate family, as in the domains of the count of Toulouse and the viscount of Béziers, there were important heretical families among his own vassals, most notably the Mirepoix, closely linked by marriage to Raymond of Pereille who, sometime between 1204 and 1208, rebuilt the fortress of Montségur in the Pyrenees, south-east of Foix, and developed it as a centre for Cathar *perfecti* and their supporters. Raymond's son-in-law, Peter Roger of Mirepoix, later claimed that, in 1206 or 1207, the town of Mirepoix had been the meeting-place for an assembly of about 600 Cathars.[63] Nevertheless, like Raymond VI and Raymond Roger Trencavel, Raymond Roger of Foix does not seem to have been a committed Cathar himself. The pro-southern anonymous continuator of the *Chanson*, who invents a series of colourful speeches for the participants in the Fourth Lateran Council held

---

59  WP, pp.24–7.
60  *Chanson*, vol. 1, laisse 15, pp.44–7; trans. Shirley, pp.18–19.
61  *HGL*, vol. 8, no. 86, cols 429–31; *Ms. 609*, f. 252r, for the presence of heretics at Saissac in 1195.
62  WP, pp.48–9; Doat, vol. 24, ff. 42–3, 241r, 251r, and *HGL*, vol. 8, no. 329, cols 1035–6, for Esclarmonda's heretication. See also J.-M. Vidal, 'Esclarmonde de Foix', *Revue de Gascogne* 11 (1911), pp.53–79, and Griffe, *Le Languedoc Cathare de 1190 à 1210*, p.155.
63  F. Pasquier, ed., *Cartulaire de Mirepoix*, vol. 1 (Paris, 1921), pp.15–16, pièces just., no. IV, pp.24–6, for the fealty to the count of Foix (1223). For Mirepoix as a meeting-place for Cathars, Doat, vol. 24, ff. 240–1. See also Vidal, 'Esclarmonde de Foix', p.57, for other houses in the county of Foix. S. Nelli, *Montségur. Mythe et histoire* (Monaco, 1996), p.81, thinks that 1207–8 is a more plausible date for the reconstruction of Montségur than the one usually given, which is 1204.

in November 1215, places Raymond Roger at the forefront of the debate. As presented by the poet, the count claimed that he had 'never befriended heretics, neither believers nor the clothed', and that if his sister had done wrong, he 'ought not to be destroyed for her fault'. When Fulk, Bishop of Toulouse, claimed that his whole county was 'seething with heresy' and that the peak of Montségur had been deliberately fortified so that he could protect heretics, Raymond Roger countered by denying that he had ever been its overlord. He also stressed the patronage given by himself and his predecessors to the Cistercian monastery of Boulbonne, just to the north-east of Pamiers, which had become the family mausoleum; it is noticeable that his son, Roger Bernard, whom Peter of Les Vaux-de-Cernay believed to be as depraved as his father, took the habit at Boulbonne as an associate before he died and, in 1241, was buried there.[64]

These Pyrenean lords formed a tightly-knit group who, although not regional powers of the first rank, were able to maintain a large degree of independence. They were closely linked by marriage: in the crusade genera-tion, for instance, Roger II of Comminges was the nephew of Raymond Roger of Foix through his mother and Bernard IV of Comminges through his father. From the mid-twelfth century both the counts of Foix and Comminges rendered homage to the counts of Toulouse, but only for the small part of their lands which lay within the diocese, Saverdun in the case of Foix, and Muret and Sammartin in the case of Comminges. Otherwise, they associated themselves as much with Aragon as with Occitania. Roger of Comminges, Viscount of Couserans, held lands in Catalonia which were joined to his northern territories by the Salou Pass.[65] Peter of Les Vaux-de-Cernay was uniformly condemnatory, since they tended to act together, usually in opposition to the crusaders; the count of Foix and his son were particularly dangerous opponents to Montfort's men.[66]

The case of Peter II of Aragon is different from those of the Languedocian lords in that he had never been associated with heretics before the Albigensian Crusade; indeed, in 1204, he was crowned by Innocent III, thus turning his lands into a papal fief, and in 1212 he played a major role in the famous Christian victory over the Moors at Las Navas de Tolosa, south of Toledo. As such, his condemnation by Peter of Les Vaux-de-Cernay in 1213 as a man 'extremely hostile to the business of the faith', is significant for the striking way in which it demonstrates the problems faced by these southern

---

64  *Chanson*, vol. 2, laisse 145, pp.48–55; trans. Shirley, pp.74–5; WP, p.165, n.2. Brenon,
    *Femmes Cathares*, pp.122–3, thinks that there must have been relatively few Cathars in the
    county of Foix in the early thirteenth century, since no Cathar bishopric was set up there.
65  Dossat, 'Le Comté de Toulouse', p.88; Bisson, *Medieval Crown of Aragon*, pp.37–8.
66  For example, in battles at Montgey (April 1211) and Castelnaudary (September 1211).

lords once Catharism had become entrenched in their territories. In the chronicler's eyes, this view was justified because, 'He [the king] took under his protection, and accepted oaths of allegiance from, all the heretics and excommunicants – the Counts of Toulouse, Comminges, and Foix, Gaston de Béarn, all the knights of Toulouse and Carcassonne who had fled to Toulouse after being deprived of their possessions for heresy, and the citizens of Toulouse.' The king then misrepresented the position of the counts of Comminges and Foix and Gaston of Béarn, resulting in a mistaken papal restoration of their lands, which had to be rapidly rescinded.[67] The kings of Aragon, though, could not ignore events beyond the Pyrenees, for they had significant interests in Roussillon, Montpellier, and Provence, as well as the fealty of the Trencavels for the viscounty of Carcassonne. Their usual policy had been to secure a foothold in the Toulousain through exploiting their rights of fealty, but Peter II changed this strategy by forming an alliance with Raymond VI, when Eleanor, the king's sister, became the count's fifth wife after the death of Joan of England. This has called into question the sincerity of Peter's apparent attempts to mediate between Raymond Roger Trencavel and the crusaders in August 1209, when the viscount was trapped in his capital at Carcassonne.[68] Whatever his long-term aims – which may even have encompassed a dream of general overlordship of Occitania – they came to an abrupt end with his death in battle at Muret in September 1213. The fact was that the southern lords could hardly avoid contact with heretics, even though their personal religious inclinations seem not to have gone beyond the conventional desire of military men for burial in the cemetery of the local house of their favoured religious order, most likely the Cistercians or the Hospitallers. For William of Puylaurens, their sin was that of omission. Nobody had opposed the heretics, he says, who were allowed to set themselves up in the towns and the countryside, acquiring fields and vineyards and large houses where they could preach publicly to their followers.[69] But, as the chronicle of Peter of Les Vaux-de-Cernay makes very clear, in the climate of Latin Christendom in the first half of the thirteenth century, there was no middle way.

---

67 PVC, vol. 2, paras 367, 389, 408, pp.65, 85, 104; trans. Sibly, pp.172, 180, 188–9.

68 *Chanson*, vol. 1, laisses 26–30, pp.68–77; trans. Shirley, pp.23–4. Cheyette, in his review of Strayer's *Albigensian Crusades*, in *Speculum*, 1973, suggests an attempt by Raymond VI and Peter II to act in concert against Raymond Roger.

69 WP, pp.22–3. William's claim is fully supported by those who, deposing before the inquisitors in the 1240s, were old enough to remember the pre-crusade era. Castelnaudary (about thirty kilometres to the north-west of Carcassonne) is an example of such a place. In 1245, Raymond Arrufat remembered that both Cathars and Waldensians had often stayed there, had taken meals with local people, and had gone about the town quite openly, *Ms. 609*, f. 251r.

As the anonymous author of the *Chanson* saw it, the crusade destroyed this world. Writing in the late 1220s he looked back nostalgically to a time when what he called *paratge* had been the central element in aristocratic society. In retrospect, the turning-point had been the defeat of the southern lords and the death of Peter II at the battle of Muret in September 1213. 'It diminished the whole world, be sure of that, for it destroyed *paratge*, it disgraced and shamed all Christendom.' This, said the Toulousans in 1218, was the fault of outsiders, primarily the pope and the prelates of the Church, for 'ordering our death and destruction at the hands of foreigners who quench the light, from whose dominion we want to be free. If God and Toulouse had let them, they would have buried worth and *paratge* deep, past recovery.' For a time it looked as if Raymond VII, both in his father's later years and during the 1220s when he became count himself, might have the means to restore the past. When Simon of Montfort was killed in June 1218, the poet saw an opportunity to 'save *paratge* and worth'. It lay in the hands of 'the brave young count, who paints the darkness with gold and brings green back to the dead world'.[70]

This concept of *paratge* was integral to the nature of aristocratic relationships in Occitania, well-understood by both William of Tudela and William of Puylaurens. Most historians believe that, until the post-crusade settlement of 1229, in most parts of the south, ties of vassalage were weak or non-existent, freemen were generally unwilling to become directly dependent upon a suzerain, and the granting of a fief in return for military service was quite rare.[71] Men did enter into agreements of mutual support, known as *convenientiae*, but participants saw themselves as equals and not dependents, and would not have interpreted them in anything like the manner that northerners understood oaths of homage and fealty. Such men held their own territories, often centred upon a *castrum* or fortified town, which they fully intended would be handed down to their descendants. Many of these were allods, quite free of outside encumbrance: even though the proportion was declining, it is estimated that just under 50 per cent of land in the Toulousain was held in this form at the end of the twelfth

---

70 *Chanson*, vol. 2, laisse 137, pp.16–17, vol. 3, laisses 196, 208, pp.104–5, 234–5; trans. Shirley, pp.68, 150, 176.

71 For a succinct summary of the historical debate, see L. Paterson, *The World of the Troubadours* (Cambridge, 1994), pp.10–19. In essence this view was established in the late nineteenth century and has only been subject to modifications since then, although debate continues. See P. Dognon, *Les Institutions politiques et administratives du pays de Languedoc du XIIIe siècle aux guerres de religion* (Toulouse, 1895), pp.16–19, and Y. Dossat, 'La Société méridionale à la veille de la croisade des Albigeois', *Revue du Languedoc* 1 (1944), pp.66–71.

century.[72] Others were free fiefs, for which relatively few services were owed, sometimes no more than render; even then many were reluctant to comply, as can be seen by Aimery of Montréal's refusal to grant such access to Peter II of Aragon in 1210, although he was in dire need of his help.[73] This pattern was reinforced by the survival of Roman influence in the south, both in law and art. Roman law allowed the free disposal of property rather than insisting on primogeniture which had become increasingly common in Francia during the twelfth century. As a consequence patrimonies were not so much divided as shared; in places the numbers of co-seigneurs could grow to unmanageable proportions.[74]

As the author of the *Chanson* saw it, however, *paratge* was not only about the right of men to hold their patrimonies and devolve them to their heirs as they wished, but was a word which encompassed a whole way of life. When the two Raymonds met at Genoa early in 1216 after gaining papal recognition of the younger Raymond's rights in Provence, they travelled first to Marseille and then to Avignon. As they set out for Avignon they rode through a picturesque natural world.

> Next morning as dew was falling, the clear light of dawn growing brighter and birds beginning to sing, as leaves unfolded and flowerbuds opened, the knights rode two and two across the grassland, talking about their weapons and equipment. But Guy of Cavaillon, riding a bay horse, said to the young count, 'Now is the time when *paratge* urgently requires you to be bad and good. The count de Montfort, who destroys men, he and the Church at Rome and the preachers are covering *paratge* with shame, they have cast it down from its high place, and if you do not raise it up, it will vanish for ever. If worth and *paratge* do not rise again through you, then *paratge* dies, in you the whole world dies. You are the true hope of all *paratge* and the choice is yours: either you show valour or *paratge* dies.

The younger Raymond pledged that this is what he would do and that evening they received an ecstatic welcome at Avignon. 'So large were the crowds and the procession that threats and sticks and stones were needed. They went into the church to say their prayers and afterwards sat down to

---

72 Dognon, *Les Institutions politiques*, p.19; P. Martel, 'Naissance de l'Occitanie', in A. Armengaud and R. Lafont, eds, *Histoire d'Occitanie* (Paris, 1979), pp.161, 165, 219–20. On *convenientiae*, see E. Magnou-Nortier, 'Fidelité et féodalité méridionales d'après les serments de Fidelité, Xe-début XIIe siècles', in *Les structures sociales de l'Aquitaine, du Languedoc et de l'Espagne au premier âge féodal* (Paris, 1969), pp.119–28.
73 See above, pp.36–7.
74 See Dossat, 'La Société méridionale', pp.69–70.

a rich and savoury banquet with many kinds of sauces and fish dishes, red and white wines, clove-scented and vermilion, with entertainers, viols, dances and songs.'[75] It is not difficult to see how the poetic conventions and sexual mores of courtly love could flourish in this atmosphere.

Nevertheless, the pre-crusade world of Languedoc, which the poet saw as reviving all too briefly under Raymond VII, was not as idyllic as he presented it or perhaps, by the late 1220s, remembered it. When, in March 1179, at the Third Lateran Council, the Church fathers brought anathema down upon the Cathars and their followers in Gascony and the territories of Albi and Toulouse, they associated them with those they called Brabanters, Aragonese, Navarrese, Basques, Coterelli, and Triaverdini. According to canon 27, these 'practise such cruelty upon Christians that they respect neither churches nor monasteries, and spare neither widows, orphans, old or young nor any age or sex, but like pagans destroy and lay everything waste'. Anyone who hired or kept them 'should be subject in every way to the same sentence and penalty as the above-mentioned heretics and that they should not be received into the communion of the church, unless they abjure their pernicious society and heresy'.[76] William of Puylaurens saw this problem as endemic in the south. According to him, Fulcrand, Bishop of Toulouse between 1179 and 1201, could not accomplish any visitation in the diocese without first pleading for protection from the lords of the lands in which he intended to travel. William did not hold the count of Toulouse entirely responsible for this state of affairs, for warfare was such that he could not secure his own lands, let alone impose a general peace. These wars attracted *routiers* from outside the region, particularly from Spain, who moved freely through the land. 'Even if by chance he [the count] very much wanted to, he was not able to extirpate the heretical weeds so strongly rooted in the land without the co-operation of his enemies.'[77] It is possible, of course, that this level of violence – although considered reprehensible by contemporary clerics – was not abnormal for the late twelfth century, but if this was so, then Stephen of Tournai, Abbot of St Geneviève in Paris, did not see it that way. When he accompanied Henry of Marcy's expedition of 1181, for most of the time he was evidently terrified of attack. In a letter to his prior he wrote: 'I am following the bishop of Albano through mountains and valleys, through vast wildernesses, through the ferocity of robbers, and the image of death, through the burning of towns and the ruins of houses,

---

75  *Chanson*, vol. 2, laisse 154, pp.94–7; trans. Shirley, pp.84–5.
76  N. J. Tanner, ed., *Decrees of the Ecumenical Councils*, vol. 1, *Nicaea I to Lateran V* (London, 1990), pp.224–5.
77  WP, pp.42–3.

where nothing is safe, nothing quiet, nothing conducive to security.' It was never possible to relax or rest properly, because they were constantly afraid of ambush.[78] The abbot may have been a timid man, given to exaggeration, but in a sense, *paratge* and mercenaries were linked, for the rarity of the obligation to provide military service meant that resort to mercenaries was the most obvious alternative.

# The clergy

William of Puylaurens placed the main responsibility for the spread of Catharism upon the count of Toulouse; paraphrasing Proverbs 24: 30–1, he claimed it could be said of him, 'I have crossed the field of the slothful man, and lo, nettles have completely filled it.'[79] Yet, William knew very well that the task of combatting heresy fell first and foremost upon the clergy and, in particular upon the episcopate. Given the geography of heresy in Languedoc, the key was the see of Toulouse which, for a crucial period, was occupied by two men whom William presents as manifestly ill-equipped for the task, both because of their own inadequacies and because of the circumstances in which they were forced to operate. Fulcrand, bishop between 1179 and 1201, he describes as living like a burgess from the little that he could collect from farm rents and his banal powers over the municipal area. He was unable to collect any tithes which all went to the nobles and the monasteries. His successor, Raymond of Rabastens, was a man tainted by simony, who spent the meagre resources of the see upon litigation and warfare with his vassal, Raymond Fort of Belpech. When he was deposed by Innocent III in 1205, the farms and the fortresses of the see were all in the hands of creditors. When Fulk of Marseille, Cistercian Abbot of Florèze and Le Thoronet, was appointed to replace him, William saw it as divine providence. He was sent, he says, to revive a dead bishopric, like another Elisha. It was not an enviable task, for the financial crisis was so acute that there were only ninety-six *sous toulzas* in cash left and the creditors were so pressing that Fulk was forced to water his four mules in the wells of his house rather than take them down to the river where they might have been seized to cover debts. Indeed, the creditors of the see demanded that Fulk present himself before the *capitouls* of the city, even though he was its bishop.[80]

---

78  *Stephani Tornacensis Episcopi Epistolarum Pars Prima (1163–77)*, in *PL*, vol. 211, no. 73, col. 371.
79  WP, pp.42–3.
80  WP, pp.40–5.

A bishop like Fulcrand, too poor and too frightened to visit the parishes, was in no position to uphold standards among the lower clergy. According to William of Puylaurens, the nobility had no wish to make their own children ecclesiastics, although they were prepared to force the sons of their subjects upon the Church so that they could take the tithes. There was, therefore, no honour or status in such a position, so that the local clergy tried to make themselves as inconspicuous as possible, even combing their hair over their tonsures. In William's view the clergy became objects of scorn: people said that they would rather be a Jew or, if faced with a really unpleasant task, that they would rather be a cleric than do that.[81] As outsiders, neither William of Tudela nor Peter of Les Vaux-de-Cernay had William of Puylaurens's knowledge of the southern clergy, but both reported local contempt for prelates as much as for parish priests. According to William of Tudela, when the papal legate, Arnald Amalric, tried to persuade the people to repent, 'they laughed at him and scorned him for a fool', while Peter of Les Vaux-de-Cernay says that wherever the legate tried to preach 'the heretics countered by pointing to the disgraceful behaviour of the clergy and argued that if the legates wanted to reform the life style of the clergy, they would have to give up their preaching campaign'.[82]

At the Council of St Félix-de-Caraman, the Cathar leaders themselves, who must have had a good grasp of where their main support lay, had defined their own bishoprics as Albi, Toulouse, Carcassonne, and Agen. The metropolitan for Toulouse and Carcassonne was the archbishop of Narbonne, while Albi lay in the province of Bourges and Agen in the province of Bordeaux. Less affected by heresy were the dioceses of Béziers, also within the province of Narbonne, and those of Comminges and Couserans, within the province of Auch.[83] Bourges and Bordeaux were quite distant, while the Cathars at St Félix had not thought to establish a bishopric at Foix, so the major task of combatting heresy fell to the archbishops of Narbonne. Here again there was a failure of leadership. The archbishops were powerful lords by any standards. Apart from Toulouse, Carcassonne, and Béziers, their suffragan bishops encompassed Elne, Lodève, Nîmes, Maguelonne, Uzès, and Agde, a vast province which stretched from Roussillon to the Rhône.

---

81  WP, pp.24–5.
82  *Chanson*, vol. 1, laisse 3, pp.12–13; trans. Shirley, p.12; PVC, vol. 1, para. 20, pp.22–3; trans. Sibly, p.17. See also J. H. Mundy, 'Urban society and culture: Toulouse and its region', in R. L. Benson and G. Constable, eds, *Renaissance and Renewal in the Twelfth Century* (Oxford, 1982), p.235. Mundy has identified a family of Tudela in Toulouse for the years 1212 to 1215, so it seems that William may have been less of an outsider than Peter of Les Vaux-de-Cernay, although he does say in the poem that he was educated in Tudela.
83  Y. Dossat, 'Le Clergé méridional à la veille de la croisade des Albigeois', *Revue du Languedoc* 1 (1944), p.265.

They dominated the city of Narbonne itself, forcing the viscounts to acknowledge their suzerainty, and they held direct lordship over a range of places in the Razès, Termes, and Pierrepertuises in the west and Hérault, Capestang, Montels, Nissan, and Poilhès, in the east.[84] Nevertheless, neither Pons of Arsac (1162–81) nor Berengar, Abbot of Mount Aragon, near Tarragona and Bishop of Lérida, who occupied the see of Narbonne from 1190 to 1212, used this financial muscle to tackle heresy, despite the fact that Catharism became entrenched in about half the province in this period. Archbishop Berengar was a great Catalan aristocrat, the son of the count of Barcelona. He revived the financial position of the see after the profligacy of Pons of Arsac within only four years of his accession, and indeed went on to develop new resources. However, in 1204, after legatine investigation, Berengar was obliged to defend himself before the pope, after accusations that he had never visited the province, nor provided any spiritual leadership. Despite promises to the contrary, there is no evidence that thereafter he conducted any visitations in the diocese or became any more active in the battle with heresy and, finally, in 1212, he was deposed and replaced by the papal legate, Arnald Amalric.[85] The relationship between the strength of the diocesan structure and the spread of heresy is not necessarily a simple one of cause and effect – indeed, there does not appear to have been any significant heresy in the city of Narbonne itself – but in this case the chief metropolitan of this part of Languedoc took no initiatives against heresy, nor provided support for the two financially weakest dioceses, those of Toulouse and Carcassonne.[86]

It is, however, an over-simplification to present Languedoc in the twelfth and early thirteenth centuries as staffed by uniformly weak clergy and riddled with anti-clericalism. Both were present, but individual bishops were aware of heresy and attempted positive action to combat it. Several complained about the situation at the Council of Tours held by Pope Alexander III in 1163 and, two years later, at the debate at Lombers, the orthodox side was represented by Bishops William of Albi and Gaucelm of Lodève, and even Archbishop Pons of Narbonne was present, together with Bishops Adelbert of Nîmes, Gerard of Toulouse, and William of Agde.[87] At Narbonne, the

---

84  Dossat, 'Le Clergé méridional', pp.265–6.
85  R. W. Emery, *Heresy and Inquisition in Narbonne* (New York, 1941), pp.55–60, for a summary of his career. See also the views of Roquebert, *L'Épopée cathare*, vol. 1, pp.151–4, and Griffe, *Le Languedoc Cathare de 1190 à 1210*, pp.197–200.
86  Dossat, 'Le Clergé méridional', p.267. It should be noted, however, that even Arnald Amalric became intensely interested in developing the power of the see after 1212, when his sweeping claims to 'the Duchy of Narbonne' brought conflict with Simon of Montfort and disapprobation from Peter of Les Vaux-de-Cernay, vol. 2, para. 561, pp.253–4; trans. Sibly, pp.250–1.
87  *Acta concilii Lumbariensis*, in *RHG*, vol. 14, pp.431–4; trans. WE, no. 28, pp.189–94.

appointment of Bernard Gaucelm, Bishop of Béziers, in 1182, seems to have been an attempt to fill the post with a man who had a good record in opposing heresy,[88] while Peter of Les Vaux-de-Cernay, who was never reluctant to express moral outrage at anyone he considered insufficiently supportive of orthodoxy, described Renaud of Montpellier, Bishop of Béziers at the time of the crusade, as a man deserving respect for his age, the conduct of his life, and his learning.[89]

Moreover, this was no religious backwater, as it has sometimes been described.[90] Indeed, like the cities of Tuscany and Lombardy, it was the centre of a rich and complex religious life in which both orthodoxy and heresy flourished, circumstances which made capable ecclesiastical leadership all the more important. Even though Languedoc was not the creative heart of twelfth-century monasticism like Burgundy, the new orders were well-represented. In the region south of the Tarn and west of the Orb, twelve Cistercian abbeys were founded between 1136 and 1165, of which Fontfroide, Grandselve, and Boulbonne were three of the most important Cistercian houses of the time. The first two produced three of the papal legates of the crusading era.[91] For the Templars and Hospitallers Languedoc was a major source of income and recruits. The Hospitallers had established their administrative centre, or priory, at St Gilles, by 1121, which governed their commanderies in the regions of Toulouse, Albi, and Béziers, among other places. Similarly, during the 1130s, the Templars appointed a regional master or *bailli* over Aragon, Toulouse, and Provence, to oversee the increasing number of preceptories they were establishing in the region. The military orders could not have achieved their great expansion in Languedoc without noble support; the establishment of new communities, and the opening up of previously uncultivated territory which was common in the twelfth century owed much to an alliance between the nobles' land and the orders' capital.[92] John Mundy's research into the foundation of hospitals and other charitable institutions in Toulouse between 1100 and 1250

88  Griffe, *Les Débuts*, p.145. There is some controversy over whether Pons was deposed or died. WE, p.705, think the former, while Griffe, p.133, says there is no evidence of deposition. There does, though, seem to have been some difficulty in finding a suitable candidate willing to take up the post, Griffe, p.135.

89  PVC, vol. 1, para. 89, p.90; trans. Sibly, p.50.

90  For example, J. Strayer, *The Albigensian Crusades* (New York, 1971), pp.24–5.

91  F. van der Meer, ed., *Atlas de l'Ordre Cistercien* (Paris and Brussels, 1965), map II; P. Wolff, ed., *Documents de l'histoire du Languedoc* (Toulouse, 1969), pp.118–19.

92  A. Luttrell, 'The earliest Hospitallers', in B. Z. Kedar, J. Riley-Smith and R. Hiestand, eds, *Montjoie. Studies in Crusade History in Honour of Hans Eberhard Mayer* (Aldershot, 1997), pp.37–54; M. Barber, *The New Knighthood. A History of the Order of the Temple* (Cambridge, 1994), pp.20–1; Mundy, 'Urban society and culture', p.241.

**Plate 4**
Basilica of Saint Sernin, Toulouse, east end

shows that there was no shortage of donors prepared to back their professed beliefs with specific material gifts in the expectation of participating in the spiritual benefits of the house. Eleven of Toulouse's fifteen hospitals were founded or renewed between the late eleventh century and the beginning of the Albigensian Crusade, while at least four of its seven leper houses were established between 1167 and 1209. In the late twelfth century the role of individual lay initiative (albeit under the aegis of canon law and episcopal jurisdiction) was particularly marked.[93] The roots of this piety ran deep; in the same region between the Tarn and the Orb there were thirty-two Benedictine houses which had been founded before the year 1000 and, among these, St Sernin of Toulouse steadily recovered its control over both churches and tithes in the course of the twelfth century, which belies the claim that Gregorian reforms had hardly touched the region.[94] The verbal jousts between the orthodox and the heretics, and among the heretics themselves, reflect the religious vitality of the region. William of Puylaurens listed Arians, Manichaeans, and Waldensians, and claimed that some 'ignorant priests', in their hatred of other heretics, tolerated the Waldensians, an observation confirmed by inquisitorial depositions.[95] Peter of Les Vaux-de-Cernay understood why. 'They were evil men, but very much less perverted than other heretics; they agreed with us in many matters, and differed in some.'[96] Although quite unconnected with the heretics, the frequent use of Jews as administrators by both the counts of Toulouse and the viscounts of Béziers, as well as their greater freedom to hold and transfer property than was the case in northern Europe, shows that Judaism was one more element in a varied religious scene.[97]

# Urban society

Traditionally, it was the cities and towns which were the most receptive to heterodox ideas, particularly during the period of economic expansion and population growth so manifest in the twelfth century. Better communication with distant places, a more rapid turnover of population, and the close

---

93  J. H. Mundy, 'Charity and social work in Toulouse, 1100–1250', *Traditio* 22 (1966), especially pp.235–8.

94  See Wolff, *Documents*, p.117 (map). For St Sernin, Dossat, 'Le Clergé méridional', p.272.

95  WP, pp.24–5.

96  PVC, vol. 1, para. 18, pp.18–19; trans. Sibly, p.14.

97  See J. O'Brien, 'Jews and Cathari in medieval France', *Comparative Studies in Society and History* 10 (1968), pp.215–20.

proximity of large numbers of people facilitated the spread of ideas as much as it accelerated the exchange of money. Historians have therefore tended to associate the rise of heresy with urban growth; indeed, the Bogomil missionaries were able to gain adherents in the towns of northern Italy and the Rhineland. Consequently, for the orthodox, heretics were particularly difficult to isolate and control in towns; with a weapon as non-selective as a crusade, the task was impossible. Towns became targets of indiscriminate attack, even though, unlike some *castra* and villages in the Toulousain, none of them actually had a majority of heretics and their supporters. As far as Peter of Les Vaux-de-Cernay was concerned the entire populations of the three main cities were irredeemably tainted by heresy; indeed, he seems to have associated urban life with sin, almost by definition. 'Béziers was a most notable city, but entirely infested with the poison of heresy. Its citizens were not only heretics, they were robbers, lawbreakers, adulterers and thieves of the worst sort, brimful of every kind of sin.' At Carcassonne the 'citizens were heretics of the worst sort and sinners before the Lord exceedingly'. As for Toulouse, this was a place which, since its foundation, had 'rarely if ever been free of this detestable plague'.[98] According to the anonymous author of the *Chanson*, the crusaders became so frustrated during their siege of Toulouse in 1218 that Foucaud of Berzy, one of Montfort's long-standing companions, proposed a radical plan of building a 'New Toulouse' where there could be a completely fresh start with new men and new oaths. Then they could destroy 'Raymond's Toulouse' and all those who lived there.[99]

In practice, it is as difficult for the historian as it was for the crusaders to identify the sources of urban heresy. Geoffrey of Auxerre, a Cistercian who had accompanied St Bernard on his visit to Toulouse in 1145, believed that there were heretics in the city before the disturbances caused by Henry the Monk and that they had been encouraged by some of the leading citizens, although he did not think that they had a great following in the city as a whole.[100] The Maurand were one such family: Peter Maurand was a prominent member who was brought before the legation of Peter of Pavia, the papal legate, and Henry of Marcy, Abbot of Clairvaux, in 1179. He is described as a rich man who owned two mansions or towers, one inside and one outside the city. They claimed that he was a leader of heretics in Toulouse and, although he at first refused to admit it, he eventually

---

98   PVC, vol. 1, paras 84, 92, 8, pp.86–7, 93–4, 7–8; trans. Sibly, pp.48–9, 51, 9.

99   *Chanson*, vol. 3, laisse 189, pp.30–3; trans. Shirley, pp.135–6.

100  Geoffrey of Auxerre, *Sancti Bernardi Abbatis Clarae-Vallensis Vita et res gestae libris septem comprehensae: Liber tertius auctore Gaufrido monacho*, in *PL*, vol. 185, cols 411–12.

confessed to the denial of the reality of the sacrifice in the Eucharist. He received a heavy penance of flogging and three years' exile in Jerusalem, although it is not known if this was ever carried out. His towers, which were 'rich and very beautiful', were to be demolished.[101] While this might mean that members of the consulate, the ruling oligarchy of Toulouse, were affected by heresy, the formation of the White Brotherhood, an orthodox militia founded in 1210 by Fulk, Bishop of Toulouse, to combat heresy and usury, suggests that their numbers were not great. According to William of Puylaurens, the White Brotherhood was supported by almost everybody in the City, and led by four men who were, at one time or another, members of the consulate.[102] Opposition to this came mainly from the Bourg, where many of the richer inhabitants had made their money through financial dealings and who therefore might be expected to oppose measures against usury.[103] It is equally difficult to determine how many heretics lived permanently in Toulouse, given the close ties between the consulate and the nobility of the *castra*. Some took refuge in the relative anonymity of the city when their presence in the *castra* became too obvious, thus temporarily increasing the size of the heretical community.[104] The only detailed list of urban heretics available is the one furnished by Renaud of Montpellier, Bishop of Béziers, to the papal legates, shortly before the fall of that city in July 1209; it was the refusal of the inhabitants to hand over these people which provoked the attack. This suggests that Catharism had some support among the crafts, although the proportion of the total population is very small.[105] The list contains between 219 and 222 names which the editor, Louis Domairon, interprets as heads of families, which might mean about 700 people were affected. Five persons are designated Waldensians, so that the others are presumed to be Cathar sympathisers. Among these it is possible to identify one noble (*baronus*) and four doctors, and a range of craftsmen, including five hosiers, two blacksmiths, two pelterers, two shoemakers, a sheep-shearer, a carpenter, a weaver, a saddler, a corn-dealer, a

101  Roger of Howden, *Chronica*, pp.150–2; trans. WE, no. 29, pp.196–7. See J. H. Mundy, *Liberty and Political Power in Toulouse, 1100–1230* (New York, 1954), pp.60–2, and Griffe, *Les Débuts*, pp.97–100.
102  WP, pp.64–5.
103  WP, pp.64–7. See Wakefield, *Heresy, Crusade and Inquisition*, p.75.
104  PVC, vol. 2, para. 359, p.57; trans. Sibly, p.168 (under the year 1212). See Griffe, *Le Languedoc Cathare de 1190 à 1210*, p.73.
105  It is not clear in this context if 'heretics' means *perfecti* or more generally Cathar sympathisers. On this issue, see J. L. Nelson, 'Religion in *"Histoire Totale"*: some recent works on medieval heresy and popular religion', *Religion* 10 (1980), p.71, and Brenon, *Le Vrai visage*, p.183. If they were all *perfecti*, then a percentage of 2.5 would be considerable but, given the references to their occupations, this seems unlikely.

cutler, a tailor, a tavern-keeper, a baker, a wool-worker, a mercer, and a money-changer. In both chronicle sources and inquisitorial depositions, *textores* (weavers) are associated with heresy. Here ten persons are employed in the textile industry, although only one is actually a weaver, perhaps because weaving was by no means an exclusively urban occupation.[106]

In fact, analysis of the evidence for Languedoc as a whole does not suggest a strong correlation between urban growth and heresy. Languedoc west of the River Orb, which was the part most affected by Catharism, was indeed relatively populous, but it was not one of the more urbanised regions of Latin Christendom in the middle ages. Even after the settlement of 1229 when there was a spurt of economic growth, only Toulouse and Narbonne, with pre-plague populations of about 35,000 and 25,000 respectively, were large enough to compare with the more important cities of Lombardy and Tuscany.[107] These two were in a class of their own in the region: the next three were Béziers at 14,500, Albi at 10,700, and Carcassonne at 8,400. Agen, on the fringes of the region, was about 6,000, but otherwise even Pamiers was only 3,500.[108] Estimates of the size of Béziers when it was attacked by the crusaders in 1209 are usually lower, at about 8,000–9,000,[109] so it is probably reasonable to scale down the other cities in proportion. Even Peter of Les Vaux-de-Cernay did not see Narbonne as a city full of Cathars, although he found the conduct of its citizens reprehensible in many ways; equally, modern research has shown that the inquisitors achieved a meagre haul in the city.[110] On the face of it, the region to the east of the River Orb, where Catharism was not widely accepted, shows some similarity in that there were only three large cities in Montpellier with 40,000, Avignon with 18,000, and Marseille with 12,000. However, it actually had what Josiah Russell calls a much higher urban index of about 11.3 per cent compared with the western part where the proportion is only 3 per cent, figures which reflect the eastern region's much greater

---

106 L. Domairon, ed., 'Role des hérétiques de la ville de Béziers à l'époque du désastre de 1209', *Cabinet historique* 9 (1863), pp.95–103. The occupations listed include those whose surname is a trade, since it suggests that they came from that type of background, even if not actually following that occupation in 1209. See J. Duvernoy, 'Les Albigeois dans la vie sociale et économique de leur temps', *Annales de l'Institut d'Études occitanes, Actes du colloque de Toulouse, années 1962–3* (Toulouse, 1964), pp.67–8, for Cathars in the textile industry.

107 J. C. Russell, *Medieval Regions and Their Cities* (Newton Abbot, 1972), pp.154–9, 162–3.

108 Ibid., pp.156, 163.

109 Estimates vary. This figure is that of A. P. Evans, 'The Albigensian Crusade', in K. M. Setton, R. Wolfe and H. Hazard, eds, *A History of the Crusades*, vol. 2 (Philadelphia, PA, 1962), p.289. It may be too low. Russell, *Medieval Regions*, pp.162–3, thinks 14,500 in 1342.

110 PVC, vol. 1, paras 264, p.262, vol. 2, paras 305, 488, 501–3, 560, pp.5–7, 179–80, 194–8, 252–3; trans. Sibly, pp.134, 149–50, 220–1, 225–6, 250; Emery, *Heresy and Inquisition*, ch. 5.

commercial activity.[111] Indeed, Innocent III believed that Montpellier, the largest of these cities, was a place particularly loyal to the Catholic Church.[112]

This pattern is confirmed by the development of consulates, oligarchies of the more powerful and wealthy citizens who had gained a series of privileges which reduced the degree of comital control. The process is not dissimilar to the development of communal institutions in the Italian cities, but it is notably later and more restricted in scope.[113] In the county of Toulouse only the city itself had a consulate by 1220, which it had established in 1152. Toulouse had grown because it was the centre of a prosperous local agriculture, in which grain and vines were the main components, and because it was the meeting-point of trade from the Mediterranean and the river traffic along the Garonne connecting it to Bordeaux.[114] As in Italy, the consulate was made up of an amalgam of mercantile and knightly families who held city property, although with the growth of the Bourg, which encompassed more money-lenders and bankers, the composition was sometimes subject to change. After 1189 Toulouse was governed by a consulate of twenty-four, representing both City and Bourg. Between 1202 and 1205 the government of Toulouse attempted to create a *contado* not dissimilar to those of the Italian cities which, if it had succeeded, would have brought twenty-three neighbouring towns and villages under the city's control.[115] In western Languedoc as a whole, only Béziers and Narbonne had their own consulates before Toulouse, in 1131 and 1132 respectively, and only three other places, Millau (1187), Carcassonne (1192), and Montauban (1195) had gained them by 1195. Agen (1197) and Albi (1220) were among ten further towns with their own consulates between 1195 and 1220. While it is evident that the region was experiencing economic growth in the twelfth and thirteenth centuries and that, consequently, certain towns were seeking greater independence from the traditional territorial authorities, it is equally clear that this growth was quite modest in comparison with the most advanced areas such as northern and central Italy and Flanders, and even perhaps eastern Languedoc. The really striking development of consulates occurred after the crusading era, when Catharism was being slowly crushed, rather than during the twelfth century, when heresy was spreading

---

111   Russell, *Medieval Regions*, pp.162, 166, 159.
112   See C. Dutton, *Aspects of the Institutional History of the Albigensian Crusades, 1198–1229* (PhD diss., Royal Holloway and Bedford New College, University of London, 1993), p.89.
113   Dossat, 'La Société méridionale', p.74.
114   Ibid., p.76. For a comprehensive analysis of the social and economic context of Catharism in Toulouse, see J. H. Mundy, *Society and Government at Toulouse in the Age of the Cathars* (Studies and Texts, 129) (Toronto, 1997).
115   Mundy, *Liberty and Political Power*, pp.68–73, and 'Urban society and culture', pp.229–33.

most vigorously. Taking the county of Toulouse alone, another fifteen con-sulates had appeared by 1249 (the death of Count Raymond VII) and an additional 145 by 1271 (the death of Alphonse of Poitiers, who had succeeded Raymond as count).[116]

## Catharism and social structure

The most favourable environment for the establishment and sustenance of Catharism was the *castra* and fortified villages of powerful local nobles. Their families were linked by marriage which often gave them widespread regional influence, enabling Cathars to preach over a large area and to establish houses for their communities in many different places. At the same time, believers provided a ready means of economic support with gifts and legacies of money, clothing, and food, and the conservation of needed resources, as well as shelter on both a long- and short-term basis.[117] The kings of Aragon, the counts of Toulouse, Foix, and Comminges, and the viscounts of Béziers and Carcassonne had seldom been able to exercise close control over these networks; consequently, when the Cathars appeared there was little hope of undermining those who supported or tolerated them, even had the will been present. Strong feudal ties which, as the Capetians showed, contained the potential for tighter control over wilful vassals, were lacking in Languedoc, where confederations among equals were much more common. The great lords could not therefore rely on contingents of vassals to fight their wars, but were more likely to employ mercenary troops, or *routiers* as the Church called them. However, these warriors were not easy to control and their activities frequently made the roads unsafe for those who did not have the resources to defend themselves. Moreover, while it is wrong to see the diocesan personnel as uniformly incapable or indifferent, in the key diocese of Toulouse the situation was exacerbated by the inability of impoverished bishops and a demoralised and ill-informed clergy to combat a well-organised and confident Cathar Church, driven forward by highly-motivated ministers who commanded the respect of a considerable proportion of the populace. This was not, however, an exclusively heretical society, but one characterised by a wide

---

116  Dossat, 'La Société méridionale', pp.72–3, for urban liberties, and Wolff, *Documents*, pp.126–8, for maps.

117  See A. Roach, 'The Cathar Economy', *Reading Medieval Studies* 12 (1986), pp.51–71, who shows that the Cathars relied mainly on bequests and that, contrary to received wisdom, usury was not an important issue.

range of successful ecclesiastical institutions, as is demonstrated by the establishment of important Cistercian monasteries and many houses of Hospitallers and Templars and by the lively debates between the orthodox and the heretics. Urbanisation was less crucial in the spread of Catharism than might be expected, for there were only two really large cities in western Languedoc, one of which was largely unaffected by heresy. Overall, quite a low proportion of the population lived in towns. The extent of heresy in the towns is inevitably difficult to measure because of the numbers and mobility of the inhabitants and the variety of their activities. In this region therefore traditional explanations for the spread of heresy are inadequate; poor clergy and urban growth made a contribution, but the interaction between society and heresy is much more complex than such simple formulae will allow.

The relationship between Catharism and social structure is not, indeed, subject to a single, monolithic explanation. Reports of dualistic belief in the Rhineland, northern France, and Flanders from the 1140s onwards suggest that its appeal was essentially to the lower classes – the association with *textores* or cloth-workers seems to confirm this – rather than to the aristocracy. Its spread by merchants along trade routes seems a quite feasible explanation, as indeed Anselm of Alessandria claims happened in Bosnia after local merchants had visited Constantinople. This would also explain why the heresy was much less successful than it became in Languedoc, where its interaction with the social structure was quite different. In Languedoc the chief protectors of heresy were the local nobles, a situation which made Catharism both more durable and, because of the likelihood that a dependent rural populace would follow the example of their social leaders, more widespread.[118] The *castrum* and village of Mas-Saintes-Puelles in the Lauragais – later the subject of intensive inquisitorial scrutiny – is a case in point. It was ruled by a noble family deeply imbued with Catharism, but it is clear that merchants, professional men, craftsmen, and peasants were all involved. Indeed, the socio-economic background of nearly half of the believers in the community is not known, which suggests that they were probably peasants. Heresy in Mas-Saintes-Puelles therefore did not arise as a result

---

118  See, Mundy, *Men and Women at Toulouse*, p.7, where he shows how the nobility responded to the decline of endogamy by the practice of primogeniture as a means of protecting their property. He notes the same trends among the lower classes, although with much less economic reason and concludes that 'the lesser imitated the behaviour of the greater'. However, Duvernoy speculates that Catharism perhaps only appears more successful in Languedoc because of the existence of important narrative sources and inquisitorial depositions but that, if better evidence were available, Germany, Champagne, or Flanders might offer 'the same sight', *Le Catharisme*, vol. 2, *L'Histoire des Cathares*, p.195.

of class or gender conflict, for it 'encompassed all social classes'.[119] It is unlikely to be a coincidence that the major turning-point for Catharism in Languedoc was the conversion of the heretics to absolute dualism at the Council of St Félix-de-Caraman by *papa* Nicetas, for Nicetas was almost certainly from that circle of upper-class Constantinopolitan families which had moulded the fairly crude Bogomilism of Cosmas's day into the more sophisticated cosmology that Nicetas seems to have presented. In contrast Bulgarian Bogomilism, with its strong attraction for oppressed peasants and craftsmen (made clear by Cosmas), readily transferred itself to a similar social milieu in the West. For one historian this difference was decisive. In Dmitri Obolensky's view: 'The seeds of the Albigensian Crusade were well and truly sown at the Council of St Félix-de-Caraman.'[120]

---

119   G. Šemkov, 'Le Contexte socio-économique du Catharisme au Mas-Saintes-Puelles dans la première moitié du 13e siècle', *Heresis* 2 (1984), pp.35–53. For the view that it was an issue of gender conflict, see G. Koch, *Frauenfrage und Ketzertum im Mittelalter. Die Frauenbewegung im Rahmen des Katharismus und des Waldensertums und ihre sozialen Wurseln (12.–14. Jahrhundert)* (Forschungen zur Mittelalterlichen Geschichte, 9) (Berlin, 1962), for example, p.20. For the various theories about the role of women in Catharism, see Mundy, *Men and Women at Toulouse*, pp.41–6.

120   D. Obolensky, 'Papa Nicetas: a Byzantine dualist in the land of the Cathars', in *Okeanos: Essays Presented to Igor Sevčenko* (Harvard Ukrainian Studies, 7) (1983), p.500.

# CHAPTER THREE

# The Cathar Church

## The Cathar hierarchy

In his querulous letter to Abbot Alexander of Cîteaux in 1177, Count Raymond V of Toulouse alleged that 'all the ecclesiastical sacraments are held for nothing and, what is sacrilege, even the two principles have been introduced . . .'.[1] He was right to be alarmed at the progress of heresy in his lands for, at the Council of St Félix-de-Caraman, probably held the previous year, the Drugunthian emissary from Constantinople, *papa* Nicetas, had indeed converted the leading representatives of the moderate Cathars of Languedoc to a belief in the two principles of absolute dualism, and he had consolidated this by drawing the previously disparate groups of Cathars in Lombardy, northern France, and Languedoc into an organised diocesan structure. While this wider unity lasted for only a brief period, Nicetas's work in Languedoc remained effective until the mid-thirteenth century, presenting the counts of Toulouse with a far greater challenge than anything they had encountered before the 1170s.

When Nicetas began his mission there were already Cathar bishops of France and of Albi, representing the Church in the Languedoïl and the Languedoc, while Mark, who was the leader of the Lombard Cathars, may have been either a bishop or a deacon. At any rate, even if he was not a bishop before Nicetas's arrival, Mark was consecrated soon after, either in

---

1 Gervase of Canterbury, *The Historical Works of Gervase of Canterbury*, vol. 1, in *The Chronicles of the Reigns of Stephen, Henry II and Richard I*, ed. W. Stubbs (Rolls Series, 73) (London, 1879), p.270. See above, ch. 2, p.49.

Lombardy or at St Félix.[2] His authority was acknowledged among the Lombard, Tuscan, and Trevisan heretics.[3] The account of the proceedings at St Félix was copied by Peter Pollan, who appears to have been the 'younger son' of the diocese of Carcassonne (that is, second in succession to the bishopric), for Peter Isarn, Cathar bishop of Carcassonne, in 1223.[4] It was taken from eye-witnesses, and describes how, at the council, the dioceses were expanded to six.

> The Church of Toulouse invited Papa Nicetas to the castle of St Félix and a great multitude of men and women of the Church of Toulouse and others of neighbouring churches assembled there, so that they could receive the *consolamentum*, which the Lord Papa Nicetas began to administer. Afterwards indeed Robert of Spernone, Bishop of the Church of the French, came with his council; Mark of Lombardy similarly came with his council, and Sicard Cellarer, Bishop of the Church of Albi, came with his council, and Bernard the Catalan came with his council of the Church of Carcassonne, and the Council of the Church of Agen was there. All thus assembled in countless numbers, the men of the Church of Toulouse wished to have a Bishop and chose Bernard Raimond: similarly, both Bernard the Catalan and the Council of the Church of Carcassonne, asked and enjoined by the Church of Toulouse, and with the advice and wish and permission of the Lord Sicard Cellarer, chose Guiraud Mercer; and the men of Agen chose Raymond of Casals.

All these bishops, both established and newly-elected, were then consoled and consecrated or reconsecrated by Nicetas.[5] Peter Pollan also provided Peter Isarn with a copy of the charter which set out the territorial extent of the dioceses, a charter probably drawn up originally at the council itself. Two panels were chosen from the members of the Churches of Toulouse and Carcassonne, before the bishops were themselves elected, and they decided to follow the existing Catholic boundary where feasible, with a dividing line between them running west from Saint-Pons between Cabaret and Hautpoul, along the line of the Black Mountain, and then south between Saissac and

---

2   B. Hamilton, 'The Cathar Council of Saint-Félix reconsidered', *Archivum Fratrum Praedicatorum* 48 (1978), pp.31–2.
3   *De heresi catharorum in Lombardia*, in A. Dondaine, 'La Hiérarchie cathare en Italie', I, *Archivum Fratrum Praedicatorum* 19 (1949), p.306; trans. WE, no. 23, p.160; Anselm of Alessandria, *Tractatus de haereticis*, in A. Dondaine, 'La Hiérarchie cathare en Italie, II', *Archivum Fratrum Praedicatorum* 20 (1950), p.309; trans. WE, no. 24, p.169.
4   Hamilton, 'Cathar Council', pp.26–7.
5   Ibid., p.52; E. Griffe, *Les Débuts de l'aventure cathare en Languedoc (1140–90)* (Paris, 1969), pp.67–76. P. Jimenez-Sanchez, 'Relire la charte de Niquinta', *Heresis* 22 (1994), p.18, regards the case for reading 'agenense' in place of 'aranense' as not proven.

Verdun and Montréal and Fanjeaux. Both, however, encompassed far more territory than their Catholic counterparts. Carcassonne included the Catholic archdiocese of Narbonne, and both extended beyond the Pyrenees into the contiguous areas to the south, so that Toulouse took in Couserans, Huesca, and Lerida, and Carcassonne extended into Catalonia, which meant Elne, Gerona, Barcelona, Tarragona, Vich, and Urgel.[6]

According to the charter, the Churches had been divided in this way 'so that they may have peace and mutual concord and one should not cause injury to another, [nor] one contradict the other'. Nicetas, indeed, seems to have made the goal of peace the central theme of the assembly, for the fragment of his sermon which survives, probably taken from accounts of those present, emphasises that 'the seven Churches of Asia were divided and distinct among themselves, and none of them did anything to the other to contradict it'. This was, he claimed, equally the case with the five other existing Bogomil Churches, those of Constantinople, Dragovitsa, Melenguia, Bulgaria, and Bosnia. In fact, as has been seen, he was not telling the entire truth: Bulgaria and Bosnia retained their belief in moderate dualism and it was not long before the arrival of Petracius in Lombardy blew apart the unity which Nicetas had hoped to create.[7] This inaugurated a complicated series of disputes which divided the Italians into two groups, under John Judeus (who succeeded Mark) and Peter of Florence. After an unsuccessful attempt at mediation by the Bishop of France, they made another attempt at reconciliation in an assembly held at Mosio, a village between Mantua and Cremona. Here they chose a man called Garattus as their bishop, but before he could go to Bulgaria to be consecrated, as planned, he was alleged to have had relations with a woman, and the whole fragile agreement collapsed. Disintegration followed: by 1190 there were six Italian Churches, at Corcorezzo (which retained Garattus), Desenzano, Mantua, Vicenza, Florence, and Spoleto. Only one of these – at Desenzano – continued to adhere to the absolute dualism which Nicetas had brought, although two of the others, the congregations of Mantua and Vicenza, sent their bishops to be consecrated in Bosnia rather than Bulgaria.[8]

Nevertheless, despite the acrimony such quarrels caused, by the end of the twelfth century the Cathars and Bogomils together had created a formidable structure of sixteen bishoprics from Toulouse in the west to Constantinople in the east. Half a century later Rainier Sacconi could still identify sixteen, thirteen of which were the same as those listed by the author of the *De heresi*

6   Hamilton, 'Cathar Council', pp.42, 52–3.
7   See above, ch. 1, pp.21–2.
8   *De heresi catharorum*, pp.307–8; trans. WE, no. 23, pp.162–3.

*catharorum.* Sacconi, however, divided the Church of Constantinople into two, that of Greeks and Latins, which must have been the case in the twelfth century as well.[9] He omits the diocese of Agen, which was probably marginal even in the later twelfth century, and that of the Milingui (the *Ecclesia Melenguiae*), which, if it was located in the Peloponnese, may have been over-whelmed (or at least isolated) by the Frankish presence after the conquest of Constantinople in 1204.[10] He does not seem to have known of the new creation in the Razès, set up in 1225. He adds one other Church, at Philadelphia in Romania, which has been tentatively identified as the ancient Philadelphia in Lydia in western Asia Minor, now known as Alashehr.[11] This may suggest a revival of dualism in Asia Minor in the thirteenth century, but it is more likely that this Church existed in the twelfth century as well, for Anselm of Alessandria lists it as one of the three original Manichaean Churches, along with Drugunthia and Bulgaria.[12]

The Cathar perception that there was a need for a formalised set of dioceses with properly recognised boundaries shows that they were prepared to establish a structured Church on this earth, whatever their views about the material excesses of the Catholic clergy. Consequently, the Cathar bishoprics were themselves founded upon a hierarchy, although it was much less complex than that of the Catholic Church. Two Catholic sources, Rainier Sacconi, and the Franciscan lector at Milan, James Capelli, writing about ten years earlier, provide the most detailed descriptions of this, although their earlier existence is confirmed by three other writers, the author of the *De heresi catharorum*, the crusader chronicler, Peter of Les Vaux-de-Cernay, and a Piacenzan layman, Salvo Burci, writing in *c.* 1200, *c.* 1213, and 1235 respectively.[13] As an ex-Cathar himself Rainier Sacconi is particularly valuable. 'The offices of the Cathars are four. He who has been established in the first and highest office is called bishop; in the second, the elder son; in the third, the younger son; and in the fourth and last, the deacon. The others among them, who are without office, are called Christian men and women.'[14]

---

9   Rainerius Sacconi, *Summa de Catharis et Pauperibus de Lugduno*, in A. Dondaine, *Un Traité néo-manichéen du XIIIe siècle: Le Liber du duobus principiis, suivi d'un fragment de rituel cathare* (Rome, 1939), p.70; trans. WE, no. 51, p.336.

10  Hamilton, 'Cathar Council', pp.38–40.

11  Dondaine, *Un Traité néo-manichéen du XIIIe siècle*, p.62.

12  Anselm of Alessandria, *Tractatus de haereticis*, p.308; trans. WE, no. 24, p.168.

13  *De heresi catharorum*, p.312; trans. WE, no. 23, p.167; PVC, vol. 1, para. 14, pp.15–16; trans. Sibly, p.7; Ilarino da Milano, 'Il "Liber supra Stella" del piacentino Salvo Burci contro i Catari e altre correnti ereticali', *Aevum* 19 (1945), p.336, trans. WE, no. 45(B), pp.273–4.

14  Rainerius Sacconi, *Summa de Catharis et Pauperibus*, p.68; trans. WE, no. 51, p.335. See A. Borst, *Die Katharer* (Schriften der Monumenta Germaniae historica) (Stuttgart, 1953), pp.202–13, on the hierarchy.

(See Map 3.) James Capelli compares the elder and younger sons to Franciscan Visitors whose duty was to travel around the convents ensuring that standards were maintained, whereas the deacons were generally responsible for administering the hospices, which acted as communal centres for the local Cathar community, as well as providing hospitality for the travelling *perfecti*.[15] The Cathars took literally the idea that Christ was present when 'two or three are gathered together' and, therefore, when they were not living in a community, they generally travelled in pairs.[16] As it is thought that nearly half the houses of the Cathars of Languedoc were occupied by women, historians have speculated that the matriarchical figures who often appear to be running these houses might be described as deaconesses. This is certainly possible, for older women did become deaconesses in the Early Christian Church and were particularly important assisting at female baptisms in an era when adult baptism was much more common than it later became. Important as such women were within the Cathar network, however, there is no solid evidence to support this idea, while research which shows that the *perfectae* were much less active and important in the Cathar Church than the *perfecti* would tend to suggest that it was unlikely.[17]

All the holders of these offices had powers of ordination, as did the *perfecti*, depending upon who was present, although it appears to have been rare for *perfectae* to have been called upon. However, it was essential to maintain the structure because, as the controversy over the origins of the ordination of Mark shows, breaks in continuity for whatever reason threw the validity of past actions into doubt. The elder and younger sons therefore also represented a line of succession. Rainier Sacconi sets this out very clearly:

---

15 James Capelli, *Summa contra haereticos*, in D. Bazzocchi, ed., *La Eresia catara: appendice* (Bologna, 1920), pp.CXXXVII–CXXXVIII; trans. WE, no. 49, pp.302–3. The rather complicated manuscript history of this material means that it is not certain that Capelli was the author.

16 B. Hamilton, 'The Cathars and Christian perfection', in P. Biller and R. B. Dobson, eds, *The Medieval Church: Universities, Heresy and the Religious Life. Essays in Honour of Gordon Leff, Studies in Church History: Subsidia* 11 (Woodbridge, 1999), p.16. See the Occitan Ritual, L. Clédat, ed., *Le Nouveau Testament traduit au XIIIe siècle en langue provençale, suivi d'un rituel cathare* (Paris, 1887), p.XII; trans. WE, no. 57(B), pp.486.

17 A. Brenon, *Les Femmes Cathares* (Paris, 1992), pp.122–31, 91, on female houses; Borst, *Die Katharer*, p.211, on speculation by historians about deaconesses; for the early Church practices, see E. Livingstone, ed., *The Oxford Dictionary of the Christian Church*, 3rd edn (Oxford, 1997), p.456; for research on the extent of active involvement of the *perfectae*, see R. Abels and E. Harrison, 'The Participation of Women in Languedocian Catharism', *Medieval Studies* 41 (1979), pp.226–7.

The ordination of a bishop once usually took place in this fashion: when a bishop died, the younger son ordained the elder son as bishop, the latter thereupon ordained the younger son as elder son. Then a younger son was elected by all the prelates and those in their charge who were gathered at the place set for the election, and he was ordained as younger son by the bishop.

This appears to have remained the system in the Balkans, but at some time before 1250 the Cathars in the West (or perhaps simply in Italy) became uneasy with this arrangement so that the bishop was required to administer an anticipatory consecration of the elder son in order to avoid the seemingly unnatural situation in which the son appeared to be installing the father. For Rainier Sacconi, however, the result of the change was an equally reprehensible creation, that of two bishops in each Church.[18]

# The *consolamentum*

Entry into this Cathar elite was through the ceremony of the *consolamentum*, the essential elements of which the westerners had received from the Bogomil missionaries. Here there do exist two Cathar versions of the ceremony, one in Latin dating from 1235–50, and a later one in Occitan, dating from the second half of the thirteenth century.[19] Again, these are relatively late in the history of the Cathars in the West, but Eckbert of Schönau's description of 'the baptism of the spirit' in 1163 shows that the Cathar initiation was known to Catholics from an early date, even if the ceremonies shown in the Rituals were more elaborate than those of the early Cathars. Moreover, Peter of Les Vaux-de-Cernay adds to his brief (and contemptuous) allusion to the unrestrained sinfulness of the believers, safe in the knowledge that they can ultimately receive 'the laying-on of hands', an account of how a heretic was first received by renouncing the cross and baptism by water, after which 'all present place their hands on his head and kiss him and clothe him in a black robe; from that time he is counted as one of them'.[20] Thereafter, a whole range of Catholic writers, including James Capelli,

---

18  Rainerius Sacconi, *Summa de Catharis et Pauperibus*, p.69; trans. WE, no. 51, pp.335–6.
19  Latin: Dondaine, *Un Traité néo-manichéen du XIIIe siècle*, pp.151–65; trans. WE, no. 57(A), pp.468–83. Occitan: Clédat, ed., *Le Nouveau Testament traduit au XIIIe siècle*, pp.IX–XXVI; trans. WE, no. 57(B), pp.483–94.
20  Eckbert of Schönau, *Sermones contra haereticos*, in *PL*, vol. 195, pp.51–5; PVC, vol. 1, paras 14, 19, pp.15–16, 19–20; trans. Sibly, pp.7, 8–9.

Anselm of Alessandria, and Bernard Gui, Inquisitor in the Toulousain from 1307, offered their versions.[21] Moreover, the ceremony is mentioned in numerous inquisitorial depositions which, in some cases, record witnesses whose memories extended back to the 1190s.[22]

The Ritual shows that the ceremony was in two parts. In the Latin the opening has disappeared and it used to be thought that this derived from the fuller Occitan version, but it is now accepted that they probably both emanated from a Latin original.[23] The Occitan version therefore sets down the words to be spoken at the beginning. These were always in Latin. 'Bless us; have mercy upon us. Amen. Let it be done unto us according to Thy word. May the Father, the Son, and the Holy Spirit forgive all your sins.' This was repeated three times, and then followed by the Lord's Prayer and the reading of the passage from John 1: 1–17, 'In the beginning was the Word . . .'. Next, in the Occitan version alone, there were a series of invocations to God for 'pardon and penance for all our sins', which were a normal part of the life of the *perfecti* who attended assemblies for monthly confession, sometimes called the *apparellamentum* by Catholic writers.[24] The next stage was the ministration of the Lord's Prayer. The Latin version begins part of the way through this, but the Occitan text shows a ceremony presided over by the most senior of the Cathars present, usually called an elder, assisted by other *perfecti* or Good Men. The elder placed the Book (meaning either the New Testament or St John's Gospel) upon a table covered with a cloth and then the postulant made his *melioramentum* or ritual greeting, before receiving the Book. The elder then explained to the postulant – who would probably have undergone a probationary period of about a year by this time – the significance of what he was about to do. In the Latin, this takes the form of a line-by-line interpretation of the meaning of the Lord's Prayer, which included the use of the phrase 'supersubstantial bread' rather than 'daily bread', meaning, according to the Ritual, 'the law of Christ', but apparently regarded by orthodox commentators as evidence of heresy.[25] In Occitan, there are a series of Scriptural injunctions intended to demonstrate how 'the presentation which you make before the sons

---

21  James Capelli, *Summa contra haereticos*, p.CXXXVIII; trans. WE., no. 49, p.303; Anselm of Alessandria, *Tractatus de haereticis*, pp.313–14; trans. WE, no. 54, pp.365–7; Bernard Gui, *Manuel de l'Inquisiteur*, ed. and trans. G. Mollat, vol. 1 (Paris, 1926), pp.12–15; trans. WE, no. 55, p.383.
22  See above ch. 2, pp.35–6.
23  B. Hamilton, 'Wisdom from the East', in P. Biller and A. Hudson, eds, *Heresy and Literacy, 1000–1530* (Cambridge, 1994), pp.46–9.
24  See WE, p.466.
25  See WE, p.778, n.8.

of Jesus Christ confirms the faith and preaching of the Church of God as Holy Scriptures give us to understand it'. At the end of the ministration the initiate is enjoined (as expressed in the Latin version): 'Now, you must understand if you would receive this prayer, that it is needful for you to repent all your sins and to forgive all men, for in the Gospel Christ says, "But if you will not forgive men their sins, neither will your Father forgive your offences"' (Matthew 6: 15).

The second part of the ceremony consisted of the actual administration of the *consolamentum*. Usually this followed immediately, but the wording of the Ritual shows that this was not always the case. In the Occitan text the elder began: 'Peter [or whatever was the name of the postulant], you wish to receive the spiritual baptism by which the Holy Spirit is given in the Church of God, together with the Holy Prayer and the imposition of hands by Good Men.' Then, drawing on Scriptural justification, the elder asserted that the baptism of the laying-on of hands had been instituted by Christ. 'This holy baptism, by which the Holy Spirit is given, the Church of God has preserved from the apostles until this time and it has passed from Good Men to Good Men until the present moment, and it will continue to do so until the end of the world.' The postulant was enjoined to keep the commandments of Christ 'to the utmost of your ability', not to commit adultery, kill, or lie, nor swear an oath or steal. He should turn the other cheek in the face of those who would persecute him. He should 'hate this world and its works and the things which are of this world'. When the believer had confirmed that he had the will to follow these injunctions, he made his *melioramentum*, and was then given the *consolamentum*. The elder placed the Book upon the believer's head and each of the Good Men placed their right hand on him. The ceremony concluded in the way customary with the Cathars, with mutual requests for forgiveness of sins known as the Pardon, and the Act of Peace in which the men embraced and kissed on each cheek and the women kissed each other and the Gospel.[26] His changed status now established, the new *perfectus* listened to the elder's exposition of the rules of conduct in the varied situations in which he might find himself.

Finally, the Occitan Ritual shows that the *perfectus* was instructed on how he should administer the *consolamentum* to the sick, which usually meant a believer who was thought to be dying. This was particularly important as it was likely to be one of the most frequent needs of the believers and was therefore an integral part of the day-to-day duties of the ordinary perfect. It was, of course, unlikely that a dying person would be able to

---

26   See WE, p.467.

undergo the extensive initiation which the Ritual lays down for the perfects themselves, so there is a much greater flexibility about the inclusion of exhortation, preaching, and the use of Scriptural texts. Nevertheless, the believer was still required to show how he had conducted himself towards the Cathar Church in the past, and to confess whether he owed debts to the Church, and whether he had done it any injury. Any debtor who could pay, but refused to do so, was not to receive the *consolamentum*, although inability to pay was not to be taken as a barrier. The believer was then asked to agree to maintain the usages and prohibitions of the Church before receiving the Prayer as the perfect himself had done. In these cases the cloth was spread out on the bed and the Book placed upon it. The believer was then consoled in the same way by the placing of the Book upon his head, together with the hands of the other believers present. Any bequests were to the Church itself and not to individuals. However, it was never easy to judge if an illness was terminal and it was accepted that if the sick person survived, then 'the Christians should present him to the order and pray that he receive the *consolamentum* again as soon as he can'.[27] By the 1240s (if not earlier) provision had also been made for the opposite circumstance in which a believer made an agreement (known as the *convenensa*) that he or she could be consoled even if they were no longer able to speak.[28]

The *consolamentum* remained the key ceremony of the Cathar Church in the West between at least the 1140s and the 1320s, for by this means it maintained the continuity of the episcopal 'ordo', continually replenished the elect class of *perfecti*, and provided the means by which dying believers could gain the salvation which had been promised. At the same time the *perfecti* acted as the focal point for believers still living in the material world, for they could make intercessionary prayers to God (which could not be done by anyone who had not taken the *consolamentum*) and they presided over communal gatherings in which they distributed bread which had been blessed in a manner not dissimilar to the *eulogia* of the early Christians. The custom, says the Franciscan James Capelli, was because they believed themselves to be the successors of the Apostles.[29] It seems certain that the Cathars had been taught the essentials by Balkan missionaries; indeed it has been shown that the opening section of the Occitan version, which

---

27  See below, ch. 6, p.188, on the issue of terminal illness.

28  See the reference by the inquisitor, Bernard Gui, *Manuel de l'Inquisiteur*, ed. and trans. Mollat, vol. 1, pp.20–3; trans. WE, no. 55, p.382, and p.756, n.5.

29  James Capelli, *Summa contra haereticos*, pp.CXLIX–CL; trans. WE., no. 49, pp.303–5, for blessed bread. See Livingstone, ed., *Oxford Dictionary of the Christian Church*, p.522, for *eulogia*, and Hamilton, 'Cathars and Christian perfection', pp.17–18, for bread and prayer. See also A. Brenon, *Le Vrai Visage du Catharisme*, 2nd edn (Portet-sur-Garonne, 1995), pp.85–6.

begins the service, is derived directly from Bogomil usage.[30] Moreover, the basic division between perfect and believers, which this ceremony creates, is little different from the Bogomils, even in the early unstructured Church described by Cosmas in the tenth century, and is very similar indeed to the description of the Bogomils of Constantinople in the early twelfth century given by Euthymius Zigabenus in the *Panoplia Dogmatica*.[31] The Latin and Occitan versions differ mainly in details, although the latter contains important additional elements, either lost from the Latin version or never included in the first place. In the Latin version, however, the postulant is told not to disdain his previous baptism in the Catholic Church or indeed any other good things done up to that time, a concession which is surprising in view of the complete dismissal of baptism by water found in other Cathar sources. It has been argued that this was intended to disguise the real nature of their beliefs,[32] although it is more likely that it reflects a changing view among the moderate dualists of Concorezzo about the role of John the Baptist.[33]

Variations of this nature notwithstanding, whatever the region or period, the *consolamentum* was universally employed by the Cathars. Sometimes it took place in large public assemblies at the castles of socially prominent believers of the Toulousain, at others in secret, furtive meetings with dying believers in rural villages deep in the Pyrenees.[34] The *consolamentum* thus provided the cement for the whole Cathar movement in the West, but it was a cement which could all too easily come loose. Misdemeanours by one of the *perfecti* or, worse still, by a member of the hierarchy, even if only alleged, could throw whole networks into doubt, for those whose *consolamentum* stemmed in any way from the individual concerned found that it could be invalidated by actions with which they had no connection or even knowledge. The failure to reunify the Italian Churches in the late twelfth century was a consequence of the allegation of sexual immorality by Garattus which led him 'to be deemed unworthy of the episcopal office by many of them,

---

30  See WE, pp.780–1, n.1.

31  HH, no. 25, pp.189–90. See above, ch. 1, p.14.

32  Dondaine, *Un Traité néo-manichéen du XIIIe siècle*, p.49. As Dondaine sees it, by this means some Christians could 'in all good faith believe that they were not renouncing the church of their fathers, but only committing themselves to a more perfect state of Christian life'.

33  Raincrius Sacconi, *Summa de Catharis et Pauperibus*, p.76; trans. WE, no. 51, p.344, says that 'many of them only recently came to believe correctly about the Blessed John the Baptist, whom they all formerly condemned'. This suggests that the Latin version of the Ritual was that used at Concorezzo in the mid-thirteenth century.

34  The Ritual presupposes that there is a gathering present, but it also allows for the pressures of circumstance. At the beginning of the ministration of the prayer, the Good Men wash their hands, and 'the believers likewise, if there be any', Clédat, ed., *Le Nouveau Testament traduit au XIIIe siècle*, p.XI; trans. WE, no. 57(B), p.485.

and therefore they did not hold themselves bound by the pledge of obedience which they had made to him'.[35] As Rainier Sacconi saw it, all Cathars lived under this shadow, for 'if their prelate, especially their bishop, may secretly have committed some mortal sin – and many such persons have been found among them in the past – all those upon whom he has imposed his hand have been misled and perish if they die in that state'. The Cathars therefore allow the *consolamentum* to be repeated once or even twice more.[36] The Catholic Church had overcome the problem of the relationship between the validity of the sacrament and the moral state of the priest as early as the second decade of the fourth century, when it had refused to accept the Donatist position, although Pope Gregory VII's boycott of sinful priests had nearly led it down that path again in the late eleventh century. Even so, donatist disputes within the Catholic Church were containable, whereas the introduction of the two principles by Nicetas brought a set of beliefs which, as Raymond V knew, were much more confrontational than the moderate or mitigated dualism to which all the Cathars had previously adhered.

# Cathar theology

Any attempt to reconstruct Cathar belief should, in the first instance, derive from the Cathars themselves, either through the parts of their own literature which have survived or through their own testimonies as recorded by the inquisitorial notaries. However, Catholic writers wrote extensively about the Cathars as well, including some individuals who themselves either may have been or were Cathars in the past, such as the anonymous Lombard who wrote the *De heresi catharorum*, or the inquisitor, Rainier Sacconi. In the latter cases their information is valuable as it stemmed from inside knowledge but, as has been pointed out, even orthodox attacks on Cathar belief are important since they were particularly concerned to define it accurately in order to give weight to their refutations.[37] Individuals appearing before the inquisitors were encouraged to say what they knew or had been taught although, as manuals such as that of the early fourteenth-century inquisitor, Bernard Gui, demonstrate, their testimony was to some extent directed

---

35 *De heresi catharorum*, pp.307–8; trans. WE, no. 23, p.162.

36 Rainerius Sacconi, *Summa de Catharis et Pauperibus*, p.70; trans. WE, no. 51, p.336.

37 On the methodology here, see Hamilton, 'Cathars and Christian perfection', p.6. Despite his great discoveries of specifically Cathar works, Antoine Dondaine did not believe that 'the conclusions already drawn from Catholic polemic ought to be seriously modified', see 'Nouvelles sources de l'histoire doctrinale du néo-manichéisme au moyen âge', *Revue des sciences philosophiques et théologiques* 28 (1939), p.488.

along lines set by their questioners.[38] Despite this, the depositions show the range of perceptions of the faith among different social classes and at different periods, offering quite another perspective from the more 'literary' approaches of the Cathar and Catholic intellectuals. Most Cathar literature emanated from north-eastern Italy, perhaps partly because controversy among the different Churches there stimulated debate, but also because the close ties with Bulgaria and Bosnia led to the importation of books already influential among the Bogomils. Such literature soon found a place in the written culture of the major Italian cities, where the development of schools was more advanced than anywhere else in the West.[39] Moreover, although reliance on Bogomil materials is particularly evident in the twelfth century, this environment encouraged the Italian Cathars to develop their own interpretations and produce their own books in the post-1200 period.[40] One such writer, the anonymous author of the *The Book of the Two Principles*, includes a substantial section of refutation of the views of a certain Master William who, although thought by some to have been a Cathar opponent, is more likely to have been William of Auvergne, Bishop of Paris, whom the author claims to have heard. If the identification is correct, Ivo of Narbonne's story that the Lombard Cathars sent their best minds to study dialectic and theology in the Parisian schools may well have some foundation.[41] Indeed,

---

38  Bernard Gui, *Manuel de l'Inquisiteur*, ed. and trans. Mollat, vol. 1, pp.26–33; trans. WE, no. 55, pp.384–6.

39  L. Paolini, 'Italian Catharism and written culture', in P. Biller and A. Hudson, eds, *Heresy and Literacy, 1000–1530* (Cambridge, 1994), pp.83–103. See also A. Roach, *The Relationship of the Italian and Southern French Cathars, 1170–1320* (DPhil diss., Wolfson College, Oxford, 1989), pp.40–4, who stresses the importance of the links which this part of Italy had with the Byzantine and Dalmatian coasts. Contact between Languedoc and Italy or Byzantium was much more irregular at this period.

40  See Hamilton, 'Wisdom from the East', pp.56–8.

41  *Le Liber du duobus principiis*, in A. Dondaine, ed., *Un Traité néo-manichéen du XIIIe siècle: Le Liber du duobus principiis, suivi d'un fragment de rituel cathare* (Rome, 1939), pp.95–7; trans. WE, no. 59, pp.531–3. See WE, pp.794–5, n.84., for debate on the identity of Master William. On this subject, see P. Biller, 'The Cathars of Languedoc and written materials', in P. Biller and A. Hudson, eds, *Heresy and Literacy, 1000–1530* (Cambridge, 1994), pp.61–82, and L. Paolini, 'Italian Catharism and written culture', pp.95–7. The story of the Cathars studying in Paris comes from a letter of Ivo of Narbonne, a clerk, to Gerald, Archbishop of Bordeaux, in 1243, reproduced by Matthew Paris. Matthew Paris, *Chronica Majora*, ed. H. R. Luard, vol. 4 (Rolls Series, 57) (London, 1877), pp.270–1; trans. WE, no. 27, pp.186–7. Ivo claimed inside knowledge derived from his time living with the Lombard Cathars, when he himself was on the run, having been (unjustly in his opinion) himself accused of heresy. However, while his story has been accepted by Borst, *Die Katharer*, p.104, J. Duvernoy, *Le Catharisme*, vol. 2, *L'Histoire des Cathares* (Toulouse, 1979), pp.184–5, believes that it has more to do with the attempt by the Imperialists to plant the label of heresy upon Frederick II's enemies in the cities of the Lombard League than with real Catharism. As he shows, the chronology will not stand up, although the concept of 'Cathar scholastics' is not inherently implausible.

despite the relative scarcity of extant Cathar writings, the existence of Cathar intellectuals was sufficiently well-known for the Cistercian, Caesarius of Heisterbach, writing in the 1220s, to use them as the basis of an *exemplum* for novices in his book of instruction, *The Dialogue on Miracles*. The novice suggests that the heretics might not have fallen into such error if they had had literate men (*literati*) among them, but the monk denies this. 'When *literati* begin to err', he says, 'at the instigation of the devil, they exhibit greater and more profound stupidity than even the illiterate.'[42] The literacy and knowledge of the French Cathars should not therefore be underestimated, as the evidence of the inquisitorial depositions shows, but survival of Cathar literature from Languedoc is scanty compared to that of Italy.[43]

Two works known to have come from the Bogomils before 1200 are *The Secret Supper* or *The Book of St. John*, and *The Vision of Isaiah*. The text of *The Secret Supper* was brought to Italy from Bulgaria by Nazarius, Elder Son and later Bishop of the Church of Concorezzo, but the beliefs described are likely to be a good reflection of those held by the moderates before the mission of Nicetas in the mid-1170s.[44] It seems originally to have been in Greek, produced in the circle established around Basil in the early twelfth century, which had so alarmed Anna Comnena and which Euthymius Zigabenus describes in his *Panoplia Dogmatica*. It must have been through a number of hands since then and it is thought that the version brought by Nazarius was in Old Slavonic which was then translated (badly, according to Anselm of Alessandria) into Latin. The two surviving western manuscripts themselves differ at various points.[45]

It takes the form of a dialogue: 'The questions of John, the apostle and evangelist, at a secret supper in the kingdom of heaven, about the governance of this world, about its ruler, and about Adam'.[46] Marginal glosses were added to elucidate certain points. It is the story of how the invisible celestial hierarchy established by God was corrupted by the sins of pride, avarice, and lust, leading to the creation of the prison of the material world.

---

42   Caesarius of Heisterbach, *Dialogus Miraculorum*, ed. J. Strange, vol. 1 (Cologne, Bonn, and Brussels, 1851), p.303.

43   See below, p.88; C. Thouzellier, *Un traité cathare inédit du début du XIIIe siècle d'après le Liber contra Manicheos de Durand de Huesca* (Louvain, 1961), pp.87–113; trans. WE, no. 58, pp.494–510.

44   On Nazarius, see *De heresi catharorum*, p.312; trans. WE, no. 23, p.167, and Anselm of Alessandria, *Tractatus de haereticis*, pp.310–12; trans. WE, no. 54, pp.362–3. See also Hamilton, 'Wisdom from the East', p.55.

45   For an analysis of this text, see E. Bozoky, ed., *Le Livre secret des cathares: Interrogatio Iohannis*, édition critique, traduction, commentaire (Paris, 1980), pp.97–217. See also WE, pp.448–9, and Hamilton, 'Wisdom from the East', pp.53–6.

46   Hamilton, 'Wisdom from the East', p.53, says John the Divine.

The cosmology of this hierarchy was the common heritage of Christians, for it was derived from the late fifth-century anonymous neo-Platonic author, now known as the Pseudo-Dionysius, but who was then thought to have been a companion of St Paul and therefore to have lived in apostolic times. This writer had assembled a coherent structure of nine hierarchical choirs of angels created by God in a perfect heavenly society.[47] According to the author of *The Secret Supper*, originally, Satan had been 'the regulator of all things and sat with the Father'; indeed, 'his power descended from the heavens even unto hell, and arose even unto the throne of the Father invisible'. However, he was not satisfied, but wished, as it says in Isaiah 14: 13–14, to be 'like the Most High'. Passing through all these layers, he began to subvert the angels' allegiance by offering them a lower scale of obligations than they owed God. Cast out by God for his treachery, Satan took a third of the angels with him, but 'could find no peace in the firmament', so he presented himself as a sinner who had repented. 'The Lord was moved with pity for him and gave him peace to do what he would until the seventh day', meaning by this the seventh age of the world.[48] It was during that time that Satan created the earth and the living things within it, including man, formed from clay, made to serve him. He ordered 'an angel of the second heaven' to enter this body. A part was then taken to form woman, entered by 'an angel of the first heaven'. These angels therefore had been forced to take mortal form and 'to perform the works of the flesh'. As they knew nothing of sin, Satan made paradise, within which was a serpent made from his spittle. Satan told the man and the woman, 'Eat of all the fruit in Paradise, but of the fruit of good and evil eat not.' The serpent, now in the form of a beautiful young man according to the marginal gloss,[49] but actually entered by the Devil, created in Eve 'a longing for sin, and Eve's desire was like a glowing oven'. The Devil then 'sated his lust on her with the serpent's tail'. The same longing was instilled in Adam and both 'were affected by a lust for debauchery', which explained why all known offspring were 'sons of the devil', a concept which inquisitorial depositions show that some *perfecti* were often very determined to impress upon pregnant believers. Christ explained to John that the spirits of heaven were trapped in the bodies of clay as a consequence of their fall, and therefore they took on the lusts of the flesh and suffered the penalty of death.

Satan's dominion, supported by Enoch and Moses, would last for seven ages. Initially, he convinced men he was the one true God, but the Lord

47  See B. Hamilton, *Religion in the Medieval West* (London, 1986), pp.87–8.
48  See WE, p.774, n.20.
49  See WE, p.774, n.30.

sent Christ 'to this world to make manifest His name to men, that they might recognise the devil and his wickedness'. Christ entered the world through the ear of Mary, an angel of the Lord, an action which the devil countered by sending his angel, 'the prophet Elijah, who baptised in water and was called John the Baptist'. The Day of Judgement would come about when 'the number of the just shall equal the number of those crowned [angels] who fell'. Although Satan would make war on the just, nevertheless all people would stand before the throne of judgement to be divided between 'those who have cherished the angelic life' and 'the servants of iniquity', the former being taken into God's kingdom, the latter thrown into everlasting fire. 'Then Satan shall be bound and all his host, and he shall be cast into the pool of fire.' Finally,

> the Son of God shall sit on the right hand of his Father, and the Father
> shall command His angels that they minister unto them [the just]; and
> He shall place them in the choir of angels and clothe them in imperishable
> raiment; and He shall give them crowns never fading and seats unmoving.
> And God shall be in their midst. 'They shall no more hunger nor thirst;
> neither shall the sun fall on them, nor any heat. And God shall wipe away
> all tears from their eyes.' And [the Son] shall reign with his Holy Father,
> and his reign shall endure forevermore.[50]

Outside commentators, both Catholic and Cathars of different persuasion, confirm the explanation of moderate dualism presented in *The Secret Supper*. Three of the most important of the Catholic writers, the mid- and late-thirteenth-century Italians, Rainier Sacconi, Moneta of Cremona, and Anselm of Alessandria, were well-versed in this cosmology. Rainier Sacconi had actually met Nazarius when he was a very old man and he had told him that 'the Blessed Virgin was an angel and that Christ did not assume human nature, but an angelic one, or a celestial body', ideas which he had received from the Bishop and Elder Son of the Church of Bulgaria sixty years before.[51] Moneta of Cremona, who was a Dominican professor at Bologna and may also have been an inquisitor, was writing about the same time as Rainier Sacconi. He was more interested in absolute dualism, but he nevertheless devoted his second book to refuting the errors of the moderate dualists. The problem with them, as he saw it, was that although they accepted the truth of God's creation, they mixed it with 'a leaven of heretical depravity'.[52] Anselm of Alessandria, in his historical

---

50   Bozoky, *Le Livre secret*, pp.58–63; trans. WE, no. 56(B), pp.458–65.
51   Rainerius Sacconi, *Summa de Catharis et Pauperibus*, p.76; trans. WE, no. 51, p.344.
52   Moneta of Cremona, *Adversus Catharos et Valdenses libri quinque I (Descriptio fidei haereticorum)*, ed. T. A. Ricchini (Rome, 1743), p.109; trans. WE, no. 50, p.317.

survey, places Nazarius as the third bishop of the Cathars at Concorezzo after John Judeus and Garattus. He had his own copy of Nazarius's text. According to him, the views which Nazarius derived from this were rejected by Desiderius, his Elder Son, thus causing a split among the Cathars of Concorezzo.[53] Bernard Hamilton sees this new generation of Cathar leaders, exemplified by Desiderius, as preferring to develop their own ideas, rather than depending upon the Bogomil literature which had become so important to the heretics in the twelfth century.[54] In this context therefore it is not surprising to find that in *The Book of the Two Principles*, which was written in the 1240s, probably by John of Lugio, a contemporary of Desiderius, and an absolute dualist from the Church of Desenzano, there is an attack on the mitigated school no less assertive about their errors than the Catholic polemicists.[55] The author found 'the Garatenses', as he calls them, deeply frustrating, for they accepted only the existence of one benevolent creator, yet repeatedly claimed that 'there is another lord, the evil prince of this world, who was a creature of the most excellent Creator'. To the author, through the testimony of Genesis (which only John of Lugio and his circle accepted among the Cathars), 'we can plainly prove the existence of an evil creator, who created heaven, earth, and all other visible bodies whatsoever'. The obstinacy of the mitigated school in not accepting what the author saw as obvious could only be the consequence of foolishness.[56]

*The Book of the Two Principles* is the most decisive evidence that the Cathars were evolving their own ideas about the nature of dualism, but half a century before the Bogomil influence had been predominant. One work – the *Vision of Isaiah* – was basic to both the moderate and absolute schools. The Cathars seem to have received it from the Bogomils before the schism of the 1170s, translated into Latin from Old Slavonic or Greek, but it had deep roots in the past, probably finding its origins among Greek Gnostics towards the end of the first century AD. References to it by thirteenth-century writers in both Languedoc and Italy and in early fourteenth-century inquisitorial depositions show that it remained an important text for the Cathars until their disappearance in the West.[57]

---

53  Anselm of Alessandria, *Tractatus de haereticis*, p.310; trans. WE, no. 54, p.362.

54  Hamilton, 'Wisdom from the East', p.56.

55  Rainerius Sacconi, *Summa de Catharis et Pauperibus*, pp.72–6; trans. WE, no. 51, pp.339–43, on John of Lugio.

56  *Le Liber du duobus principiis*, pp.132–4; trans. WE, no. 59, pp.567–9. For the acceptance of Genesis, see Hamilton, 'Cathars and Christian perfection', p.8.

57  Hamilton, 'Wisdom from the East', pp.52–3, for the argument that it was known before the schism. See WE, no. 56(A), pp.456–8, for a retelling in the early fourteenth century.

When Isaiah 'had ceased to behold the vision', he was able to recount his experience. This was of great value to the Cathars for he had been taken on a journey through the visible and invisible worlds by an angel, who had told him that 'no one who desires to return to the flesh of that world has seen what you see nor is able to see what you have seen'. The angel took Isaiah by the hand and, as they ascended through the firmament, they saw a great battle raging between Satan and the followers of God. 'For just as it is on earth, so also is it in the firmament, because replicas of what are in the firmament are on earth.' The angel told him that the world would not end until God 'comes to slay him [Satan] with the spirit of His virtue'. Beyond the firmament he was conducted through the seven heavens, each one inhabited by angels praising God and each more glorious than the one below until, reaching the seventh, he saw 'the righteous who, stripped of fleshly robes, were in heavenly robes and standing in great glory'. They had not, however, received their 'thrones and crowns of glory', which would not happen, the angel said, until the Son of God took on human likeness.

> And the prince of that world will stretch forth his hand upon the Son of God and will kill Him and hang Him on a tree, and he will kill Him not knowing who He is. And He will descend into hell and lay it waste, with all the phantoms of hell. And He will seize the prince of death and despoil him, and crush all his powers, and will rise again on the third day; having with him certain of the righteous. And He will send His preachers into the whole world, and will ascend into heaven. Then these will receive their thrones and crowns.

In the seventh heaven Isaiah saw an angel more glorious than all the others: this was the Archangel Michael, who held a book in which the works of all men were contained, including Isaiah's own. Finally, he saw 'the Lord in great glory and I was most sorely afraid'. Isaiah saw too the Son of God descending through the heavens and his transfiguration, saw him 'like the Son of Man dwelling with men and in the world', and saw his ascent back through the heavens. He saw 'a wonderful angel sit at His left hand', who told him that he had seen what 'no other son of the flesh had seen' and that he must now return his robe 'until the time of your days shall be fulfilled and then you shall come here'.[58]

Although the Bogomils had made their own modifications to this story, both moderate and absolute Cathars accepted the theological landscape it

---

58   R. H. Charles, ed., *The Ascension of Isaiah, Translated from the Ethiopic Version, Which Together with the New Greek Fragment, the Latin Versions and the Latin Translation of the Slavonic, Is Here Published in Full* (London, 1900), pp.98–139; trans. WE, no. 56(A), pp.449–56.

depicted, for it showed a material world and a firmament riven by the battle between Satanic and Godly forces, but it did not tackle the question of the devil's origins, which was the central issue of dispute between them. In the thirteenth century, however, the surviving Cathar literature is dominated by those who believed in absolute dualism. Cathars in both Languedoc and Lombardy produced major books expounding this point of view. The Languedocian treatise is an anonymous exposition by a leading Cathar from the Albi, Toulouse, and Carcassonne triangle, copied out for the purpose of refutation in the *Liber contra Manicheos* by Durand of Huesca, a former Waldensian reclaimed by the Catholic Church, and was probably written between 1218 and 1222.[59] The Lombard version is *The Book of the Two Principles*, written perhaps twenty years later. Neither author can be certainly identified. Speculation that the author of the Albigensian treatise might have been 'Theoderic' (formerly William of Châteauneuf, a canon from Nevers), who is described by Peter of Les Vaux-de-Cernay as debating with Bishop Diego of Osma in 1206, or Bartholomew of Carcassonne, a leading Cathar of the region in the 1220s, fails to take account of Duvernoy's point that Durand of Huesca would almost certainly have known if either of these two were behind it.[60] The idea that John of Lugio was the author of *The Book of the Two Principles* is, however, much more likely, for Rainier Sacconi says that he possessed a copy of 'a large volume of ten quires' written by John of Lugio, and indeed *The Book of the Two Principles* is much more comprehensible in the light of Sacconi's detailed commentary upon John of Lugio's beliefs. Since Sacconi had himself been a Cathar for seventeen years, it is quite possible that he knew John of Lugio personally. He was certainly well-aware of the divisions within their ranks, for he differentiates between the two parties of the Albanenses, based at Desenzano on Lake Garda, by his day the only Italian Cathar Church still adhering to absolute dualism. Most of the older Cathars followed Bishop Belesmanza of Verona, whose views had commanded general support among the Albanenses between 1200 and 1230, but who by the 1240s found himself in a minority in the face of a group of 'modernisers', led by John of Lugio of Bergamo.[61]

59 Thouzellier, *Un traité*, pp.17–84. For a detailed analysis of the *Liber contra Manicheos* and its author, see Thouzellier, *Catharisme et Valdéisme en Languedoc à la fin du XIIe et au début du XIIIe siècle*, 2nd edn (Louvain and Paris, 1969), pp.303–424. In 1208 Durand of Huesca made a profession of faith and was allowed by the papacy to form a religious society called 'the Poor Catholics'. From this base, he and other leading former Waldensians, such as Ermengaud of Béziers and Bernard Prim, launched a powerful polemical attack upon the Cathars. See PVC, vol. 1, para. 10, pp.9–10; trans. Sibly, p.11, for absolute dualism in Languedoc.
60 WE, p.783, n.8.
61 Rainerius Sacconi, *Summa de Catharis et Pauperibus*, pp.70–1, 76; trans. WE, no. 51, pp.337, 343.

According to Rainier Sacconi, the Languedocian Churches maintained 'the errors of Belesmanza and the old Albanenses' which, as these evidently represented the established view, suggests that they best reflect the teaching of Nicetas at the Council of St Félix-de-Caraman. John of Lugio held to some of these, but he had changed others 'for the worse', while 'some errors he has devised for himself'.[62] However, neither author seems to have been writing for the mass of believers, anymore than the scholastics of the Catholic Church intended their thoughts to be communicated directly to the faithful. The Albigensian author saw himself as the upholder of the truth in the face of the Catholics, whom he saw as heretics, 'blind leaders of the blind', as in Matthew 15: 14. He probably intended his work to fortify the *perfecti*, for it is buttressed throughout with careful and detailed Scriptural quotation. The author of *The Book of the Two Principles* is equally keen to provide biblical justification, although he is more directly combative, and had evidently debated the issues with both Catholics and Albanenses on many occasions. Indeed, he appears to have been quite capable of goading opponents whom, at one point, he describes as 'speaking calmly at first and then shouting'. Rainier Sacconi's reference to members of the Albanenses, 'who were less well informed, to whom special points were not revealed', suggests that these writers were part of a Cathar elite aiming to provide the intellectual underpinning of their faith.[63] Neither the Catholic nor the Cathar leaders expected the mass of people in their Churches to be able to explicate the whole range of their respective theologies.

The absolute dualists believed in the existence of two worlds, one visible, vain, and corruptible, and one invisible, incorruptible, and eternal. John's Gospel says that Christ's kingdom is not of this world (18: 36), but is the New Heaven and the New Earth which the Lord spoke of in Isaiah (66: 22).[64] The idea that God created all things had been grossly misinterpreted by the Catholic Church. 'It should be clearly realised', says *The Book of the Two Principles*, 'that these universal symbols which refer to what is evil, vain, and transitory are not of the same sort as those other universal symbols already mentioned, which designate the good, clean, and highly desirable, and which persist forever'.[65] They therefore argued that the two principles,

---

62  Rainerius Sacconi, *Summa de Catharis et Pauperibus*, pp.77, 72; trans. WE, no. 51, pp.345, 339.

63  Thouzellier, *Un traité*, pp.104–5; trans. WE, no. 58, p.506; *Le Liber du duobus principiis*, p.92; trans. WE, no. 59, p.527; Rainerius Sacconi, *Summa de Catharis et Pauperibus*, p.72; trans. WE, no. 51, p.339.

64  Thouzellier, *Un traité*, pp.87–95; trans. WE, no. 58, pp.497–500.

65  *Le Liber du duobus principiis*, p.111; trans. WE, no. 59, p.547; Thouzellier, *Un traité*, pp.101–2; trans. WE, no. 58, pp.503–4.

good and evil, existed from eternity, and that each principle had created his own world.[66] Consequently, as the Albigensian author says, 'the devil engendered the children of this world, who are born of the flesh of sin, who are born of blood and of the will of the flesh and of the pleasure of man'.[67] For the author of *The Book of the Two Principles*, the logic of this was inescapable. There could not be a single, omnipotent God. 'For one who knows fully all things that shall come to pass is powerless, in so far as he is self-consistent, to do anything except that which he himself has known from eternity that he shall do.' Given the evident existence of evil, it was therefore obvious that a single God would have 'knowingly and in full awareness created and made His angels of such imperfection from the beginning that they could in no way escape evil'. In other words, God would have been 'the whole cause and origin of evil – which is obviously to be denied'.[68] Although the literature of the Cathars shows that they used the same text of the New Testament as the Catholics and the Waldensians, there was, as a consequence of these beliefs about creation, one significant difference. According to the orthodox, John 1: 3, 4 should be rendered as 'All things were made by him; and without him was not any thing made that was made. In him was life, and the life was the light of men.' For those who believed that the material world was the work of the Devil, this was clearly unacceptable, for the Albigensian author, for example, this passage meant that 'nothing' (*nihil*) had been made without him (i.e. without God's involvement), interpreting 'nothing' to be the transitory world which contrasted with the true reality which was the creation of God.[69]

Then, the Devil and his angels invaded the heavenly world, did battle with the Archangel Michael, and came away with a third of the creatures of God. 'These he [the Devil]', says Rainier Sacconi, 'implants daily in human bodies and in those of lower animals, and also transfers them from one body to another until such time as all shall be brought back to heaven.'[70] Rainier is referring here to the idea that souls transmigrated until they reached the body of a consoled Cathar, preparatory to reintegration with their guardian spirit, although it is not clear how widely accepted this belief

---

66  Rainerius Sacconi, *Summa de Catharis et Pauperibus*, p.71; trans. WE, no. 51, p.338.
67  Thouzellier, *Un traité*, p.96; trans. WE, no. 58, p.501.
68  *Le Liber du duobus principiis*, p.84; trans. WE, no. 59, pp.518–19.
69  Thouzellier, *Un traité*, pp.102–3; trans. WE, no. 58, pp.504–5, and comment, p.787, n.138, and Brenon, *Le Vrai Visage*, pp.58–62.
70  Rainerius Sacconi, *Summa de Catharis et Pauperibus*, p.71; trans. WE, no. 51, p.338. The idea of a third comes from Revelations 12: 4. On these events, see Borst, *Die Katharer*, pp.143–6.

was among Cathar intellectuals.[71] This devil's attack seems to be what the Albigensian author is referring to when he speaks of the spread of terror in 'the land of the living'.[72] The author of *The Book of the Two Principles* uses the Parable of the Sower from Matthew 13: 24–5 to make the same point: 'The kingdom of heaven is likened to a man that sowed good seed in his field; but while men were asleep, his enemy came by night and oversowed cockle among the wheat, and went his way.'[73] Here was another fundamental question – that of how angels could have sinned – which equally exercised contemporary Catholic theologians.[74] For the Cathars it followed that God's angels in no way had free will, for God 'would have known that from this cause alone His kingdom would be corrupted'. The corruption therefore was the consequence of this invasion of evil.[75] For the author of *The Book of the Two Principles*, therefore, there would be no cataclysmic Last Judgement at some arbitrary point in the future, where all would be judged in accordance with their actions based on free will. On the contrary, the finite number of souls which had been entrapped would all eventually be delivered from their prisons and only then would the material world come to an end. Otherwise, 'there would be an untold multitude of children of all races, four years of age or less, and an astonishing multitude of the dumb, the deaf, and the simple-minded, none of whom were ever able to do penance, none of whom had from God in any measure either the ability or knowledge to do good'. For the author this was manifestly absurd.[76]

---

71  On transmigration, see R. Poupin, 'De metempsycose en réincarnation ou la transmigration des âmes des temps cathares à nos jours', in *CEI*, pp.145–64, where it is argued that, as there is no evidence for this in Cathar literature, it was largely a popular belief, presented to convey the idea that the perfects lived on the frontier of the tenth heaven. Brenon, *Le Vrai Visage*, pp.286–91, also thinks that the idea of transmigration through the bodies of animals was specific to the 'Catharism of the mountains' of the early fourteenth century, but Sacconi obviously thought differently. Caesarius of Heisterbach, *Dialogus Miraculorum*, p.301, tells his novice that the Albigensians all foolishly believed in transmigration, 'that in relation to its merit the soul will pass through various bodies, even animals and serpents'. Hamilton, 'Cathars and Christian perfection', pp.21–2, prefers to follow Sacconi, arguing that the strict Cathar prohibition on the killing of animals largely derived from their belief that fallen souls were in the bodies of animals and birds.
72  Thouzellier, *Un traité*, pp.105–6; WE, no. 58, pp.496, 506–7.
73  *Le Liber du duobus principiis*, p.91; trans. WE, no. 59, p.526. Implicit in the 'Manichaean treatise', Thouzellier, *Un traité*, pp.96–7; trans. WE, no. 58, p.501.
74  See Borst, *Die Katharer*, p.145–6. On angels, Livingstone, ed., *Oxford Dictionary of the Christian Church*, pp.61–2.
75  *Le Liber du duobus principiis*, pp.89, 93, 97–8; trans. WE, no. 59, pp.523, 528, 532–3; Moneta of Cremona, *Adversus Catharos et Valdenses*, pp.63–5; trans. WE, no. 50, pp.313–17, including his refutation.
76  *Le Liber du duobus principiis*, p.142; trans. WE, no. 59, pp.577–8. See Brenon, *Le Vrai Visage*, pp.70–2.

The Cathars accepted the Trinity, but not as one God, for 'the Father is greater than the Son and than the Holy Spirit'.[77] Salvation came through Christ. What the Cathars actually understood by this however is difficult to interpret. Using the text from Matthew 26: 31, 'For it is written, "I will strike the shepherd, and the sheep of the flock shall be dispersed"', the author of *The Book of the Two Principles* explained that God ' "struck" His Son by enduring His death' because he 'was unable in a better way to deliver His people from the power of the enemy'. He did not, he stressed, 'by His own act absolutely and directly strike His Son Jesus Christ'.[78] Both Rainier Sacconi and Moneta of Cremona say that the Cathars did not believe that the Incarnation, Crucifixion, and Resurrection had literally taken place. Christ did not, says Rainier Sacconi, 'acquire human nature in reality but only its semblance from the Blessed Virgin, who, they say, was an angel. Neither did he really eat, drink, or suffer, nor was he really dead and buried, nor was His resurrection real, but all these things were in appearance only'.[79] However, Bernard Hamilton has recently argued that, while this was the Cathar belief about the role of Christ in this world, they nevertheless believed that these events really had occurred in the other world, that is the 'Land of the Living'.[80] 'The tribulation and persecution and passion and death of our Lord Jesus Christ', says *The Book of the Two Principles*, in a section which consists almost entirely of biblical quotation, '. . . is manifestly displayed in Holy Scriptures'.[81] It is not easy to discern how widespread this view was among the Cathars. Rainier Sacconi saw it as a particular tenet of John of Lugio, 'that Christ was born according to the flesh of the fathers of old, just named [i.e. the Old Testament prophets], and that He really assumed flesh from the Blessed Virgin and really suffered, was crucified, dead, and buried, and rose again on the third day, but he thinks that all these things took place in another, higher world, not in this one'.[82] According to Sacconi, John of Lugio believed that the other world was entirely comparable with the visible realm: 'marriages, fornications and adulteries take place there, from which children are born'.[83]

As the copious quotation deployed by the Cathar writers shows, the heretics rested their arguments exclusively upon certain books of the Bible.

---

77  Rainerius Sacconi, *Summa de Catharis et Pauperibus*, p.71; trans. WE, no. 51, p.338.

78  *Le Liber du duobus principiis*, p.143; trans. WE, no. 59, p.578.

79  Rainerius Sacconi, *Summa de Catharis et Pauperibus*, p.71; trans. WE, no. 51, p.338; Moneta of Cremona, *Adversus Catharos et Valdenses*, p.5; trans. WE, no. 50, p.311.

80  Hamilton, 'Cathars and Christian perfection', pp.11–12. See also WE, p.496.

81  *Le Liber du duobus principiis*, p.145; trans. WE, no. 59, pp.581–5.

82  Rainerius Sacconi, *Summa de Catharis et Pauperibus*, p.75; trans. WE, no. 51, pp.342–3.

83  Rainerius Sacconi, *Summa de Catharis et Pauperibus*, p.73; trans. WE, no. 51, p.340.

Rainier Sacconi says that they believed that the devil was the author of the Old Testament, 'except these books: Job, the Psalms, the books of Solomon, of Jesus son of Sirach, of Isaiah, Jeremiah, Ezeckiel, Daniel, and of the twelve prophets. Some of these, they say, were written in heaven, to wit, those which were written before the destruction of Jerusalem, which, they say, was the heavenly land'.[84] In keeping with his view that 'whatever in the whole Bible is stated to have been in this world he changes to have actually taken place in that other world', John of Lugio dissented from this, accepting the whole of the Old Testament and, indeed, that all the patriarchs and the prophets were 'pleasing to God', but that 'they were men in another world'.[85] As Hamilton points out, John of Lugio's school nevertheless understood the version of creation in the Old Testament to be the work of the devil, even though they did not ascribe this part of the Old Testament to diabolic origin.[86] They found it inconceivable that the God of the Old Testament, who had 'caused the manifest and merciless destruction of so many men and women with all their children', could be the same as the true creator.[87]

# Moral and ethical teaching

Apart from the anonymous exposition of the nature of the true Church, *La Gleisa de Dio*, which is exceptional in that it is probably to be dated to the third quarter of the fourteenth century, none of the surviving Cathar writings set down their moral code in any systematic or detailed way although, as has been seen, the Occitan Ritual reiterated what the Cathars saw as basic New Testament commandments (the prohibitions on adultery, killing, lying, oath-taking, and stealing). The Ritual also contains guidance on the practical application of some of these beliefs for *perfecti* who are travelling from place to place. Therefore, for example,

> if they find some personal belonging along the road, let them not touch it
> unless they know that they can return it. If they see that persons to whom
> the object may be returned have passed that way ahead of them, let them

---

84  Rainerius Sacconi, *Summa de Catharis et Pauperibus*, p.71; trans. WE, no. 51, p.338. See also Moneta of Cremona, *Adversus Catharos et Valdenses*, p.3; trans. WE, no. 50, pp.308–9.

85  Rainerius Sacconi, *Summa de Catharis et Pauperibus*, p.75; trans. WE, no. 51, pp.342–3.

86  Hamilton, 'Cathars and Christian perfection', p.8.

87  *Le Liber du duobus principiis*, p.128; trans. WE, no. 59, p.564.

take it to return it if they can. If this is not possible, they should put it back in the place where it was found.[88]

Catholic writers saw matters differently. They were familiar with Cathar ethical and moral teaching and, indeed, many had observed the behaviour of the *perfecti* at first hand. Nevertheless, few were prepared to accept it at face value. One of the most virulent was the Cistercian, Peter of Les Vaux-de-Cernay, whose close connection with the Albigensian Crusade hardened his already uncompromising stance on the heretics.

> The 'perfected' heretics wore a black robe, claimed (falsely) to practise chastity, and renounced meat, eggs and cheese. They wished it to appear that they were not liars although they lied, especially about God, almost unceasingly! They also said that no one should take oaths for any reason. The term 'believers' was applied to those who lived a secular existence and did not try to copy the way of life of the 'perfected', but hoped that by following their faith they would attain salvation; they were separated in the way they lived, but united in their beliefs – or rather unbelief! Those called 'believers' were dedicated to usury, robbery, murder and illicit love – and to all kinds of perjury and perversity; indeed they felt they could sin in safety and without restraint, because they believed they could be saved without restitution of what they had stolen and without confession and penitence, so long as they were able to recite the Lord's prayer and ensure a 'laying-on of hands' by their masters, in the final moments of their lives.

Among his other points he reported that 'some of the heretics declared that no one could sin from the navel downwards; they characterised images in churches as idolatry; they maintained that church bells were the trumpets of devils; and they said that it was no greater sin for a man to sleep with his mother or his sister than with any other woman'.[89] Rainier Sacconi was more sophisticated in his presentation, but equally outraged by what he saw as the Cathar indifference to sins committed before their *consolamentum* and their consequent rejection of the Catholic system of penance involving contrition, confession, and works. After the *consolamentum*, he says, they make

88  For *La Gleisa de Dio*, see T. Venckeleer, 'Un Recueil cathare. Le manuscrit A.6.10 de la "Collection Vaudoise" de Dublin, I: Une Apologie', *Revue belge de philologie et d'histoire* 38 (1960), pp.820–31; trans. WE, no. 60(A), pp.592–602. On the moral code in *La Gleisa de Dio*, see A. Brenon, 'Syncrétisme hérétique dans les refuges Alpins? Un Livre cathare parmi les recueils vaudois de la fin du moyen âge: Le Manuscrit 269 de Dublin', *Heresis* 7 (1986), p.11. For the thirteenth-century Occitan Ritual, see Clédat, ed., *Le Nouveau Testament traduit au XIIIe siècle*, pp.XIX, XXI–XXII; trans. WE, no. 57(B), pp.489–90, 491.
89  PVC, vol. 1, paras 13, 17, pp.13–15, 17–18; trans. Sibly, pp.12–13, 14.

no restitution for past usury, theft, or rapine, leaving any gains from these activities to their relatives.[90]

Not all were as consistently antagonistic as Peter of Les Vaux-de-Cernay though. The Franciscan James Capelli, for example, shows a willingness to take a more objective view. Although hostile to 'the ferocious rabies of the heretics', he nevertheless affirmed their adherence to chastity and to dietary restrictions and fasts. Rumours of sexual orgies were quite false, he said; their gatherings were for preaching, confession, and prayer. Both Capelli and Sacconi agreed that they refused to eat meat, eggs, fowls, and cheese.[91] Sacconi says that this was because they were 'begotten of coition', although it may be that it had more to do with Cathar belief in the transmigration of souls to warm-blooded creatures, inducing a consideration for animal life among them.[92] This would answer the question posed by the Cistercian theologian, Alan of Lille, in the late twelfth century, who thought it illogical for them to eat fish, which were also the product of generation.[93] Over and above the dietary prohibitions, it was also admitted that the Cathar *perfecti* were expected to endure rigorous fasts; according to Anselm of Alessandria, three days per week on bread and water, as well as three forty-day fasts in the course of the year.[94]

Naturally, a Church which believed in the continuity of the Old and New Testaments was for the Cathars, as for the Bogomils, an object, first, of distaste, and then, after the crusade, of hatred. According to Moneta of Cremona, the Cathars believed that almost all of what is found in Revelations 16, 17, and the first part of 19, applied to the Catholic Church.

For they interpret 'the beast' and 'the woman' as references to the Roman Church. The beast, we read, was scarlet; likewise, we find in verse 4 that the woman was clothed with 'scarlet and purple, and gilt with gold, and precious stones and pearls, having a golden cup in her hand'. These words are applicable to the lord pope, who is the head of the Roman Church. The woman 'drunk with the blood of the saints' (verse 6) is referred to in the same connection. This symbol they attach to the Roman Church because it orders their death, for they believe that they are saints.[95]

90  Rainerius Sacconi, *Summa de Catharis et Pauperibus*, p.66; trans. WE, no. 51, p.332. See also, Borst, *Die Katharer*, pp.173–7.
91  James Capelli, *Summa contra haereticos*, pp.clvii–clviii, clxxvi–clxxviii; trans. WE., no. 49, pp.305–6; Rainerius Sacconi, *Summa de Catharis et Pauperibus*, p.64; trans. WE, no. 51, p.330.
92  See Hamilton, 'Cathars and Christian perfection', p.21, and J. Guiraud, *Histoire de l'Inquisition au moyen âge*, vol. 1 (Paris, 1935), pp.85–6.
93  Alan of Lille, *De fide catholica*, in *PL*, vol. 210, cols 377–8.
94  Anselm of Alessandria, *Tractatus de haereticis*, p.315; trans. WE, no. 54, p.367; Bernard Gui, *Manuel de l'Inquisiteur*, ed. and trans. Mollat, vol. 1, pp.18–19; trans. WE, no. 55, p.381.
95  Moneta of Cremona, *Adversus Catharos et Valdenses*, p.397; trans. WE, no. 50, p.328.

# Popular Cathar belief

Moneta may have derived some of his information about Cathar views of the Roman Church from the testimonies of witnesses before the inquisitors, for important and well-educated Cathars deposed before the tribunals in both France and Italy. However, the inquisitors also swept up many more ordinary believers, whose answers to questions on belief offer some idea of the way dualism was understood at a popular level, as well as suggesting the content of the preaching of the *perfecti* to their supporters. Among Cathar supporters in Languedoc, not surprisingly, less effort was expended in the attempt to unravel the origins of evil power than was the case with the intellectuals. The most important messages which were absorbed were the attribution of the material world to the Devil and, in turn, the identification of the Catholic Church with that materialism. It has been suggested, indeed, that the reason for the greater unity of the Cathar Church in Languedoc lies in its lack of doctrinal dogmatism, which is in sharp contrast to the quarrels among the Italians. In this view, the example set by the lifestyle of the *perfecti* was more important than dualistic belief as such.[96] It is probable that Nicetas's absolute dualism was comprehended more fully among the leaders of the Cathars in southern France than it was by the majority of the believers: an anonymous treatise describing the heretics of Languedoc, probably dating from the early years of the Albigensian Crusade, while outlining their belief in absolute dualism, nevertheless also says that some of them believed in one god, who had two sons, 'Christ and the prince of this world'.[97]

William Faber of *Podio Hermer*, who appeared three times before Friar Ferrier at Toulouse during November and December 1243, offers a pertinent case history, since he not only testified himself, but was one of a group of men who discussed these issues, a circumstance known to others. Moreover, he admitted that he had been involved with heretics for as long as he could remember; he had believed their errors, as he put it, 'as soon as he could distinguish between good and evil'. References in the document suggest he was unlikely to have been younger than his early forties at the time of

---

96 Roach, *Relationship*, pp.37–8, 47–50. See, too, Duvernoy, *Le Catharisme*, vol. 1, *La Religion des cathares*, p.39, who warns that it would be erroneous to think that Cathar theology was imparted to the faithful 'in the logical order of a manual of theology', and M. G. Pegg, *The Corruption of Angels: Inquisitors and Heretics in Thirteenth-Century Europe* (Ph.D. diss., Princeton University, NJ, 1997), p.149, who argues that 'heresy in the Lauragais loses all historical specificity through being seen as nothing more than a set of stable ideas'.

97 A. Dondaine, 'Durand de Huesca et la polémique anti-cathare', *Archivum Fratrum Praedicatorum* 29 (1959), p.271; trans. WE, no. 37, p.234. The author may have been Ermengaud of Béziers who, together with Durand of Huesca, founded 'the Poor Catholics'.

his deposition, so his testimony and those of the other witnesses are relevant to most of the earlier thirteenth century. He had often assisted at heretical gatherings in Toulouse and in the area to the north in and around Castelsarrasin and Moissac, and he had been a witness of 'a disputation' about faith between three *bonhommes* and two priests in a house at Castelsarrasin some twenty-five years before. Marriage to Petronilla, a woman who did not share his views, apparently made no difference, except that he had often shouted at her because of it. He said that he had heard the heretics preaching that God did not make visible things, that baptism and marriage were of no value, that the consecrated host was not the body of Christ, and that there was no resurrection of the dead.[98] According to another witness, John Vitalis, William was among those seen celebrating the news of the murder of the inquisitors at the village of Avignonet (south-east of Toulouse) in May 1242, by a band emanating from the Pyrenean fortress of Montségur.[99] These included William's nephew, William Audebert, a man who had, according to John Vitalis, 'written a great deal' about Cathar belief, and who had explained to him what he called the truth of the Upper and Lower Worlds.

> On a certain day, while the Lord was preaching in the sky to his people, a messenger came to him from earth, saying that he would lose this world unless he sent someone at once, and the Lord immediately sent Lucibel to this world, and received him for a brother, and afterwards Lucibel wished to have a part of the Lower and Upper possessions, and the Lord did not wish it, and on this account there was a war for a long time.

Thus, as a consequence of pride, conflict still continues between them every day.[100] A third witness, William Feraut, had been present when, some years earlier, in 1234, William Faber had discussed the issue of salvation in this world, while at the house of a John of Toulouse, where William Audebert was lying ill. 'When God saw the poverty of his kingdom on account of the fall of the evil spirits', said William Faber,

> he asked those around him, 'Does anyone wish to be my true son and that I be his father', and when no one replied, Christ, who was the *bailli* of God, replied, 'I wish to be your son and I will go wherever you shall send me', and then God, as if [he were] his son, sent Christ to the world to preach the name of God, and thus Christ came.

---

98 Doat, vol. 22, ff.4r–5v. See the very similar list reported of preachers at Villemur, south-east of Castelsarrasin, Doat, vol. 22, ff.65v–66r.
99 See below, ch. 5, p.154.
100 Doat, vol. 22, ff.11r–12v.

William Audebert was not too ill to make his own contribution, in which he showed an appreciation of the Cathar belief in two parallel worlds. The heretics taught, he said, that oxen and *roncins* grazed and ploughed the soil and worked on the sky as on earth.[101]

Such conversations were not uncommon among the believers of Castelsarrasin and there is no reason to believe that this town was untypical. Aymeric of Naregina had said that God had not come in the Blessed Virgin, but had adumbrated himself; nor had he instituted the mass, which was the invention of the cardinals and the clergy 'for the love of the great oblations'. Sometimes, it was simply part of everyday gossip, as in the following explanation of the creation of man overheard in the market-place:

> the devil made man from the clay of the land, and said to God that he should send a soul to man, and God said to the devil he will be stronger than me and you if he is made of clay, but make him from the mud of the sea, and the devil made him from the mud of the sea, and God said, he is good, for he is not too strong and not too weak, and God sent a soul to man.[102]

Discussion of this kind remained frequent despite the attentions of the inquisitors. In 1274 Guillelma, wife of Thomas of St Flour, a carpenter from Toulouse, alleged that her neighbours, Fabrissa and her daughter, Philippa, regularly sheltered heretics, both male and female. Guillelma claimed that Fabrissa had said that Lucifer made man and God had told him to make man speak. Lucifer replied that he could not do this, 'so God breathed in the man's mouth, and the man spoke'. Moreover, she had heard Fabrissa speak ill of the clergy, saying that their teaching was in bad faith and that it was untrue for them to say that 'they gave the bread which was the body of God'. On a number of occasions, Fabrissa and Philippa had planned to go secretly to Lombardy (with which they had contact through the heretics who frequently stayed with them) in order to perform penance, but they had never done so. These women lived in houses attached to each other and it seems unlikely that Fabrissa would have allowed heretics to stay if Guillelma had not been trustworthy or even complicit, so this testimony suggests that at some time they must have quarrelled. Perhaps the key to it lay in the Cathar view of the creation of new material bodies. When Guillelma was pregnant, Fabrissa had apparently told her that 'she should ask God to free her from the demon which she had in her belly'.[103]

---

101  Doat, vol. 22, ff.26r–26v.
102  Doat, vol. 22, ff.31r–32v.
103  Doat, vol. 25, ff.38v–44r.

If the testimony of 1274 seems more simplistic than that of 1243–44, it was not only because it might have stemmed from antagonism between neighbours. By the 1270s the pressures brought to bear by the inquisitors, the monarchy, and the new count, the king's brother, Alphonse of Poitiers, combined with a series of failed attempts at resistance, had largely broken up the Cathar hierarchy in Languedoc.[104] Those who had survived had fled to Lombardy, as Fabrissa indicates, so there was no core of *perfecti* the believers could turn to for guidance. However, in 1299, two brothers, notaries from the Pyrenean spa town of Ax, Peter and William Autier, having been to Italy for several years' instruction and training, returned to the county of Foix and began a new preaching campaign in an effort to revive their ailing faith. Although this lasted for barely a decade, it was sufficiently vigorous to have a real impact upon the rural society of the northern Pyrenees south of Foix and Carcassonne, an impact which can be seen in the depositions made before James Fournier, Bishop of Pamiers, recorded between 1318 and 1325.[105] One witness, Sibylla, wife of Raymond Peter, a farmer from the Sabarthès region in the upper Ariège valley, lived in the village of Arques, a substantial village, south-east of Limoux, situated in the valley of the River Sals, a tributary of the Aude. Drawn into Catharism by her husband's interest, she was able to give first-hand accounts of the teaching of the Autiers and their circle in the early years of the fourteenth century, some 130 years after Nicetas had furnished the Cathar Church in the West with new doctrines and a systematic organisation.

Sibylla and Raymond Peter were familiar with both the heretics' conversation and their more formal preaching, for they stayed at their house and were frequent visitors to others in the village. Not surprisingly, given the circumstances in which they found themselves, the Autiers were particularly vehement about the Roman Church. The priests were 'evil men . . . since although they taught the way of God, nevertheless they departed from the way and despoiled and stole everything which men had'. Indeed, 'they did not say masses nor do anything except for money'. Since they did not live properly, 'they had lost the power of absolving from sins'.[106] On another occasion, the Autiers had compared the Roman clergy to a cow, which does good by delivering milk, but then destroys it by placing her foot in the milk vessel or kicking it over. In contrast, the Autiers represented the Church of God, for 'the other Church was a house of idols, . . . and they said that adoring such images was fatuous, since the images themselves were made with axes and other metal tools'.[107]

---

104  See below, ch. 5, pp.172–5.
105  See below, ch. 6, pp.178–82.
106  *RF*, vol. 2, p.404.
107  *RF*, vol. 2, p.420.

But the Cathar Church of the early fourteenth century was not based on mere anti-clericalism, for the positive teaching on creation remained. The technique of the Autiers was for one of them to read from a book, while the other explained what it meant in the vernacular; in this case, Peter's son, James, did the reading and Peter made the exposition.[108] One evening, Peter had told them that 'in the beginning the celestial Father had made all the spirits and souls in Heaven', but then

> the devil came to the gate of paradise, wishing to enter there, but he was not able to, remaining at the gate for a thousand years; then he fraudulently entered paradise and, when he was there, persuaded the spirits and souls made by the celestial Father that it was not good for them, since they were subject to the celestial Father, but if they wished to follow him and go to his world, he could give them possessions, namely fields, vineyards, gold and silver, wives, and other good things of the visible world.

Many of the souls and spirits were seduced by this and fell from heaven for nine days and nine nights until God, seeing that he had been almost deserted, put his foot upon the hole through which they had fallen, and said to those who remained that from now on if any others left 'they would never have pause or rest'. As for those who had already fallen, they would be allowed to return, although it would be a difficult and prolonged pro-cess for those spirits of bishops and other great clerics, who had knowingly deserted, whereas those of simple men (and here the Autiers must have been very aware of their audience), who had been more or less tricked out of heaven, would be able to return quickly and easily.

After their fall the spirits remembered the good they had lost and were sad about the evil they had found. The Devil saw that they were sad and told them that they should sing a canticle to the Lord, as they had been accustomed to do, but they replied 'how could they sing a canticle to the Lord in an alien land?' Then one of the spirits asked the Devil why he had deceived them into following him when all could now return to heaven, but the Devil replied that they would not be returning to heaven, 'since he had made for the spirits and souls such a husk (*tunica*) from which they could not escape, and in these husks the spirits would forget all the good and joys which they had had in heaven'. The Devil then made bodies, but he was unable to make them move, so he asked God to do this for him. God consented only on condition that what he placed in the bodies, which

---

108    On the books used and carried by the Autiers, see J.-M. Vidal, 'Doctrine et morale des derniers ministres albigeois', *Revue des Questions historiques* 86 (1909), pp.23–5.

enabled them to move, belonged to him; consequently, 'since then souls are of God and bodies are of the Devil'. No one could be saved unless 'he had been touched by the hand of the good Christians, that is the heretics, and had been received by them'. Without this the souls or spirits would pass from body to body until they reached one which had been received by the good Christians 'and when they left that body, they would return to heaven'. This seems to have been considered enough for one session. The Autiers ended by telling anecdotes about the transmigration of souls, including one which they had often repeated about a man who had previously been a horse and was able to prove it by identifying the place in the mountains where he had once lost a shoe. This amused the company and seems to have been part of their repertoire aimed at lightening the mood at the end of an evening of serious preaching and instruction, a technique not dissimilar from that used by contemporary Dominicans and Franciscans.[109] They then performed the *melioramentum*, 'adoring' (as the inquisitors preferred to express it) the heretics three times and receiving the blessing in return.

The following evening the Autiers developed these themes further. It was not worthy to believe that 'the Son of God was born of a woman, or that the Son of God adumbrated himself in a thing so vile as a woman'. Peter Autier said that 'he who was called the Son of St Mary came to earth and preached, but nevertheless did not eat or drink, nor experience hunger or thirst or cold or heat'. Then the Jews crucified him, but he suffered no harm, since he was only 'apparently' crucified. He did not die or suffer, but he disappeared and was believed to be dead. He ascended to the celestial Father 'from whom he obtained that he could give his disciples power that what they should do on earth be done by the celestial Father in heaven'. Returning to the disciples after three days, he said to them that he had given them nothing and that they should ask, 'since he would give to them'. But when one of them asked that they should be without fear and evil in the world, Christ said that he could not grant this since 'as he had had evil in the world, it was necessary that they should also have it'. Then one of the disciples, representing all of them, asked that he should grant that what they do on earth be done in heaven and 'the same for others who came after them until the end of the world'. Peter Autier saw himself as one of these successors.[110]

These views had implications for the behaviour of contemporary Cathars. They should not revere the cross or images of the crucifixion or other

---

109 See Vidal, 'Doctrine et morale', *Revue des Questions historiques* 85 (1909), p.379, for other occasions when they told this story.

110 For a very full evaluation of Cathar belief at this period, see ibid., pp.357–91.

images of the saints, 'since such images were idols, and as a man ought to break with an axe gallows on which the father of that man had been hung, so ought they to endeavour to break crosses since, according to appearances, Christ was suspended on the cross'. He told them too that the Catholic baptism was not valid as it was done with water which was material and accompanied by many lies, for a child cannot consent when it did not have 'the use of reason'. Only their baptism of the Holy Spirit, given to adults, was good. In the sacrament of the altar, there was only bread and wine, and 'he added derisively that if the said sacrament was the body of Christ and was as great as the mountain of Bugarach [a well-known peak in the Aude], there were so many chaplains that they had already eaten it, nor would it be sufficient for them'.[111] Good matrimony was when 'our soul was joined to God through good will, and that was the sacrament of matrimony'. In contrast, 'carnal matrimony' was not matrimony at all, and carnal intercourse between husband and wife was 'always a sin', even more than if a man had intercourse with a woman who was a stranger, as carnal acts between those who were married were more frequent and therefore engendered greater shame. Hasty anger was not a sin, but it was better that men conducted their affairs and work through discussion together. He also said that since men ate meat, it made little difference whether they ate it one day or another as it was just as much a sin. Peter Autier drew all this together around the theme of salvation and the end of the world. Those who were saved through their hands, that is through the Cathar Church, would never return to the flesh or to this world, for there never had been resurrection of the flesh. 'After the end of the world the whole visible world would be full of fire, sulphur, and pitch, and it would burn, and this was called the inferno. But all the souls of men would then be in paradise, and one soul would have as great a good in heaven as another, and all would be one.'[112]

Such a detailed presentation from a believer, herself a peasant who was almost certainly illiterate, shows that, in this case at least, the Autiers had been highly successful. Despite claiming from time to time that she did not remember certain things that had been said, Sibylla of Arques nevertheless shows a remarkable recall of the basic teaching which had been conveyed to her in the course of two evenings. When comparison is made both with the intellectual expositions of Catharism and with earlier deposition evidence, it seems clear that the Autiers, if only for a brief period, managed to sustain

---

111  This, however, seems to have been a commonplace since at least the eleventh century, although it was popularised by the Cathars, see W. L. Wakefield, 'Some unorthodox popular ideas of the thirteenth century', *Medievalia et Humanistica* 4 (1973), pp.30–1.

112  *RF*, vol. 2, pp.406–11.

the content and level of past teaching, belief, and morality in the Cathar Church, even though their Italian training seems to have infused them with something of a mixture of mitigated and absolute dualism.[113] There is no doubt that some of those whom they hereticated failed to reach these standards[114] – and indeed the lack of suitable personnel remained a major weakness of the early fourteenth-century Cathar Church – but it is difficult, nevertheless, to argue that Cathar belief was 'decadent' while the Autiers lived. Although Sibylla of Arques's witness is admittedly late evidence of popular Cathar belief, it is arguably a valid reflection of what it had meant to most of the populace since the last quarter of the twelfth century.

On one issue, however, historians have claimed that there had been a change in attitude, which is on the question of the *endura*, or 'the suicide' of those who had received the *consolamentum*.[115] This was later to cause Sibylla of Arques much misery when Prades Tavernier, one of the *perfecti* of the Autier circle, hereticated her infant daughter, although as Peter Autier clearly regarded Prades as having acted wrongly in this case, it cannot be said that giving the *consolamentum* to infants was approved practice in the contemporary Cathar Church.[116] Jean Duvernoy is undoubtedly correct in saying that the *endura* was not a special rite and that, in most cases, it was simply 'the normal consequence of the *consolamentum*' in that some dying believers survived for long periods after receiving the *consolamentum*.[117] Usually, they did not expect to take anything other than water, but if they broke their fast, they would need to be reconsoled. As the numbers of the *perfecti* in Languedoc in the second half of the thirteenth century dwindled, it was increasingly difficult to find another opportunity to do this, so there was more pressure to maintain their abstinence after *c.* 1250, a situation which may convey the impression that the *endura* was a peculiarity of late Catharism when it was not actually the case. In one sense it depends upon how suicide is defined. Rainier Sacconi argued that this could be done passively. 'Since many of them when ill have sometimes asked those who nursed them not to put any food or drink into their mouths if the invalids could not at least say the Lord's Prayer, it is quite evident that many of them commit suicide.'[118] This does not preclude the possibility that some

113  On this, see Vidal, 'Doctrine et morale', *Revue des Questions historiques* 85 (1909), pp.366–7.
114  See Vidal, 'Doctrine et morale', *Revue des Questions historiques* 86 (1909), pp.39–40, and below, ch. 6, pp.189, 198.
115  See Borst, *Die Katharer*, p.197; Hamilton, 'Cathars and Christian perfection', p.14, and M. D. Lambert, *The Cathars* (Oxford, 1998), pp.240–4.
116  See below, ch. 6, pp.188–9.
117  *RF*, vol. 1, pp.235–6, n.93, for Duvernoy's comments. See also below, ch. 6, p.188.
118  Rainerius Sacconi, *Summa de Catharis et Pauperibus*, p.68; trans. WE, no. 51, p.334.

believers chose deliberately to let themselves die in an action akin to a hunger strike: the woman from Coustaussa (south of Limoux in the Aude) who, in c. 1300, fled from her husband and went to stay at the house of Sibylla den Balle, a well-known Cathar supporter who lived at Ax in the Sabarthès, where she took twelve weeks to die, may be such a case, since there is no mention of illness.[119] In this she was surely not dissimilar to some ascetics in the monastic world.

## The attraction of Catharism

As they could find no virtue or truth in them, Catholic writers waste little time trying to discern the attraction of these doctrines to those of their contemporaries who adhered to them. To them Cathar supporters were either fools or dupes, or probably both. The Piacenzan layman, Salvo Burci, writing in 1235, commenting on the Cathar practice of breaking bread, thought it inconceivable that anyone could believe that Christ would have done this at the Last Supper if the bread had been created by the Devil. 'How well even dullards may see that you are the worst of heretics!'[120] Even James Capelli believed that people had been fooled by 'cunning serpents'. 'Because no truth adheres to the pernicious traditions of the heretics, they flavour them in consequence with a certain seasoning of simulated virtue so that the underlying poison is less perceptible through the pleasing sweetness of the honey.'[121] To him 'the underlying poison' was obvious, but for many believers what he calls the 'simulated virtue' of the Cathars seemed completely genuine. When the moral probity of the *perfecti* was presented within a familiar context it is not difficult to understand the attraction to contemporaries. Borst has pointed out the parallels with the Catholic Church which provided that context: penitence (confession), confirmation (*consolamentum*), extreme unction (*consolamentum* for the dying), and priests (*perfecti*). Institutions such as dioceses, patterns of the year in determining periods of fasting, and the cults of relics and prayers for the dead reflected in the memorial of martyrs and the use of their own cemeteries, all provided the comfort of recognition.[122]

---

119  J. J. I. von Doellinger, *Beiträge zur Sektengeschichte des Mittelalters*, vol. 2 (Munich, 1890), p.25. See Vidal, 'Doctrine et morale', *Revue des Questions historiques* 86 (1909), pp.36–7, on the cases of Amiel of Perles and William Belibaste after their capture in 1309.
120  Ilarino da Milano, 'Il "Liber supra Stella"', *Aevum* 19 (1945), p.336; trans. WE, no. 45(B), p.273.
121  James Capelli, *Summa contra haereticos*, pp.clxxvi–clxxvii; trans. WE, no. 49, p.306.
122  Borst, *Die Katharer*, pp.218–22.

Although often denied by the polemicists on both sides, the extent to which the Catholic and Cathar worlds overlapped was often considerable. It might be thought that, for instance, Cathars would be uninterested in what happened to their earthly bodies after death, yet their use both of local Catholic cemeteries and of their own burial grounds contradicts this, while the inquisitors cannot have been wrong in every case when they ordered the disinterment and burning of the bodies of the dead, suspected of heresy.[123] Moreover, the Cathar stress on the Gospels in their preaching offered, as Raoul Manselli puts it, a yardstick by which the behaviour of the Catholic priests could be measured, and in that sense did not invariably appear very different from reformist preachers within the Roman Church itself. Reinforced with colourful myths explaining the creation of the world, it is not difficult to see the relevance of Cathar evangelism to the daily lives of many contemporaries. Even if Cathar theology did derive from a past dualistic tradition (and, as has been seen, many historians do not accept that it did), this need not have been of great concern to many members of the audience of the Cathar preachers.[124]

This is, to an extent, encapsulated in the story told by William Pelhisson, a Dominican inquisitor from Toulouse, who describes how, on the Feast Day of St Dominic, 5 August 1234, the friars had just finished celebrating mass in their house in the city, when a citizen came to tell Raymond of Le Fauga, the Dominican Bishop of Toulouse, that some heretics had been seen entering the house of a sick woman who lived in a street nearby. This turned out to be the mother-in-law of a man called Peitavin Boursier, apparently known for his services to heretics. The bishop hurried to the house and 'seating himself beside the invalid, began to talk to her at length about contempt for the world and for earthly things and, perhaps because she understood what had been said to mean that it was the bishop of heretics who visited her, for she had already been hereticated, she freely responded to the bishop in all things'. It is not surprising that the old lady was confused but, even when he revealed who he was, she remained obstinate. The appropriate authorities were called and she was taken out of the house, still in her bed, and was burned to death in a field outside the city.[125]

It would be superficial to argue that the majority of Cathar adherents were attracted simply by what they saw as a Church similar to that of Rome,

---

123   W. L. Wakefield, 'Burial of heretics in the Middle Ages', *Heresis* 5 (1985), pp.29–32.
124   See R. Manselli, 'Evangelisme et mythe dans la foi Cathare', *Heresis* 5 (1985), pp.5–17. See also R. Abels and E. Harrison, 'The Participation of Women in Languedocian Catharism', *Medieval Studies* 41 (1979), pp.244–5, on the levels of knowledge of Cathar beliefs.
125   Pelhisson, pp.60–5; trans. Wakefield, pp.215–16.

but staffed by a better-behaved and less demanding elite, important as this was in gaining support. Sibylla of Arques was a peasant woman from a small village in the Razès, far removed from the world of men like John of Lugio or Rainier Sacconi, yet she listened to and absorbed the teaching of Peter Autier and his son, itself based on intensive study by literate and intelligent men among the Lombard Cathars. Women like Sibylla were not as dull as men like Salvo Burci liked to think. The attraction of Catharism lay not only in the transparent morality of most of the *perfecti*, but also in the assertion that the *consolamentum* would enable their souls to be readmitted to the heavenly kingdom and thus escape the miseries of the world.[126] Moreover, in an era when the Catholic Church itself vigorously promoted the cult of the Virgin and the life of the human Christ, the identification of this figure with the avenging Jehovah of the Old Testament was always likely to create problems for many thinking persons, whether they were peasants or lords.

---

126  Hamilton, 'Cathars and Christian perfection', pp.12–13.

# CHAPTER FOUR

# The Catholic Reaction

## The justification for force

'Attack the followers of heresy', wrote Pope Innocent III in March 1208, 'more fearlessly even than the Saracens – since they are more evil – with a strong hand and a stretched out arm'. Thus, in militant Old Testament language, the pope called upon the nobility and people of the ecclesiastical provinces of Narbonne, Arles, Embrun, Aix, and Vienne, 'to avenge this righteous blood', by which he meant the murder of the papal legate, Peter of Castelnau, two months before, by a vassal of Raymond VI, Count of Toulouse. 'Forward then soldiers of Christ! Forward, brave recruits to the Christian army! Let the universal cry of grief of the Holy Church arouse you, let pious zeal inspire you to avenge this monstrous crime against your God!'[1] Consciously evoking the imagery of the jealous God of Deuteronomy, whose faithful shall have no other gods, he presents the crusade against the enemy within Latin Christendom as more vital than the war against the external enemy, Islam, which had dominated papal thinking for more than a hundred years. The pope's resort to violence in these circumstances rested on respectable foundations. In the late fourth and early fifth centuries, St Augustine, faced with the widespread acceptance in Christian circles of the necessity for warfare, had established specific criteria for the just war, which he had come to see as a regrettable necessity if the proper order of society was to be maintained. The covenant that God had made with Moses and the Israelites showed that the faithful were obliged to act against those

---

1 Quoted by PVC, vol. 1, paras 56–65, pp.52–65; trans. Sibly, pp.31–8. Also *Innocentii III Registrorum sive Epistolarum*, in *PL*, vol. 215, cols 1354–8.

who rebelled against God. For Augustine bad will could not be left 'to its own freedom'; if this were the case 'why were the disobedient and murmuring Israelites restrained from evil by such severe chastisements, and compelled to come into the land of promise?'[2] Just as Augustine had responded to the threat of Manichaeism to his own society, so in the early thirteenth century 'the plague of heresy' had reappeared, creating 'this unprecedented storm' which was battering 'the ship of the Church'. In this sense Innocent was returning to the original purpose of the just war, developed more than two centuries before the rise of Islam, but he was couching his appeal in the language of vengeance easily comprehensible to those feudal lords he wished to attract to his crusading army.[3] The call for 'soldiers of Christ' was reinforced by a vigorous propaganda campaign. For Innocent, a pope deeply imbued with the idea of personal sacrifice for the faith, Peter of Castelnau was a Christian martyr; indeed, he presents his death quite overtly as the means by which Christians could be awakened to the danger which they faced:

> we believe it is expedient that one man should die for it rather than that it should all perish; for it is indeed so contaminated by the contagion of heresy that it may well be recalled from error more readily by the voice of the blood of its victim than by anything he could have done had he gone on living.

Peter of Les Vaux-de-Cernay, who quotes this letter verbatim in his chronicle, eagerly followed the papal lead. According to him, when, after a long period, Peter of Castelnau's body was transferred from the monks' cloister at St Gilles to the church proper, 'it was found to be as whole and unimpaired as if it had been buried that very day. A marvellous perfume arose from his body and clothing'.[4] In contrast the heretics were utterly depraved. Peter claimed that one, called Hugo Faber, 'fell into such depths of madness that he emptied his bowels beside the altar in a church and by way of showing his contempt for God wiped himself with the altar cloth'.[5]

---

2  See R. A. Markus, 'Saint Augustine's views on the "Just War"', in W. J. Shiels, ed., *The Church and War. Studies in Church History* 20 (1983), pp.1–13, and F. H. Russell, *The Just War in the Middle Ages* (Cambridge, 1975), ch. 1.

3  See J. Gilchrist, 'The Lord's war as the proving ground of faith: Pope Innocent III and the propagation of violence (1198–1216)', in M. Shatzmiller, ed., *Crusaders and Muslims in Twelfth-Century Syria* (Leiden, 1993), pp.65–83, in which he argues that Innocent used the idea of the just war as a means of calling upon the faithful to prove their commitment to the defeat of Christ's enemies. On Innocent's own wish for martyrdom on crusade, see R. Foreville, 'Innocent III et la Croisade des Albigeois', in *CF* 4 (1969), p.185. See, too, C. Dutton, *Aspects of the Institutional History of the Albigensian Crusades, 1198–1229* (PhD diss., Royal Holloway and Bedford New College, University of London, 1993), pp.15–24.

4  PVC, vol. 1, para. 79, p.79; trans. Sibly, p.45.

5  PVC, vol. 1, para. 40, pp.37–8; trans. Sibly, p.24.

For Peter, the count of Toulouse was the evil counterpart to the good avenger, Simon of Montfort who, after the fall of Carcassonne in August 1209, became the leader of the crusade.

> Moreover, the Count was a vicious and lecherous man to the extent
> that – we can take it as an established fact – he abused his own sister as a
> way of showing contempt for the Christian religion. Again, from early
> youth he lost no opportunity to seek out his father's concubines and felt
> no compunction about bedding them – indeed none of them could please
> him unless he knew his father had previously slept with her. So it came
> about that his father frequently threatened to disinherit him, for this
> enormity as much as for his heresy.[6]

Just as the Church drew on its long tradition of just wars to legitimise the crusade against heretics, so too were there many precedents for salacious stories. Peter of Les Vaux-de-Cernay's claim that Cathars believed they 'could sin in safety and without restraint' was the lineal descendent of stories like that of the Chartrain monk, Paul of St Père de Chartres who, writing some half-century after the events, alleged that the heretics discovered in Orléans in 1022 held orgies at night in which indiscriminate sexual intercourse took place and that the ashes derived from the cremation of children born of such unions were used as a viaticum for the terminally ill.[7] Byzantine sources confirm that, for the orthodox, perverse behaviour was an inevitable concomitant of foul heresy. Peter of Sicily, writing his history of the Paulicians in 870, claimed that their leader, Carbeas, 'summoned to himself to the same place the greediest and most licentious and foolish people from the frontier areas near Tefrice, by promising freedom for their most shameful feelings', and that 'they sleep with both sexes without distinction and without fear. They say that some of them abstain from their parents, and from them alone'.[8]

Not all Catholics, though, were as convinced as Peter of Les Vaux-de-Cernay. King Philip II of France, aware that Raymond of Toulouse had not been formally condemned as a heretic and, at the same time, determined not to allow King John the opportunity to regain Normandy and Anjou which he had seized from him between 1204 and 1206, did not respond to papal pleas in 1204 and 1205, nor was he willing 'to eliminate such harmful filth',

---

6   PVC, vol. 1, para. 41, p.38; trans. Sibly, p.24.
7   PVC, vol. 1, para. 13, p.15; trans. Sibly, p.13; Paul of Saint-Père de Chartres, *Vetus Aganon*, ed. B.-E.-C. Guérard, in *Cartulaire de l'abbaye de Saint-Père de Chartres* (Collection des cartulaires de France, 1) (Paris, 1840), p.112; trans. WE, no. 3(B), p.79.
8   HH, no. 7, pp.91–2, no. 8, p.96. For a general survey, see J. Duvernoy, 'L'air de la calomnie', in *CEI*, pp.21–38.

as Innocent put it, when called upon directly in 1207.[9] Even so, the king was not voicing an objection in principle and, indeed, there is no evidence of widespread opposition to the idea that a crusade could be used in this way, even among the troubadours where it might be expected. Those who did actually participate took the matter very seriously, making careful arrangements for their dependents and appropriate grants either to local monasteries or to important foundations in the south like St Dominic's nunnery at Prouille.[10]

Thus two armies were assembled, the more formidable of which mustered at Lyon in July 1209, led by the papal legate, Arnald Amalric, Abbot of Cîteaux, and including two of the king's leading vassals, Odo III, Duke of Burgundy, and Hervé of Donzy, Count of Nevers, as well as Walter of Châtillon, Count of Saint Pol, and Rainald of Dammartin, Count of Boulogne. The three major narrative accounts of the Albigensian Crusade all accept, with varying degrees of enthusiasm, that the use of force had become inevitable. Naturally, Peter of Les Vaux-de-Cernay was the most unequivocal.

> With so many thousands of the faithful in France already taking up the cross to avenge the wrong done to our God, and others yet to join the Crusade, nothing remained but for the Lord God of Hosts to dispatch his armies to destroy the cruel murderers – God who with his customary goodness and inborn love had shown compassion to his enemies, the heretics and their supporters, and sent his preachers to them – not one, but many, not once, but often; but they persisted in their perversity and were obstinate in their wickedness; some of the preachers they heaped with abuse, others they even killed.[11]

William of Tudela claims that he foresaw it all.

> He [William himself] had long studied geomancy and was skilled in this art, so that he knew that fire and devastation would lay the whole region waste, that the rich citizens would lose all the wealth they had stored up, and the knights would flee, sad and defeated, into exile in other lands, all because of the insane belief held in that country.

---

9 *Innocentii III Registrorum sive Epistolarum*, in *PL*, vol. 215, cols 361–2 (1204), 526–8 (1205), 1246–7 (1207). There is a partial translation of Innocent's letter to Philip II in 1207, in L. Riley-Smith and J. Riley-Smith, trans., *The Crusades. Idea and Reality, 1095–1274* (Documents of Medieval History, 4) (London, 1981), no. 15(i), pp.78–80, and of Philip's reaction to a further request following the death of the papal legate, Peter of Castelnau, in which the king stresses that Raymond VI had not been condemned for heresy, W. A. and M. D. Sibly, trans., *The History of the Albigensian Crusade* (Woodbridge, 1998), Appendix F, pp.305–6 (Latin text, *HGL*, vol. 8, no. 138(ii), cols 558–9). For a discussion of Philip II's attitude, see Dutton, *Aspects*, pp.28–32.
10 See E. Siberry, *Criticism of Crusading, 1095–1274* (Oxford, 1985), pp.6–8, 158–68. For the participants, see Dutton, *Aspects*, pp.176–7.
11 PVC, vol. 1, para. 81, pp.80–1; trans. Sibly, pp.45–6.

Thus it was in Rome that they [the pope, Arnald Amalric, and Master Milo, papal notary and legate from March 1209] 'made the decision that led to so much sorrow, that left so many men dead with their guts spilled out and so many great ladies and pretty girls naked and cold, stripped of gown and cloak. From beyond Montpellier as far as Bordeaux, any that rebelled were to be utterly destroyed'.[12] William of Puylaurens, who was born just before the crusade in *c.* 1200 and who did not die until at least 1274, was able to take a longer view than both the others, seeing the campaign to extirpate heresy as covering a period of seventy years, apparently dating its beginning to 1203 when Peter of Castelnau was first appointed legate in the region. He says that he was setting this down in writing, 'so that from these events the great, the middling, and the low, might understand, by the judgement of God, how on account of the sins of the people, He decreed that miseries scourge these lands'.[13]

## The campaigns against heresy in the twelfth and early thirteenth centuries

The fatalism of these writers was rooted in the belief that it was axiomatic that heresy should be overcome, and in the knowledge that past efforts had failed to do so. From the time of his accession to the papal throne ten years before Innocent III had given the matter high priority, for unity under Rome was essential in order to continue the just war against external enemies, a war which was the path to salvation for all those who sincerely took up God's cause.[14] Indeed, one of his first acts had been to promise those

---

12   *Chanson*, vol. 1, laisses 1, 5, pp.3–5, 18–19; trans. Shirley, pp.11, 13.
13   WP, pp.23–4 and n.2.
14   Gilchrist, 'The Lord's war', p.83, and Foreville, 'Innocent III', pp.184–217. Michel
     Roquebert has linked the stories of the Grail cycle to this phase of crusading history, for
     he sees a chronological convergence between the development of Church militancy
     towards the Cathars, which he dates from the Third Lateran Council of 1179, and the
     appearance of the Grail stories which, until *c.* 1215 at least, he believes promoted the
     importance of the 'soldier of Christ', fighting to defend the Church and assured of eternal
     salvation if he is killed during that fight. Others have associated these stories with the
     crusades to the East; Roquebert believes they apply equally well to the Albigensian
     Crusades. Indeed, the stories were especially prominent in areas associated with
     recruitment for the Albigensian wars, in particular Champagne and Flanders. Moreover,
     the assertion of the dogma of transubstantiation at the Fourth Lateran Council of 1215
     was a direct answer to the anti-eucharistic views of the Cathars and contributed towards
     the internalisation of the concept of the soldier of Christ which Roquebert discerns around
     1225. This 'mystical stage' in the Grail cycle he attributes to the crusading failures – both
     in the East and in Languedoc – between 1218 and 1225. See M. Roquebert, *Les Cathares
     et le Graal* (Toulouse, 1994), esp. pp.66–8, 179–88.

who were willing to respond to his legates' request for help when combatting heretics in Languedoc the indulgence 'which we accord to those visiting the sanctuaries of Sts Peter and James', putting such activity on an equal footing with the great pilgrimages to Rome and Compostela, although it is most unlikely that he had yet formed the idea of instigating a crusade in the manner of 1209, as has sometimes been argued.[15] There had been no lack of previous demands for secular support in tackling heresy. In 1119 at Toulouse and in 1139 at the Lateran, there had been calls for the civil power to repress those who, 'simulating a kind of religiosity', rejected the Eucharist, infant baptism, the priesthood, and marriage, while in 1148 at Reims, Pope Eugenius III had forbidden anyone to defend or help heretics in Gascony, Provence, or elsewhere.[16] In 1145 Bernard of Clairvaux himself went on a mission to Toulouse, apparently because he believed that Alfonso-Jordan, the reigning count, had neglected to make much effort to prevent the spread of heresy. He succeeded in frightening away Henry of Lausanne, but could not really confront the underlying problems of the region, which suggests that dualist belief had already begun to find adherents there, even if it was not as evidently as at Cologne. At the Council of Tours in 1163, ten years after St Bernard's death, the exiled pope, Alexander III, again condemned heresy in the Toulousain and Gascony.[17]

In 1178 Count Raymond V finally responded, asking for help against the ravages of the heretics. Most historians see this as a piece of opportunism by an unsuccessful ruler anxious to gain some credit with the Church, but he did have reason to think that the threat was genuine. The mission, led by Peter of Pavia, papal legate in France, and Henry of Marcy, Abbot of Clairvaux, did succeed in indicting and condemning the important Toulousan citizen Peter Maurand, as well as excommunicating two heretics who had been persuaded to come to Toulouse from Castres to put their views.[18] This experience seems to have convinced Henry of Marcy that more consistent pressure was needed and, in his report, he called for military action: 'We know that the triumph will not be denied to those who struggle for us, if

---

15   *Innocentii III Registrorum sive Epistolarum*, in *PL*, vol. 214, cols 81–3. Innocent uses the word *accingantur*, but this does not necessarily mean that the pope was calling on them to fight in a literal sense, although it has sometimes been interpreted in that way. See the discussions in Sibly, *History*, p.316, n.3, and Dutton, *Aspects*, p.25, who points out that, at this time, the pope was chiefly concerned to recruit for his proposed crusade to the East.

16   See C. J. Hefele and H. Leclercq, *Histoire des Conciles*, vol. 5(i), 5(ii) (Paris, 1912, 1913), pp.570–3, 731–2, and N. J. Tanner, ed., *Decrees of the Ecumenical Councils*, vol. 1, *Nicaea I to Lateran V* (London, 1990), p.202, for canon 23 of the Lateran Council of 1139.

17   See above, ch. 1, pp.24, 31–2.

18   See above, ch. 2, pp.64–5.

they are willing to fight in the love of Christ.'[19] He appears to have had some effect, for in canon 27 of the Third Lateran Council, held in March 1179, there is a clear threat of force.

> As St Leo says, though the discipline of the church should be satisfied with the judgment of the priest and should not cause the shedding of blood, yet it is helped by the laws of catholic princes so that people often seek a salutary remedy when they fear that a corporal punishment will overtake them. For this reason, since in Gascony and the regions of Albi and Toulouse and in other places this loathsome heresy of those whom some call Cathars, others the Patarenes, others the Publicani, and others by different names, has grown so strong that they no longer practise their wickedness in secret, as others do, but proclaim their error publicly and draw the simple and weak to join them, we declare that they and their defenders and those who receive them are under anathema, and we forbid under pain of anathema that anyone should keep or support them in their houses or lands or should trade with them. If anyone dies in this sin, then neither under cover of our privileges granted to anyone, nor for any other reason, is mass to be offered for them or are they to receive burial among Christians.[20]

This canon lays down the framework for the use of force at the very beginning, but then within this framework offers specific privileges to those who actually take up arms. They will receive two years' remission of penance and ecclesiastical protection of their persons and lands, 'as we do those who visit the Lord's sepulchre'. Moreover, 'those who in true sorrow for their sins die in such a conflict should not doubt that they will receive forgiveness for their sins and the fruit of eternal reward'. The conventional view of historians therefore is that, a generation before the Albigensian Crusade began, Pope Alexander III and the fathers at the council had already incorporated the language of crusading ideology into the official policy of the Church. However, the interpretation of the canon is complicated by the fact that it condemns not only heretics, but also *routiers*. Elie Griffe argues that the use of force applies to the *routiers*, whereas the heretics are to be tackled by the traditional methods of discipline and expulsion, so the decree of 1179 cannot be regarded as the beginning of the violent repression of heretics.[21] This is a possible interpretation of the canon, but it is difficult to

---

19 *Epistolae Domni Henrici Claraevallensis quodam Abbatis postmodum Episcopi Albanensis*, in *PL*, vol. 204, cols 235–40 (quotation col. 235).
20 Tanner, ed., *Decrees of the Ecumenical Councils*, vol. 1, *Nicaea I to Lateran V*, p.224.
21 E. Griffe, *Les Débuts de l'aventure cathare en Languedoc (1140–90)* (Paris, 1969), pp.118–19. See also ch. 2, p.57.

sustain given the initial statement of intent which must apply to both heretics and *routiers* and the evident context provided by the report of the legatine mission of the previous year. Moreover, measures to impose the peace of God, such as those promulgated by Bernard Gaucelm, Bishop of Béziers, probably in the same year,[22] are not dissimilar to those developed in the course of the eleventh century and taken up by Urban II when preaching the First Crusade in 1095. In the past attempts to impose internal peace were closely connected to the development of crusading, and the same presumably applied in the case of heresy. The fathers at the council may well have been correct to connect the two; in an insecure society there was less chance of any systematic repression of heresy. Indeed, the decree illustrates the problem very well, for heresy had become so embedded in sections of Languedocian society it was often impossible to avoid contact with it, even for the orthodox. Thus, in the November following, at the Council of Narbonne, which was undoubtedly the province most affected by Catharism, Archbishop Pons of Arsace felt obliged to warn the Templars, Hospitallers, and other clerics, that burial of excommunicates would mean an interdict for the parish in which it took place and excommunication for those concerned until the body had been exhumed from sacred ground. The military orders in particular were obliged to take this seriously, for they were the institutions of the Church most closely identified with the crusade. Although in his will in 1218 Raymond VI expressed his desire to be buried as a Hospitaller, and indeed they placed their mantle on his shoulders as he lay dying four years later, he was never allowed burial in their house at Toulouse.[23] The intent of the canon was clarified in 1181, when an attempt was made to put its provisions into practice in an action which certainly has some crusading characteristics. Henry of Marcy now led an army into the Albigeois and attacked Lavaur. Two *bonhommes* were handed over and, apparently convinced of their error, thereafter became canons in Toulouse.[24]

These initiatives suggest that the ecclesiastical authorities were about to embark upon a vigorous campaign against heresy, but circumstances prevented this from happening. Five popes in the period between the death of Alexander III in 1181 and the accession of Innocent III in 1198 did little to encourage continuity of policy, especially as the chief causes for concern seemed elsewhere. The battle of Hattin in July 1187, and the subsequent

---

22   Griffe, *Les Débuts*, pp.122–3, dates this 1179.
23   J. Delaville Le Roux, ed., *Cartulaire général de l'Ordre des Hospitaliers de Saint-Jean de Jérusalem, 1100–1310*, vol. 1 (Paris, 1894), no. 572, p.388; vol. 2, no. 1617, p.246. See also the discussion in Sibly, *History*, Appendix D, pp.299–301. See above, ch. 2, p.50.
24   WP, pp.28–31. See above, ch. 2, pp.39–40.

conquests made by Saladin, devastated the Latin states in the East, and their possessions were only partially rebuilt by the Third Crusade between 1189 and 1192. The Holy Sepulchre itself remained out of Christian reach. Soon after, the problem of the overweening empire of the Staufen, Frederick Barbarossa, which seemed to have been solved by the peace settlement made in 1177, reappeared in the person of his son, Henry VI, who, in 1194, revived papal fears of encirclement by conquering the Kingdom of Sicily. The only papal lead given during these years predated these troubles, when Lucius III issued the decretal *Ad abolendam* in 1184. This anathematised a whole range of heretics and their defenders, defining heresy under a wide variety of names which included *Cathari* and *Patarini*, and referred to those who favour 'heretical depravity', whether they be called *consolati*, *credentes*, or *perfecti*.[25] However, it depended upon the episcopacy to enforce it by annual visits and, whatever his other qualities, a good example can hardly be said to have been set by Berengar, appointed to the archbishopric of Narbonne in 1191, but unable to find time even to visit his province for the first ten years of his episcopate. Within his province lay the two key dioceses of Toulouse and Carcassonne.[26] The one prelate to have led a military expedition into the region, Henry of Marcy, died in 1189. These years were crucial for the spread of Catharism in Languedoc, for in the mid-1170s Nicetas had established a diocesan structure within which the *bonhommes* could operate and there seems no reason to doubt William of Puylaurens's view that they had become an accepted part of the everyday scene (at least in the lands of Toulouse and Trencavel) within a generation of the Council of St Félix-de-Caraman.[27] Here may lie the reasons for the difference in attitude between Raymond V and Raymond VI, with the former anxious to call in outside ecclesiastical help, while the latter was apparently indifferent to the appeals of the Church. By the time of Raymond VI's succession in 1194 there really was little he could do about Catharism in his lands. As Peter of Les Vaux-de-Cernay saw it: by 1203, 'the root of bitterness springing up was now so strongly and deeply embedded in the hearts of men that it could no longer be easily dug out'.[28]

When Celestine III died in 1198 he was about ninety-two years old and, not surprisingly, those prelates of Languedoc who were alarmed at the spread of Catharism were quick to petition Innocent III who, at thirty-seven, seemed to offer hope of a more dynamic pontificate. The pope

---

25  J. Fearns, ed., *Ketzer und Ketzerbekämpfung im Hochmittelalter* (Historische Texte, Mittelalter, 8) (Göttingen, 1968), pp.61–3.

26  See above, ch. 2, p.60.

27  WP, pp.22–7, 46–51.

28  PVC, vol. 1, para. 6, p.6; trans. Sibly, p.8.

responded with a series of legatine missions in 1198, 1200–1, and 1203–4, the last of which saw the appointment of two Cistercians from Fontfroide, Peter of Castelnau and Master Ralph. William of Puylaurens's view that this was a turning-point seems to be justified, for Bernard Hamilton points out that at this time the Bosnian and Bulgarian Churches recognised papal primacy and this may well have alerted the pope to the extent of Bogomil belief in the Christian world and therefore given the matter much greater urgency. In 1199, soon after Innocent became pope, King Vukan of Zeta (a son of Stephen Nemanja, ruler of Serbia) was claiming that 'an uncontrolled heresy' was spreading in Bosnia and that the ruler, Kulin, Ban of Bosnia, 'has introduced more than 10,000 Christians to this heresy'. Innocent responded with vigour: in October 1200, he wrote to King Imre of Hungary warning him that the disease would spread to the surrounding area if he did not act for, although Archbishop Bernard of Split had already cleansed the city of 'Paterenes', nevertheless they were finding that Bosnia was 'an open shelter'. By 1203 Innocent had also sent a legate to Bosnia where, in April, at Bolino-Polje, John of Casamaris persuaded the local heretical leaders to renounce their beliefs and live in accordance with 'the ordinances and commands of the holy Roman Church'.[29] From Rome dualist heresy must have looked to be endemic in the lands east of the Adriatic for, as well as Dalmatia, Bosnia, and Bulgaria, the pope knew very well that a powerful Paulician community still existed in Philippopolis, for he was heavily involved in the affairs of the Latin settlers in the former Byzantine lands following the fall of Constantinople in April 1204.[30]

The legates in Languedoc had some initial success in persuading the consuls and people of Toulouse to swear an oath to defend orthodoxy and expel heretics, although in the view of Peter of Les Vaux-de-Cernay 'treacherous Toulouse' never had any intention of keeping its promises.[31] By 1204 Innocent III seems to have taken a similar view, for he had moved radically beyond his position of 1198, increasing the status of action against

---

29  B. Hamilton, *The Albigensian Crusade* (Historical Association, 1974), p.17; HH, pp.47–8 and no. 29, pp.254–9; R. Manselli, 'Les "chrétiens" de Bosnie: le catharisme en Europe orientale', *Revue d'histoire ecclésiastique* 72 (1977), pp.600–14. Innocent may, too, have been influenced by the presence of Cathars nearer at hand, especially in central Italian strongholds like Viterbo and Orvieto, where opposition to the extension of papal sovereignty must sometimes have appeared to the pope as linked to heresy, see C. Lansing, *Power and Purity. Cathar Heresy in Medieval Italy* (New York and Oxford, 1998), pp.33, 41. From the papal perspective dualism seemed to be gaining ground everywhere.

30  M. Barber, 'Western attitudes to Frankish Greece in the thirteenth century', in B. Hamilton, B. Arbel and D. Jacoby, eds, *Latins and Greeks in the Eastern Mediterranean after 1204* (London, 1989), pp.111–28.

31  PVC, vol. 1, paras 7, 8, pp.7–8; trans. Sibly, p.9.

heretics from a minor good work to a major penitential act. In a letter to his new legate, Arnald Amalric, full of the imagery of the sword and bloodshed, the pope told him that 'those who will have laboured faithfully against the heretics, we wish to enjoy the same indulgences which we concede to those crossing to the aid of the Holy Land'. To the legate himself 'we concede the power to destroy, ruin, and root out that which you know needs to be destroyed, ruined or rooted out'.[32] The next year in a letter to Philip II he said that the heretics were 'raging so freely among Christ's flock that they do not fear the amputation of their right ear by means of the sword which Peter himself wields'.[33] From this time the pope did what he could to induce such dread. In May 1207, he told Raymond VI that his body was like any other man's, vulnerable to fever, leprosy, paralysis, possession by demons, or incurable disease. That he was not immune to misfortune would soon be seen for

> we will enjoin all the neighbouring princes to rise up against you as an enemy of Christ and persecutor of the Church, retaining from you whatever lands of yours they are able to occupy, in case more of those places under your lordship be infected with the stain of heretical depravity. Nor in all these things should the fury of the Lord be averted from you; but already his hand will be extended to strike you, and show how difficult it will be for you to fly from the face of his anger, which you have gravely provoked.[34]

For William of Puylaurens, Francia was the natural place to turn for there they were 'accustomed to wage the wars of the Lord'.[35]

Simultaneously, however, there were continued attempts to engage the heretics directly in the form of public debates, an activity which had never been seen as incompatible with the strident language of the papal chancery and the ecclesiastical councils. William of Tudela thought they were futile. At Carcassonne in 1204 there was a formal confrontation between the orthodox, led by Berengar of Pomas, the bishop, and Peter II, King of Aragon, the overlord of the region, and 'the Bulgars', but the king soon abandoned the debate once he heard what the heretics had to say. They kept trying, however: 'Led by Brother Arnald, Abbot of Cîteaux, friend of God, the preachers travelled on foot and on horseback among the wicked

---

32  *Innocentii III Registrorum sive Epistolarum*, in *PL*, vol. 215, cols 358–60. The offer of 1198 had not, in any case, produced any results. See G. G. Coulton, *The Death Penalty for Heresy from 1184 to 1917* (London, 1924), p.4.
33  *Innocentii III Registrorum sive Epistolarum*, in *PL*, vol. 215, cols 526–8.
34  Ibid., cols 1166–8.
35  WP, pp.54–5.

and misbelieving heretics, arguing with them and vigorously challenging their errors, but these fools paid no attention and despised everything they said.'[36]

Yet, despite a long string of disappointments, debates had been taking place since at least 1165, nearly half a century before, when a meeting had been convened at Lombers before assessors chosen by both sides. This was certainly taken seriously by the Catholic Church, whose assessors were led by William III, Bishop of Albi (1157–85), in whose diocese Lombers was situated, supported by a bishop, three abbots, and a layman, as well as observers which included the archbishop of Narbonne, three other bishops, and four abbots, and a range of seculars, the most important of whom was Raymond Trencavel, Viscount of Béziers. It was claimed that almost the entire population of Lombers and Albi was present. In the end, though, it fell into mutual recrimination with the Catholic bishops condemning the *bonhommes* and demanding that they prove their innocence, and the *bonhommes* calling their opponents 'ravening wolves, hypocrites, and seducers, lovers of salutations in the marketplace, of the chief seats and the higher places at table, desirous of being called rabbis and masters'. The main sticking points seem to have been the refusal of the *bonhommes* (as the heretics are called on this occasion, apparently for the first time) to accept the Old Testament and their unwillingness to take oaths, although on a number of other crucial points they were apparently not prepared to offer definitive answers. Written into the record is their statement of belief in one God and in the humanity of Christ which has led some historians to doubt whether they were actually Cathars as such, although it is clear from the line of questioning adopted by the bishop of Lodève that the ecclesiastical authorities thought they were.[37] The memory of this confrontation may well explain the reluctance of his successor as bishop, William IV (1185–1227), to participate in another debate at Lombers, at an unknown date, but probably fairly near the beginning of his episcopate. According to William of Puylaurens, one day, when he was visiting the town, the nobles and bourgeois insisted that the bishop debate with Sicard the Cellarer, who had lived there openly as Cathar bishop of the Albigeois since the time of the Council of St Félix-de-Caraman. It is possible that this is the same person as Oliver, who had

36 *Chanson*, vol. 1, laisses 2, 4, pp.8–11, 12–13; trans. Shirley, p.12. See also above, ch. 1, p.6.
37 *Acta concilii Lumbariensis*, in *RHG*, vol. 14, pp.431–4, trans. WE, no. 28, pp.189–94. For the succession of the bishops of Albi, see J. Dufour, *Les Évêques d'Albi, de Cahors et de Rodez des origines à la fin du XIIe siècle* (Mémoires et documents d'histoire médiévale et de la philologie) (Paris, 1989), pp.38–41. On doubts about the extent to which these men can really be called Cathars, see M. Costen, *The Cathars and the Albigensian Crusade* (Manchester, 1997), p.60. See also above, ch. 1, pp.24–5.

led the heretics' side in 1165. The bishop thought that it was pointless, but agreed in order not to look as if he were afraid. It was not a meeting of minds. As the bishop saw it, Sicard was intent on presenting everything the wrong way round, so that he believed that, whereas Abel, Noah, Abraham, Moses, and David were not saved, nevertheless the late William Peyre of Brens, whom the bishop had known and described as 'a man accustomed as long as he lived to rapine and evil deeds', had been.[38]

More promising – if only because the Catholic participants were eager to be involved – were three debates described by William of Puylaurens at Verfeil and Pamiers, probably in late 1206, and at Montréal, in April 1207. These were led by Diego, Bishop of Osma, who pioneered this approach among the orthodox, supported by Dominic Guzman, then a canon of Osma, and the Cistercian legates, Peter of Castelnau and Ralph of Fontfroide. William admired Diego and Dominic as they went out 'not pompously and with a multitude of horsemen, but along the footpaths, from castle to castle, walking with bare feet, to the disputations arranged'.[39] Peter of Les Vaux-de-Cernay knew of four debates at Servian (just to the north of Béziers), Béziers, Carcassonne, and the one at Montréal, held between September 1206 and April 1207. At Servian, Peter claimed that the two heresiarchs, Baldwin and Theoderic (formerly William of Châteauneuf, a canon from Nevers) had been routed and the Catholic preachers had 'succeeded in turning the whole population of the town in hatred of the heretics', at Béziers the heretics were confounded, and at Montréal, the judges, who were supporters of the heretics, refused to give a verdict 'since they could see that the heretics had already lost the contest'.[40] These disputations were marathons, lasting eight days at Servian and Carcassonne, and fifteen days at Béziers and Montréal. Both Peter and William agree that the debates at Montréal had been recorded in writing, although they did not know what had happened to the documents afterwards. William had asked Bernard, the co-seigneur of Villeneuve la Comtal, who had been one of the judges, about this, and he told him that they were lost when everyone fled at the time of the crusade, which accords with Peter's view that they had been in the possession of the heretics. Despite this, according to Bernard, 150 heretics had been converted as a consequence of the debate.[41] Indeed, for Peter of Les Vaux-de-Cernay, it was not only the murder of Peter of Castelnau which had led to the crusade, but the collective impact of the

---

38  WP, pp.34–7. Duvernoy, n.2, for the possible identification of Oliver and Sicard.
39  WP, pp.46–51.
40  PVC, vol. 1, paras 22, 23, 26, pp.24–6, 28–9; trans. Sibly, pp.18, 18–19, 20.
41  WP, pp.51–3.

deaths of the legate Ralph of Fontfroide and Bishop Diego of Osma within the space of only eighteen months. According to Peter, the prelates of the Narbonne province had come to the conclusion that, after this, this particular preaching campaign had run its course, for 'the outcome they had looked for had almost entirely failed to materialise'.[42] Even so, although the violence of the crusade inevitably stifled open debate during the next twenty years, the Church never relented in the intellectual battle. It is noticeable that when Raymond VII was eventually forced to come to a settlement in 1229 one of the conditions was that he contribute 4,000 marks for the salaries of professors of theology, canon law, liberal arts, and grammar, who were to be established in Toulouse.[43] With the war over, debates of the kind seen before 1209 did not resume but during the middle decades of the thirteenth century the Catholics did produce more comprehensive analyses of the defects of Cathar belief than ever before.

# The Albigensian Crusades

The pope had promised the crusaders not only a full indulgence equivalent to that received by those fighting for the cross in the East, but also the right to occupy lands confiscated from the heretics, including those of the count of Toulouse. The pope's thinking here had already been formulated in the decretal *Vergentis*, issued to the clergy and people of Viterbo at the beginning of his pontificate. In this decretal he had equated heresy with the Roman crime of treason against the emperor, the punishment for which was confiscation of property and the disinheritance of descendants. In July 1200, he had extended this to cover Languedoc, although, significantly for the future, excluding the sanction against a heretic's descendants.[44] However, Raymond VI, after a fruitless attempt to persuade Raymond Roger Trencavel to make common cause with him, decided to cut his losses by undergoing a penitential scourging and then, in June, joining the crusaders.[45] This was

---

42  PVC, vol. 1, para. 67, pp.65–6; trans. Sibly, p.38, and n.48. Ralph died in early July 1207, and Diego on 30 December, the same year.

43  A. Teulet, ed., *Layettes du Trésor des Chartes*, vol. 2 (Paris, 1866), no. 1992, pp.147–52 (12 April), p.149, for the masters.

44  PVC, vol. 1, para. 62, pp.60–2; trans. Sibly, p.36. See also Sibly, n.36, and the discussion in Appendix G, pp.313–20. For *Vergentis*, see W. Ullmann, 'The significance of Innocent III's decretal "Vergentis"', in *Études d'histoire du droit canonique dédiées à Gabriel Le Bras* (Paris, 1965), pp.729–41, and C. Thouzellier, *Catharisme et Valdéisme en Languedoc à la fin du XIIe siècle et au début du XIIIe siècle*, 2nd edn (Louvain and Paris, 1969), pp.155–6.

45  *Chanson*, vol. 1, laisse 9, pp.26–7; trans. Shirley, p.15; PVC, vol. 1, paras 77–8, 80, pp.77–80; trans. Sibly, pp.44–5.

not welcomed by Peter of Les Vaux-de-Cernay, who calls him 'a false and faithless crusader', using the crusading vow as a cover for his wickedness, although Innocent III's correspondence suggests that the pope thought that this mattered little as long as the southern lords were divided.[46] Nevertheless, this did mean that the main force of the crusade was initially directed against the two chief Trencavel cities of Béziers and Carcassonne, despite William of Tudela's view that Raymond Roger was 'certainly Catholic', and despite the fact that, until this time, the pope had been almost exclusively concerned with placing the blame on the shoulders of Raymond of Toulouse.[47] By turning to the weapon of the crusade, the Catholic authorities had in practice abandoned the attempt to unpick the strands of Languedocian society and thus isolate the heretics. (See Map 4.)

The nature of the conflict is encapsulated in the first and last acts. The attack on Béziers on 22 July 1209 was led by those described by Peter of Les Vaux-de-Cernay as *ribauds* rather than the noble and knightly leaders of the army, a distinction which perhaps suggests that even this most grim and unforgiving of Catholic observers felt a need to distance himself from the massacre which followed. Indeed, Peter knew very well that the bishop, Renaud of Montpellier, had a list of known heretics, and although the chronicler may not have seen the details, he must have realised that the numbers could constitute only a very small minority. In fact, as has been seen, a fairly generous extrapolation from this source cannot take the figure much above 700, whereas the total number of inhabitants was between eight and nine thousand.[48] Yet, according to William of Tudela, 'they killed everyone who fled into the church [cathedral church of St Nazaire]; no cross or altar or crucifix could save them. And these raving beggarly lads, they killed the clergy too, and the women and the children. I doubt if one person came out alive.' His conclusion suggests that he doubted many were actually heretics. 'God, if it be his will, receive their souls in paradise.'[49] Twenty years later, Fulk, Bishop of Toulouse, is pictured by William of Puylaurens feeding the populace of the city, starving in a famine artificially created by the systematic devastation of the vineyards and cornfields upon which Toulouse depended. The previous year, forces led by the royal seneschal, Humbert of Beaujeu, and supported by the archbishops of Auch and Bordeaux, attended mass at dawn each day and then, led by crossbowmen and followed by the knights, they advanced to the outskirts of the town. Here they turned round and set off back to their camp, destroying the harvest all along the front

---

46  See J. Strayer, *The Albigensian Crusades* (New York, 1971), pp.58–9.
47  *Chanson*, vol. 1, laisse 15, pp.44–5; trans. Shirley, p.18.
48  See above, ch. 2, pp.65–6.
49  *Chanson*, vol. 1, laisse 21, pp.58–9; trans. Shirley, p.21.

covered by their forces, their rear protected by the crossbowmen. 'And they proceeded in this manner every day, until almost three months having passed, on all sides almost everything was destroyed.'[50] (See Table 1.)

After the bloodshed at Béziers, the capture of Carcassonne on 15 August was accomplished with relatively little violence. Raymond Roger had decided to make his stand in his chief city, but he was effectively isolated after attempts by his overlord, Peter II of Aragon, to mediate, broke down. After a siege of two weeks Raymond Roger voluntarily gave himself up as a hostage, a decision which William of Tudela described as 'lunatic', but was probably taken in the light of what had happened at Béziers. 'It's nothing but a few fools and their folly that have brought you into such danger and distress', Peter of Aragon is supposed to have said, although this probably reflects William of Tudela's opinion more closely than that of the king.[51] If this was so, the mass of the inhabitants of Carcassonne paid dearly for these 'few fools', for the capitulation meant that they lost everything. 'All the inhabitants came naked out of the city', says Peter of Les Vaux-de-Cernay, 'bearing nothing but their sins'. Raymond Roger was imprisoned and died on 10 November, apparently of dysentery.[52]

Crusades, however, need constant renewal if the gains made are to be sustained and the lands conquered are to be permanently occupied. The fall of Béziers and Carcassonne and the subsequent death of the viscount destroyed the Trencavel fortunes for the foreseeable future and, by implication, posed a great threat to Raymond of Toulouse, but the problem of heresy remained. If the crusade was to be effective against Catharism and its adherents, it needed not only one or two spectacular successes of this kind, but also a prolonged and tedious war of attrition aimed at destroying the social and political infrastructure which made the existence of an organised Cathar Church possible. However, none of the major secular lords – and consequently their vassals, most of whom were obligated to forty days of service only – were willing to stay in the south for the winter. These were the circumstances which led to the grant of the Trencavel titles (and thus effective responsibility for the continuation of the crusade) to Simon, lord of Montfort l'Amaury, a ruler of some local importance whose power was based mainly upon a group of castles in the diocese of Chartres, about forty kilometres west of Paris. Although Peter of Les Vaux-de-Cernay liked to

---

50  WP, pp.140–1, 130–1. Cf. the standard Roman methods as set out in the second half of the tenth century by the Byzantines, G. T. Dennis, ed. and trans., *Three Byzantine Military Treatises* (Washington, DC, 1985), pp.303–5.

51  *Chanson*, vol. 1, laisses 32, 28, pp.78–81, 70–3; trans. Shirley, pp.25–6, 24.

52  PVC, vol. 1, paras 98, 124, pp.99, 128; trans. Sibly, pp.54, 69; *Chanson*, vol. 1, laisse 37, pp.94–5; trans. Shirley, p.28.

refer to him as 'Count' and he did have a claim to the earldom of Leicester through his mother's family, he was not a ruler of regional status and he was certainly not known in Languedoc at this time. Nevertheless, in the north he had an established reputation as a crusader, having taken part in the Fourth Crusade during which he showed his independence of mind by his refusal to take part in the Venetian-inspired attack on Zara in 1202–3. He was, moreover, well known to Odo III, Duke of Burgundy, one of the most important of the crusaders in 1209; indeed, Peter of Les Vaux-de-Cernay says that it was the duke who had originally urged him to join the expedition.[53] From late August 1209 until his death while besieging Toulouse nearly nine years later, Montfort personified the crusade, driven on by his conviction that he was doing God's work and his consequent belief that he was entitled to the lands which he had seized from a nobility which had forfeited all rights as *fautors* or protectors of heretics. That Montfort quite consciously fused his religious and military roles can be seen in the striking ceremony he organised at Castelnaudary in high summer on the Feast of John the Baptist, 1213. There his son, Amaury, was, as Peter of Les Vaux-de-Cernay expresses it, installed as 'a knight of Christ'. The initiative very obviously came from Montfort himself, for the Bishop of Orléans, Maurice of Seignelay, was at first reluctant to perform a ceremony which was 'new and without precedent', but was persuaded to do so by Montfort. It took place in the open before a huge crowd.

> On the day of the feast the Bishop of Orleans donned his robes of office to celebrate a solemn Mass in one of the pavilions. Everyone, knights as well as clergy, gathered to hear the Mass. As the Bishop stood at the altar performing the Mass, the Count took Amaury, his eldest son, by his right hand, and the Countess by his left hand; they approached the altar and offered him to the Lord, requesting the Bishop to appoint him a knight in the service of Christ. The Bishops of Orleans and Auxerre, bowing before the altar, put the belt of knighthood round the youth, and with great devotion led the *Veni Creator Spiritus*.[54]

As the winter of 1209–10 came on, Montfort was, according to Peter of Les Vaux-de-Cernay, 'left alone and almost unsupported', for the core of his forces amounted to no more than thirty knights, largely drawn from among his vassals and neighbours in the Ile-de-France. 'Our people in Carcassonne

---

53   PVC, vol. 1, para. 103, p.102; trans. Sibly, p.56. On Montfort and his family see
     Y. Dossat, 'Simon de Montfort', in *CF* 4 (1969), pp.281–302, and Sibly, *History*,
     Appendix C, pp.294–8.
54   PVC, vol. 2, paras 429, 430, pp.122–3; trans. Sibly, pp.196–7. See the comments of
     M. Keen, *Chivalry* (New Haven, CT and London, 1984), pp.74–5.

were in such confusion and fear that they had almost abandoned hope and could think only of flight; indeed they were surrounded on all sides by innumerable powerful enemies.' Smaller fortresses and towns which had submitted to the crusader army now abandoned him and threw out or killed his representatives, so that 'almost all the local people became affected by the same ill-will and deserted our Count'. Peter of Les Vaux-de-Cernay could name only eight places, including Carcassonne and Albi, retained by the crusaders during this period.[55] However, when new crusaders appeared in the successive springs, 1210 and 1211, Montfort was able to return to the attack, steadily picking off the *castra* of the local nobility one by one. Between the spring of 1210 and the summer of 1211, all the main *castra* of the former Trencavel lords were either taken by siege or submitted voluntarily, including Minerve, Montréal, Termes, Cabaret, Lavaur, and Puylaurens. In the circumstances Peter of Aragon at last accepted Montfort's homage for these lords, confirming him as the Trencavel successor.[56]

The counts of Toulouse and Foix though remained, both wicked defenders of heretics in the eyes of Peter of Les Vaux-de-Cernay. Indeed, in a diversion from his main narrative, Peter gave himself space for his prolonged tirade about the crimes of Raymond Roger of Foix, a man, he said, 'who helped and encouraged them [heretics] as much as he could',[57] his anger perhaps exacerbated by the relative impotence of the crusaders in the count's lands. In the late summer of 1211 the crusader army spent eight days in the region around Foix 'doing all the damage it could', but there was little opportunity of establishing a permanent presence there.[58] In fact, Montfort saw the count of Toulouse as his more immediate problem and, as soon as he had taken Lavaur in May 1211, began to encroach upon his lands. Raymond VI had left the crusade after the fall of Carcassonne and had then been excommunicated for his failure to show real commitment in the battle with heresy. If, as has been argued, Raymond VI and Peter II of Aragon had quite deliberately stood aside while the Trencavels were

---

55 PVC, vol. 1, paras 115, 128, 136, pp.119, 132–3, 139–40; trans. Sibly, pp.63–4, 71, 74; *Innocentii III Registrorum sive Epistolarum*, in *PL*, vol. 216, cols 141–2. Dutton, *Aspects*, pp.12, 93–4, 213, argues that the idea of a limited 40-day service was the invention of the legates and had not been intended by the pope.

56 PVC, vol. 1, paras 151–7 (Minerve), 167 (Montréal), 168–89 (Termes), 214 (Cabaret), pp.154–61, 170–92, 212–14; trans. Sibly, pp.82–5, 90, 90–9, 110–11. See also M. Barber, 'Catharism and the Occitan nobility: the lordships of Cabaret, Minerve and Termes', in C. Harper-Bill and R. Harvey, eds, *The Ideals and Practice of Medieval Knighthood 3, Papers from the Fourth Strawberry Hill Conference, 1988* (Woodbridge, 1990), pp.1–19.

57 PVC, vol. 1, paras 197–209, pp.199–208; trans. Sibly, pp.103–7. See also ch. 2, pp.50–1.

58 PVC, vol. 1, para. 245, pp.244–5, trans. Sibly, p.125; *Chanson*, vol. 1, laisse 84, pp.202–3; trans. Shirley, p.48. Béarn presented a similar problem, *Chanson*, vol. 1, laisse 126, pp.280–1; trans. Shirley, p.63 (autumn 1212).

**Plate 5**

The four castles of Lastours from the south. Cabaret is the most northerly

**Plate 6**
Cabaret from the south-east

**Plate 7** Cabaret from the south-west

**Plate 8**
The keep at Cabaret

ruined,[59] then both were to pay heavily for their miscalculation. During the summer and autumn of 1211 Montfort took Les Cassès, Montferrand, and Castelnaudary, although in June he found his attack on Toulouse itself a step too far and abandoned the siege after two weeks. Nevertheless, the Trencavel lands remained under his control, and the city of Toulouse could be weakened by attacking the count's possessions to the east and the north. A foray north to Cahors in the late summer of 1211 at the request of the bishop, showed the possibilities, for the crusaders were able to destroy the count's castle of Caylus *en route*. Retaliation was inevitable. In September Raymond attacked Castelnaudary and Raymond Roger of Foix engaged some of Montfort's men at Saint-Martin-Lalande. Widespread defections followed on a scale similar to that of the winter of 1209–10. But neither succeeded and the arrival of crusader reinforcements from the north – unusually in December – 'nobly revived His business which', as Peter of Les Vaux-de-Cernay put it, 'at that time had reached a low ebb'.[60]

Further reinforcements arrived in the spring; according to William of Tudela from as far afield as Germany, Lombardy, and Slavonia as well as from the Auvergne.[61] During the campaigns of 1212 therefore the crusaders took Hautpoul and Sorèze to the east, and a whole swathe of towns to the north, including St Marcel, St Antonin, Montcuq, Penne, Biron, Castelsarrasin, and Moissac. By November Montfort had returned south to Pamiers, strong enough to enact a series of statutes which were intended to replace southern customary law with the practices with which Montfort was familiar in Francia. Toulouse itself may have eluded him, but the techniques which had brought the submission of the Trencavel lords seemed about to work just as effectively in the Toulousan territories as well. These were the circumstances which at last provoked Peter of Aragon, backed by the counts of Toulouse, Foix, and Comminges, to draw Montfort to the battlefield at Muret (south-west of Toulouse) on 12 September 1213. Despite the disparity in the size of the forces – the allied army was probably three times the size of the crusader contingent – Montfort nevertheless attacked and once again triumphed, leaving the king of Aragon dead on the field.[62]

59  See F. L. Cheyette, review of J. Strayer, *The Albigensian Crusades, Speculum* 48 (1973), pp.411–15.
60  PVC, vol. 1, paras 251–86, pp.250–83; trans. Sibly, pp.129–43; *Chanson*, vol. 1, laisses 87–111, pp.204–49; trans. Shirley, pp.49–56.
61  *Chanson*, vol. 1, laisse 111, pp.248–9; trans. Shirley, p.57.
62  For these events, see PVC, vols 1 and 2, paras 231–486, pp.230–93, 1–179; trans. Sibly, pp.119–219, and *Chanson*, vol. 1, laisses 79–131, pp.190–291, vol. 2, laisses 132–41, pp.2–37; trans. Shirley, pp.46–72 (paras 132 ff. are by the anonymous continuator). See A. P. Evans, 'The Albigensian Crusade', in K. M. Setton, R. Wolfe and H. Hazard, eds, *A History of the Crusades*, vol. 2 (Philadelphia, PA, 1962), p.302, for an estimate of the numbers involved. On the circumstances which led Peter II to take this action, see E. Griffe, *Le Languedoc Cathare au temps de la Croisade (1209–1229)* (Paris, 1973), pp.75–97.

Confident now of his military position, in the summer of 1214, helped again by northern reinforcements, Montfort moved north again, attacking any town which allegedly held heretics or mercenaries from Morhlon to Mondenard and Marmande, and then back to Casseneuil. For the first time the crusaders took the war into the Dordogne valley. 'In this way', says Peter of Les Vaux-de-Cernay, 'we achieved the subjugation of four *castra*, Domme, Montfort, Castelnaud, and Beynac. For a hundred years and more Satan's seat had been in these four places.' In Peter's view 'the valour and skill' of Montfort had now restored 'peace and tranquillity . . . not only to the inhabitants of Périgord, but also to the people of Quercy, the Agenais, and most of the Limousin'.[63] Montfort then swept east into the diocese of Rodez, capturing Capedenac (near Figeac) and Sévérac, before returning to the south to attend the Council of Montpellier, held in January 1215. Despite the increasing papal doubts, such impressive military success was difficult to dispute and, at the Lateran Council held in November, Simon of Montfort was confirmed as Count of Toulouse by the pope and, at Melun, his homage for this position was accepted by King Philip II.[64]

But to Montfort Languedoc must have seemed like a pot which was never less than simmering and which all too frequently came to the boil. The only way that the lid could be kept down was by constant pressure which, in Montfort's case meant an unremitting war of movement. At the Lateran Council Innocent III, deeply troubled by the legitimacy of disinheriting Raymond VI's son, who had been only a small boy when the wars began and could hardly be held responsible for their development, had left the lands east of the Rhône within the count's Provençal domains to be held in trust for the younger Raymond. The southerners took quick advantage of this concession: while Montfort was in the north securing his position with Philip II, the younger Raymond besieged his troops in Beaucaire, and his father went to Spain to gather new forces. For the last twenty months of his life Montfort was obliged to grapple with a double threat, on the west in Toulouse and on the east in Provence. Despite immense effort he failed to relieve the garrison at Beaucaire and an uprising of the citizens of Toulouse against the French forced him to turn west again. Although this was put down in March 1217, the French forces were insufficient to maintain a proper grip on the city and, in September, Raymond VI was able to enter and rally support. Montfort, who believed that he had gained time to return to the conflict in Provence, was obliged to invest Toulouse once again,

---

63   PVC, vol. 2, para. 534, p.229; trans. Sibly, p.239.
64   PVC, vol. 2, paras 537–49, 570–3, pp.230–42, 259–65; trans. Sibly, pp.239–45, 253–6; *Chanson*, vol. 2, laisses 143–50, pp.40–77; trans. Shirley, pp.72–80.

although neither side had the strength to win a quick victory. It was during this siege, on 25 June 1218, that Simon of Montfort was killed, struck on the head by a stone from a catapult.[65]

Not surprisingly, the opinions of contemporaries are sharply polarised. For Peter of Les Vaux-de-Cernay, whose monastery was so closely linked to the Montfort family, he was the ultimate crusading hero: 'he was eloquent of speech, eminently approachable, a most congenial comrade-in-arms, of impeccable chastity, outstanding in humility, wise, firm of purpose, prudent in counsel, fair in giving judgment, diligent in the pursuit of military duties, circumspect in his actions, eager to set about a task, tireless in completing it, and totally dedicated to the service of God.' Faced with the apparent inconstancy of a God who only appeared to support Montfort sometimes, the chronicler presents the prolongation of the wars as God's means of preventing him from succumbing to the sin of pride, while at the same time providing opportunities for the salvation of sinners.[66] This contrasts dramatically with the depiction of Montfort which the anonymous continuator of the *Chanson* puts in the mouth of the count of Foix when he speaks before Innocent III at the Lateran Council in November 1215. He was a man 'who binds and hangs there [Provence, Toulouse, and Montauban], who destroys and devastates, a man devoid of pity'. After his death, the crusading army disintegrated. 'The cross is broken in two', says the author of the *Chanson*, 'and parts in hatred'.[67] Both these men were close to the time and the action. William of Puylaurens lived through the crusade, but his viewpoint is shaped by the perspective of fifty years.

> See, he who was dreaded from the Mediterranean to the sea of Britain fell under a blow from a stone, as a result of which those who previously had stood firm were overthrown, and through him, who was good, was brought down the pride of his subordinates. I say now what I heard in the course of time that the count of Toulouse who died last [Raymond VII], although he was his enemy, marvellously commended him for his faith, foresight, and strength, and in everything which is fitting in a leader.

Nevertheless, William of Puylaurens presents Simon of Montfort at the last as disillusioned and weary. 'However, the count was burdened by toil

---

65   PVC, vol. 2, paras 574–612, pp.266–316; trans. Sibly, pp.257–77; *Chanson*, vol. 2, laisses
      152–86, pp.82–309, vol. 3, laisses 187–205, pp.8–212; trans. Shirley, pp.82–173.
66   PVC, vol. 1, paras 104, 109, pp.104–5, 113–14; trans. Sibly, pp.56–7, 60.
67   *Chanson*, vol. 2, laisse 144, pp.46–7; trans. Shirley, pp.73–4. See vol. 3, laisse 208,
      pp.228–9; trans. Shirley, p.176, for this author's famous epitaph on Montfort as a man
      of blood, who slaughtered men, women, and children, and seized the lands of others.
      See also below, ch. 7, p.217.

and grief and worn down and exhausted by the expense, nor did he easily bear the constant goading of the legate, who said he was careless and slack, which annoyed him very much. Thus, as was said, he prayed to God that he should give him peace by the remedy of death.'[68] Table 2 puts this in perspective, showing his constant movement over a wide area for the entire nine years which he was on crusade. His military activity consists almost entirely of sieges and the skirmishing which was their inevitable accompaniment, for he was involved in only two battles, in one of which (at Saint-Martin-Lalande) he played a minor role at best. Between September 1209 and June 1218 he led thirty-nine sieges, all but six of which were successful; some lasted no more than a few hours while others went on for months, culminating in the eight months spent in the fruitless attack on Toulouse in which he met his death. In addition, Peter of Les Vaux-de-Cernay lists another forty-eight places which either submitted voluntarily or capitulated as soon as he and his forces approached.[69] This involved an area which extended from the Razès and the Sault in the south to the middle Dordogne in the north, and from Lourdes in the west to the Rhône in the east. Statistics cannot convey, however, that it was a war fought with particular brutality. Two examples are sufficient to gain some idea of this. As might be expected, Peter of Les Vaux-de-Cernay claims that the other side started it, but whatever the truth of this, it is clear from his narrative that both sides were involved. In the winter of 1209, Guiraud of Pépieux, a knight from Béziers who had apparently at first sided with the crusaders, suddenly seized the fortress of Puisserguier from the crusader garrison. When Montfort brought up forces to threaten him, Guiraud fled, having left the sergeants for dead covered with debris in the fosse. The two knights who had commanded them were taken to Minerve where they were stripped naked, their eyes put out, and their noses, ears, and upper lips cut off. Thrown out in this condition, one died of exposure, while the other was saved by a poor man who took him to Carcassonne. The defenders of Bram paid for this the following March. When, after a three-day siege, the fortress fell, the captured men were blinded, their noses cut off, and sent to Cabaret under the guidance of a man who had been left with one eye for the purpose.[70] The verdict of William of Puylaurens rings true. Montfort had endured nine years which would have taxed the resolution of even so iron-willed and single-minded a man.

---

68   WP, pp.102–5.
69   See Table 2. The list is not definitive. PVC refers to other, unnamed places which were taken or submitted.
70   PVC, vol. 1, paras 125–7, 142, pp.128–32, 147–9; trans. Sibly, pp.69–70, 78–9.

However, while his determination is not in doubt, whatever may have been the views of Cardinal Bertrand of St Priscus, the legate, there remains the question of what impact Montfort and his crusaders actually had on Catharism itself. Innocent III predeceased Simon of Montfort by just under two years. He had, in his letter of March 1208, presented the death of Peter of Castelnau as a necessary sacrifice if 'the evil and corrupt generation' of heretics was to be overcome.[71] Nevertheless, the relationship between Montfort's unceasing military activity and the actual extirpation of the Cathars is much more complex than the pope's rhetoric suggests. As Table 2 shows, the main crusade chroniclers mention only three places from the thirty-seven (Toulouse was besieged three times) which he is known to have besieged, in which the existence of *perfecti* is explicitly recorded. There were executions of 140 *perfecti* at Minerve in July 1210, of between 300 and 400 at Lavaur in May 1211, and, soon after, between fifty and one hundred at Les Cassès.[72] Nowhere else are heretics specifically mentioned, although it is probable that the crusaders took it for granted that the defenders of places which resisted them must by definition at least be sympathetic to the heretics and their teaching. In this sense, Peter of Les Vaux-de-Cernay seems to be using Les Cassès as a symbol for them all. 'This was a clear demonstration of the love of the Count of Toulouse for heretics – in this insignificant *castrum* of his there were found more than fifty perfected heretics.'[73] If this is an accurate reflection of the mentality of the crusaders, then another possible way of measuring this is to compare the list of the places which Montfort besieged or which voluntarily submitted to him with Michel Roquebert's survey of the heretic presence 'on the eve of the crusade'.[74] Roquebert found eighty-six places (excluding Carcassonne and Béziers), of which Montfort held twenty-three at one time or another, having tried but failed to take one other, that of Saint-Marcel.

These figures are difficult to interpret. They suggest that, for all his dynamic activity, Montfort does not seem to have tried to gain control of sixty-two places now known to have contained heretics at or before 1209. As some of the evidence comes from inquisitorial records, however, it is possible that Montfort was unaware of this at the time. They may, of course, have been beyond his resources for, despite the revolution effected in crusade taxation during the pontificate of Innocent III, the Albigensian

---

71  PVC, vol. 1, para. 60, pp.56–8; trans. Sibly, p.33. See above, p.108.
72  See above, ch. 2, pp.41, 43. William of Tudela, *Chanson*, vol. 1, laisse 84, pp.200–1; trans. Shirley, p.48, says that there were at least ninety-four heretics at Les Cassès.
73  PVC, vol. 1, para. 233, pp.232–3; trans. Sibly, pp.119–20.
74  M. Roquebert, *L'Épopée cathare*, vol. 1, *1198–1212: L'Invasion* (Toulouse, 1970), appendice, pp.525–37.

Crusades were not properly financed, and Montfort found himself more reliant on private bankers like Raymond of Cahors and upon booty than any regular incomes from clerical taxation.[75] Even so, he did manage either to seize or to gain the submission of another sixty-three places for which there is no evidence of heresy during his nine years of crusading and, at one point, in January 1213, following protests from envoys of Peter of Aragon, Innocent III himself accused Montfort, together with Arnald Amalric, of extending 'greedy hands into lands which had no ill reputation for heresy'.[76] This may be significant for assessing Montfort's motivation, but it also suggests that there were distinct limits to the military solution of 'the contagion of heresy' since, in fact, it is highly unlikely that the Church could have found a secular champion of greater commitment and military skill than Montfort. The failure of his son, Amaury, after his father's death in June 1218, serves to underline this. Southern lords sympathetic to Catharism could not easily escape Montfort if he chose to turn his attention to them, but the figures show that there were in fact odds of between three and four to one against being attacked. Individual *bonhommes* therefore had plenty of places to take refuge from the butchery if they chose, which perhaps explains why there are no mass burnings of heretics by the crusaders after May 1211.

However, there is another way to assess the impact of Montfort's campaign upon Catharism. Although he only held just over a quarter of the places listed as 'heretical' by Roquebert, the map shows that they are concentrated in the Trencavel lands and around Raymond VI's chief city of Toulouse. Montfort, for reasons of his own, spent a proportion of his time campaigning in Provence, the Agenais, and the Dordogne, where there were relatively few Cathars as far as can be seen, but by subjugating many of the *castra* and fortified villages of the Lauragais, the Toulousain, the Carcassès, and the Albigeois, where the Cathars were solidly established, he did try to break up at least part of the infrastructure upon which the *perfecti* depended.[77] If the gaps in the Cathar hierarchy during these years are any indication,

---

75  On crusade financing, see Dutton, *Aspects*, ch. 6 and p.299.

76  *Innocentii III Registrorum sive Epistolarum*, in *PL*, vol. 216, cols 741–3; trans. Sibly, *History*, Appendix F, pp.309–10.

77  The evidence for the 'heretical' places identified by Roquebert (see above, n.74) is largely drawn from a report of the papal legates and the inquisitorial registers, which are concentrated in these areas, so that the argument can become circular. However, as will be seen, there does not seem to have been a necessity for extensive inquisitorial activity outside these areas. If Catharism really was strong to the north and east, then the historian is left with the unlikely hypothesis that it died out spontaneously there in the years after Montfort's death in 1218 and that the same would have happened in the regions in and around Toulouse and Carcassonne without any need for inquisitors or political changes.

Montfort was at least partially successful. There are no known Cathar bishops of Albi, Carcassonne, and Agen during the period he led the crusade, and only one deacon (in the diocese of Carcassonne). Toulouse fared better in that here the continuity was maintained by Bishops Gaucelm (1204–c. 1220) and Guilhabert of Castres (c. 1220–c. 1241), but they only survived because they were able to take refuge at Montségur during the crusade, together with some of the deacons from the diocese and other leading *perfecti*.[78] Indeed, Montfort's policy was doubly important after the fall of major cities like Béziers and Carcassonne, for many of those associated with heresy had fled to the *castra* before the crusade could catch them, only to find themselves facing further military pressure. Once gone, it was not easy for them to return, for any property was confiscated and granted to orthodox institutions: the house and property of the heretical sympathiser, Bernard of Lerida, in Carcassonne itself and nearby Beriac, for example, were ceded to the Cistercians.[79]

In 1208, after the murder of his legate, the pope had appealed to Philip II to establish 'Catholic inhabitants who, in accordance with your orthodoxy will preserve the discipline of the faith in holiness and justice under your felicitous governance in the presence of God'.[80] He failed to persuade the king, but Montfort did replace at least some of the rural lords and castellans with the limited number of crusaders willing to stay in the south for more than one campaigning season, men like Alan of Roucy who gained Termes, Montréal, and Bram, and Bouchard of Marly, who held Saissac and Cabaret. That he took this seriously can be seen by the enactment of the statutes of Pamiers in 1212 intended, as Claire Dutton says, to establish a 'new order' in the south. Among the provisions was the requirement for 'robed heretics, even if reconciled' to remove themselves from the town in which they had lived; they could resettle elsewhere, but only with Montfort's permission. The stipulation that heiresses and widows of 'high rank' who held fortresses needed licence to marry indigenous lords but not Frenchmen was obviously intended to reinforce this new orthodox environment. At the same time Montfort did begin to establish some kind of administrative structure, although it appears fairly rudimentary in comparison with the practices of more sophisticated contemporary

---

78  See M. Roquebert, *L'Épopée cathare*, vol. 4, *1230–1249: Mourir à Montségur* (Toulouse, 1994), pp.107–8; J. Duvernoy, *Le Catharisme*, vol. 2, *L'Histoire des Cathares* (Toulouse, 1979), appendice II, pp.347–51; S. Nelli, 'L'Évêque Cathare, Guilhabert de Castres', *Heresis* 4 (1985), pp.11–24. The vicissitudes of the career of Guilhabert are a good index of the structural state of the Cathar Church in Languedoc during the first four decades of the thirteenth century.

79  See Griffe, *Les Débuts*, p.160 and Costen, *The Cathars*, pp.68–9.

80  *Innocentii III Registrorum sive Epistolarum*, in *PL*, vol. 215, col. 1359.

regimes.[81] Nevertheless, the problems of resources and manpower remained. Few settlers survived to found long-term dynasties in the south and, indeed, in the early 1220s, the reappearance of Cathar preachers in some of the *castra* shows how limited such settlement had been.[82] It was the royal conquest of 1226 to 1229 which curtailed this revival, rather than any permanent legacy of Montfort's activities.

The course of the crusade, however, had never been solely in the hands of the military. Montfort's position had throughout been affected by the lobbying of the various parties involved at the papal curia and by the vacillations of a pope who, for all his reputation as a man of clear vision and decisive action, sometimes seems to have formulated policy on the basis of the views of the most recent lobbyist to have gained access to him. Innocent III's own troubled conscience was assaulted from two sides: on the one hand, the Aragonese–Toulousan axis, which sought to convince him that the crusade had achieved its objective and that therefore no further action need be taken, on the other, by vociferous papal legates on the ground who tried to persuade the pope that he was being misled by the cunning manoeuvres of those who protected heretics. On three key occasions – in 1211, 1213, and 1215 – the pope's decision finally favoured the crusaders, and each time that decision served to prolong the crusade. Arnald Amalric, who had always held Raymond VI personally responsible for the death of Peter of Castelnau, believed that the conquest of the Trencavel lands was insufficient while those of the perfidious count of Toulouse remained untouched. Although the legate can justly be charged with duplicity on more than one occasion in his dealings with Raymond VI,[83] the pattern of 'heretical' sites which emerges from Roquebert's list seems to vindicate Arnald Amalric's belief that, in the spring of 1211, Catharism in Languedoc was far from conquered. Assiduous campaigning at the papal curia by Raymond VI combined with Montfort's preoccupation with a stubborn Trencavel nobility delayed a direct attack upon him, but when at the Councils of Narbonne and Montpellier in January and February 1211 the count once more refused to give a direct promise of aid against the Cathars of the Toulousain, the legates took the opportunity to excommunicate him and

---

81   As Dutton, *Aspects*, pp.173–4, points out, settlement in the south was 'not a major motivation for the crusaders', see esp. her ch. 7 on this subject. Text of the Statutes of Pamiers, *HGL*, vol. 8, no. 165, cols 625–35, trans. Sibly, *History*, Appendix H, pp.321–9. Clause XV concerned robed heretics. This prefigures the conditions laid down by the Cardinal, Romanus of Sant' Angelo, at the Council of Toulouse, sixteen years later, see below, ch. 5, p.145.

82   See Evans, 'Albigensian Crusade', p.294, esp. n.23.

83   The legates seem to have felt that the circumstances justified such conduct. See PVC, vol. 1, paras 163, 164, pp.166–9; trans. Sibly, pp.88–9, on the legate Thedisius in 1210.

directed the crusade into his lands for the first time.[84] At the same time, with the Trencavel resistance apparently over, Peter of Aragon finally accepted Montfort's homage for these lands.

However, as Montfort increasingly squeezed Toulouse itself through his strategy against the count's lands to the north and east of the city, Peter of Aragon's doubts resurfaced. Taking advantage of the prestige gained by his key role in the victory over the Moors at Las Navas de Tolosa in July 1212, the king sent his envoys to Rome and, on 17 January 1213, obtained a papal letter suspending the crusade and censuring Montfort for his indiscriminate use of force. For the king the moment was propitious, in that the pope had the ultimate goal of a new crusade to the Holy Land at the forefront of his mind. In April, he issued the encyclical *Quia maior* for this purpose, in the course of which he revoked the privileges for the crusaders in Spain and Languedoc on the grounds that the reasons for them no longer existed.[85] Although indicative of Innocent's increasing uncertainty about the direction and nature of the Albigensian Crusade, his change of attitude was brief. Peter of Les Vaux-de-Cernay describes the pope as 'too ready to believe the false accounts of the King's envoys', and records with satisfaction how the legates and prelates persuaded Innocent to change his mind. In May 1213, the pope wrote to Peter of Aragon:

> We are amazed and disturbed that, by using your envoys to suppress the truth and give a false account of matters you have extorted from us a papal letter ordering the restitution of their territories to the Counts of Comminges and Foix and Gaston de Béarn, bearing in mind that – to pass over their many other monstrous misdeeds – they have been bound with the chain of excommunication for their support of the heretics, whom they openly defend.[86]

This failure of his diplomatic efforts must have been a substantial element in the king's decision to act against Montfort himself. As described by William of Tudela, the king 'announced to them all [his men] that he intended to go to Toulouse to fight against the crusade because it was wasting and destroying the whole country. Furthermore, he said, the count of Toulouse had appealed to their compassion to prevent his land being burned and laid waste, for he had done no harm or wrong to any living soul.'[87]

---

84  See Evans, 'Albigensian Crusade', pp.291–2, and Strayer, *Albigensian Crusades*, p.74–9.
85  G. Tangl, *Studien zum Register Innocenz' III* (Weimar, 1929), pp.88–97; Riley-Smith and Riley-Smith, trans., *The Crusades*, pp.118–24. See the analysis of Dutton, *Aspects*, pp.38–44.
86  PVC, vol. 2, paras 400, 406, pp.97–8, 103; trans. Sibly, pp.185, 188–9.
87  *Chanson*, vol. 1, laisse 131, pp.290–1; trans. Shirley, p.65.

The papal fear of the political nature of the crusade which had temporarily influenced Innocent's judgement in 1211, reappeared at the Lateran Council of November 1215. The pro-southern continuator of the *Chanson* includes a dramatic set-piece which purports to be an account of the arguments put forward before the pope at the council. All the participants are endowed with an eloquence seldom found in real life, but it is likely that beneath the vivid words the poet puts into their mouths, he is conveying a fundamental truth about their respective positions.[88] A flavour of this presentation can be gained from the confrontation between Fulk, Bishop of Toulouse, and Raymond Roger, Count of Foix. 'My lords', said the bishop

> you have all heard the Count of Foix declare that he is free of this heresy
> and untainted by it. But I tell you that his fief is its major root, that he
> has cherished, supported and been gracious to them, that his whole county
> is crammed and seething with heresy, that the peak of Montségur was
> deliberately fortified so that he could protect them, and he has made them
> welcome there. And his sister [Esclarmonda] became a heretic when her
> husband died and she then lived more than three years at Pamiers where
> she converted many to her evil doctrine.

Raymond Roger replied in language equally extreme. 'And once he [Fulk] was elected bishop of Toulouse, a fire raged throughout the land that no water anywhere can quench, for he has destroyed the souls and bodies of more than five hundred people, great and small. In his deeds, his words and his whole conduct, I promise you he is more like Antichrist than a messenger from Rome.'[89] After considerable personal agonising the pope's award of the fiefs of the count of Toulouse to Montfort combined with his guardianship of 'the remaining lands, which were not obtained by the crusaders' on behalf of the count's son until he came of age, served once more to reignite the war.[90]

Simon of Montfort excited extremes of admiration and loathing from contemporaries, but whatever their opinion of him they all recognised his key role in sustaining the crusade. This meant that, while he lived, the Cathars could no longer proselytise in the way that they had before 1209. The crusade did not eliminate heresy – indeed, as has been seen, there were many known heretical centres which remained untouched – but it did

---

88  *Chanson*, vol. 2, laisses 144–52, pp.44–89; trans. Shirley, pp.73–83. See above, ch. 2, pp.52–3.

89  *Chanson*, vol. 2, laisse 145, pp.54–5; trans. Shirley, p.75.

90  Teulet, ed., *Layettes du Trésor des Chartes*, vol. 1, nos 1113–15, pp.413–16 (award of fiefs to Montfort) (April 1215), no. 1132, p.420 (saving rights of the young Raymond) (December 1215). Trans. no. 1132 in Sibly, *History*, Appendix F, pp.311–12.

change the whole environment. After 1209 Languedoc would never be the same for the Cathar Church; from then, once expansionist and confident, it became defensive and beleaguered. Montfort's death might have changed this, even if the world of *paratge* yearned for by the nostalgic poet of the *Chanson* could never be revived.[91] This did not happen because there finally occurred what Innocent III had wanted in the first place, which was the intervention of the French Crown. The main interest came from Philip II's son, Louis. He had already taken a force south in 1215 and did so again in the summer of 1219, when he took Marmande from Raymond VI's garrison and was involved in an unsuccessful siege of Toulouse. The latter expedition did little to check the revival of the Toulousan fortunes: by 1224 Raymond VII had recaptured most of his dynasty's hereditary lands. It was not an impressive record and even Peter of Les Vaux-de-Cernay admits Philip II's lack of enthusiasm, although he does not dare to criticise the king for what he obviously saw as a serious failing. When Louis took the cross in 1215, Peter describes Philip as 'very sad to hear that his son had joined the Crusade, but it is not for me to explain the reasons for his grief'.[92]

With his father's death in 1223, Louis was much freer to pursue his own policies; the will for the continuation of the fighting came less from Raymond VII and Amaury of Montfort who, if William of Puylaurens is correct, were close to compromise and a marriage alliance in 1223,[93] than from Louis VIII and Pope Honorius III. Indeed, not only did Amaury lack his father's dominant personality, he was also faced with declining enthusiasm for a cause which had been dragging on since 1209. He relied more on mercenaries than his father had done and this may have led, in 1221, to an attempt to found a military religious order on the model of the Templars but devoted to the fight against heresy.[94] Honorius III at first showed some enthusiasm for the project, but the interest of Louis VIII in the crusade may have overshadowed it. If, as seems likely, the initial impetus had come from Amaury of Montfort, its total disappearance from the sources may be explained by his decision in 1225 to retire from the scene and to grant his rights in Languedoc to the king. At the Council of Bourges in November 1225, the new papal legate, Romanus, cardinal-deacon of Sant' Angelo – a man firmly in the tradition of Peter of Castelnau and Arnald Amalric – refused to accept Raymond's case and, early in 1226, excommunicated him. Louis could now begin his planned crusade. The

---

91  *Chanson*, vol. 2, laisse 137, pp.16–17; trans. Shirley, p.68.
92  PVC, vol. 2, para. 417, p.110; trans. Sibly, p.191.
93  WP, pp.114–15.
94  See Dutton, *Aspects*, pp.226–32.

king was initially baulked at Avignon but forced its submission, along with Beaucaire, in September 1226, and then moved on to Albi. Many southern lords then decided that they had no alternative but to accept royal authority. Although Louis did not follow up his gains by attacking Toulouse – perhaps because he was already undermined by the illness from which he died in October, or perhaps because of his memory of the frustrations of the siege of 1219 – he was able to leave a permanent presence under his cousin, Humbert of Beaujeu, whose systematic ravaging of the land was in turn made possible because he could draw on royal resources. It was this destruction of the Toulousan hinterland which finally brought Raymond VII to negotiation.

# CHAPTER FIVE

# The Decline of Catharism

## The Treaty of Paris, 1229

'For, just at the moment when the church thought to have peace in that land, heretics and their believers girded themselves more and more for numerous ventures and stratagems against her and against Catholics, with the result that the heretics did more harm by far in Toulouse and that region than they had even during the war.'[1] William Pelhisson was a Dominican from Toulouse who, writing probably in the mid-thirteenth century, recalled the work of the inquisitors appointed to investigate heresy in Languedoc – of whom he was one – in the early 1230s. Naturally, he wished to show the achievements of his order, so he was certainly not interested in underplaying the opposition to the forces of orthodoxy; nevertheless, he was often an eye-witness, sometimes himself directly involved in events, and his evaluation of the problem of heresy at that time is significant.

In 1229 the Church had been well aware that the Cathars were not beaten; the clauses of the Treaty of Paris, forced on Count Raymond VII of Toulouse in April, show how the authorities intended to tackle the problem from now on.[2] In one sense, this document underlined the political and military defeat of the house of Toulouse: Raymond conceded the marquisate of Provence to the Church in perpetuity and most of the southern and eastern parts of his lands in Bas Languedoc to the Crown. Most importantly, he agreed that his daughter, Jeanne, would marry one of King Louis IX's brothers (this took place in 1236 or 1237 when she married Alphonse of

---

1 Pelhisson, pp.36–9; trans. Wakefield, p.209.
2 *HGL*, vol. 8, no. 271, pp.883–94.

Poitiers), the remaining lands falling to them and their heirs after Raymond's death. However, in another sense, the treaty was an attempt to solve the problem of Catharism which had frustrated both Innocent III and Simon of Montfort. The Catholic powers needed to undermine the political and social infrastructure which enabled the Cathar Church and its ministers to continue to operate. The war had manifestly failed to do that, for there were evident signs of a reviving Cathar hierarchy. In 1223, the new Cathar bishop of Carcassonne, Peter Isarn, had had copies made of key records of the Council of St Félix-de-Caraman, so that he could re-establish the jurisdictional boundaries of his diocese after the intervening disruption. Two years later, a new council held at Pieusse, on the River Aude just down-stream from Limoux, created a new bishopric, that of the Razès, apparently because Peter Isarn had been unable to sort out the problem. Peter Isarn's interest in these records was not simply jurisdictional, however, for at the same time he was determined to combat an attempt to reintroduce moderate dualism into Languedoc, and he needed the authority of St Félix to help him to do this.[3] While the council at Pieusse was not on the scale of St Félix and the threat of schism a real worry for Peter Isarn, for the historian neverthe-less there are evident signs of the continuing intellectual vitality of Catharism in the mid-1220s.

Therefore, in the lands which Raymond VII was allowed to retain dur-ing his lifetime – that is those within the diocese of Toulouse, including the city itself, the dioceses of Agen and Rodez, and those of Albi, north of the Tarn, and Cahors, including the cities of Albi and Cahors themselves – it is revealing to see the places which were particularly targeted. Tou-louse itself was to be overseen by the royal officials who were to garrison the Château Narbonnais for ten years, partly financed by Raymond himself with a sum of 6,000 marks. Yet again, the walls were to be removed and the ditches filled. Verfeil, on the River Agout east of Toulouse, and the village of Lasbordes and its dependencies to the north-west of Carcassonne were to be ceded to the bishop of Toulouse and the son of the crusader, Oliver of Lillers, in conformity with a grant previously made by King Louis VIII and Amaury of Montfort, although the count still retained certain rights over them. Equally significantly, twenty-five named *castra* were to receive the same treatment as Toulouse, plus five others to be chosen by the legate. The twenty-five were: Fanjeaux, Castelnaudary, Labécède, Avignonet, Puylaurens, Saint-Paul-Cap-de-Joux, Lavaur, Rabastens, Gaillac, Montégut, Puycelci, Verdun, Castelsarrasin, Moissac, Montauban, Montcuq, Agen,

---

3   See B. Hamilton, 'The Cathar Council of Saint-Félix reconsidered', *Archivum Fratrum Praedicatorum* 48 (1978), pp.43–9.

Condom, Saverdun, Auterive, Casseneuil, Pujols, Auvillar, Peyrusse, and Laurac. Five of these – Castelnaudary, Lavaur, Montcuq, Peyrusse, and Verdun – together with three others, Penne d'Agenais, Cordes, and Villemur, would, however, be garrisoned by royal forces for ten years, five of which would be paid for by the count. The king reserved the right to destroy four of them – Castelnaudary, Lavaur, Villemur, and Verdun – although the count would still be required to pay the expenses of garrisons. These provisions must give a good idea of the perceived geography of Catharism in the diocese in 1229, even if some were included as much for their past record (and therefore their potential rather than actual danger) as for their present heretical population. Indeed, there was an ominous sign for the Church: one of them, Penne d'Albigeois, was still holding out, and Raymond had to commit himself to capturing it by force.

If the Cathars could be deprived of their customary refuges, they would be vulnerable to an active policy of heresy hunting. 'We will purge', promised Count Raymond, 'these lands of heretics and of the stench of heresy, and we will also aid the purgation of the lands which the lord king will hold.' Bounties were to be offered to those who took the hunt seriously. 'In order better and more easily to unmask them [these heretics], we [the count] promise to pay two marks of silver for the next two years and, after that, one mark to every person who causes a heretic to be arrested, on condition that the heretic is condemned as such by the bishop of the place or by a competent authority.' At the same time Raymond would provide solid support for the Church both by establishing peace through the expulsion of *routiers*, and by defending the rights and property of individual churches. The count's full administrative system was to be deployed to make this a reality, especially in enforcing sentences of excommunication; indeed, his officials were to give bite to these sentences by confiscating the property of those who obstinately ignored excommunication for more than a year. Nobody would be employed as a *bayle* therefore if there was any doubt about their commitment, including Jews and anybody suspected of heretical sympathies. All ecclesiastical lands and tithes were to be restored to the Church. All this was to be sustained out of the count's own pocket: 10,000 marks were to be paid to the Church as reparation for damage done to its property, 4,000 marks to specific monasteries, and another 4,000 marks to support fourteen masters in a new university to be established at Toulouse.

The land would therefore be filled with bastions of orthodoxy where heretics could find no comfort or protection. Deprived of an infrastructure, they could more easily be isolated and identified and appropriate measures could then be taken to stop their activity. In the new post-crusade Languedoc, Toulouse would be transformed from a city which Peter of Les Vaux-de-Cernay had believed to be 'the chief source of the poison of faithlessness' into what John of Garland, a Parisian grammarian who came to take up a post at the new university, described as 'a second promised land'.[4] Even so, past experience had taught that reliance on local secular powers was often misplaced, especially when the principal figure belonged to the house of Toulouse; the difference in 1229 was that now the royal power had a substantial interest in the direct government of Languedoc. Initially, at least, it does not seem as if Raymond VII was expected to play much of a role once he had financed the required structure. Clause fourteen of the Treaty of Paris laid down that sometime between August 1229 and August 1230 he was to leave for Outremer, from which he was not to return for five years. This would have left the royal officials as the predominant influence in the region, especially as they occupied key centres in the count's designated lands. Nor was this confined to castles, for the promulgation of the treaty was immediately followed by the statute *Cupientes*, which gave 'the barons of the land, our officers and other subjects present and future' the obligation to work 'with diligence and fidelity to search out and discover heretics and when they have discovered any, to deliver them without delay to the ecclesiastical authorities'.[5]

# The inquisitors

These measures attempted to address the basic problem of lay support for Catharism in Languedoc, but it was the task of those 'ecclesiastical authorities' to deal with the heresy itself. Most historians see the influence of the papal legate, the Cardinal Romanus of Sant'Angelo, behind the issue of *Cupientes*; he was certainly the guiding hand in November when he convened a council at Toulouse. Here, eighteen of the forty-five canons of the council dealt with the pursuit of heretics, giving the authorities very explicit powers of search and arrest.[6] These canons give some insight into the Church's perception of where its past weaknesses lay in the pursuit of Cathars. Preaching, debate, and even military action could all be avoided by those who wanted to escape detection; the measures taken at Toulouse were devised to uncover what the legate evidently saw as the hidden structure of heresy by creating

---

4  PVC, vol. 1, para. 6, p.6; trans. Sibly, p.8; H. Denifle, ed., *Chartularium Universitatis Parisiensis*, vol. 1 (Paris, 1899) (reprint Brussels, 1964), no. 72, p.129.
5  J. D. Mansi, ed., *Sacrorum conciliorum nova et amplissima collectio*, vol. 23 (Florence, Venice, and Paris, 1799), cols 185–6.
6  Mansi, ed., *Sacrorum conciliorum*, vol. 13, cols 192–3. See C. J. Hefele and H. Leclercq, *Histoire des Conciles*, vol. 5(ii) (Paris, 1913), pp.1494–501.

the mechanisms for the active pursuit of individuals. The local prelates should swear in a priest and two trustworthy laymen in every parish, who should search for heretics in their area. This seems to have been based on a similar idea instituted at the Council of Narbonne in 1227. It leaves no doubt about the seriousness of intent, for it was to be no infrequent episcopal parade; from 1229 homes could be systematically turned over, their cellars, roofs, and outbuildings inspected, as well as anywhere else which might be used as a hiding place. Anywhere in which a heretic had been found was to be destroyed, a provision which must have acted as a considerable deterrent to any casual hospitality. The cardinal was determined to follow up the attack on communal support presaged in the Treaty of Paris. *Bonhommes* who had voluntarily confessed were to be resettled in Catholic towns where heresy had never been suspected. Once there, they were to wear two crosses, 'in detestation of their recent error'. The detail is significant because of what it reveals about how the Church thought heretics might react to this legislation. The crosses had to be a different colour from the garments and written permission was needed from the bishop before a former heretic could stop wearing them. There was to be no public role for such persons, for they could not hold any office, nor play a part in any legal process until they had, in the eyes of the pope or his legate, performed sufficient penance. No trust was placed in heretics whose confessions were not accepted as voluntary: they were to be imprisoned and do penance. The prison was 'to prevent them having the power of corrupting others', and was to be paid for by the person who had obtained the confiscated property.

Once heresy had been excised from the community, no opportunity was to be offered for it to creep back in again. Everybody who reached the 'years of discretion' was obliged to swear an oath against heresy and to go to confession three times a year. The possession of an Old or New Testament was in itself seen as grounds for suspicion and was forbidden; only the Psalter and a Breviary were allowed and then not in translation. It was thought particularly important to cut off access to the sick and dying, because it was claimed that this was the most likely time for the occurrence of 'wicked and abominable things'. Thus heretics or suspected persons could not act as physicians and wills were not valid unless witnessed by a priest and other 'men of good credit'.

William of Puylaurens may have been present at the council, judging by his detailed account of the way that, at its end, the cardinal brought forward a man whom he evidently considered to be his star witness, William of Solier, a former Cathar *perfectus* who had now re-established his reputation. The purpose was 'in order that his witness should be efficacious against those about whom he knew the truth'. Other witnesses were produced by

Fulk, Bishop of Toulouse, and the bishops at the council were invited to interrogate them. The results were to be written down and stored so that they could 'expedite much in a short time'. In the past some bishops had shown little grasp of what was needed; this looks like an attempt to persuade them to practise this approach under supervision before they returned to put the legislation into effect in their own dioceses. Some witnesses deposed freely but others remained obdurate. Similarly, while some put themselves at the mercy of the legate and were given a full indulgence, others had to be forced to attend and were given heavy penances. Some wanted to mount a defence in law and asked for the names of the witnesses deposing against them. The legate appears to have been reluctant to do this, for they had to pursue him to Montpellier before they could obtain an answer. In the end he gave them a general list of witnesses, rather than those who had deposed against them specifically, for he assumed 'that they would kill the witnesses whom they knew had specially deposed against them'. They should then see if they recognised any of their enemies from the entire list. The list must have been formidable for, according to William, they then gave up the litigation and submitted to the legate.[7] Contemporaries could see that the Albigensian wars had not eliminated heresy, but it was equally evident that post-crusade Languedoc no longer offered the hospitable environment which the Cathars had once enjoyed. The actions of the Church and Crown in 1229 created a world which thereafter became more and more uncomfortable and dangerous for the Cathar Church.

Nevertheless, although the framework had changed, the conflict between orthodoxy and Catharism had not disappeared. Indeed, as William Pelhisson saw it, the strategy for eliminating heresy formulated in 1229 engendered a new wave of resistance, and the Church's drive in the 1230s was only sustained by the efforts of his own order, the Friars Preachers. As one who became an inquisitor himself, he presents the Dominicans as the front-line in an assault upon a society which was soon found to be less than accommodating. William did not think very highly of the newly-arrived professors at Toulouse, whom he castigates as 'ineffective in uprooting heresy', and he remained deeply suspicious of the court of Raymond VII, whose entourage he believed to be 'notably corrupted in the faith'. For him the real keepers of the flame were the Dominicans, who had first been established in Toulouse in 1215. They had received three houses near the Narbonne Gate, given to them by a wealthy citizen called Peter Seila, who later joined the order himself, and the church of St Romain, granted to them by Bishop Fulk. In 1230 they moved to a new site along the Saracen Wall, called Garrigue's

---

7  WP, pp.138–9.

Garden, again benefiting from the patronage of a wealthy citizen, Pons of Capdenier. By 1234 there were more than forty friars in residence, forming a powerful preaching cohort in the city. They were supported in this by Bishop Fulk, 'father and friend of the order'; when he died in 1231 he was replaced by a Dominican, Raymond of Le Fauga, a former provincial prior.[8]

At the same time, Pope Gregory IX who, until his temporary reconciliation with the Emperor Frederick II in 1230, had been deeply preoccupied by his battle with the Staufen, turned his mind to the campaign against heresy. The Dominicans were well-suited to his purposes, since they had been founded primarily to combat heresy, they were well-educated in theology and law and, in several places, had already taken the initiative. Real or imagined threats to the faith had been discerned in Germany and France, as well as in Languedoc; in 1231 the pope had authorised the Dominicans to act in Germany and, two years later, in France, although to an extent he was regularising an already existing situation. At La Charité-sur-Loire the leader of the heresy hunters was himself an ex-Cathar, Robert 'the Bulgar', a man who seems to have interpreted his mission entirely in his own terms.[9] In Languedoc inquiries were set up by two papal bulls, issued in April 1233, which informed the archbishops of Bourges, Bordeaux, Narbonne, and Auch that Dominicans would be sent to support episcopal action against heresy, and then ordered the Dominican priors to find suitable persons to fulfil this role.[10] Historians have stressed that the inquisition which developed from this was never an entirely Dominican affair for, over time, it involved both Franciscans and local prelates,[11] and William Pelhisson himself was anxious to counter any claim by 'a detractor or rival or envious person' that he was describing these events for 'the exaltation of members of our order'. Nevertheless, the work had already been started in Languedoc before the papal instructions and it took little time for the Dominicans to find appropriate personnel.

---

8   Pelhisson, pp.38–49; trans. Wakefield, pp.209–12. See also pp.137–40.
9   See A. Brenon, *Le Vrai Visage du Catharisme*, 2nd edn (Portet-sur-Garonne, 1995), pp.49–50, on the destruction of the Cathar bishopric of 'France', which had effectively disappeared by *c.* 1240.
10  T. Ripoll, ed., *Bullarium ordinis fratrum praedicatorum*, vol. 1 (Rome, 1779), nos 71 and 72, p.47.
11  B. Hamilton, *The Medieval Inquisition* (London, 1981), pp.36–9. It may be more accurate to speak of 'inquisitors' rather than of 'the Inquisition' in that, initially, there was a lack of institutional structures and set procedures. It has therefore been argued that, for the thirteenth century at least, the Inquisition is a historical construct, see R. Kieckhefer, 'The office of inquisition and medieval heresy: the transition from personal to institutional jurisdiction', *Journal of Ecclesiastical History* 46 (1995), pp.36–61. However, the appearance of a manual of procedure as early as 1244 and the continual emphasis on the need for proper record-keeping, does suggest an awareness of the need for consistency and a strong sense of common purpose.

Also, Friar Pons of St Gilles was chosen as prior at Toulouse. He bore himself courageously and vigorously in the business of the faith against heretics, together with Friar Peter Seila, who was a Toulousan, and Friar William Arnold, a jurist, who was from Montpellier. Them the lord pope appointed as inquisitors against heretics in the dioceses of Toulouse and in Cahors as well. The lord legate, archbishop of Vienne [John of Bernin], also made Arnold Catalan, who was then of the convent at Toulouse, an inquisitor against heretics in the diocese of Albi, where manfully and fearlessly he preached and sought to conduct the inquisition as best he could.[12]

The impact of this new system now became a matter of crucial importance for the Cathars. The first surviving manual of procedure seems to have been compiled by the Dominican inquisitor, Friar Ferrier, in 1244,[13] although, as will be seen, this cool and methodical textbook often belies the reality of actually conducting such inquisitions in the face of hostile communities and unco-operative secular rulers. Judging by the account of William Pelhisson, who was appointed to the circuit in and around Albi together with Arnold Catalan, the manual reflects methods which had been developed as a result of the experiences of the inquisitors during the 1230s and early 1240s. The first step was to drive a wedge into the façade of community solidarity, so that the loyalties and fears which had held it together could be undermined. Under the year 1235, Pelhisson describes how 'all the inquisitors came to Toulouse and called many to confess, giving them a time of grace. If, within this period, they made a good and full confession without deceit, the inquisitors offered solid hope that they would not be imprisoned, be exiled, or lose property, because Lord Raymond had agreed with the friars that any penitent who confessed the truth would lose nothing. Subsequently, those who had honestly confessed found this to be true.'[14]

In these circumstances the temptation to denounce others was almost overwhelming, if only for defensive reasons. In a community that had had frequent contact with heretics – and the provisions of the Treaty of Paris show how well-known were these places – nobody was likely to be innocent in the eyes of the Church, and therefore anybody could have been written into the inquisitors' copious records. Evidently such records were kept: in

---

12  Pelhisson, pp.34–47; trans. Wakefield, pp.208–11.
13  A. Tardif, 'Document pour l'histoire du *processus per inquisitionem* et de l'*inquisitio heretice pravitatis*', *Nouvelle revue historique du droit français et étranger* 7 (1883), pp.669–78; trans. W. L. Wakefield, *Heresy, Crusade and Inquisition in Southern France, 1100–1250* (London, 1974), Appendix 6, pp.250–8. For dating and attribution, see L. Kölmer, *Ad capiendos Vulpes. Die Ketzerbekämpfung in Südfrankreich in der ersten Hälfte des 13. Jahrhunderts und die Ausbildung des Inquisitionverfahrens* (Deutsches Historisches Institut in Paris, Historische Studien, 19) (Bonn, 1982), pp.198–203.
14  Pelhisson, pp.68–9; trans. Wakefield, p.217.

1234 many of the living had received penances as a consequence of the names given by William of Solier at the Council of Toulouse, while some of the dead, previously thought orthodox, had been disinterred and their bones burnt. Conversions of former heretics like William of Solier were especially valuable. In April 1236, Raymond Gros, whom William Pelhisson says had been a perfected heretic for about twenty-two years, suddenly went to the Dominican house at Toulouse, even though he had not been summoned or cited, and made such an extensive confession that it took the friars several days to write it all down. William Pelhisson can offer no reason for his conversion, beyond a feeling that it must have been divine providence, but instead is content to celebrate the huge catch this netted. 'Many came of their own volition, fearing arrest', he says.[15] To keep quiet in the hope of evading the notice of the inquisitors was an immense gamble, for the penalties for silence or dissembling once the period of grace had been announced were far greater than early confession and ready denunciation of others. Speaking of an inquisition conducted by Peter Seila and William Arnold at Moissac in 1234, when various men were condemned as contumacious heretics, William Pelhisson says that 'great fear was aroused among the heretics and their believers in that land'.[16]

The manual of 1244 reflects the experience gained through adopting these methods. Having chosen the place at which they wished to begin, the inquisitors assembled the people and clergy and presented a general sermon, before issuing citations to appear to the entire population of the parish from the age of fourteen in the case of males and twelve in the case of females, 'or younger if perchance they shall have been guilty of an offence'. The device described by Pelhisson to force open the can of worms is here built into the system. If no previous inquisition had been there 'we will grant indulgence from imprisonment to all from that place who have not been cited by name or who have not yet earned the indulgence, if, within a specified time, they come voluntarily as penitents to tell the exact and full truth about themselves and about others'. All those who presented themselves were to abjure all heresy and swear to take active steps to aid in the pursuit and seizure of other heretics. Then the persons concerned were to be 'diligently questioned', that is an attempt was made to cover all possible contacts with heretics including listening to preaching, guiding, providing hospitality, eating and drinking with them, holding deposits of money, or making gifts. 'And when a region is widely infected we make general inquisition of all persons in the manner just described, entering the names of all of them in the record, even

---

15  Pelhisson, pp.52–5, 92–5; trans. Wakefield, pp.213, 223–4; WP, pp.138–9.
16  Pelhisson, pp.58–9; trans. Wakefield, p.214.

of those who insist that they know nothing about others and have themselves committed no crime, so that if they have lied or if subsequently they commit an offence, as is often found true of a number of persons, it is on record that they have abjured and have been interrogated in detail.' Summonses were set out according to a prescribed legal formula, which included 'a limit of delay without contempt', obviously intended to cut off another possible avenue of excuses. A legitimate defence was allowed, but the names of witnesses remained secret. Penance and condemnations were then issued, following another abjuration. Penances for those who were not to be imprisoned meant wearing yellow crosses, attending mass and vespers on Sundays for the remainder of one's life, following processions, and pilgrimage to a set number of sanctuaries. A prohibition on molesting penitents suggests that this was in fact another form of pressure, albeit an indirect consequence of inquisitional condemnation. Those, however, who could not be recalled from their heresy they relinquished to 'secular judgement', as well as condemning deceased heretics whose bones were to be burned 'in detestation of so heinous an offence'. Finally, they caused the goods of heretics and those imprisoned to be confiscated. This, they stated, was their legal obligation, but they stressed its importance because 'it is in this way that heretics and believers are particularly confounded'.[17]

## Resistance

The subtle construction of this system was such as to leave little possibility of legal evasion; the alternative was much more direct and, at times, violent resistance. It is not surprising to find, therefore, that the enduring theme of

---

17  The use of imprisonment and social stigmatisation were effective means of detaching a heretic from the community which had enabled him to sustain his beliefs and role in the past. Individuals isolated in this way often found they had little alternative but to work for the inquisitors. See J. Given, 'The inquisitors of Languedoc and the medieval technology of power', *American Historical Review* 94 (1989), pp.336–59, and 'Social stress, social strain, and the inquisitors of Medieval Languedoc', in S. C. Waugh and P. D. Diehl, eds, *Christendom and Its Discontents. Exclusion, Persecution, and Rebellion, 1000–1500* (Cambridge, 1996), pp.67–85; H. A. Kelly, 'Inquisition and the prosecution of heresy: misconceptions and abuses', *Church History* 58 (1989), pp.439–51, argues that originally the procedural rules for heresy cases 'did not privilege heresy cases' over others, except in the use of summary procedure and the concealment of the names of witnesses. However, he also shows that the rules were often abused to the extent that such abuses seem to have become 'normal' in the course of the thirteenth century. What is evident is the skill with which the inquisitors developed the means which were available to them to obtain the results they sought, see J. Given, *Inquisition and Medieval Society. Power, Discipline and Resistance in Languedoc* (Ithaca, NY and London, 1997), esp. chs 1–3.

William Pelhisson's chronicle is that of the heroic triumph of his order in the face of the blows of the wicked. 'I write so that successors in our order and whatsoever other faithful persons who examine these matters may know how many and what sufferings came to their predecessors for the faith and name of Christ.'[18] Exhumations, which started in Toulouse as early as 1230 and continued throughout the decade, were particularly provocative. One incident in Albi in 1234, described by both William Pelhisson and an anonymous contemporary, encapsulates the type of reaction to this sort of inquisitorial activity. Here, a crowd attempted to throw the inquisitor Arnold Catalan into the River Tarn, although in the end some of them relented, leaving him badly beaten, his face bloody and his clothes torn.[19] The anonymous account (possibly by Isarn of Denat, a priest who was caught up in the incident and injured as a result) gives an idea of the atmosphere an order for exhumation created. The officials were too frightened to go to the cemetery to carry out Arnold Catalan's sentence on a deceased woman called Boyssene, so he himself went there and struck the first symbolic blows with a mattock, leaving the actual digging to the bishop's servants. Almost immediately they were back to say that they had been driven out by a crowd led by a knight called Pons Bernard. He had at least twenty-five people with him (whose names are carefully recorded in the anonymous account), and was soon joined by others. When Arnold Catalan confronted them, they turned on him and beat him, 'some striking him with their fists on the chest, some slapping his face; some dragged him by the hood, others tore his cloak, as was to be seen for many days thereafter'. Only the intervention of others prevented him being thrown into the Tarn. By the time the inquisitor had struggled back to the cathedral the crowd had grown to two or three hundred, some demanding that they cut off his head, put it in a sack, and throw it into the river. Arnold Catalan's reaction was to excommunicate the town's inhabitants, a move which led to an attempt to make amends. Arnold's reply was that he forgave the attack on his person, but could not do so on behalf of the Church. However, he did withdraw the sentence.[20]

The speed and apparent spontaneity of the reactions to exhumation suggest that a climate of confrontation already existed. This was particularly true of Toulouse, where the consulate claimed that respectable Catholics were being wrongly accused. This came to a head when, in mid-October 1235, William Arnold, whose high profile as an inquisitor in Toulouse and Carcassonne during the 1230s may have contributed to his murder in 1242,

---

18  Pelhisson, pp.36–7; trans. Wakefield, p.208. For an analysis of violent resistance, see
     Given, *Inquisition and Medieval Society*, pp.112–17.
19  Pelhisson, pp.46–7; trans. Wakefield, p.211.
20  Pelhisson, pp.112–22; trans. Wakefield, pp.226–8.

cited twelve believers of heretics from the city, including Maurand the Elder, a member of a leading family with a record of heretical sympathies who had crossed swords with the authorities before.[21] They refused to appear and 'uttered threats and dire warnings to make him desist from his activities'. When he would not he was literally marched out of the city. An attempt to issue the citation a second time from Carcassonne led to the expulsion of the priests entrusted with the task. Although the Dominicans were allowed to stay, their convent was effectively placed in quarantine, cut off from water and food, except for what could be lowered over the walls by their supporters. As this applied to the bishop as well, he too left the city, as 'no one dared to take him bread or do other such things'. Eventually, the Dominicans were also expelled: dragged from their cloister by the sergeants of the consuls, according to William Pelhisson. Only at the beginning of March 1236, after a protest before the pope at Perugia and consequent papal pressure upon Raymond VII, were the inquisitors and other Dominicans restored to the city.[22] The bitterness of the conflict was a reflection of the importance of the matters at stake for, as John Mundy shows, the inquisitors rightly perceived that the most wealthy and powerful families in the city were disproportionately important in the sustenance of Catharism there. They therefore seem to have adopted a conscious policy of pursuing these families from the outset. At the same time, Raymond VII, although no friend of the inquisitors, had his own agenda, for he was anxious to re-assert comital power in the chief possession left to him under the terms of the Treaty of Paris. Not surprisingly, the consuls found themselves far more seriously squeezed than their contemporaries in the Italian cities. The tension continued throughout the 1230s: on the one hand, the consuls accused the inquisitors of bringing false accusations against 'decent married men', while on the other, William Pelhisson claims that the consuls were prompted by the heretics among whom 'great fear' had been aroused.[23]

---

21  See above, ch. 2, p.64.
22  Pelhisson, pp.52–3, 72–87; trans. Wakefield, pp.213, 218–23. See also E. Griffe, *Le Languedoc Cathare et l'Inquisition (1229–1329)* (Paris, 1980), p.56, and Y. Dossat, 'La Crise de l'Inquisition toulousaine en 1235–1236 et l'expulsion des Dominicains', *Bulletin philologique et historique (jusqu'à 1715), années 1953 et 1954* (Paris, 1955), pp.391–8, who revises the chronology of these events.
23  Pelhisson, pp.52–3, 58–9; trans. Wakefield, pp.213, 214. See J. H. Mundy, *The Repression of Catharism at Toulouse. The Royal Diploma of 1279* (Studies and Texts, 74) (Toronto, 1985), esp. pp.28–32, 50–5. In his view, 'the back of Toulousan Catharism had been broken by the end of September 1237', a success which he believes made the attack on the rural lordships much easier. However, not all historians are convinced by Mundy's analysis, see M. D. Lambert, *The Cathars* (Oxford, 1998), p.140 and n.33. E. Griffe, *Le Languedoc Cathare au temps de la Croisade (1209–1229)* (Paris, 1973), pp.160–6, presents a very similar social profile to that of Mundy.

Resistance by vested interests like the *consuls* of Toulouse, whatever their motives, was quite overt; however, it was underpinned by a more clandestine violence, frequent enough to give threats uttered publicly real menace. William of Puylaurens claims that this began soon after the departure of the legate, Romanus of Sant'Angelo after the Council of Toulouse in November 1229. An immediate victim was Andreas Chaulet, a royal seneschal, ambushed in a wood at La Centenière, near Coudons, south of Carcassonne, apparently in retaliation for his conversion of a Cathar *perfectus*, whom he was holding in prison. Many others, he says, were assassinated on 'suspicion alone', so that Raymond VII was accused of crass negligence. As William of Puylaurens saw it, these people sought to lead the land back to the bad times of the past, 'so that once the peace was disturbed they were able to indulge in their accustomed rapine and to support heretics and, although they pretended to love him, prepare the fall of the count. Consequently, these sons of Belial burst out from their hiding places, disrupted the tithes of the bishop, persecuted his clergy, and infected his territory of Verfeil.'[24] As a native of the area, William knew the territory to the east of Toulouse very well, which suggests that the *pays* around Verfeil still contained many Cathars and their supporters, despite the inquisitorial circuits and the presence of a royal garrison at Lavaur.

Cardinal Romanus had been well-aware of the dangers and, when he had returned to Rome in November 1229, he had taken the entire documentation of his inquiry with him, 'since, if at any time it had been found by evil-doers in that land, it might result in the death of witnesses who had deposed against such persons'.[25] Inexperienced heresy hunters were, however, more vulnerable, especially those such as the vicar of Toulouse and the abbot of Saint-Sernin, drafted in to help the Dominicans in Toulouse at Easter 1235, at that time overwhelmed by the numbers of those wanting to make their confessions. A wine-seller called Arnold Dominic, under pressure from the vicar of Toulouse, led him and the abbot to Les Cassès in the Lauragais about half-way between Toulouse and Carcassonne. There they captured seven heretics, but some escaped with the help of local peasants. Arnold Dominic then made his confession and was released, in accordance with the procedures described by William Pelhisson, but he was now a marked man whose identity was well-known, and he was murdered in his bed at Aigrefeuille, near Lanta, which is about twelve kilometres north of Verfeil. The abbot and the vicar were similarly thwarted when they arrested Peter William Delort in the bourg of Saint-Sernin, whom William

---

24  WP, pp.140–1.
25  Ibid., pp.140–1.

Pelhisson says was 'a noted believer of heretics'. He was snatched away from them by his friends and fled, although he was later condemned as a heretic.[26]

This violence culminated in a direct attack upon inquisitors themselves when, on the night of 28 May 1242, an entire inquisitorial team led by a Dominican, William Arnold, and a Franciscan, Stephen of St Thibéry, was wiped out at the small town of Avignonet, about forty kilometres to the south-east of Toulouse. The inquisitors were on circuit from Toulouse, covering the eastern part of the diocese. Between November 1241 and the date of their murder they had covered most of the region from Lavaur in the north to Fanjeaux in the south, so their presence must have been well-known. Their stay in Avignonet was communicated to the Pyrenean castle of Montségur, another seventy kilometres to the south, by a message from Raymond of Alfaro, the comtal *bayle*. Montségur had been rebuilt by Raymond of Pereille in *c*. 1204 and it had developed into a focal point for Cathars from all over Languedoc. By 1242 it was one of the few places left which offered the kind of environment which had been commonplace before 1209. The message evoked an immediate response from Peter Roger of Mirepoix, its lord and son-in-law of Raymond of Pereille. Peter Roger gathered more men from Gaja *en route*, and from Avignonet itself, who vented their hatred of the inquisitors by smashing their victims to death with swords, axes, and lances. Several of them claimed to be personally responsible for the deaths of William Arnold and Stephen of St Thibéry themselves. Afterwards pillage ranging from horses to books was distributed among the murderers, some of which was later sold on. Nevertheless, profit was not the motive. As one participant, William Golairon, later said, they hoped that by this means 'the affair of the inquisition could be extinguished, and the whole land would be freed, and there would not be another inquisition'.[27] Indeed, although the attack may have been opportunistic, the target may not have been random. In William Pelhisson's account, William Arnold appears as the single most active inquisitor during the 1230s, when he led inquiries in Toulouse, Carcassonne, and Cahors, and his attackers may have imagined that his elimination would have broken the backbone of the campaign.

The idea that this measure would put an end to inquisitions forever appears, in retrospect, to have been a naive hope. In fact, inquiries were reinstituted within months, led by the Dominican, Friar Ferrier. Between

---

26  Pelhisson, pp.66–7; trans. Wakefield, p.217.

27  For an account of Avignonet, see Y. Dossat, *Les Crises de l'Inquisition toulousaine en XIIIe siècle (1233–1273)* (Bordeaux, 1959), pp.146–51. For the pillage, Doat, vol. 24, ff.165r–165v, and for William Golarion, Bibliothèque municipale, Toulouse, *Manuscript 609* (hereafter *Ms. 609*), f.140v.

December 1242 and September 1244, together with various colleagues – Peter of Alès, William Raymond, Pons Gary, and Peter Durand – he questioned at least 700 people. Significantly, in the aftermath of Avignonet, they showed little interest in actual belief, concentrating instead largely upon actions. Ferrier was the most experienced inquisitor of his time, having been involved in the prosecution of heresy since 1229 and remaining active in Narbonne, Caunes, and Elne throughout the 1230s. He had a reputation for severity and was no stranger to the violence his actions could provoke. His appointment so soon after Avignonet therefore was clearly meant as a signal that the inquisitors would not be intimidated, and certainly helped make possible the huge inquiry conducted by Bernard of Caux and John of St Pierre in 1245 and 1246. The only real effect that the murders seem to have had was – temporarily at least – to restrict the inquisitors' itineracy, for Ferrier's investigations were largely based at Conques, Limoux, and Saissac, to which witnesses were required to travel.[28]

Peter Roger and his men may also have been encouraged to act by the political circumstances prevailing in the late spring of 1242. At that time Raymond VII had entered into a coalition of the enemies of the French Crown, which encompassed the English king, Henry III, and Hugh of Lusignan, Count of La Marche in Poitou. All three at their different levels saw themselves as victims of Capetian rapacity, although they had little else in common. William of Puylaurens's claim that the violence of the Cathar supporters in fact prepared the way for 'the fall of the count' once more highlights the dilemma of the house of Toulouse ever since Catharism had penetrated its territories. Raymond VII was caught between the orthodox authorities who saw Languedoc as an evil land which needed to be purged, and his subjects, among whom a substantial minority at least were sympathetic to heretics and who, even if they were not pro-Cathar, were prepared to resist to protect their own patrimonies. William of Puylaurens is both hostile to heretics and pro-Capetian in his sympathies, positions which make his view of Raymond's situation all the more valuable. In his opinion, the conditions of the Treaty of Paris were such that, if the king had defeated the count in battle and made him his prisoner, 'any one on its own should have sufficed as the price of redemption'.[29] Raymond's actions in the 1230s and 1240s reflect these conflicting pressures and it is understandable that they could have been misinterpreted by those southerners so filled with zeal

---

28  See J. Duvernoy, 'Confirmation d'aveux devant les Inquisiteurs Ferrier et Pons Gary ( Juillet–Août 1243)', *Hérésis* 1 (1983), pp.9–23; W. L. Wakefield, 'Friar Ferrier, Inquisition at Caunes, and escapes from prison at Carcassonne', *Catholic Historical Review* 58 (1972), pp.220–37, and 'Friar Ferrier, Inquisitor', *Heresis* 7 (1986), pp.33–41.

29  WP, pp.132–5.

for their own cause that they would fail to see the wider consequences of their actions. Raymond had failed to fulfil his promise to remove himself to Outremer for five years and, in 1236, he had been reproved by the pope for not preventing the expulsion of the inquisitors from Toulouse. Yet, in 1238, Gregory IX, harassed by the Emperor Frederick II, was apparently sufficiently persuaded by Raymond's complaints about the conduct of the inquisitors to suspend their activities. The count then refrained from involving himself in the revolt of Raymond Trencavel in September 1240, and the revolt failed, leaving Trencavel no alternative but to retreat once more to exile in Catalonia. Raymond must have seen the coalition of 1242 as a better opportunity than Trencavel's isolated effort, but it can hardly have gone unnoticed by the Cathars that he seemed unwilling to act once the inquisitions had restarted in 1241. However, by October 1242, the coalition too had fallen apart and, in January 1243, Raymond had been obliged to make a new settlement with Louis IX.[30]

During the decade following, some of the Cathars, as William of Puylaurens expressed it, 'wished to return to the vomit of war'.[31] If so, the following ten years must have extinguished even that hope. The failure of the revolts of 1240 and 1242 left no figureheads in which they could invest any faith, however misplaced, and, more importantly for the Cathar cause, Avignonet provoked a royal attack upon Montségur itself. The siege of Montségur, which began in mid-summer 1243, and ended with its fall in mid-March 1244, has been invested with immense significance by historians of Catharism. There are good reasons for this. If, as seems likely, the ultimate decline of Catharism in Languedoc can be partially explained by the destruction of its supporting infrastructure, then Montségur can be seen as the last real representative of the traditional refuge of a Cathar community. It had been a Cathar redoubt from the time of its rebuilding. Raymond of Pereille's mother, Fournière, wife of William Roger of Mirepoix, was a perfected heretic, and at the time of the siege forty of the 415 inhabitants, spanning four generations, belonged to the family of Mirepoix-Pereille.[32] The castle was situated on top of a rocky outcrop in the Ariège region of the Pyrenees, 1,216 metres above sea level. It is by no means inaccessible, but evidently it is not so close to the main centres of population as to be an obvious target of military action. It had been well-known as a heretical centre since the era of the crusade. At the Lateran Council of 1215, Fulk,

---

30   See Wakefield, *Heresy, Crusade and Inquisition*, pp.153–61, for an outline of these events.
31   WP, pp.140–1.
32   M. Roquebert, 'Le Catharisme comme tradition dans la "familia" languedocienne', in *CF* 20 (1985), pp.226–8. See also A. Brenon, *Les Femmes Cathares* (Paris, 1992), pp.242–9, on the nature of Montségur and the community there.

Bishop of Toulouse, had tried to prove that Raymond Roger, Count of Foix, was a heretic by accusing him of giving his protection to the castle. Raymond Roger was equally vehement in his denial, rightly pointing out that he was not its overlord.[33] Both sides, though, accepted that association with Montségur was evidence of Cathar sympathies. In the view of William of Puylaurens it remained 'a public refuge for all sorts of malefactors and heretics, like "the synagogue of Satan"'.[34]

When it fell, its significance for Catharism became very evident. Over half the population were *perfecti* or *perfectae*, that is 210 of the 415 persons who were in the castle, including Bertrand Marty, Bishop of Toulouse, and Raymond Agulher, Bishop of the Razès. The presence of the bishop of Toulouse is a measure of the pressure which had been exerted upon the Cathar Church since 1229, for this position had been maintained in the much more vulnerable Lauragais, albeit intermittently, at Saint-Paul-Cap-de-Joux in the Tarn region, throughout the crusades and even beyond the peace down to 1232, when Bertrand Marty's predecessor, Guilhabert of Castres, had been forced to make his base at Montségur.[35] According to William of Puylaurens, 'about 200' perfected heretics, men and women, were burned to death in March 1244, a figure largely confirmed by William Pelhisson. Those executed included Bertrand Marty.[36] The viability of the Cathar hierarchical structure in Languedoc was undermined, and those who escaped or were not present were forced to take refuge in Lombardy where they formed a Church in exile, which meant that they could hardly expect to influence and encourage their supporters in the Toulousain and the Carcassès in the way they had done in the past.

Montségur therefore represents the type of lordship which had been common in Languedoc in the past, controlled by powerful but local seigneurs, little concerned by outside authority. As at Lavaur, these lords favoured heretics, allowed them to live and preach within the enclosure, and had several family members who were 'clothed heretics'. Lavaur, however, was

---

33  *Chanson*, vol. 2, laisse 145, pp.48–55; trans. Shirley, pp.74–5. See above ch. 2, p.53, and ch. 4, p.138. There is an ambiguity about the feudal position of the lords of Pereille, since the suzerainty of this region was divided between the counts of Foix, and the viscounts of Carcassonne. Ultimately, however, the overlord was the count of Toulouse, see M. Roquebert, *L'Épopée cathare*, vol. 4, *1230–1249: Mourir à Montségur* (Toulouse, 1994), pp.32–3.

34  WP, pp.174–5.

35  These are Duvernoy's figures, WP, p.174, n.4. Roquebert, *L'Épopée cathare*, vol. 4, pp.366–7, calculates that there were 211 *perfecti* and at least 150 lay persons, so that the minimum figure was 361.

36  WP, pp.174–7; Pelhisson, pp.56–7; trans. Wakefield, p.214. Duvernoy has gathered together the texts of the depositions of the survivors of the fall of Montségur, as well as references to the castle in other inquisitorial testimonies, J. Duvernoy, ed. and trans., *Le Dossier de Montségur. Interrogatoires d'inquisition (1242–1247)* (Toulouse, 1997).

too close to Toulouse and to the main arena of crusading action to survive, whereas an attack on Montségur would not have seemed worth the resources when there were more pressing matters. In 1243–44, however, Hugh of Arcis, Seneschal of Carcassonne, put together a powerful force, supported by such prominent ecclesiastics as Peter Amiel, Archbishop of Narbonne, and Durand, Bishop of Albi, which suggests that they now thought that Montségur represented Catharism in a way which could not be allowed to continue. An attempt had been made to persuade Raymond VII to take action against it in 1241; the murder of the inquisitors the next year was the trigger for a serious campaign. Indeed, historians from Henry C. Lea in the late nineteenth century to Jean Duvernoy and Elie Griffe in the 1970s and 1980s have seen the expedition as having 'the character of a crusade'.[37] Even so, the fall of Montségur needs to be kept in perspective. Not all historians accept that contemporaries saw it in crusading terms; indeed, some are sceptical that the executions after the fall of the castle ever took place, suggesting that this is too reminiscent of 'the Béziers mentality' and thus quite unlikely in the circumstances prevailing in 1244.[38] Moreover, as Delaruelle has pointed out, the chronicles of 'Capetian France' and of the reign of St Louis paid no attention to the event. The St Denis monk, William of Nangis, for example, devotes half a chapter to the Trencavel revolt and the siege of Raymond Trencavel in Montréal by royal forces, but does not mention Montségur. For the northerners the event of the year was the taking of the cross by the king to fight Muslims in the East.[39]

Yet, for the Cathars, Louis IX's momentous decision to take the cross and the localised war being fought on his behalf in the mountains of the Ariège were in fact connected, for the two events together determined the future of the Languedocian heretics. The fate of the lordships which underpinned Catharism had been in the balance since 1209; after 1244 almost all those lords who still survived saw no alternative but to accept what the king was prepared to offer. The history of the lords of Termes in the thirteenth century illustrates how these outside pressures shaped their fate and therefore that of the Cathars they protected. The castle of Termes is about twenty-eight kilometres south-east of Carcassonne as the crow flies, but because

---

37 H. C. Lea, *A History of the Inquisition in the Middle Ages*, vol. 2 (New York, 1889), p.42; Duvernoy, WP, p.173, n.4; Griffe, *Le Languedoc Cathare et l'Inquisition*, p.80.

38 See Wakefield, *Heresy, Crusade and Inquisition*, p.173, and Duvernoy, *Le Dossier de Montségur*, pp.13–17.

39 See E. Delaruelle, 'Saint Louis devant les Cathares', in *Septième Centenaire de la Mort de Saint Louis. Actes des Colloques de Royaumont et de Paris (21–27 mai 1970)* (Paris, 1976), pp.277–80. For an assessment of the contemporary importance of Montségur, see Roquebert, *L'Épopée cathare*, vol. 4, pp.21–2.

of its position in the mountains of the Corbières it is nearly twice that distance by any feasible modern road. Consequently, its lords, who were Trencavel vassals, had been accustomed to their independence, confident that they could not be successfully attacked. Even when under threat from the crusade in the summer of 1210, the head of the family, Raymond of Termes, together with Peter Roger of Cabaret and Aimery of Montréal, had been unwilling to allow that independence to be eroded, so that negotiations intended to lead to the rendering of homage to Peter II of Aragon failed when it became clear that the king was insisting upon the rendability of their castles as a condition of acceptance.[40] The place itself clearly terrified Peter of Les Vaux-de-Cernay who describes with awe the precipitous terrain and the climatic extremes, while William of Tudela believed that Simon of Montfort was only able to take what he called 'a wonderful castle' after a siege lasting four months between late July and late November 1210, because of divine intervention.[41] As far as Peter of Les Vaux-de-Cernay was concerned, Raymond of Termes was a manifest heretic, fully deserving his ultimate end, which was to die in prison in Carcassonne. Whether or not this was true, he certainly tolerated Cathars in his castle. Men like Benedict of Termes, a garbed heretic since 1207 who, in 1226, became Cathar bishop of the Razès, came from this community, while during the siege Bernard Raymond of Roquebert, the Catholic Bishop of Carcassonne, had tried to mediate, since his mother and brother, who were both heretics, were in the castle at the time.[42] Peter of Les Vaux-de-Cernay had a particular hatred of William of Roquebert, the bishop's brother, whom he describes as 'a most tenacious persecutor of the Church', holding him responsible for the murder of a party of unarmed Cistercians from the abbey of Eaunes (between Toulouse and Foix) in late 1209.[43] The castle was eventually abandoned on 22 November 1210, after an outbreak of dysentery, and Raymond was among those captured while trying to flee. This had an immediate effect on the Cathars of the region since, according to William of Tudela, 'When it was known that Termes had fallen, all the strongest castles were abandoned, and Le Bézu [between Coustaussa and Puivert] was taken, without any need for sieges.'[44] In 1213, Termes, together with Montréal and Bram the

---

40    See above, ch. 2, pp.36–7. See, too, G. Langlois, 'La Formation de la seigneurie de Termes', *Heresis* 17 (1991), pp.51–72.

41    PVC, vol. 1, paras 171–90, pp.173–93; trans. Sibly, pp.91–100, and *Chanson*, vol. 1, laisses 56–7, pp.132–41; trans. Sibly, pp.36–7, for accounts of the siege.

42    PVC, vol. 1, para. 185, pp.187–9; trans. Sibly, p.98. On Benedict of Termes, see Duvernoy, WP, p.50, n.3.

43    PVC, vol. 1, para. 130, pp.134–6; trans. Sibly, pp.71–2.

44    *Chanson*, vol. 1, laisse 58, pp.140–1; trans. Shirley, p.57.

following year, was granted to Alan of Roucy, a vassal of the count of Champagne, who joined the crusade in 1211.[45]

However, Raymond's sons, Oliver and Bernard, had regained their father's lordship by 1220 or 1221, apparently as a consequence of Alan of Roucy's death while fighting at Montréal.[46] Thereafter, the vicissitudes of Oliver's long career, which lasted until his death in Outremer in 1275, are a good reflection of the shifting politics and changing military fortunes of the people of Languedoc.[47] Under pressure from Capetian power in 1219 and 1228, he and his brother submitted to the king's marshal, Guy of Lévis. Between these dates Oliver had supported first Raymond Trencavel and then, when Trencavel had been forced to leave Carcassonne in 1226, he had joined Raymond VII. It was on the count's behalf that he had helped in the unsuccessful defence of the fortress of Labécède in the Lauragais just to the north of Castelnaudary in 1227. Here again there were important Cathars: the deacon, Gerard of Lamothe, was burnt to death after the fall of the fortress to Humbert of Beaujeu. It had a history of heretical association since a former lord, Pagan of Labécède, had been a *perfectus*.[48] This miscalculation cost Oliver Termes itself, as well as a promise that he and Bernard 'would always remain *fideles* to the lord king of the French and his heirs'. In fact he no more remained faithful than he had in 1219. Although he no longer held Termes, he retained lands and influence in the Corbières where, together with a *faidit* lord, Chabert of Barbéra, he held the castle of Quéribus, perched on a mountain-top 729 metres above sea level in a situation not dissimilar to that of Montségur. Here they provided a refuge for Benedict of Termes, who probably died there in about 1241, as well as other Cathar deacons and *perfecti* who fled there, especially in the early 1240s.[49] Moreover, together with another of the Pyrenean lords, Gerald of Niort, he took an active role in the prolonged and sometimes violent opposition to the inquisitional activities of Friar Ferrier in the *bourg* of Narbonne between 1234 and 1237.[50] Most serious of all, he played a leading part in both the Trencavel revolt of 1240 and that of Raymond VII in 1242. The price of the first was the loss of another of his fortresses, that of Aguilar, a short distance to the north-east of Quéribus, while the second

---

45   PVC, vol. 1, para. 279, pp.274–5 and n.1; trans. Sibly, pp.139–40, n.58.

46   *HGL*, vol. 8, no. 269, p.877, for the act of submission which refers to their cession of the lands in 1228. WP, pp.110–11, gives 1220/21.

47   See A. Peal, 'Olivier de Termes and the Occitan nobility', *Reading Medieval Studies* 12 (1986), pp.109–29.

48   WP, pp.124–7.

49   See below, p.166.

50   See R. W. Emery, *Heresy and Inquisition in Narbonne* (New York, 1941), pp.77–101; Wakefield, *Heresy, Crusade and Inquisition*, pp.143–6; Peal, 'Olivier de Termes', pp.116–17.

**Plate 9**
The castle of Peyrepertuse from the west

**Plate 10**
Peyrepertuse from the north

**Plate 11**
The chapel at Peyrepertuse

led to his excommunication. After 1240 Capetian power was able to extend itself into the Corbières more effectively than ever before: one of Raymond Trencavel's other leading supporters in the revolt, William of Peyrepertuse, whose castle was about equidistant from Aguilar and Quéribus, also suffered confiscation.[51]

Oliver of Termes had broken oaths to the Crown three times over a period of twenty-two years, he had defended fortresses containing leading Cathar ministers, and he had joined major uprisings against the king. All these efforts had been defeated: Raymond VII submitted in 1243 and Raymond Trencavel in 1247. This time there was no escape and it is therefore not surprising to find that, in 1247, he agreed to join Louis IX's crusade to Egypt, from which he did not return until 1255. This time the king retained his fidelity and, in 1250, he was rewarded with the return of Aguilar and other lands in the Corbières, together with revenues of 250 *livres tournois*.[52] Thereafter, he three times campaigned in Outremer on behalf of the Crown – in 1264, 1267–70, and 1273–75 – and he was with Louis IX in Tunis when the king died on crusade there. As early as 1257 he expressed a wish to be buried at the Cistercian abbey of Fontfroide. Oliver of Termes knew that he would not have had another chance: in the charter by which some of his lands were restored in July 1250, it is stated quite explicitly: 'that if any of them [i.e. members of the family] should be held to be suspect of heresy or commit another enormity, we do not wish any restitution of the aforesaid lands to be made to them'. He may have had to pay in another way as well. It was his ambush and capture of his former co-lord of Quéribus, Chabert of Barbéra, which enabled Peter of Auteuil, Seneschal of Carcassonne, to take over Quéribus and probably its western neighbour, Puylaurens, as well in the winter of 1255–56, in return for Chabert's freedom.[53] After this there were no more independent Pyrenean castles for Cathars driven down from the north to fall back on.

## The Italian connection

By the mid-1240s the Cathars of Languedoc were oppressed from three sides: by the weight of royal military and bureaucratic power, by the loss of their traditional secular supporters, and by the determined and systematic

---

51   *HGL*, vol. 8, nos 333 and 334, cols 1045–6.
52   *HGL*, vol. 8, no. 420, pp.1276–7.
53   See M. Roquebert, *Les Cathares. De la chute de Montségur aux derniers bûchers (1244–1329)* (Paris, 1998), pp.288–92.

prosecutions of the inquisitors. As a result almost all their surviving ministers fled to Lombardy so that neither instruction nor spiritual comfort could be obtained near at hand. In these circumstances recruitment for the next generation was severely impeded. Ties which the violence of Montfort's crusaders had failed to sever were now stretched to breaking-point. However, in contrast to Languedoc, the Cathar Church in Italy, although far from united, had retained its shape. Rainier Sacconi thought that in 1250 there were less than 4,000 perfected heretics in west and east, but that about 2,550 of them were in Italy. This compares with his estimate of about 200 in the Churches of Toulouse, Albi, and Carcassonne, formerly the most active of the western Cathar communities.[54] In Lombardy, despite the inquisitors, the four main Churches of Concorezzo (near Milan), Desenzano (on Lake Garda), Bagnolo (near Mantua), and Vicenza, were still operating.[55] (See Map 5.) Moreover, there appears to have been at least one colony of Cathars in Apulia as well. William of Puylaurens claimed that under Frederick II's son, Manfred, the region was 'a "hood" and a refuge for every kind of infidel and evil-doer', but that this was brought to an end with the defeat and death of Manfred by Charles of Anjou, Louis IX's brother, in 1266.[56] In fact, the Staufen had been notably active in their promulgation of anti-heresy laws, ever since the decrees issued by Frederick II in 1224, which predated the papacy's use of especially designated inquisitors. In 1264 Manfred also acted against the Cathars grouped around Vivent, Cathar Bishop of Toulouse, at the bastide of Guardia-Lombardi, near Naples.[57] It is even possible that some were living in Rome: William Pelhisson describes how, in 1234, the inquiries conducted by Peter Seila and William Arnold in Cahors had caused the flight of Raymond of Broelles, 'an important believer of heretics', to Rome where, he claimed, Raymond had drowned in the River Tiber.[58]

---

54  Rainerius Sacconi, *Summa de Catharis et Pauperibus de Lugduno*, in A. Dondaine, *Un Traité néo-manichéen du XIIIe siècle: Le Liber du duobus principiis, suivi d'un fragment de rituel cathare* (Rome, 1939), p.70; trans. WE, no. 51, p.336.

55  See E. Dupré-Theseider, 'Le Catharisme languedocien et l'Italie', in *CF* 3 (1968), pp.302–3; A. Roach, *The Relationship of the Italian and Southern French Cathars, 1170–1320* (DPhil diss., Wolfson College, Oxford, 1989), pp.129–47.

56  WP, pp.190–1.

57  Doat, vol. 25, ff.140v–143r. See Roach, *Relationship*, pp.185–7, who argues that, in 1264, Manfred was under threat from the papal ally, Charles of Anjou, and therefore did not wish to alienate his orthodox friends by appearing to protect heretics. He sees the fall of Guardia-Lombardi as a great blow to the Languedocian Church in exile, since it appears to have been an attempt to establish a stronghold in Apulia not dissimilar to that of Montségur. There is no doubt that the Cathars had been well-established in southern Italy, as they had provoked a violent outburst against them as long ago as *c.* 1200 by the Calabrian abbot, Joachim of Fiore. See C. Thouzellier, *Catharisme et Valdéisme en Languedoc à la fin du XIIe siècle et au début du XIIIe siècle*, 2nd edn (Louvain and Paris, 1969), pp.114–17.

58  Pelhisson, pp.56–7; trans. Wakefield, p.214.

Nevertheless, Lombardy remained the most active Cathar area in western Christendom in the mid-thirteenth century and therefore the main place of refuge. References in William Pelhisson's account show that, from 1234 at least, the threat of the inquisitors had already caused targeted individuals in Toulouse and Moissac to escape to Italy, while Bertrand Marty, the Cathar Bishop of Toulouse who was executed after the fall of Montségur in 1244, had previously been offered a haven at Cremona by the Cathar bishop there.[59] Bertrand Marty may have preferred to risk martyrdom rather than abandon his responsibilities, but the fall of Montségur in 1244 and Quéribus in 1255 left no alternative but to look elsewhere if any kind of hierarchy were to be maintained. Both Bernard Oliba, Cathar Bishop of Toulouse, and Aymeric of Collet, Cathar Bishop of Albi, are known to have been in Lombardy in 1272–73. Bernard Oliba had been at Sirmione, on the southern shore of Lake Garda, since at least 1255. By this time Sirmione, which was part of the Church of Bagnolo, had become a major Cathar centre. In 1255, apart from Bernard Oliba, a witness had seen William Peter of Verona, Bishop of France, and Henry, described rather vaguely as 'Bishop of the Heretics of Lombardy'.[60] Money was collected among the believers in Languedoc to help maintain this Church in exile.[61]

Believers visited the bishops and 'the good men' on a regular basis. Some, like Peter of Bauville and Bernard of Quidiers, had been directly involved in the Avignonet massacre, and when the inquisitional effort did not collapse as they appear to have hoped, had to flee at once. Peter of Bauville went first to Clermont and then to Lagny in Champagne before travelling to Cúneo in the Alpine foothills in western Lombardy. In an exile which lasted until 1277, he lived and worked at Cúneo, Pavia, Piacenza, and Cremona, as well as visiting many other cities, including Alessandria, Genoa, and Milan.[62] Peter of Bauville's departure had been hasty and unplanned, but others saved up for visits to 'the good men', to see relatives, or to transact business.[63] Traffic was great enough to provide a full-time living for men like

---

59   Pelhisson, pp.50–1, 58–9; trans. Wakefield, pp.212, 214; J. J. I. von Doellinger, *Beiträge zur Sektengeschichte des Mittelalters*, vol. 2 (Munich, 1890), pp.34–5, for the contact with Cremona. See also Roach, *Relationship*, pp.139–44, who points out that there was no known Cathar 'bishop of Cremona' and suggests that this offer probably came from Languedocian exiles rather than from Cathars of the Italian Church.

60   Doat, vol. 25, ff.5r–5v, 244v–246v; vol. 26, ff.15r–15v.

61   Doat, vol. 25, ff.71v–72v, 264v, 311r–311v. Dupré-Theseider, 'Le Catharisme languedocien et l'Italie', p.310, believes that they had a proper treasury.

62   Doat, vol. 25, ff.308r–313r. See J. Guiraud, *Histoire de l'Inquisition au moyen âge*, vol. 2 (Paris, 1938), pp.247–8, 253–9, and G. Boffito, 'Gli Eretici di Cuneo', *Bullettino Storico-Bibliografico Subalpino* 1 (1985), pp.329–32.

63   For example, William Rafford of Roquevidal, Doat, vol. 26, ff.15r–15v.

Peter Maurel, who acted as a guide, called a *nuntius* or *ductor* in inquisitional documents. Peter Maurel was sufficiently skilled and discreet to have survived in this hazardous occupation for at least nineteen years between 1255 and 1274, when he was finally caught by the inquisitors.[64] Although the existence of such persons was known to the inquisitors from an early date – William Pelhisson, for example, knew that Peitavin Boursier had, even in 1234, 'for a long time been something of a general courier for the heretics in Toulouse' and that he was 'a messenger and agent of heretics'[65] – they developed a structure of sufficient strength as to make them difficult to catch. Peter Maurel, for instance, utilised 'safe houses' in both Languedoc and Lombardy, in the latter case making use of a family network based upon his brothers. The most frequent route appears to have been along the Via Domitia, the old Roman road which linked Narbonne, Béziers, Montpellier, and Nîmes across Bas Languedoc. Travellers from Toulouse and Carcassonne could join it at Narbonne and those from Cahors at Béziers. The Rhône was crossed by ferry from Beaucaire and from there they went over the Alps to Cúneo, from which they could reach all the important northern Italian cities, as well as the smaller towns which the Cathar hierarchy seems to have preferred.[66]

This was, of course, only a makeshift solution to the problems faced by the Cathars of Languedoc. The journeys were risky in themselves, while those exiles who returned to see their families or conduct business were often arrested, since the inquisitors had created an environment in which no one could regard themselves as 'safe' once their presence was known to anyone. In 1274 the career of Peter Maurel ended in this way, causing panic among the many known to him.[67] Indeed, it is possible that by the 1270s the Cathar Church was being squeezed at both ends, for in November 1276 the members of the heretic community at Sirmione were seized, and in February 1278 'about 200' were burnt at Verona, which must have dealt a huge blow to the Toulousan Church based there.[68] Moreover, the inquisitors

---

64  Doat, vol. 25, ff.18r–19v.
65  Pelhisson, pp.60–3; trans. Wakefield, pp.215–16.
66  See P. A. Clément, *Les chemins à travers les âges en Cevennes et Bas Languedoc* (Montpellier, 1984), esp. pp.89–91, 112–13, 130–6, 172–6, 189, 213–24, and Y. Renouard, 'Les Voies de communication entre la France et le Piémont au moyen âge', *Bullettino Storico-Bibliografico Subalpino* 61 (1963), pp.233–56.
67  Doat, vol. 25, ff.122v–123v.
68  See Dupré-Theseider, 'Le Catharisme languedocien et l'Italie', p.303, and Roach, *Relationship*, pp.218–19. Roach attributes this coup to the desire of Mastino della Scala, *capitano del popolo* at Verona since 1262, to gain favour with the papacy, which had laid an interdict on the city in 1267.

had been operating in Italy as long as they had been in Languedoc, although the effects had been mitigated by the presence of urban governments more powerful than the consuls of Toulouse, which were jealous of their juris-dictional rights.[69] A measure of the perceived threat among the Cathars can be seen by the murder of the inquisitor Peter of Verona and his compan-ion Dominic while travelling from Cúneo to Milan on 6 April 1252, victims of a conspiracy planned and financed in several Lombard cities, including Milan, Cúneo, Lodi, Bergamo, and Pavia. Like William Arnold, Peter of Verona had drawn attention to himself because of his exceptionally energetic pursuit of heretics, which he combined with a talent for publicity. Peter of Verona's own parents were allegedly Cathars, but he himself became a Dominican in the convent of St Eustorge in Milan; by the early 1230s he was already well-known as a public preacher and debater with heretics. He was inquisitor in Milan from 1234 and in Florence between 1244 and 1246, where he converted the former Cathar, Rainier Sacconi, who himself became an inquisitor. In 1234 in Milan and ten years later in Florence he was responsible for founding orthodox militias to fight heresy, thus encour-aging popular participation. The idea was taken up in other cities. In 1251 he was commissioned to operate across all of northern Italy from Genoa to Venice. The plot was also aimed at Rainier Sacconi, working then at Pavia, but it failed.[70] The Dominican Order duly received its reward for its first martyr, when Peter was canonised in 1253. By the late 1250s he had already reached legendary status, included in James of Voragine's *Golden Legend*, where he is described as 'a radiant light in a cloud of smoke', and his miracles are described in detail. The explanation for his murder, how-ever, may well lie beneath the hagiography. According to *The Golden Legend* the heretics in Milan were very numerous, occupying positions of power where they 'made effective use of their fraudulent eloquence and devilish knowledge', but when Peter of Verona arrived he gave them 'neither rest nor quarter'.[71]

---

69  Dupré-Theseider, 'Le Catharisme languedocien et l'Italie', p.306. For example, the regime of Oberto Pelavicino, an ally of the Emperor Frederick II, who dominated Cremona and Piacenza between 1250 and 1266. His opposition to the inquisitors meant that they could not operate in these cities during this period, see Roach, *Relationship*, pp.163–6. Imperial anti-heresy laws were less effective than diligent inquisitors and therefore the Cathars, both Italian and southern French, tended to survive best in cities with Ghibelline (anti-papal) sympathies.

70  On his career, see A. Dondaine, 'Saint Pierre Martyr', *Archivum Fratrum Praedicatorum* 23 (1953), pp.66–162.

71  Jacobus de Voragine, *The Golden Legend. Readings on the Saints*, trans. W. G. Ryan, vol. 1 (Princeton, NJ, 1993), pp.254–66.

# The operation of the Inquisition

The demeanour of the inquisitors in Languedoc during the 1240s suggests an increasing confidence that they were winning the battle with heresy. Most of the evidence indicates that they were correct, although sporadic acts of violence still occurred: late in 1247, for example, a clerk and a courier working for the inquisitors at Carcassonne were murdered at Caunes, near Narbonne, and significantly, the register they were carrying was burned.[72] During this period inquisitors were based in the two cities of Toulouse and Carcassonne. Those operating from Toulouse also took in part of Quercy and the Agenais, while the Carcassonne inquisition covered most of the province of Narbonne except for the diocese of Toulouse. The dioceses of Albi and Rodez appear to have been divided between them.[73] Both tribunals were backed by secular power, although perhaps with varying degrees of enthusiasm. In Toulouse, Raymond VII, despite a continuing feud with the Dominicans, saw little alternative after 1242 but to co-operate with the Church, and at Béziers in April 1243 took an oath to this effect, while in Carcassonne the inquisitors could call upon royal officials established there by a resolute monarchy.

An idea of how this operated in practice can be gained from Walter Wakefield's study of the two surviving registers of the inquisition carried out by Bernard of Caux and John of St Pierre in Toulouse in 1245–46.[74] He shows how this affected one village, Mas-Saintes-Puelles in the Lauragais just to the west of Castelnaudary, where 420 persons deposed, which was probably about two-thirds of the inhabitants. This is more than any other place in the surviving records of this inquiry, but then, as the depositions show, this had been a village where, since at least 1180, heresy had been accepted by most people as part of everyday life. Moreover, a substantial minority had been fully committed to it, handing the beliefs on to their children, and marrying within a defined group. The scale of the summonses in 1245–46 may have been because the authorities already knew this to have been the case, for seventy-five of the witnesses said that they had already confessed to other inquisitors in the past, reflecting the fact that investigations had been made and confessions gained on several occasions going back to 1209. In fact, as Wakefield points out, the two inquisitors did not

---

72 Dossat, *Les Crises*, p.169.
73 Ibid., p.152.
74 W. L. Wakefield, 'Heretics and inquisitors: the case of Le Mas-Saintes-Puelles', *Catholic Historical Review* 69 (1983), pp.209–26, based on *Ms. 609*.

follow up potential lines of inquiry as rigorously as might be expected. This is not surprising given the sheer scale of the inquiry overall, since even the two surviving registers encompass over 5,500 persons from 104 different places, and it is known that there were once ten registers.[75] Nevertheless, the inquisitors seem to have secured at least an outward acquiescence to orthodoxy thereafter which, in this case at least, suggests that the circumstances undermining Catharism across the region as a whole were crucial in creating a context in which inquisitors could operate effectively.

Examples taken from the sentences issued by these two inquisitors between March 1246 and June 1248, following this inquiry, show how they applied what they had learned.[76] On 24 June 1246, they took measures to prevent what they evidently saw as heretical infection within the convent of Lespinasse of the Order of Fontevrault, where Joanna, widow of Bernard of Latour, who had probably been a *consul* in Toulouse, was living as nun. This was not itself any protection from inquisitorial sentence.

> Since Joanna . . . saw and adored many heretics and heard their preaching in many places, received them many times, gave them things from their own property, believed them to be good men, gave alms to Waldensians, and denied the truth against her own oath, she is to be enclosed within the precincts of the monastery of Lespinasse in another separate room, so that others cannot gain access to her nor she to them; but necessities are to be administered to her from the outside; and we order the prioress of Lespinasse to make provision for her in accordance with the aforesaid manner.[77]

If even entry into the Order of Fontevrault did not enable a former believer to evade the eye of the inquisitors, there was little likelihood that other widows who admitted that they believed the heretics to be 'good men' could avoid a sentence of perpetual prison. A list of seven people condemned at Toulouse on 18 August 1247, for instance, included Berengaria, widow of Assalit of Monts, who 'had given a legacy of a certain *perfecta* to

---

75   Ibid., p.209; C. Douais, ed., *Documents pour servir à l'histoire de l'Inquisition dans le Languedoc* (Société de l'histoire de France), vol. 2 (Paris, 1900), p.ccxlviii. Moreover, as J. H. Mundy, 'Village, town and city in the region of Toulouse', in J. Raftis, ed., *Pathways to Medieval Peasants* (Toronto, 1981), p.156, shows, such villages were no longer served by compliant or timid priests, for the parish system had been comprehensively overhauled. For a thorough analysis of *Ms. 609*, see M. G. Pegg, *The Corruption of Angels: Inquisitors and Heretics in Thirteenth-Century Europe* (Ph.D diss., Princeton University, NJ, 1997).

76   Douais, ed., *Documents pour servir*, vol. 2, pp.1–89. All the sentences are within this period, except for one anomaly, no. XVI, which seems to have been given at Cahors on 26 August 1244. Neither place nor date are consistent with the rest of the register.

77   Ibid., p.cclxi and no. XI, p.31.

the heretics', and Marin, widow of Hugh, 'who sought to buy cloth in which a certain dead heretic could be buried'.[78] In these circumstances flight was the only alternative, a course followed by William Garnier, a doctor from Mas-Saintes-Puelles, who was excommunicated on 16 February 1248, having been condemned for seeing and 'adoring' heretics and bringing them food.[79] These sentences represent only a fraction of the total handed out, yet they show that 190 people were condemned, not only for their belief in Catharism and their respect for the 'good men', but also for the help they gave in the form of food, shelter, clothing, and money. Each time these tribunals completed their work they cut off more possible sources of sustenance for the ministers of the Cathar Church.

The same process was taking place in the Carcassès, where the register of the *greffier* or clerk of the inquisitors at Carcassonne recorded sentences and depositions of tribunals operating over a seventeen-year period from 1250 to 1267. It is possible to reconstruct from these records something of the life of a Cathar perfect, Bernard Acier, who, from at least 1241 down to his arrest in 1259, attempted to keep the Cathar faith alive in a small part of the Razès just to the south of Carcassonne (see Map 6). Bernard Acier came from the village of Couffoulens on the right bank of the Aude River about seven kilometres from Carcassonne. He appears to have been careful to have stayed within a quite specific area: there is no record of him further east than Rieux-en-Val or further west than Belvèze-du-Razès, a distance of only about forty kilometres, while the most southerly place he was seen in was Limoux, about fifteen kilometres from his home village. Within this rather narrow band of territory he knew he could find places to stay, food and clothing, and guides whom he could trust. The inquisitors had made it dangerous to venture further afield or to stay too long in one place. Even then, although he was on home ground, he often seems to have been very uncertain of the situation, which suggests a man forced to react to events rather than initiating them. In October 1254, Bernard Acier was at Belvèze, from which he sent a message to a believer called William Sicred, a near neighbour of his at Cavanac, only about two kilometres from Couffoulens. William therefore went to Belvèze, where he found Bernard Acier and his companion. Bernard then asked him 'about the state of the land and of the believers of heretics', apparently because the itinerant and clandestine life he had been forced to follow had given him little opportunity to assess the general condition of the Cathar Church even in this relatively small region.

---

78  Ibid., no. XVIII, pp.44–5.
79  Ibid., no. XXXVII, pp.74–5.

William Sicred and other witnesses show that, over an eighteen-year period, Bernard Acier, as well as other *perfecti*, had moved from one hiding-place to another, sometimes finding shelter in houses, but also in cellars, sheds and barns, often meeting sympathisers at night in a local wood or vineyard before being taken to the next place. Where possible Bernard Acier performed the spiritual functions of his office at small gatherings of believers or, on one occasion, at Limoux in 1257, he was called in by a man whose wife was dying, apparently to administer the *consolamentum*. However, these activities were done very much on an individual basis, for there was little left of the organisational structure of the Cathar Church. Bernard Acier did sometimes travel in a party of as many as half a dozen *perfecti*, but they did not form a consistent or coherent group, while the only reference to Peter Pollan, Cathar Bishop of the Razès, in October 1258, was when a *perfectus* called Bernard of Montolieu (a village just to the north of Carcassonne) told William Sicred that the bishop had secretly left them and 'absconded with all the money and all the treasure'. In fact, after some searching on a mountain above a wood near La Bezole, about ten kilometres south-west of Limoux, William Sicred found three bottles buried in the ground containing various sums of money which, a couple of days later, he gave to Bernard of Montolieu and Bernard Acier. Eventually, Bernard Acier seems to have decided he could carry on no longer in this manner and, together with another perfect, Peter of *Camia*, met William Sicred at Corrèze, another village on the Aude about three kilometres upstream from Couffoulens, and proposed that he went with them to Lombardy. William, though, told them that he could not go as he did not have any money ready. Bernard Acier himself never reached Lombardy. This discussion took place about the middle of Lent in 1258; within the year he had been captured and taken to Carcassonne. There he had been converted and made confessions which implicated others, including William Sicred. With some of the others, William therefore left for Rocamadour 'to visit the church and oratory of the Blessed Virgin Mary', which may possibly have been a belated attempt to undertake a penitential pilgrimage he had promised when previously questioned by inquisitors in 1250. However, by October 1259, William Sicred too was in the hands of the inquisitors.[80]

The profound change in the milieu of the Cathar Church in the mountains south of Carcassonne offers in microcosm a view of what had happened in the wider world. In the early thirteenth century this region had been

---

80   Ibid., pp.255, 256, 264, 265, 272, 277, 279–85. See also Griffe, *Le Languedoc Cathare et l'Inquisition*, pp.110–14, who suggests that the flight to Rocamadour might have been an unfulfilled pilgrimage.

dominated by powerful Trencavel vassals such as the lords of Termes, of Fanjeaux, and of Montréal. Such men allowed Cathar ministers to travel openly in their territories, welcomed them in their *castra*, listened to their preaching, and even permitted family members to become *perfecti* or *perfectae*. By the 1250s all that had been swept away: a *perfectus* like Bernard Acier lived in a state of constant insecurity and fear, unable to rely on either the local nobility or the Cathar hierarchy. Catharism had been driven down the social scale, leaving few noble supporters, while most of its ministers had been captured or had fled to Lombardy. Bernard Acier, even if he had had the capability, was in no position to study the literature of his faith or to convey such learning to others; instead, he functioned only in small and unco-ordinated gatherings of believers or in meetings with individuals.[81] The history of the inquisitors in Languedoc during their first twenty-five years was not, it is true, an unqualified success; violent attacks on inquisitors on the one hand and periodic suspensions of activity on the other, highlight the problems. Nevertheless, the inquisitional machinery functioned well enough and often enough to make successful resistance ever more difficult. Again, the case of Bernard Acier is instructive. When the *perfectus* was captured, William Sicred had rushed to Carcassonne to try to find out what he had said. Here he was told by another Cathar believer, Vital of *Paulmiano*, that Bernard Acier had already told the inquisitors about him [Vital] and that 'he presumed that, if he had not yet spoken about this witness [William Sicred], he would do so now and would expose this witness and his doings; and he advised him to flee and go away from this land'.[82]

At the same time as the Cathar Church was trying and largely failing to maintain a coherent structure and ideology, the forces of orthodoxy were rapidly gaining strength. Although the structure of the Italian city-states was less favourable to the Catholic Church than the political and religious settlement imposed on Languedoc in 1229, nevertheless even in Italy there is a noticeable inquisitorial drive, backed by powerful refutations of Cathar belief. Sometimes the two were combined in the person of impressive individuals like the former Cathar Rainier Sacconi or the professor of theology, Moneta of Cremona. Even the murder of a leading inquisitor like Peter of Verona could be turned to advantage: Peter 'the Martyr' was rapidly

---

81   See R. Abels and E. Harrison, 'The participation of women in Languedocian Catharism', *Medieval Studies* 41 (1979), pp.238–540, for the steep decline in the numbers of both *perfecti* and *perfectae* in the 1240s and 1250s. The itinerant life made *perfectae* particularly conspicuous and they were frequently captured. See A. Borst, *Die Katharer* (Schriften der Monumenta Germaniae historica) (Stuttgart, 1953), pp.211–12, for the decline in the numbers of deacons.

82   Douais, ed., *Documents pour servir*, vol. 2, no. XXXII, p.284.

promoted to cult status as a symbol of good struck down by evil. More mundanely, the Catholic Church in Languedoc, so often despised and impotent before 1209, was now heavily patronized by a king who regarded Simon of Montfort as a hero of the faith, and benefited both from royal generosity and the restoration of its tithes.[83] The most obvious effects were seen in the cities and towns, particularly those with episcopal seats, where confident bishops took a role in inquisitorial proceedings beside the specialists from the preaching orders.[84] However, rural areas were also affected, particularly by the enactment of synodal statutes from the mid-thirteenth century onwards. Such statutes reflect prescriptions laid down at the Fourth Lateran Council in 1215 and are part of a general trend of French episcopal legislation since that time. They aimed to set standards both for the clergy and for the practice of the faith throughout the diocese, not only through ordinance but by visitation and the calling of clerical assemblies as well.[85] These changes took place in a surprisingly favourable economic climate. In his study of charitable provision in Toulouse in the twelfth and thirteenth centuries, John Mundy has shown that recovery from the Albigensian wars was remarkably rapid, enabling new charitable institutions to be founded and sustained between 1230 and 1250.[86]

It is often the case that economic prosperity does much to reconcile the populace to a new regime. Louis IX reinforced this by a shrewd series of restitutions, particularly between 1259 and 1262,[87] as well as rehabilitations of nobles like Oliver of Termes. Although he continued to complain about the Dominicans, Raymond VII's resistance effectively ended after 1242; when he died in 1249 the whole region fell to Alphonse of Poitiers, obliterating the ambivalence of the house of Toulouse. Alphonse was a zealous promoter of orthodoxy whose opposition to pecuniary substitutions for inquisitorial penalties manifested itself in the much greater provision of prisons. His officials followed this up with a rigorous enforcement of

---

83   See Griffe, *Le Languedoc Cathare et l'Inquisition*, pp.123–5, and Delaruelle, 'Saint Louis', pp.275–6.

84   The *greffier*'s register of 1250–67 (above, n.76), for example, records not only the work of the Dominicans and Franciscans, but also that of two successive bishops of Carcassonne as well.

85   See, for example, J. Avril, ed., *Les Statuts Synodales Français du XIIIe siècle*, vol. 4, *Les Statuts Synodaux de l'Ancienne Province de Reims (Cambrai, Arras, Noyon, Soissons et Tournai)* (Collection de Documents inédits sur l'histoire de France, Section d'Histoire Médiévale et de Philologie, vol. 23) (Paris, 1995).

86   J. H. Mundy, 'Charity and social work in Toulouse, 1100–1250', *Traditio* 22 (1966), esp. p.236. This view of the post-crusade economy of Languedoc is confirmed by P. Wolff, 'Rôle de l'essor économique dans les ralliement social et religieux', in *CF* 20 (1985), pp.243–55.

87   See Griffe, *Le Languedoc Cathare et l'Inquisition*, p.123.

the confiscations of the property of convicted heretics.[88] Moreover, the accession of the new government of Alphonse of Poitiers coincided with the concession of greater freedom of action to the inquisitors, after a period when they had withdrawn their co-operation in 1248 and 1249. This had been a protest against what they considered to be Pope Innocent IV's leniency towards convicted heretics and it had been maintained until 1254 when the new pope, Alexander IV, had acceded to their demands. Most significantly, in 1256, they were even granted permission to absolve each other from irregular actions in canon law.[89] In fifty years the environment had been transformed, changing the Cathars first from reformers to *maquisards*, and then from *maquisards* to fugitives.

---

88   Douais, ed., *Documents pour servir*, vol. 1, pp.ccxiii–ccxix, on the policy of Alphonse of Poitiers.
89   See Dossat, *Les Crises*, pp.175–88.

# CHAPTER SIX

## The Last Cathars

### The Autier revival

Bertrand of Taix was a knight from Pamiers in the *pays de* Foix. He was probably born around 1250 into a heretical family, for his father, Isarn, had been condemned as a contumacious heretic, possibly as long ago as 1236, while his mother, Ava, had been sentenced to wear penitential crosses for heresy. Bertrand himself died an unrepentant heretic, still believing in 'the errors of the Manichaeans'. In about 1300 Bertrand boasted to his maidservant, Margarita, that, when he was young, he had acted as a guide for heretics, frequently leading them to 'diverse places'. Such was his reputation that Roger Bernard III, Count of Foix, had once warned him that he might lose his lands as a consequence, but Bertrand had replied that 'he was not afraid of this, as long as his mother, whose lands they were, was alive'.

However, by the time he told Margarita this story, he had lost most of this insouciance. In 1272 he had been cited to appear before the inquisitor, William Raymond, operating from Carcassonne, but sitting then at Varilhes, about half-way between Pamiers and Foix. He had made a confession which had been recorded by the notary, and presumably had undergone some type of penance. By 1300 he was married to Hugeta, a woman who did not share his beliefs and in whom he could not therefore confide, and lacking other like-minded cronies in Pamiers itself, he felt isolated and depressed. The marriage to Hugeta was his second. Six years before, in 1294, his first wife, Flors, had reproached him for speaking favourably of the 'good men', blaming the downfall and destruction of many people in the region on their support for the heretics. He had hoped for better from Hugeta, so she must have been a particular disappointment to him, for this was an arranged marriage which appears to have been made on the basis of mistaken identity. Bertrand was willing to tell anyone whom he thought might be sympathetic that he had thought she was the daughter of Poncius Esshaura of Larnat (apparently a family of known Cathar persuasion), whereas she turned out to be the daughter of En Esshaura of Larcat. The close proximity of these two mountain villages – they are about three kilometres apart as the crow flies – and the similarity of the names might explain his error. Around 1301 he broke down in tears when he was explaining this to Blanca, wife of his nephew, William of Rodes, and one of Poncius's daughters. She does not seem to have indulged him though, telling him that, in fact, all her sisters were married, except for one who had become a nun. His regret was compounded by the disappearance of Cathar society in the town, for which he may have hoped his new marriage would have compensated. In 1294 he had complained to a young relative of his, William Bernard of Luzenac, a village farther up the Ariège Valley, that such were the times that there was only one man, Peter Soquerii, in the whole of Pamiers with whom he could discuss the faith. Yet, he went on, in the past, 'he was able to speak with many nobles of these parts, believers of the good men, as he wished'. Sometime before 1301 he had been able to talk to a woman from Foix, then living in Pamiers, but she had been discovered and her house burnt down as a convicted heretic.

By the early years of the fourteenth century therefore the once bold *ductor* of heretics was reduced to crabby complaints about his wife and his neighbours. He was well-known locally for his anti-clericalism; once reproached by Bonet Davy, the father of John Davy, a burgess of Pamiers, for his language, he had replied bitterly that he [Bonet] had been responsible for destroying the town by introducing the Dominicans there. According to William Bernard, when Bernard Saisset, the first Bishop of Pamiers, had asked him whom he hated, the clergy or the French, he had replied that 'he hated clerics more, since the clerics had introduced the French into these parts, and if there were no clergy, there would never have been any French in these parts'. Bernard Saisset himself was notoriously outspoken about the French and particularly insulting about the king, Philip IV, a characteristic which led to his arrest by royal officials in October 1301, and which subsequently blew up into a major quarrel between the king and Pope Boniface VIII. Nevertheless, Saisset was sent to Rome in February 1302, and, if local memory was accurate, back officiating in the Church of St Antonin at Pamiers by 1304. During a mass conducted by Bernard Saisset on one of the feast days of that year, William Saisset, the bishop's brother, recited a *cobla* or poem to Bertrand of Taix which so pleased him that he learned it by heart himself. It was based on a poem by the troubadour Peire Cardenal and, a couple of years later, Bertrand passed it on to his nephew, William

Bernard. The main theme of the *cobla* was the hypocrisy of a clergy who passed themselves off as pastors when they were in fact murderers.

Only one piece of news heartened Bertrand of Taix. In 1298 or 1299, Peter and William Autier, from Ax, a small town in the Sabarthès situated about sixty kilometres upstream from Pamiers, returned to the region from Lombardy. There, for the previous three or four years, they had been taking instruction in the Cathar faith and had finally received the *consolamentum*. The presence of two active *bonhommes* in an area recently devoid of any Cathar ministers was a great encouragement to Bertrand, who arranged for a consignment of wine to be carried to them, and who frequently spoke of going to Ax to see them himself, using the story that he was going to take the waters as a cover, for the town had been famous for its thermal springs since Roman times. One indirect contact he had was through Peter Autier's illegitimate daughter, Guillelma, whom he first met in *c.* 1301, when she was still a young girl. At that time she had come to Pamiers with Bartholomew Barravi of Tarascon to buy linen thread for Raymunda of Tarascon, Peter Autier's sister, who had brought her up, and she had been waiting in the kitchen of Bertrand's home while Bartholomew had sought out a sumpter animal to carry the purchases back up the valley. According to Guillelma, when Bertrand was told who she was, 'placing a hand on her head he said that, since she was the daughter of Peter Autier, he loved her very much, since Peter Autier was a good man and accustomed to provide good hospitality'. About three years later, Guillelma, together with her new husband, William Carramati, a tailor from Tarascon, again visited Bertrand. William was Bertrand's nephew, the son of his late brother, Isarn, and Bertrand tried hard to persuade them to settle in Pamiers, even offering them a house if they would do so. Then, he said, he would be able to involve himself properly in Cathar affairs, including those of her father, 'whom he had not been able to see since his return to the land, although he had many times tried to see him'. It does not appear that the offer was taken up. When Guillelma told Raymond of Rodes and Blanca, the wife of William of Rodes, after his return to Tarascon, they said that 'she should not speak of this, since if she did, evil would befall her'. Here, indeed, was the nub of Bertrand of Taix's continuing resentment. 'The faith of Peter and William Autier is good', he had told William of Rodes in 1300, but 'they were sustaining many evils and dangers on God's behalf, nor did they dare go about openly, since the Church was persecuting them, as a result of which it was committing a great sin'.[1]

---

1  *RF*, vol. 3, pp.312–30, for the depositions against Bertrand of Taix; Pelhisson, pp.106–7; trans. Wakefield, p.225, for Isarn of Taix (condemned 1236). See the commentary by E. Griffe, *Le Languedoc Cathare et l'Inquisition (1229–1329)* (Paris, 1980), pp.172–6.

Bertrand of Taix was a minor urban noble who was a lifelong Cathar believer. He was not always as discreet as he should have been but, from the 1270s until his death sometime after 1306, he offered no real threat to orthodoxy. He was mainly occupied with ineffective grumbling about the potential treachery of his wife and the malice of the clergy. He was unable to play an active role in the Cathar Church and, indeed, for all his anti-clericalism, he actually continued to go to church. However, further up the Ariège Valley, the Autier brothers had decided that they could no longer remain passive, that their souls were in danger, and that they must act both for themselves and for others. In most other ways they were quite similar to Bertrand. Neither was young for they were Bertrand's con-temporaries, and they came from a heretical background, for two of their forebears, Peter and his son, Raymond, had been identified as Cathars as long ago as 1234. Both were quite prominent socially, since the Autier brothers were successful notaries, while Bertrand appears to have lived off his revenues. Both were known to Roger Bernard, Count of Foix. All three men had families; in Peter's case more than one, since he had a mistress and illegitimate children as well.[2] Neither, however, was in a position to provide extensive patronage for the Cathar Church so, as the contrasting careers of Bertrand of Taix and Peter Autier show very clearly, Cathar-ism in Languedoc in the early fourteenth century was entirely dependent upon the character and actions of a quite limited number of individuals. By chance rather than by design, when the Autiers began their ministry in about 1299, circumstances were temporarily favourable for such an initiative. Bernard Saisset was more concerned with his hatred of the French than he was with pursuing Cathars. Roger Bernard, despite an outward appearance of orthodoxy, was evidently a secret sympathiser, since he was hereticated on his death-bed at Tarascon by Peter Autier in 1302.[3] Both Geoffrey of Ablis, Inquisitor in Carcassonne from c. 1303, and Bernard Gui, appointed to the Toulousain in 1307, were well-aware of the role of such individuals; it was their determination to eliminate the group assembled

---

2  *RF*, vol. 1, p.217 (notaries); vol. 2, p.403 (wives and sons); J.J. I. von Doellinger, *Beiträge zur Sektengeschichte des Mittelalters*, vol. 2 (Munich, 1890), p.24 (mistress); Doat, vol. 24, f.209v (for heretical ancestors). The fundamental research on this was carried out by J.-M. Vidal, 'Les Derniers ministres de l'albigéisme en Languedoc', *Revue des Questions historiques* 79 (1906), pp.57–107. For modern analyses, see J. Duvernoy, *Le Catharisme*, vol. 2, *L'Histoire des Cathares* (Toulouse, 1979), pp.321–33, and M. D. Lambert, *The Cathars* (Oxford, 1998), pp.230–71, and for the Autier family, see A. Pales-Gobilliard, *L'Inquisiteur Geoffrey d'Ablis et les Cathares du Comté de Foix (1308–9)*, texte ed., traduis, et annoté (Paris, 1984), pp.44–8.
3  *RF*, vol. 2, p.427.

by the Autiers, successful by 1312, which broke up the revival the brothers had sustained for a decade. (See Table 3.)

Once they had decided to leave for Lombardy, the Autier brothers made a number of careful arrangements. Peter, for example, went to see his son-in-law and fellow notary, Arnold Textor, at nearby Lordat, as well as selling his cattle in the market at Tarascon. Once they had left, the absence of such public figures from these small communities was certain to be noticed, but the reason remained a matter of speculation and gossip, some believing that they had become leprous, others that they had committed some crime, and some, 'on account of heresy'.[4] In Lombardy they spent time at Cúneo, Asti, and Como, where they finally received the *consolamentum* after a period of study lasting three or four years.[5] Their return was equally discreet. Some family members had accompanied them, but contact had been maintained with other relatives and a close circle of friends in the Sabarthès, some of whom had visited them in Lombardy.[6] William Bonus, Peter Autier's illegitimate son, had preceded them to Ax to check if it was safe and, on their arrival, they had stayed at the house of their brother, Raymond, for about two weeks, before making their presence known to Arnold Textor.[7] These first cautious moves were quite justified for, within a year or so they were nearly captured, escaping only because of their network of relatives and friends. In 1300 they were denounced to the Dominicans at Pamiers by a beguin called William Déjean, who had pretended to be a believer. However, they were alerted by Raymond of Rodes – described as 'a great friend' of Peter and William Autier – who was himself a Dominican at Pamiers. Raymond is described in inquisitorial records as an *explorator* or spy for the heretics so that 'if anything occurred or was done against them at Pamiers or the surrounding area, he would at once notify them or send a messenger to warn them'. In these circumstances help sometimes took the form of deterrence. Although there is no evidence to implicate the Autier family, William Déjean was later beaten up so badly by two believers, Philip of Larnat and Peter of Area, that he could not speak. He was then taken into the mountains above Larnat and thrown off a cliff into a deep ravine where his body would never be found.[8] On another occasion, Arnold Lizier, from Montaillou, an isolated village on the western edge of the plateau between the upper reaches of the Ariège and the Aude, was found dead at the gate

---

4  *RF*, vol. 2, pp.196, 202, 19.
5  Doellinger, *Beiträge zur Sektengeschichte*, vol. 2, p.27.
6  *RF*, vol. 2, p.19. See Vidal, 'Les Derniers ministres', pp.64–6.
7  *RF*, vol. 2, pp.206–8.
8  *RF*, vol. 2, p.423; Pales-Gobilliard, *L'Inquisiteur Geoffrey d'Ablis*, pp.150–5.

of the castle there, apparently as a consequence of a remark by William Autier that if it were not for Arnold Lizier he could appear publicly in the square of Montaillou, so extensive was Cathar support in the village.[9] Not surprisingly the heretics were sometimes very nervous. When, in 1304 or 1305, William Escaunier, of Arques, heard one evening that Peter Autier was staying at the home of William Botolh, his brother-in-law, he determined to visit him. The next morning, he and his mother surprised Peter sitting alone in front of the fire, frying little fish in a pan. When William Escaunier shouted out, 'Who's there?' Peter Autier was so alarmed that he jumped up and was about to run away before Marquesia, William's sister, told him not to be afraid.[10]

It is therefore to be expected that the most intense activity of the Autier group is to be found in their own home territory of the Sabarthès, from which they extended their influence eastwards into the *pays* d'Aillon, the Razès, and the Fenouillèdes, south of Carcassonne. (See Map 7.) These lands are noticeably deeper into the mountains than the country covered by Bernard Acier in the 1250s and, because of their extensive local connections, they were able to create a better support structure and system of communication than Bernard and his supporters had managed. However, they were not confined to these regions for, despite the dangers, Peter Autier's sometimes ambitious itinerary took him north along the Ariège Valley to Toulouse (where the Cathars had a permanent presence in a house in the rue de l'Etoile), and to many of the former centres of heresy east of the city in the Lauragais and in the valleys of the Agout and the Tarn. Occasionally, Peter travelled even farther: in 1302 he went to Cahors to hereticate two dying believers and, when he was captured in August 1309, he was hiding on a farm at Beaupuy-en-Lomagne, thirty-six kilometres to the north-west of Toulouse. In all, Vidal identified 125 places where believers could still be found in the early fourteenth century.[11] In addition to Peter Autier himself, who seems to have been regarded as the leader, Vidal found fourteen other *perfecti* or *bonhommes* in this group, including Peter's younger brother, William, and his son, James, whom they hereticated

9 *RF*, vol. 2, p.427 (for the treachery); vol. 2, p.423, n.380 (for the murder); vol. 1, p.296. Arnold Lizier appears to have been killed in 1309, vol. 3, p.63. See also E. Le Roy Ladurie, *Montaillou. Cathars and Catholics in a French Village, 1294–1324*, trans. B. Bray (London, 1978) (originally Paris, 1975), p.267.
10 *RF*, vol. 2, p.13.
11 Vidal, 'Les Derniers ministres', pp.85–6. For the house in Toulouse and the capture in Beaupuy, see A. Brenon, *Les Femmes Cathares* (Paris, 1992), pp.332, 340. For the longevity of Catharism in the Sabarthès, see A. Cazenave, 'Les Cathares en Catalogne et Sabarthès d'après les registres de l'Inquisition: La Hiérarchie cathare en Sabarthès après Montségur', *Bulletin philologique et historique* (1969), pp.387–436.

in 1301. At least eight of these were given the *consolamentum* by the Autiers after their return from Lombardy.[12]

These heretics usually travelled by night or adopted some form of cover, such as pretending to be shepherds or, as James Autier once did, putting on a green surcoat belonging to a believer in order to go into the town square at Arques.[13] Where possible, they used known safe houses. Peter Autier said that they had three 'houses of friends' in Châteauverdun, a village about sixteen kilometres downstream from Ax, while in Montaillou, above Ax on the edge of the Sault Plateau, where the local priest, Peter Clergue, was a secret believer, they could enter his home by removing a post which had been especially loosened for the purpose.[14] Nevertheless, it was an inherently unstable existence for supporters could not always be relied upon. On one occasion, when Peter Autier sent William Bonus to ask Arnold Textor if he could stay on a certain night, Arnold responded with 'Get out, devil! Get out, devil!' As a consequence Peter said that he 'had acted evilly in not receiving him when he was his son-in-law'. The issue was probably personal rather than religious as Peter had complained to Arnold about his harsh treatment of his wife, Guillelma, Peter's daughter.[15] Even with the willing help of believers though, there were short-term problems. On another occasion, when Peter and James Autier were expected at Quié, bedding, wine, and food had to be brought from Tarascon across the other side of the River Ariège, since they were not available where they were intending to stay. Most of the food came from believers. The heretics did not eat 'meat, nor fat, nor anything in which fat or meat was cooked'; believers gave them fish, apples, plums, figs, grapes, nuts, hazel-nuts, bread, oil, and wine. In such a diet fish was particularly important: once it was salted mullet, another time it had been made into a *paté*, on another occasion it was trout and salmon. When they were stranded at Quié, a female believer in Tarascon had sent them two pieces of turbot, a palm in size, which must have been an expensive gift, especially deep in the Pyrenees.[16] Believers frequently made other gifts, either in kind (as might be expected in this region, this was often in the form of wool) or in money, on a sufficient scale for reserves to be accumulated. Some money was kept at Ax, while the shepherd, Peter Maury, described one of the *bonhommes*, Raymond of Toulouse, as holding 'the treasure of the heretics', and claimed that

---

12  Vidal, 'Les Derniers ministres', pp.74–83.
13  *RF*, vol. 1, p.471; vol. 2, p.405 (travel by night); vol. 2, p.412 (shepherds, green surcoat).
14  *RF*, vol. 2, p.425 (Châteauverdun), p.419 (Clergue's house).
15  *RF*, vol. 2, p.213; vol. 1, p.301.
16  *RF*, vol. 2, pp.404, 406, 412; vol. 3, p.370; vol. 1, p.301; Pales-Gobilliard, *L'Inquisiteur Geoffrey d'Ablis*, pp.182–7, 372–3.

**Plate 12**
The remains of the castle of Montaillou

this contained more than 16,000 gold pieces. When the pressure from inquisitors at Toulouse became too great, he entrusted this to a nephew, who took it to Sicily or Lombardy. As late as 1323 rumour had it that the Cathars had a great treasure of 100,000 *livres* hidden in Toulouse, Mirande, and Castelsarrasin.[17]

The experience of William Escaunier when he went to fetch a *bonhomme* to hereticate his mother, Galharda, whom he thought was dying, illustrates the precautions taken by the heretics even in familiar territory. William knew that a likely place to look was at the home of Sibylla den Balle at Ax, for she was well-known among believers as a key link in the Autier network, but he seems to have had little idea beyond this.[18] He first went a few kilometres down the road to the nearby village of Coustaussa where, in a tavern, he met a number of men he knew to be believers. One of them, a young man called Peter, said that he should not go to Ax alone, and accompanied him the rest of the way. It was not, indeed, an easy journey. After Coustaussa, they followed the Aude Valley to Quillan, before the steep climb up to the exposed Sault Plateau, and then the descent into Ax, on the western side, a distance of nearly eighty kilometres. In Ax itself he stopped at the home of his brother, Raymond, before going to see Sibylla den Balle. She asked him if he was a believer and who was accompanying him, and then said she would see if anybody was available. He should return after dinner. This he did, only to be told to go and wait at the cemetery. 'He, Peter, and his brother went to the cemetery and waited there for a long time for Sibylla and, as he said, it was raining and it was a dark night, and then his brother said to him, "What are we doing here?" and he replied that he was waiting for Sibylla den Balle who ought to be bringing a certain man who would go with them, and his brother, who was very suspicious of the affair, said to him, "And who is this man?" and he replied, "I don't know", and while they were talking in this way in the cemetery, Sibylla came with the heretic Prades Tavernier, otherwise called Andreas of Prades. And because it was a dark night they could not see each other and Sibylla said, "Who's there?" and he told her who he was, and Sibylla then said to him, "So, here he is, go with him, but do not go along

---

17  *RF*, vol. 3, pp.144–5 (wool, money); vol. 2, pp.416–17 (money); vol. 2, pp.59–60 ('treasurer of Toulouse'); vol. 2, p.484 (rumour of the 100,000 *livres*). The sums mentioned are obviously fantasy, but there were Languedocian Cathars in Sicily with which the Autier group had contact. There were no inquisitors on the island until after the treaty of Caltabellotta in 1302, A. Roach, *The Relationship of the Italian and Southern French Cathars, 1170–1320* (DPhil diss., Wolfson College, Oxford, 1989), pp.256–60.

18  See Brenon, *Les Femmes Cathares*, pp.319–20, on Sibylla den Balle, and Vidal, 'Les Derniers ministres', p.75, on her son, Pons, hereticated by Peter Autier in 1301.

the *via de Balneis*, but by way of the old *Villa*, so that you cannot be seen by anybody."' There followed an altercation between William and his brother Raymond, in which Raymond threatened to tell the priests, but in the end Raymond reluctantly agreed to come with them, although grumbling under his breath and walking behind.

They spent the night on a wooded mountain called 'Concaga', before making their way to Coustaussa the next morning. Here they reached another of the Cathar safe houses, but they did not move on in daylight. Meanwhile, Prades Tavernier received a number of believers who came to visit him there. 'And after midnight they went out with the heretic and others, and they went to Arques and, entering the house in which his sick mother lay, they found her very gravely ill, and not fully in her senses. And then the heretic went up to the bed of the sick woman, and spoke with her, but she did not make any sense, only repeating, "O, o!" and the heretic began to wonder whether he should receive her into his sect. And since he was in doubt and it was around dawn, Raymonda, mother-in-law of Peter, was called, who was also a believer of heretics, and at length the heretic decided that he should receive her into his sect, and made many genuflections on a certain bench in front of the bed of the sick woman. Then, taking a certain book, he placed it upon her head and hereticated her.'[19]

Within this world the Autiers and their fellow *bonhommes* struggled to revive the Cathar Church, converting, preaching, and hereticating the dying. The Autier family formed the core of this revival and, while that remained the case, Cathar teaching still rested upon a literary culture with which the brothers were quite at ease. They were, as the believer Sibylla of Arques put it, 'clerks and they knew law'. As she understood it, they had determined to devote themselves to the faith 'when, on a certain day, Peter had read in a certain book in his house in the presence of his brother William, and said to him that he should [also] read the book'. The book itself was left in the safe-keeping of Peter Autier's son-in-law, Arnold Textor, while they were in Lombardy, and retrieved on their return. It may have been the smart book with red leather covers mentioned by one of the witnesses before the inquisition of the bishop of Pamiers. Sometimes Peter Autier made use of a book as a starting-point for his teaching, once when his son, James, read from a book and Peter explained this in the vernacular. Where possible it was to educated families that the Cathars turned for help in spreading the faith. Their friend, William Bayard of Tarascon, described by Peter Autier as 'a valiant man and good clerk [who] had read

---

19  *RF*, vol. 2, pp.13–15.

their books and knew their faith and sect well', had two sons, Richard and Matthew. Peter Autier said they were like those described by Christ in the parable of the talents, 'since, as far as they could, they persuaded other persons to believe in the faith of the heretics, so that whatever they received from the heretics they duplicated'.[20]

Not all the *bonhommes* of the Autier circle were educated to this extent: Prades Tavernier, for example, was a former weaver, described as a simple man who did not know letters.[21] Although they initiated him, the Autiers did not rate him very highly, largely because they saw him as ignorant. For them literacy was in itself a powerful weapon among the many illiterate believers, who respected knowledge gained from books. Sibylla of Arques's naive retelling of the story of how the Autier brothers were convinced by reading a book is indicative, but more overt is William Balle's recall of a conversation he had with Peter Maury. Both men were itinerant shepherds from Montaillou. Discussing the recent arrest of two other shepherds, William and Arnold Maurs, Peter Maury had said that it was the work of the bishop of Pamiers, a man 'whose spirit after his death would never have peace or repose' because he persecuted 'those who we called heretics'. William Balle conceded the truth of what Peter Maury had said, but was perplexed, as he said were other shepherds, as to 'why it could be that the bishop, who was a literate man, as was said, did not know if the heretic held a better faith than he or vice-versa'. Peter Maury replied that the bishop knew nothing in comparison with the heretics: indeed, Peter Autier, just before he was burnt to death, had said that 'if he had been allowed to speak and preach to the people, he would have converted the whole populace to his faith'.[22]

In practice, Peter Autier never had such an opportunity, for circumstances determined that the *bonhommes* had to rely upon the cumulative effect of many small gatherings, often held before or after a meal in the house of a trusted believer. A typical meeting took place at the home of Martin Francissi in Limoux, when a small party from Arques consisting of William Escaunier, his sister, Marquesia, wife of William Botolh, and Sibylla of Arques, travelled to see Peter Autier. They brought him a gift of fish, which he later ate in a communal meal. The audience here seems to have consisted of five people, the three visitors and Martin and his wife or concubine. Peter Autier talked to them about the faith before the meal,

20   *RF*, vol. 2, pp.403–4, 207, 406, 419, 426 (parable of the talents); vol. 3, p.370 (red covers). Other references, vol. 1, pp.280, 285–6. See also Pales-Gobilliard, *L'Inquisiteur Geoffrey d'Ablis*, pp.112–13, 316–17, 390–1.
21   *RF*, vol. 2, p.416.
22   *RF*, vol. 2, p.393.

although William Escaunier claimed he could not recall much of what he said. If he was telling the truth, then Peter Autier either confined himself to a series of moral precepts which William did remember or William had not really grasped (and therefore retained) the fundamentals of the faith from which these precepts were derived. Probably the talk was geared to the audience. Peter Autier said that 'in no way should they touch the naked flesh of a woman, and that they should not return evil for evil, since God had forbidden it, and that they should not lie or kill anything except that which drags itself along on its belly across the ground, and if they were going along the road and found a purse or a money-bag, they should not touch it unless they knew or believed it belonged to one of their believers, and then they should take it and return it to them'. Later that evening, before bed, Peter Autier and Martin Francissi had taught William Escaunier how to perform the *melioramentum*.[23]

Word spread by this means, for Sibylla of Arques's original involvement with the Cathars had stemmed from preaching and instruction in just such a small gathering, after her husband, Raymond Peter, a farmer in the village, had listened to Peter and William Autier in the house of Sibylla den Balle at Ax. He had been so convinced by their assertions that, when he returned home, he had told his wife that 'if the good Christians should come to their home, they should be well-received'. On this occasion the Autiers stressed that salvation could only be attained through the Cathar Church, whose ministers lived ascetic and moral lives, and not through the Catholic Church, whose priests were evil men who did nothing except receive money and whose sacraments were worthless. When the world ended the whole earth would be 'a fiery hell', Raymond Peter told his wife, and 'the blessed would be he who had been well-shod'. By this he meant those who were heretics or hereticated at their deaths.[24]

Few of the artisans and shepherds who made up the majority of the audience in these meetings were likely to become *bonhommes* during their lifetime, but those who were convinced that the Cathar Church was the only path to salvation, naturally wished that they and their families should be hereticated before death.[25] Stories such as that of Bernard Arquié of Ax who claimed that during one such heretication a miracle occurred when 'a great light descended from the sky upon the house and reached

---

23  *RF*, vol. 2, p.12.

24  *RF*, vol. 2, pp.404–5.

25  Brenon, *Les Femmes Cathares*, pp.299–300, argues that, from the 1270s, there was a change in the nature of the *consolamentum*, which became largely a ceremony to hereticate the dying rather than a means of creating new ministers. However, see Pales-Gobilliard, *L'Inquisiteur Geoffrey d'Ablis*, pp.70–1, 314–15.

to the sick woman who lay upon the bed', served to reinforce the desire of believers to receive the *consolamentum* before death.[26] For Raymond Peter and his family and neighbours however, no such miracle blessed their connection with the Cathars; for them death-bed heretications became a source of great misery and domestic conflict. The Autier group believed in the *endura* for those hereticated,[27] but in a society in which there was often great difficulty judging whether an illness was final, the Cathar ministers and their supporters were often presented with impossible choices. Galharda, whose son, William Escaunier, had been urged to fetch the good men by Raymond Peter, had been hereticated by Prades Tavernier when she was in no state to understand what was happening. He had left instructions that from then on she was to be given nothing except cold water. However, having remained between six and eight days in this state, Galharda began to recover and demanded food. The refusal of her daughter, Marquesia, to bring any, led to a bitter quarrel, leading James Autier, who was staying at Raymond Peter's home at the time, to call Galharda 'an evil old woman'. In the end it was Sibylla, Raymond Peter's wife, who brought her bread, wine, and cooked cabbage, although she would not eat any meat. Both women concluded that to starve in these circumstances was 'very stupid and fatuous'.[28]

Almost immediately Sibylla suffered a trauma of her own, when her daughter, Jacoba, a baby only a few months old, became so ill that her father wanted her, too, hereticated. Prades Tavernier was still in Arques, staying in the home of another neighbour, Raymond Mauleon, while waiting for the death of Galharda, and he came that night. After hereticating the child, he said that Sibylla 'should not give the girl food or milk, or anything which is born of flesh, and that, if she lived, she should from then on feed her with Lenten food'. Raymond Peter, her husband, was very pleased, 'saying that if his daughter died in this state, she would be an angel of God', but Sibylla could not, as she said 'see her daughter die in this way', and she suckled her when her husband was out of the room. The resulting quarrel was so serious that 'her husband did not love her or her daughter, nor speak to them for a long time until', as Sibylla put it, 'he recognised his error'. At the time he was supported by Peter Maury, who called her a bad mother and said that women were demons. The

---

26   *RF*, vol. 1, pp.285, 297. This was the heretication of Sibylla, wife of Peter Pauc of Ax, who did not in fact die at this time. When she did die, two years later, she had 'already lost her memory' and could not be reconsoled.

27   For views and literature on the *endura*, see W. L. Wakefield, *Heresy, Crusade and Inquisition in Southern France, 1100–1250* (London, 1974), pp.40–1. See also above, ch. 3, pp.103–4.

28   *RF*, vol. 2, pp.15–16, 414.

child survived until it was almost a year old, but then died, unconsoled. If the incident provoked a masculine reaction against her, Sibylla found emotional support in Galharda. 'And when Galharda Escaunier heard what had happened to her daughter, that is after heretication she had given her milk, she became her great friend, and wished to return to eating meat, which Sibylla also gave her, as a result of which her husband and the other believers were very upset.'[29]

Peter Autier was later critical of the whole process since, in his view, it was not legitimate to hereticate a child 'who did not have understanding' and, indeed, it had always been the contention of the Cathars that the Roman Church was corrupt to baptise the unknowing infant. Prades Tavernier, though, remained defiant, claiming that God had wished him to do it. His rider adding that Peter and William Autier wished to dominate the group and that they always took the better part of the cloth made from the wool donated by the believers suggests an underlying rivalry that went beyond a conflict of interpretation over the *consolamentum*.[30] Nevertheless, Prades Tavernier was more cautious the next time. When Raymond Peter himself fell ill and sent Raymond Mauleon to Ax to fetch a *bonhomme*, Prades made the journey, but refused to give him the *consolamentum* until he was sure he was dying. He was right to be circumspect, for Raymond Peter recovered after a few days.[31] There is some irony in the story of this family's involvement with the Cathars, for it had been Galharda Escaunier who had first persuaded Raymond Peter and Sibylla to seek comfort in the Cathar Church in their great sadness following the premature death of a previous infant daughter, Marquesia, in 1306. Raymond Peter's enthusiastic conversion had led directly to the heretications of Galharda and Jacoba and to the temporary estrangement with his wife. Sibylla herself became disillusioned with the Cathars after this, believing them too avaricious and envious. As far as she could tell, Peter and William Autier did not live as they ought, but accumulated money, even though according to their own precepts, they should receive only enough for immediate necessities. Indeed, since that time she had heard heretics say to believers that they should betray and kill those who persecuted them since 'the tree of evil' ought to be cut off and killed. She nevertheless allowed them to continue to use her house, 'since she was very much afraid and loved her husband, and did not wish to offend him'.[32]

---

29   *RF*, vol. 2, pp.414–15. On Sibylla of Arques, see Brenon, *Les Femmes Cathares*, pp.327–9.
30   *RF*, vol. 3, pp.144–5.
31   *RF*, vol. 2, p.416.
32   *RF*, vol. 2, pp.417, 424. For 'the tree of evil', Matthew 7: 19.

The Autier brothers were not the first to try to revive the Cathar networks in Languedoc. Between the arrest of Bernard Acier in 1259 and the return of the Autiers in 1299, there were at least thirty-five *bonhommes* in the traditional Cathar areas of the Albigeois, the Toulousain, the Lauragais, and the Ariège.[33] Some, like William Pagès, survived for a quarter of a century; between 1260 and 1285, he was particularly active in the region of Saissac and in the Minervois to the west, although his presence was known in places as far apart as Albi and Carcassonne. His involvement in a futile plot to seize and destroy inquisitorial registers at Carcassonne in 1285 finally led to his arrest.[34] It seems certain that this is a considerable underestimate of the number of active *bonhommes* in Languedoc in the last forty years of the thirteenth century, but even so the numbers are very small, showing a sharp decline from Rainier Sacconi's already modest figure of 200 in 1250. As even the Autier group found, it was by this time extremely difficult to create any form of permanent organisation or hierarchy. By the 1260s few *bonhommes* ventured back from Lombardy on a long-term basis, while the last known Cathar bishops of Toulouse and Albi settled at Sirmione. Deacons, whose functions were closely tied to local communities, disappear after 1270.[35] Although some believers were prepared to make great sacrifices to maintain their links with their Church in Italy, there must have been many more like Philip, a believer from Auriac, who complained that they had been abandoned by the *perfecti*, leaving no one to administer the *consolamentum*.[36]

## Heresy in Carcassonne and Albi

The new generation of inquisitors of the late thirteenth and early fourteenth centuries exacerbated their plight, for their investigations were frequent, relentless, and uncompromising, leading one believer, Bernard Castelnau of Dreuille, to ask in despair if the persecution of the *bonhommes* would last for ever.[37] Bolstered by the independence granted them by Pope Alexander IV

---

33 These are *bonhommes* whose names are known. The list is compiled from Vidal, 'Les Derniers ministres', pp.73–4. See also J. Guiraud, *Histoire de l'Inquisition au moyen âge*, vol. 2 (Paris, 1938), pp.267–333, and Brenon, *Les Femmes Cathares*, p.282.

34 There are accounts of the plot in Griffe, *Le Languedoc Cathare et l'Inquisition*, pp.152–4; Guiraud, *Histoire de l'Inquisition*, vol. 2, pp.303–33, and G. W. Davis, *The Inquisition at Albi, 1299–1300. Text of Register and Analysis* (New York, 1948) (reprint 1974), pp.52–3.

35 See above, ch. 5, p.173, n.81.

36 Doat, vol. 25, f.268v.

37 Doat, vol. 25, f.268r.

in 1255, the inquisitors were unafraid of any vested interest, still less of the scattered rural communities upon which the Autier revival was based. In the late thirteenth century, therefore, the battles between inquisitors and urban consulates which had characterised the 1230s reappeared, dragging in outside powers as each side strived to justify its position. The most bitter manifestations of the conflict occurred in Carcassonne and Albi: in both cases it was alleged that important and wealthy citizens had been subjected to harsh imprisonment on quite unjustified suspicions of heresy. Between 1280 and *c.* 1286, three appeals were made by the *consuls* of Carcassonne against the inquisitorial operations in the city, addressed to the pope, the king, and the royal chancellor and, on the third occasion, the Dominican prior in Paris, who had overall responsibility for the Inquisition in France.[38] The *consuls* were particularly aggrieved at what they claimed was the irregular conduct of the inquisitor, John Galand, who, they said, greeted those who were convoked to appear before him with 'an evil and leonine countenance'. He based his enquiries, they claimed, on depositions given by people of any type, whether they were enemies, persons of bad repute, or of 'vile condition'.[39] The repercussions of this were still being felt in the 1290s and the conflict did not die down until the 'reconciliation' of 1299.[40]

The protests at Albi emanated from the proceedings conducted by the bishop, Bernard of Castenet, and Nicholas of Abbeville, Inquisitor of Carcassonne, between December 1299 and the spring of 1301, and were directed to both king and pope. Some of the accusations might have been stimulated by information obtained in the earlier hearings at Carcassonne. In both cities the *consuls* were particularly indignant about the conditions of imprisonment, an issue which had been less important in the 1230s when there were few prisons available. These complaints eventually led Pope Clement V to appoint a commission of inquiry into inquisitorial prisons in March 1306.[41] It has been argued that the zeal of the inquisitors – and thus the violence of the reaction – was partly fuelled by economic considerations, for the inquisitors needed to cover the high costs of their operations, which they could expect to retrieve from confiscations taken by the secular authorities. At Albi, Bernard of Castenet's direct aggrandisement of the see was

---

38   Davis, *Inquisition at Albi*, pp.51–2.
39   J.-M. Vidal, *Un Inquisiteur jugé par ses "victimes": Jean Galand et les Carcassonais, 1285–1286* (Paris, 1903), pp.39–43.
40   Davis, *Inquisition at Albi*, pp.57–9.
41   C. Douais, ed., *Documents pour servir à l'histoire de l'Inquisition dans le Languedoc* (Société de l'histoire de France), vol. 2 (Paris, 1900), pp.302–49, for letters and reports from 1306. This inquiry began energetically but, as is typical of this most procrastinatory of popes, it did not finish.

particularly obvious for, in 1285, he began the building of the great brick fortress which became the cathedral of St Cecilia.[42] The confiscated property of the twenty-five men known to have been convicted in the Albi inquiry would certainly have been worth having, for these were not itinerant shepherds or weavers from country villages, but mostly judges, lawyers, notaries, and merchants, several of whom were from important consular families.[43] In fact, despite their social prominence, the appeals to the Crown ultimately proved fruitless for, although King Philip IV was interested in exercising some control over the inquisitors, he was not disposed to conciliate what he evidently saw as urban agitators, a belief which seems to have been reinforced by a Languedocian tour he conducted in December 1303. It seems to have been this attitude which, in 1304, provoked a group of *consuls* in Carcassonne into a reckless attempt to persuade Fernand, son of James II of Majorca, to become their ruler. The leaders were hanged as traitors in November 1304.[44] There is no doubt therefore that these conflicts were as much concerned with property, jurisdiction, and local politics as with Cathar belief.

Nevertheless, the *bourgeoisie* of these two cities were not quite as innocent of association with heresy as their protests made out, and it is arguable that the inquisitorial attack upon members of these urban elites was a calculated move to break the remaining powerful patrons of Catharism in the towns, rather as had been done in Toulouse in the 1230s.[45] The third protest from Carcassonne, for instance, which is almost certainly related to the proceedings against the alleged plotters of 1285, was drawn up by the notary Bartholomew Vézian, who had himself been accused of involvement in the conspiracy.[46] At Albi, the deposition of Stephen Mascoti, made on 27 January 1300, shows that, although the Cathar Church itself was not functioning in any organised way in Languedoc, nevertheless important citizens were prepared to go to considerable risk to maintain contact. In 1297 this man was employed by two merchants of Albi, Bertrand of Monte Acuto and William Golferii, to fetch a *bonhomme* called Raymond Andree from Lombardy. He was paid 35 *livres* of Albi for this. Raymond Andree was obviously known to them and, indeed, appears to have come

---

42  B. Hamilton, *The Medieval Inquisition* (London, 1981), p.69; Davis, *Inquisition at Albi*, pp.44, 88–90.

43  Davis, *Inquisition at Albi*, pp.22–3.

44  See ibid., pp.69–75.

45  On the validity of these depositions, see Davis, *Inquisition at Albi*, pp.36–8. See, too, J. G. Biget, 'L'extinction du catharisme urbain: les points chauds de la répression', in *CF* 20 (1985), p.324, who argues that Catharism failed in the towns when the urban élites abandoned it. For the case of Toulouse, see above ch. 5, n.23.

46  Vidal, *Un Inquisiteur jugé par ses "victimes"*, p.12.

**Plate 13**
The cathedral of Saint Cecilia, Albi, from the south

**Plate 14**
Albi cathedral from the north

from the Albigeois, but they were not in regular communication with him because they did not know where to find him and were prepared to receive another *bonhomme* in his place. Stephen Mascoti went to Genoa where, in what must have been a prearranged meeting, he made contact with Bernard Fabri, a tailor from Albi. They in turn travelled to the baths at Acqui, about seventy kilometres to the north-west over the Ligurian Apennines, where they found two other men. After some cautious opening conversation they established that these two men were part of the exiled heretical community, also from Albi. They took Stephen Mascoti and Bernard Fabri to a wooded hill a few kilometres from the baths, where there were three or four hospices in which Cathars were living. Here they performed the *melioramentum* to 'the lord of the heretics'. The next morning this man introduced them to a *perfectus* called William Pagani, who was a Lombard, since they could not find Raymond Andree. Stephen Mascoti and Bernard Fabri then took William Pagani back to Albi, where he was greeted 'with joy' by Bertrand of Monte Acuto. After a meal at William Golferii's house, a small party went to a barn used for pressing grapes belonging to William, where they performed the *melioramentum*. The process was apparently repeated the following morning in the house of a local cobbler who was a friend of Bertrand of Monte Acuto. William Pagani stayed only a short time, setting out immediately for Lombardy. Bertrand of Monte Acuto's version broadly accords with that of Stephen Mascoti, although he implicates a further five people. Even so, the total number of those who knew of William Pagani's presence was only fourteen.[47] The repercussions were serious for the participants: seven of the nine named by Bertrand of Monte Acuto, including himself, were still in prison at Carcassonne in 1306, one had been burnt to death before 1305, and one was later executed.[48] This incident – minor in itself – shows how fragmented the Cathar Church had become. The Albigensian *consuls* and their associates knew nothing of the Autier brothers, who were still in Lombardy in 1297, but even when they returned there is no evidence of any contact between the rural network set up in the *pays de* Foix and the cities of Albi and Carcassonne. Indeed, the meeting with William Pagani itself seems to have been quite unconnected with the contacts which most of the accused in the Albi proceedings (including the two merchants in this case) had had with two local *bonhommes*, Raymond del Boc and Raymond Desiderii.[49]

---

47 Davis, *Inquisition at Albi*, pp.165–8, 190.
48 Douais, ed., *Documents pour servir*, pp.322–6.
49 Davis, *Inquisition at Albi*, p.13 and the map between pp.38 and 39 showing some of the areas covered by these two *bonhommes*.

# The end of Catharism in Languedoc

The Cathar revival of the late thirteenth and early fourteenth centuries never rested on firm foundations. A king of Philip IV's autocratic temperament and religious conviction was unlikely to sympathise with urban communities which combined aspirations towards autonomy with the taint of Catharism, while the inquisitors took little more than a decade to see off the Autier mission. Indeed, the Autier campaign was always balanced on a knife-edge, for the brothers were denounced to the Dominicans in Pamiers as early as 1300, and five years later another betrayal in Limoux led to the imprisonment of James Autier and Prades Tavernier, an event which set off panic among some believers and led them to travel to Lyon to seek absolution from Pope Clement V.[50] Two other *bonhommes* from the Autier circle, William Belibaste and Philip of Alairac (of Coustaussa), were captured in the spring of 1309.[51] Although on both occasions the heretics managed to escape, intense pressure was exerted thereafter by the tribunals of the Dominicans Bernard Gui and Geoffrey of Ablis at Toulouse and Carcassonne respectively,[52] greatly reducing the effectiveness of the *bonhommes*, and forcing Peter Autier into hiding for almost a year before his capture in early September 1309. By the end of the year most of the rest of the *bonhommes* had been taken and, in December, William Autier was burnt to death. Peter Autier was remitted to the secular arm before the church of St Sernin in Toulouse and executed on 9 April 1310, after having provided much additional information to the inquisitors over the previous seven months.[53] For Bernard Gui the defeat of the Autiers was akin to a crusade: analysis of his sentences between 1308 and 1323 (when he ceased to be an inquisitor) reflects this determination. In his entire career as an inquisitor he is known to have handed heretics over to the secular arm on forty-two occasions, twenty-nine of which occurred between March 1308 and September 1313,

---

50   *RF*, vol. 2, p.423; vol. 3, pp.145–6. One of the leaders on this journey was Raymond
      Peter, husband of Sibylla of Arques.
51   See Vidal, 'Les Derniers ministres', p.76.
52   On the tribunal at Carcassonne under Geoffrey of Ablis, see Pales-Gobilliard, *L'Inquisiteur
      Geoffrey d'Ablis*, pp.4–44. See also Douais, ed., *Documents pour servir*, vol. 1, pp.cxcviii–ccvi,
      and C. Molinier, *L'Inquisition dans le Midi de la France au XIIIe et au XIVe siècle* (Paris, 1880)
      (reprint 1974), pp.108–22.
53   For a survey of Peter Autier's career, see Vidal, 'Les Derniers ministres', pp.61–73;
      J. Given, *Inquisition and Medieval Society. Power, Discipline and Resistance in Languedoc*
      (Ithaca, NY and London, 1997), pp.56–7, for the great importance of the information
      which Peter Autier provided for Bernard Gui. After this it was only a matter of time
      before the inquisitors destroyed his whole network.

the period when he was concentrating upon breaking up the Autier campaign. In the four years between March 1308 and April 1312 he issued 459 sentences, nearly half of his total of 930 sentences during his time in office.[54] On the one hand, he was evidently concerned to wipe out the *bonhommes* completely, while on the other, he was intent upon intimidating those who supported them. James Given has shown that nearly three-quarters of those who appeared before him were accused of association with Catharism, most of whom were *credentes*. Sentences ordering the destruction of the houses of those who had sheltered *bonhommes* or allowed the *consolamentum* to be administered under their roofs are exclusively during this period, amounting to twenty-two in all. Women had clearly played an important role in providing this kind of hospitality and this is reflected in the fact that forty per cent of those who appeared before him were female, and that forty-six per cent of those were accused of Catharism, at a time when in other types of judicial cases women hardly figure at all.[55] Forty-nine of his sixty-nine exhumations and burning of the dead also occurred during this period. This last figure is perhaps a measure of his success in suppressing popular resistance for, in the 1230s, exhumations above all had provoked violence against the inquisitors, whereas there appears to have been no overt reaction in Bernard Gui's time.[56]

The massive inquiry undertaken by James Fournier, Bernard Saisset's successor as Bishop of Pamiers, which began in 1318 and lasted until 1325, was therefore left to chase ghosts, peasants, and one confused and ignorant *bonhomme*. Vidal's calculations show that the combined efforts of Geoffrey of Ablis, Bernard Gui, and James Fournier, produced a list of 650 believers, to which can be added between three and four hundred denounced by others, but never questioned. Although this by no means provides a definitive measure of Cathar support over the period, it does offer a large sample for

---

54    The original figures were set out by Douais, ed., *Documents pour servir*, vol. 1, p.ccv, but
      see a fresh analysis by J. Given, 'A medieval inquisitor at work: Bernard Gui, 3 March
      1308 to 19 June 1323', in S. K. Cohn, Jr. and S. A. Epstein, eds, *Portraits of Medieval and
      Renaissance Living. Essays in Memory of David Herlihy* (Ann Arbor, MI, 1996), pp.207–32.
      He points out that Douais does not make clear that 'acts' do not equal individuals, some
      of whom appear twice or even three times, p.210. It should also be pointed out that,
      between 1316 and 1318, although still nominally an inquisitor, he was acting as
      procurator general of the Dominican Order at the papal court, and that he was fully
      occupied with this task during those years, see B. Guenée, *Between Church and State.*
      *The Lives of Four French Prelates in the Late Middle Ages*, trans. A. Goldhammer
      (Chicago, IL, 1991) (originally 1987), pp.51–7.
55    Given, 'Medieval inquisitor', pp.210, 226–32. See also R. Abels and E. Harrison, 'The
      participation of women in Languedocian Catharism', *Medieval Studies* 41 (1979), p.243, on
      the high proportion of women acting as 'receivers of heretics' from the 1240s onwards.
56    See above, ch. 5, p.151.

social analysis. Nine-tenths were peasants, shepherds, artisans, and labourers. Examples of even minor nobles are rare and there are few other property-owners or professionals. Fournier's seventy Cathar suspects, for example, produce two nobles, four clerics, one notary, and one lawyer.[57]

The *bonhomme* was William Belibaste who, with Philip of Alairac, had been captured in the spring of 1309, but had escaped, fleeing over the Pyrenees into Catalonia. Although Philip of Alairac was incautious enough to return, William Belibaste remained out of sight and thus escaped the arrests of the autumn of 1309, and the holocaust which followed. The fate of the Autiers showed how difficult it was to revive Catharism even for educated men, well-prepared to take advantage of temporarily favourable political and religious circumstances. Even had he thought in such terms, William Belibaste had none of these opportunities, for he was a poor representative of the Cathar tradition. His heretication by the Autiers took place towards the end of the decade and may in itself reflect their increasingly desperate situation, for his lack of both morals and education meant that he was manifestly unsuitable for the task, and in fact he seems to have contributed nothing to the campaign. He had originally come from the village of Cubières, not far south of Arques, where he had been a shepherd and, while in exile, he maintained himself by this means and by carding and weaving. His lifestyle, however, did not stimulate the admiration which had enabled *bonhommes* of the past to gather support. Even the believers came to recognise that his 'servant', Raymonda Marty, the wife of Arnold Piquier of Tarascon, was in fact his mistress, while his attitude to money and goods does not suggest an indifference to material things. Before his *consolamentum* he had been on the run for murder and while he was in Catalonia he was party to an unsuccessful plot to murder the daughter of a believer it was feared might betray them. However, after 1314, when Raymond of Toulouse died, he was the only known *perfectus*, and this still carried some resonance, even in a man like William Belibaste. Believers continued to want the *consolamentum* when near death and they were glad to listen to William Belibaste's invectives against the Catholic Church and the inquisitors. He did therefore manage to attract a loosely-knit group largely made up of members of about half a dozen families from the Ariège, living a rather impoverished existence mostly in and around Morella and San Mateo in northern Valencia. It is not, though, surprising to find the shepherd, Peter Maury, regretting the passing of the Autiers who, unlike 'the lord of Morella', as he called William Belibaste, knew how to preach.[58]

---

57   Vidal, 'Les Derniers ministres', pp.87–92.
58   *RF*, vol. 2, pp.28–9.

At the other extreme there appear to have been times when William slipped into pure fantasy, prophesying that 'one of the people of the king of Aragon would bring his horse to eat upon the altar of Rome', and then the Cathar Church would be exalted.[59]

William Belibaste and his fluctuating band of believers survived in this way until 1321, when William was tricked into travelling to Tirvia, west of Andorra, which, although on the southern side of the Pyrenees, was located within the lands of the count of Foix. His betrayer was Arnold Sicre, one of the four sons of Sibylla den Balle of Ax, who had devoted herself to the Autier group. Arnold Sicre came from a family riven by the choices the Cathar revival forced upon them, for his father had been a Catholic who, as a comital official, had been involved in the arrest of suspected Cathars, and he had separated from his mother as a consequence. Arnold and Peter were the two youngest children and, because Sibylla feared that they might inadvertently give the heretics away, she had sent Arnold to live with his father in Tarascon and Peter to her sister, Alazais, in Urgel. The two elder brothers, Pons and Bernard, were old enough to understand the situation, and had grown up committed to the Cathars.[60] Arnold's brother, Peter, had suggested that the delivery of a 'garbed heretic' might help them to regain their mother's property, confiscated because of her heresy; rewards of 50 *livres tournois* had been promised for the capture of lesser persons. Initially, Arnold Sicre's search in Catalonia was unsuccessful, probably because he was expecting to find them farther north. In 1318, however, a chance meeting with one of the believers, Guillemetta, Peter Maury's cousin, while he was working as a shoemaker in San Mateo, led him to William Belibaste. Even then, at first he was exceptionally clumsy for one who claimed to have been a long-term believer, at one point offering to entertain William Belibaste with a supper of mutton and cabbage. Arnold Sicre's real advantage, though, was the high reputation his mother retained among the believers, and he was able to play on this to survive in company in which he was never fully trusted. Early in 1319, when he returned to Pamiers to tell the bishop of his discovery and obtain permission and money to fulfil what they called 'a pious fraud', he convinced the Belibaste group that he had been seeking out his aunt, Alazais, and his brother, Bernard. At Christmas 1320, he returned to tell them that his aunt and sister, Raymonda, were living in the mountainous region of Palhars on the southern side of the Pyrenees. A proposed marriage between Raymonda and Arnold Maury, son of Guillemetta, had been agreed, but his aunt was

---

59 *RF*, vol. 2, p.63.
60 *RF*, vol. 2, p.28.

in no physical state to travel to San Mateo. With some misgivings, William Belibaste agreed to lead their group to see her. He was arrested when they reached Tirvia, and taken to Castelbó. From there he was escorted to Carcassonne and condemned as an obstinate heretic by the archbishop of Narbonne. He was burnt to death at Villerouge-Termènes, not far from his own birth-place, in the spring of 1321. Arnold Sicre himself was solemnly absolved by Fournier and the inquisitors Bernard Gui and John of Beaune on 14 January 1322. It was not, their instrument said, easy to find those 'hiding in secret places, . . . unless they are detected through accomplices or through such persons who know their devious ways'.[61]

On 29 April 1321, at about the same time as William Belibaste was executed in the Termènes, a woman called Alazais from the village of Vernaux, about ten kilometres downstream from Ax, was appearing before James Fournier in the episcopal camera at Pamiers. It was the second time she had appeared to answer accusations of heresy; on the first occasion, in front of the inquisitors at Carcassonne, she had been less than totally frank. According to her, her interest in Catharism had begun in 1305 or 1306, when Mengarda Alverniis, of Lordat, 'who is now a fugitive for heresy', came to her house and began to commend the heretics to her, as 'they alone held the way to God'. They could, Mengarda told her, 'save souls and absolve men from all sins, and those received among them immediately entered Paradise after death'. They discussed these matters for some time between themselves, for no one else was present, and at length Mengarda persuaded her to send measures of wheat and rye to William Autier, who was staying at Mengarda's house at that time. Later, Mengarda took her to meet the two heretics at her house, one of whom she recognised as William Autier, the other was 'a fat man with a plump and round face', whom she did not know, but who nevertheless was also a heretic. She claimed she could not remember what the heretics had said, but accepted that, at the time, she believed them to be good and holy, and that what Mengarda had told her was true. Mengarda then instructed her to 'lead as many persons as she could to place faith and credence in the good Christians, that is the heretics, since the more who could be induced to the belief, the more there would be deserving of reward'. Alazais's flirtation with heresy lasted, by her account, for only a year or so, but her offence was compounded by her previous dissembling before the tribunal at Carcassonne. She was imprisoned and not released until August 1324.[62]

---

61   *RF*, vol. 2, pp.20–81. The detailed account in Vidal, 'Les Derniers ministres', pp.92–105, is largely based on this deposition of Arnold Sicre. For the execution of William Belibaste, *RF*, vol. 2, p.416.
62   *RF*, vol. 1, pp.482–7.

The case of Alazais of Vernaux, while of no particular importance in itself, nevertheless encapsulates the fate of the Autier revival and the believers who were drawn into it. By the time Alazais appeared before the bishop of Pamiers there were no more 'good Christians' to admire in Languedoc, and there was therefore little point in trying to spread the word. The remaining believers who had assembled around William Belibaste were either themselves captured (some through the efforts of Arnold Sicre, who seems to have found he could make a living in this way) or dispersed. Among these, Raymonda Marty and her daughter fled to Peñiscola, on the Valencian coast, while Peter Maury went as far as Majorca. Guillemetta Maury and her relatives simply disappeared. In 1323 the Maury brothers, John and Peter (who had returned from Majorca) were arrested in Catalonia, and they appeared before James Fournier during 1324. On 12 August they were both sentenced to perpetual prison.[63]

Some may never have been known to Fournier. In 1325 Pope John XXII wrote to Prince Stephen of Bosnia, asking him to support the Franciscan Brother Fabian, appointed as inquisitor in his territories. 'A great company of heretics', said the pope, 'has come together from many different places to the principality of Bosnia, in the confident hope of disseminating their foul error and of remaining there in safety.'[64] While it may well be the case that this pope was more susceptible to such stories than some of his predecessors, there is nevertheless solid evidence of continuing contacts between the Cathars and the Bosnian dualists during the twelfth and thirteenth centuries, and it is clear, too, that the Bogomil Church continued to function there at least until the Ottoman conquests in the mid-fifteenth century.[65]

Some Cathars may not have fled so far, for the existence of Cathar literature among the materials conserved by the Alpine Waldensian communities of the late fourteenth century suggests that some may have settled in the Piedmont, an idea made all the more plausible by the evident frequency with which the Cathars of Languedoc passed through this region while trying to maintain their contacts with the Cathar Church in exile in Lombardy. Two Occitan texts – *La Gleisa de Dio* and the *Glosa Pater*

---

63  See Vidal, 'Les Derniers ministres', pp.105–7, and A. Brenon, *Le Vrai visage du Catharisme*, 2nd edn (Portet-sur-Garonne, 1995), p.300, on this last round-up. The last executions seem to have been in 1329.

64  HH, no. 457, pp.276–8.

65  F. Sanjek, 'L'Initiation Cathare dans l'Occident médiéval', *Heresis* 5 (1985), p.23, points to the similarity between the form of the Latin and Occitan Rituals of the thirteenth centuries and that of Radoslav, 'the Christian' in mid-fifteenth-century Bosnia. See also Lambert, *The Cathars*, pp.297–313.

– written shortly before 1376, suggest belief in a form of mitigated dualism (quite different from the rigorist position of John of Lugio's school) which may have been assimilated by the heterodox communities of the late fourteenth century to the extent that the Waldensians seem to have regarded these works as part of their own literature. Indeed, the strong eschatological theme of *La Gleisa de Dio*, which presents the Cathars as a persecuted and martyred Church, suffering before the appearance of Antichrist and the Last Judgement, is quite in keeping with other late medieval heresies, influenced as they were by Joachimite ideas. Cathars may or may not have been a distinguishable element among the heretics of these Alpine communities, but the composition of two texts which suggest a form of Cathar Ritual (for the *Glosa Pater* is an elaborate commentary on the Lord's Prayer, which generally preceded the ceremony of the *consolamentum*) offers the intriguing possibility that in the late fourteenth century the remote valleys of the Alps still harboured the two classes which had characterised the Cathar Church in its prime.[66]

---

66 A. Brenon, 'Syncrétisme hérétique dans les refuges Alpins? Un Livre cathare parmi les recueils vaudois de la fin du moyen âge: Le Manuscrit 269 de Dublin', *Heresis* 7 (1986), pp.5–23. The dating of these works remains problematical. They were first identified as Cathar literature by the Belgian historian, Theo Venckeleer, in 1960, 'Un Recueil cathare. Le manuscrit A.6.10 de la "Collection Vaudoise" de Dublin, II: Une glose sur le Pater', *Revue belge de philologie et d'histoire* 39 (1961), pp.762–85, but his suggested date of between 1210 and 1240 has been rejected both by Brenon and by WE, pp.592–3. WE, who do not see the two works as connected, suggest *c.* 1250 for *La Gleisa de Dio*, but clearly lean towards a later date for the *Glossa Pater*, pp.595–6. For the evidence of syncretistic beliefs in Piedmont in the fourteenth century, see Lambert, *The Cathars*, pp.290–6.

# CHAPTER SEVEN

# Cathars after Catharism

## Déodat Roché, Simone Weil, and Otto Rahn

On the west side of the Place de l'Eglise in the village of Arques is the house of Déodat Roché, born and brought up in the village and, at various times, its *maire*. Roché died in January 1978, having just reached his hundredth birthday, leaving a large and controversial legacy of literature on the world of the Cathars, both by himself and those he inspired or who admired him, including a journal, *Cahiers d'Etudes Cathares*, which he founded in 1948. Throughout his life Roché stayed close to his roots in the Hautes-Corbières, gaining his *license* in Law and Philosophy at the University of Toulouse, and serving as a magistrate in Limoux and Carcassonne until he was removed by the Vichy government on the grounds that 'he occupies himself too much with the history of religions and spiritualism'. These may or may not be good reasons for dismissal from the magistracy, but it was certainly true that Roché had been deeply concerned with such subjects since his youth when, heavily influenced by his father, a local notary, he had begun to study the Egyptian mystery cults and Persian Mithraism, moving on to research into the manifold religious and moral influences upon Christianity. When he was dismissed he was already in late middle age, so Vichy's arbitrary action gave him the opportunity to devote himself full-time to the subject which had been of central interest to him since at least the late 1890s, that is 'the true visage of Catharism, the heir of Manichaeism', which he fervently believed had been obscured by what he saw as the lies and calumnies of the Inquisition and the intolerance of the medieval Church. In the words of his obituarist, Lucienne Julien, 'Déodat Roché wanted to bring to our twentieth century the light which the Cathars wished to see illuminate medieval society.'[1]

For Roché this was a serious intellectual and, indeed, moral endeavour, but he had arrived at this interest by a route which had led him to identify powerfully with his subject. In 1950 he had established the *Société du Souvenir et des Etudes Cathares*, significantly at the highly emotive site of Montségur, creating a structure which complemented the bulletin founded two years before. He had already written two strongly pro-Cathar books, *L'Eglise romane et les Cathares albigeois* (1937) and *Le Catharisme* (1938), while as early as 1899 he had founded a short-lived journal, *Le Réveil des Albigeois*, intended to promote a revival of interest in Cathar morality and beliefs. Moreover, after he had met the Austrian scientist, Rudolf Steiner, the founder of 'anthroposophy', and editor of another review, *Die Gnosis*, in 1922, he attempted to create an underpinning for his own life and interest in Catharism by adopting Steiner's philosophy that man's development of his intellect could ultimately lead to the rediscovery of the ability (which Steiner thought to be innate) to perceive and participate in spiritual things, partially lost because of the growth of material concerns.[2] Like most proponents of a cause he was concerned, too, to establish its legitimacy through historical continuity and therefore envisaged a link from Gnosticism and Manichaeism through Catharism down to the Freemasons, in whose lodge at Carcassonne he played a prominent role. Indeed, for Roché, the Cathar treasure removed from Montségur during the siege of 1243–44 was not the Grail in the sense used in literature – a chalice or a stone – nor the more mundane precious metals and money which the sergeant, Imbert of Salles (who was one of the defenders of Montségur), described to the inquisitors, but the ancient literature which, as heirs of the original dualists, the Cathars had a duty to protect.

Roché's interest is that he spans two cultures – the scholarly and the popular – for he undoubtedly saw his work as serious research, but at the same time his status as the leading 'neo-Cathar' helped to popularise the myths upon which present-day tourism trades. One person who took his views very seriously was Simone Weil, the young French philosopher of the inter-war years, who died aged only thirty-four at Ashford in Kent in August 1943. It is not true, as has sometimes been said, that she starved herself to death in imitation of the Cathar *endura*, although her refusal (or inability) to eat properly certainly contributed to her death from tuberculosis. It is the case, however, that during the last years of her life, she became captivated by

---

1 See L. Julien, 'Celui qui fut Déodat Roché', *Cahiers d'Etudes Cathares* 29 (1978), pp.3–12.
2 J.-G. Biget, 'Mythographie du Catharisme (1870–1960)', in *CF* 14 (1979), pp.308–9, and Y. Hagman, 'Les Historiens des religions et les constructions des ésotéristes', in *CEI*, pp.142–3.

twelfth-century Occitan culture and with the Catharism which she believed to be one of its major distinguishing characteristics. At the suggestion of her friend, Simone Pétrement, she had been reading about Manichaeism since 1939, but it appears that her interest in the Cathars was really stimulated by two of Roché's articles, drawn to her attention by Jean Ballard, editor of the journal, *Cahiers du Sud*. As a consequence, in January 1941, she wrote to Roché, telling him what a great impression his articles had made upon her, in particular his explanation of the Cathar rejection of the Old Testament Jehovah, whom she saw as a god of 'pitiless cruelty', incompatible with 'the Father who is invoked in the Gospel'. It was, she said, the importance given to these stories in Judaism and Christianity which had kept her away from these faiths. 'The influence of the Old Testament and of the Roman Empire, whose tradition was continued by the Papacy, are to my mind the two essential sources of the corruption of Christianity.' Entering on to a theme which she developed further in two articles for Ballard's *Cahiers*, she told Roché how the Cathars fitted into her world view, based upon her belief that the best minds of the ancient world – of whom Plato was the finest – adhered to a single philosophical and religious tradition. 'It is from this thought that Christianity issued; but only the Gnostics, Manichaeans, and Cathars seemed to have kept really faithful to it. They alone really escaped the coarseness of mind and baseness of heart which were disseminated over vast territories by the Roman domination and which still, today, compose the atmosphere of Europe.' Catharism, she thought, was not simply a philosophy, pursued by a number of individuals, but a religion which pervaded the whole environment. Weil felt that a revival of the kind of spiritual life which the Cathars represented was urgently needed in her own time, and encouraged Roché to try to publish texts for the general public which would attract the attention his studies deserved.[3]

Simone Weil wrote two articles on the subject, probably during 1941, for a special edition of the *Cahiers du Sud*, published in 1943 to celebrate 'Le Génie d'oc'. The first of these – *L'Agonie d'une civilisation vue à travers un poème épique* – was largely inspired by her reading of the *Chanson de la croisade albigeoise*, in particular the second, pro-southern part of the poem. She saw the theme of the poem as epic because, for her, it was concerned with the delivery of a death-blow to 'an entire civilization in its prime'. The Albigensian Crusade was a religious war in which there was 'no question of religion'; it was rather another demonstration of one of the major themes of her writing, that of the triumph of 'the empire of force'. Greek civilisation

---

3   Simone Weil, 'Letter to Déodat Roché', in G. Panichas, ed., *The Simone Weil Reader* (New York, 1977), pp.82–5.

had been 'almost the only light we possess', but had been crushed by Roman arms which had 'brought sterility to the Mediterranean basin'. Only once in the last twenty-two centuries was there a Mediterranean civilisation which might – had it been given the chance – have attained 'a degree of freedom and spiritual creativity as high as that of ancient Greece', and that was the Languedoc of the Cathars. 'Little as we know about the Cathars, it seems clear that they were in some way the heirs of Platonic thought, of the esoteric teachings and mysteries of that pre-Roman civilization which embraced the Mediterranean and the Near East.' She saw the diverse elements within these lands as bound together by chivalry, tolerance, and dignity. Indeed, it was the feeling of 'patriotism' for a country described by its language, which predominated. All this was brought down by the violence and bad faith of Simon of Montfort and the crusaders. The Catholic Church, which sought to obtain religious unity by offering 'unconditional salvation to those who should fall', bore a heavy responsibility, creating the circumstances which turned the war into one of conquest. 'Thus a shady deal in salvation and the acquisitiveness of a rather mediocre man were all that was required to destroy a world.'[4]

The second essay aimed at a wider context. In *En quoi consiste l'inspiration occitanienne?* she repeats her assertion that 'Rome destroyed every vestige of spiritual life in Greece', and that only Israel's revelation had been able to survive the onslaught. However, the true mission of Christianity was prevented from appearing at first both by its Jewish content and its association with Rome. The destruction of the Empire by the barbarians offered another opportunity and it was then that Romanesque civilisation was able to flourish in the tenth and eleventh centuries. This formed the true Renaissance, not the false one of the fifteenth century. Between these two the country which was the centre of this Romanesque civilisation – the *langue d'oc* – was destroyed, breaking the last living link with the traditions of India, Persia, Egypt, and Greece. 'The Gothic Middle Ages, which began after the destruction of Languedoc, were an essay in totalitarian spirituality.' Again, the Church was to blame for 'the assassination' of the Romanesque world, a choice of evil, for which 'now we are suffering evil'. Weil does admit that social life was polluted in Toulouse as everywhere, but 'at least the inspiration, composed solely of civic spirit and obedience, was pure'. This purity had found its most extreme form in Catharism. 'Their horror of force was carried to the point of practising non-violence and to the doctrine

---

4  Simone Weil, 'A Medieval Epic Poem' (L'Agonie d'une civilisation vue à travers un poème epique'), in *Selected Essays, 1934–1943*, trans. R. Rees (Oxford, 1962), pp.33–44. The articles appeared under the pseudonym Emile Novis.

which sees everything associated with the domain of force as originating in evil: namely, everything carnal and everything social.'[5]

It is not surprising that a personality such as Simone Weil should have been attracted by the asceticism of the Cathar *perfecti*. Her rejection of a materialistic lifestyle and her dislike of physical contact, established while she was still a child, were reinforced by a vigorous pacifism engendered by the First World War and by a deep pessimism about what she saw as the essentially evil nature of the human social order. Moreover, Weil's interest in Catharism coincided with her efforts to explain the rise of Hitler within the wider context of Western history.[6] In a letter to her friend, the Dominican Father J.-M. Perrin, written shortly before she left Marseille in May 1942, she seemed to be blaming the Catholic Church as well as the Roman Empire, for the contemporary plight of Europe, presenting it as the originator of totalitarianism in the form of the Inquisition. 'This tree', she says, 'bore much fruit.'[7]

For both Déodat Roché and Simone Weil therefore Catharism had become a vehicle for their philosophical and moral attitudes. Weil's claim that the Cathars, although little was known about them, were 'in some way the heirs of Platonic thought',[8] shows both in its cavalier disregard for evidence and its vagueness that her approach was fundamentally unhistorical; indeed, even in her teens, her history teacher described her as 'an intelligent girl who visibly feels herself to be above history'.[9] Unlike Roché, however, Simone Weil can in no way be seen as a neo-Cathar, despite her claim that she could see no real difference 'between the Manichaean and Christian conceptions concerning the relationship between good and evil'.[10] Throughout her life she seems to have been seeking a spiritual solution to the distress she felt at the condition of the world in which she lived, for she had learned early on that neither conventional political institutions nor revolutionary movements offered her the answers she sought. This solution, ultimately, though, did not lie in Catharism, for she remained convinced of the humanity of Christ and of his Crucifixion, as well as maintaining an appreciation of the world and of many of the human achievements within it.[11]

---

5  Simone Weil, 'The Romanesque Renaissance' ('En quoi consiste l'inspiration occitanienne?'), in *Selected Essays*, trans. Rees, pp.45–54.

6  For this phase of her life, see D. McLellan, *Utopian Pessimist. The Life and Thought of Simone Weil* (New York, 1990), pp.154–7, 164–89, 195–200, and J. Hellman, *Simone Weil. An Introduction to Her Thought* (Waterloo, Ontario, 1982), pp.65–73.

7  Simone Weil, 'Spiritual Autobiography', in Panichas, ed., *Simone Weil Reader*, p.25.

8  Weil, 'Medieval Epic Poem', p.38.

9  McLellan, *Utopian Pessimist*, p.17 and pp.151–2. See also Hellman, *Simone Weil*, p.58.

10  Simone Weil, 'Letter to a Priest', in D. Raper, ed., *Gateway to God* (London, 1974), p.121. Written September 1942.

11  See McLellan, *Utopian Pessimist*, pp.196–7.

For both Roché and Weil the Cathars became an integral part of their own moral universes: for one this meant almost complete identification, for the other a key place in her view of history. For a third contemporary – the German Otto Rahn – they were one side of an eternal struggle between two religious traditions, a struggle which formed the basis of his cosmology. Rahn was born in Hesse in 1904. As a young adult he had researched in various European libraries before first coming to the Ariège in 1930. He spent much of 1931 and 1932 exploring the region with his friend, Antonin Gadal, a local teacher from Ussat. For a short time he himself ran a small hotel in the town, but left owing many debts. In 1933 he published *Kreuzzuge gegen den Graal*, apparently hoping that earnings from this would at least offset some of what he owed. In this book he presented his interpretation of Wolfram von Eschenbach's famous *Parzival*, completed around 1210. In the sense that the story is generally interpreted in ethical terms – Parzival's gradual realisation of the true nature of God by means of the hermit, Trevrizent – Rahn maintains the central theme. The startling difference, however, is that he saw this in relation to the Albigensian Crusade and the personalities involved in it, an approach not easy to justify if only because of the evident chronological problems it presents. Thus Repanse de Schoye is seen as Esclarmonda of Foix, her brothers, Anfortas, the Grail king, and Trevrizent, the hermit, are Raymond Roger of Foix and (probably) Guilhabert of Castres, Cathar Bishop of Toulouse, and Raymond Roger Trencavel, the young *vicomte* of Béziers, who died in prison in 1209, is the model for Parzival. The two classes within Catharism are represented by the Templars (the Believers) and Trevrizent (the *Perfecti*). At the heart is the castle of the Grail at Montsalvaesche in Wolfram's story, but transformed into Montségur by Rahn. Here is kept the Grail, seen as a precious stone symbolising a dualist tradition which long predated Christianity.

Rahn therefore rejected the view that Bogomil missionaries may have spread Catharism to the west since, for him, the fundamental ideas were already embedded in Languedoc and had been since the era of the Celts and the Iberians, themselves heirs to the Persians. The Council of St Félix-de-Caraman was an attempt to consolidate their position and to unify doctrine in the face of what the Cathars perceived to be the growing threat of the Catholic Church. The setting for these events is a Languedoc where there is intellectual independence and religious tolerance, and where the spiritual and material demands of the Catholic Church are rejected as incompatible with the honour and independence of the inhabitants. The Albigensian Crusade therefore was a campaign to destroy this noble (and much older) civilisation, 'condemned to death' by men like Bishop Fulk of Toulouse, a former troubadour, whose whole life had been dedicated to exploiting any

opportunity which would bring him money and glory. The character of
the crusade was clear after the initial attack: 'Thus died Béziers, thus began
the crusade against the Grail.' After the conference at Pamiers in 1207, the
Cathars had suspected that the Catholic Church was about to use force,
and therefore inaugurated the building of Montségur, to be presided over
by Esclarmonda of Foix. Just before the castle fell in March 1244, the
Grail itself was smuggled out by four Cathars – this was the Cathar treasure
– and hidden in one of the many caves of the Ornolac region.[12] It may well
be, as Jean-Louis Biget argues, that Rahn was seeking to exploit the nostalgia
of a disillusioned Weimar audience, for he presents Guyot of Provins, a
northern poet who had extensive connections at the Aragonese and Toulousan
courts, as the major influence upon Wolfram, postulating a lost original,
suppressed by the Inquisition. There is a strong appeal to pangermanism
here, for the ultimate derivation can be seen as another Germanic source,
that of the Visigoths who, in the fifth century, had settled in Septimania,
the southern and south-western regions of Roman Gaul.[13] In fact, in some
senses, he was doing no more than exploit the ideas of Joséphin Péladin who,
in 1906, had turned Montségur into 'Montsalvat' and the Cathars into a
group of initiates and, more immediately, the novels of Maurice Magre,
whom he had met in Paris.[14] Much of the rest of the book is a straight-
forward, if not always accurate, account of the troubadours, the crusaders,
and the inquisitors.

However, Rahn has developed a notoriety since that time as a consequence
of a second book, *Luzifers Hofgesind*, published in 1937, which moulded his
previous theories to the contemporary racist climate of Hitler's Germany:
the two civilisations remain in conflict, as in the previous book, but now the
true God is Lucifer, the Bringer of Light, venerated by the Cathars. Around
him Lucifer gathers his 'court', which is pitted against the wicked Jehovah,
God of the 'Judaic' Catholic Church. 'With Catharism', he says,

12 O. Rahn, *Kreuzzug gegen den Gral* (Freiburg im Breisgau, 1933) (reprint 1985), esp. pp.246–
    7, n.38, 254, n.68, 135–8, 149–50, 157, 201.
13 Biget, 'Mythographie', p.312.
14 Not that either of them had much claim to originality. As Francesco Zambon expresses
    it, Péladan 'pillaged' the book of Eugene Aroux, *Les mystères de la chevalerie et l'amour
    platonique en Môyen Age* (Paris, 1858). For the context of the development of the myth,
    see F. Zambon, 'Le Catharisme et les mythes du Graal', in *CEI*, pp.215–43. For a recent
    popularisation of this idea, see M. Bertand, *Le Soleil des Cathares. Montségur, Citadel du Graal*
    (Paris, 1982), which accepts Péladan's claim that the Cathars and the Templars were
    secretly connected. On the historical, chronological, and linguistic flaws in Rahn's thesis,
    see M. Roquebert, *Les Cathares et le Graal* (Toulouse, 1994), pp.33–4, 101–2, 206.
    Roquebert sees quite the opposite significance in the Grail Cycle, see above, ch. 5,
    p.111, n.14. See also S. Nelli, *Montségur. Mythe et histoire* (Monaco, 1996), pp.99–128.

a power independent of Judaism and the Roman See was active until the thirteenth century, a force which did not need to be purified of all Jewish mythology because it had never adopted it. . . . This force united men, regions, and nations which were very different from one another but which were of all the same race and had the same origin.[15]

At the very least Rahn – like so many others – was bending with the wind; during this period he worked for Himmler, first in a civil capacity and then as a staff officer in the SS. It is for this reason that Biget accuses Rahn of opportunism for, as René Nelli pointed out in his preface to the reprint of the French translation of *Kreuzzuge gegen den Graal*, it is only the second book which is infused with political propaganda and anti-Semitism.[16]

*Luzifers Hofgesind* appears as a very minor footnote in the history of Nazi Germany; unlike *Kreuzzuge gegen den Graal*, which was translated into French within a year of publication, it was not translated until 1974. However, in more recent times it has stimulated a whole genre of books claiming to have found the key to historical events which has eluded the more 'conventional outlooks and methodologies' of academic historians. Many of these seek to exploit a post-war obsession – particularly apparent in Britain and the USA – with Hitler and the Nazi regime. One such example is *The Occult and the Third Reich* by two cousins whose names have been elided as Jean-Michel Angebert. This was published in English in 1974, although the title for French readers in the original work of 1971 was *Hitler et la tradition cathare*.[17] Heavily influenced by the novel, *Nouveaux cathares pour Montségur* by 'Saint-Loup' (Marc Augier), published in 1969, the work purports to show that Rahn was not an opportunist, but was rather the means by which Hitler 'actualized a

---

15   O. Rahn, *Luzifers Hofgesind. Eine Reise zu Europas guten Geistern* (Leipzig and Berlin, 1937), quotation p.255. French trans. *La Cour de Lucifer. Les Cathars Gardiens du Graal*, trans. R. Nelli (Paris, 1974). Rahn became a staff officer in the SS in March 1936, although he was apparently linked to it before this time, see C. Bernadac, *Le Mystère de Otto Rahn (Le Graal et Montségur). Du catharisme au Nazisme* (Paris, 1978), pp.246 ff, 347 ff.

16   Biget, 'Mythographie', p.312. O. Rahn, *La Croisade contre le Graal (Grandeur et chute des Albigeois)*, trans. R. Pitrou, new edn, C. Roy, preface R. Nelli (Paris, 1974), pp.16–17. See also Nelli's comments in the preface to his translation of *Luzifers Hofgesind*, pp.38–40. However, Bernadac, *Le Mystère de Otto Rahn*, p.392, believes that he was a convinced Nazi, but that his inability to provide proof of racial purity led to his resignation from the SS in 1939.

17   J.-M. Angebert, *The Occult and the Third Reich. The Mystical Origins of Nazism and the Search for the Holy Grail* (New York, 1974) (trans. L. A. M. Sumberg from *Hitler et la tradition cathare*, 1971). The authors are Michel Bertrand (see n.14) and Jean Angelini. According to Biget, 'Mythographie', p.314, the original perpetrator of these ideas seems to have been Philéas Lebesque in an article entitled, 'Sources secrètes de l'Hitlerisme', in the review *L'Age nouveau*, reprinted in Bernadac, *Le Mystère de Otto Rahn*, annexe II, pp.457–61. This article is not cited in Angebert's book. For information about the fictions upon which Angebert's book is based, see M.-C. Viguier, 'Otto Rahn entre Wolfram von Eschenbach et les néo-Nazis', in *CEI*, pp.165–89.

Gnostic racism', as the translator puts it. In this version of Rahn's life, he was twice sent (in 1931 and 1937) by Alfred Rosenberg to try to discover if Montségur really was the Grail castle.[18] The authors are uncertain whether Rahn actually found the Grail, but believe that it was eventually removed to Germany in March 1944, the seventh centenary of the ending of the siege, by an SS group acting on Himmler's orders. In Germany it would form the core of a special 'Black Order' derived from the SS. Thus Hitlerism could be explained as a manifestation of a long dualistic tradition – locked for centuries in combat with the Christian Church – stretching from the Gnostics to the Cathars and into the modern era via the Rosicrucians (founded in the fifteenth century), the Illuminati of Bavaria (founded in the eighteenth century), and the Thule Society (founded in 1914). The appeal of dualism to Hitler lay in the concept of the Sun (Light) as a symbol of the Aryan race in contrast to the Moon (Darkness), revered by the Semitic peoples. The link was consolidated when Rahn adopted the theory of Fernand Niel who, on the basis of measurements made at Montségur in relation to the position of the sun at various times of the year, argued that it was like a Temple of the Manichaeans for whom the Sun occupied a central symbolic role.[19]

It may be unnecessary to add, given Umberto Eco's dictum that the Templars have something to do with everything, that the Order of the Temple, founded in the Kingdom of Jerusalem in 1119 by a group of knights dedicated to the protection of pilgrims, while pursuing an ascetic, quasi-monastic lifestyle, can be considered an ally of the Cathars, albeit in secret. Proof was furnished by the Austrian Orientalist, Joseph von Hammer-Purgstall, in 1818 in the form of four 'Gnostic idols', allegedly once in the possession of the Templars. Just as once the secret of the Cathars was known the Albigensian Crusade was called by the Catholic Church to 'kill them all', words allegedly uttered by Arnald Amalric, the papal legate, at Béziers, so too were the Templars suppressed by a 'collaborationist' pope, Clement V, in 1312.[20] Again, what the authors see as the militaristic and

---

18 As Biget, 'Mythographie', pp.314–15, points out, Rosenberg's *Der Mythus des 20. Jahrhunderts. Eine Wertung der seelisch geistigen Gestaltenkampfe unserer Zeit*, 4th edn (Munich, 1932) makes only brief mention of the Cathars, although his comment that only the Albigensians and the Protestants (both ill-treated by the decadent French) adhered to true civilised values, can be fitted into this picture. However, it was hardly a central issue for Rosenberg.

19 For F. Niel's theories, see, for example, *Montségur. Temple et Forteresse des Cathares d'Occitanie* (Grenoble, 1967). On his ideas, see S. Nelli, *Montségur*, pp.131–2.

20 The notorious phrase, 'Kill them all, God will know his own' derives originally from the *Dialogue on miracles* by the Cistercian Caesarius of Heisterbach and is usually (although not invariably) discounted by serious historians. However, the quotation is frequently used by those wishing to promote the idea of northern brutality intent upon crushing southern civilisation. The passage in question reads as follows: 'Knowing from confessions of these Catholics that they were mixed up with heretics, they [the crusaders] said to the abbot

initiatory character of the Order of the Temple made a significant contribution to Hitler's conception of an elite order created to underpin his
theocratic self-image. It should not deter those who adhere to this explanation of the psychology of Nazism to learn that Hammer-Purgstall's 'idols'
have long since been demonstrated as forgeries, while the present structure
of the castle of Montségur has been shown to post-date the Cathar era.[21]

## Protestantism and Catharism

Although the differences between Roché, Weil, and Rahn are very evident
– Simone Weil described the Roman Empire as 'a totalitarian and grossly
materialistic regime, founded upon the exclusive worship of the state, like
Nazism'[22] – nevertheless, all three writers demonstrate how Catharism has
been deployed to underpin a world picture quite unconnected with that of
the original heretics. They were not, however, the first to do this; indeed, they
were part of a long tradition, established almost as soon as the real Cathars
had been extinguished. Hardly a generation had passed since the execution
of William Belibaste before the Dominican, Nicholas Eymeric, himself an
inquisitor and author of a manual on inquisitorial procedure, was falling
into the kind of confusion which had overtaken eleventh-century chroniclers.
Although he knew Bernard Gui's exposition, he still managed to place Mani
in the pontificate of Innocent III, making him the leader of the 'modern

---

[Arnald Amalric]: What shall we do, lord? We cannot tell the good from the bad.
The abbot, as well as others, fearing that as they were in such great fear of death they
[the heretics] would pretend to be Catholics, and after they had left again return to their
perfidy, is said to have said (*fertur dixisse*): Kill them. For God knows who are his. Thus
innumerable persons were killed in that city' (book V, cap. XXI, p.302). See also below,
n.39. It is noticeable that most commentators insert 'all' for the sake of emphasis and omit
*fertur dixisse* by which Caesarius makes clear that this is hearsay. On the other hand,
Caesarius was, like Arnald Amalric, a Cistercian, and therefore may have had some
knowledge of this, particularly as his reference to the role of Conrad of Urach as legate
(1220–24) shows that he was not writing later than 1224. For a discussion of the sources
for the fall of Béziers, see M. Roquebert, *L'Épopée cathare*, vol. 1, *1198–1212: L'Invasion*
(Toulouse, 1970), pp.258–61, and W. A. and M. D. Sibly, trans., *The History of the
Albigensian Crusade* (Woodbridge, 1998), Appendix B, pp.289–93.

21  On the 'disappearing stones' of Montségur and their alleged removal by neo-Nazis, see
Bernadac, *Montségur et le Graal* (1994 re-edition of *Le Mystère de Otto Rahn*), annexe VI,
pp.481–3. On the Templar 'idols', see M. Barber, *The New Knighthood. A History of the
Order of the Temple* (Cambridge, 1994), pp.320–3. On the dating of Montségur, see
M. Roquebert, *L'Épopée cathare*, vol. 4, *1230–1249: Mourir à Montségur* (Toulouse, 1994),
pp.26–7, 79–87, and S. Nelli, *Montségur*, pp.79–96. The new lord, Guy II of Lévis, totally
rebuilt the castle erected by Raymond of Pereille.

22  Weil, 'Letter to a Priest', p.143.

Manichees'.[23] However, the main themes were established from the sixteenth century onwards and, for Simone Weil at least, they still retained their resonance in the early 1940s. In her last work, *The Need for Roots*, she wrote:

> History can show us deeds of atrocity equal to, but not greater than –
> save perhaps a few rare exceptions – that of the conquest by the French
> of the lands situated to the south of the Loire, at the beginning of the
> thirteenth century. These lands, where a high level of culture, tolerance,
> liberty, and spiritual life prevailed, were filled with an intensely patriotic
> feeling for what they termed their 'language' – a word that, for them,
> was synonymous with native land. To them, the French were as much
> foreigners and barbarians as the Germans are to us. In order to drive
> terror immediately into every heart, the French began by destroying the
> town of Béziers *in toto*, and obtained the results sought. Once the country
> had been conquered, they installed the Inquisition there. A muffled spirit
> of unrest went on smoldering among these people, and later on induced
> them to embrace with fervor the Protestant religion, which, according
> to D'Aubigné, in spite of very great divergencies in doctrine, is directly
> traceable to the Albigenses.[24]

The first real impetus was indeed a consequence of the Protestant Reformation of the sixteenth century. Luther's Catholic contemporaries accused him of reviving 'sleeping heresies', although in fact it was they themselves who drew attention to what had, until then, been largely forgotten conflicts of the past. Influenced by collections such as the catalogue of heresies assembled by the Cologne inquisitor, Bernard of Luxembourg, published in 1522, they tried to demonstrate that Luther was part of a continuous tradition of wicked dissent which reached back to the Manichaeans but could be traced through the preceding centuries in the form of Waldensians, Albigensians, and Hussites, among others.[25] The polemicists had little in

---

23  M.-H., Vicaire, 'Les Albigeois ancêtres des protestants: Assimilations catholiques', in *CF* 14 (1979), pp.23–5, for the views of later medieval writers on Catharism. For overviews of writing on the Cathars and the Albigensian Crusade from the late middle ages onwards, see A. Borst, *Die Katharer* (Schriften der Monumenta Germaniae historica) (Stuttgart, 1953), pp.25–58, and P. Martel, 'Les Cathares et les historiens', in R. Lafont and R. Pech, eds, *Les Cathares en Occitanie* (Paris, 1982), pp.403–77.

24  Simone Weil, *The Need for Roots*, in G. Panichas, ed., *The Simone Weil Reader* (New York, 1977), p.191.

25  Some historians can still see vestiges of Cathar belief in the sixteenth century (such as that of the shepherd, Hans Thon, in Thuringia in the 1560s and again in the 1580s), but there seems little possibility that they had any connection with dualism of previous centuries, or indeed that the Catholic Church ever recognised them as such. See C.-P. Clasen, 'Medieval heresies in the Reformation', *Church History* 32 (1963), pp.392–414. Bernard of Luxembourg was probably influenced by the Imperial edict of the previous year, which claimed that such a tradition existed, see Martel, 'Les Cathares et les historiens', p.431.

the way of source material – and therefore nothing to undermine their concepts of the Church's past – but what they did have they deployed to the same end; thus, in 1561, as Calvinism spread across Languedoc, Jean Gay, a lawyer in the *parlement* of Toulouse, published extracts from Peter of Les Vaux-de-Cernay's chronicle as a warning to Catherine de Medici of the contemporary dangers which Catholics faced, especially if she pursued a policy of toleration. For their part the Protestants had initially been concerned to counter accusations of novelty, arguing that a true (although invisible) Church had always existed. It was not until the Lutheran Matthias Flacius Illyricus published his *Catalogus testium veritatis* at Strasbourg in 1562 that they too provided a concrete formulation for a continuity with the past. Flacius Illyricus emphasised the similarities between the Waldensians and the Protestants, while at the same time distinguishing the Cathars from the former; even so, he presented the Cathars as part of the same process in that both seemed to be denying the apostolic validity of the Catholic Church and rejecting priestly intercession. On this basis, at the synod of the Reformed Churches held at La Rochelle in 1607, the French Protestants commissioned a history from Jean-Paul Perrin, pastor of Nyons in the Dauphiné, which appeared as the *Histoire des Vaudois* in 1618. He claimed that Waldensians and Cathars did not differ in their beliefs, and that both were falsely accused of Manichaeism by a Catholic Church intent upon crushing and discrediting these proponents of the true faith. By this means he was able to construct a formidable martyrology for Protestants.[26] Perrin's misrepresentation had a long life. Catholic scholarship in the seventeenth century, culminating in the *Histoire des variations des églises protestantes*, by Jacques Bénigne Bossuet, Bishop of Meaux, published in 1688, offered convincing evidence that the Waldensians and the Cathars were not the same but, perhaps because positions had become so entrenched, its impact upon Protestants was not really felt until the mid-eighteenth century. Only then did Protestant writers begin to turn upon the Cathars, in the words of Arno Borst, 'with the complete aversion of disappointed love'.[27]

---

26  See Vicaire, 'Les Albigeois ancêtres', and G. Bedouelle, 'Les Albigeois témoins du véritable Evangile: l'Historiographie Protestante', in *CF* 14 (1979), pp.23–46 and pp.47–70 respectively, and D. Walther, 'Were the Albigenses and Waldenses forerunners of the Reformation?', *Andrews University Seminary Studies* 6 (1968), pp.178–202.

27  Borst, *Die Katharer*, p.34. See also R. Darricau, 'De l'histoire théologienne à la grande érudition: Bossuet (XVIe–XVIIIes)', in *CF* 14 (1979), pp.85–118.

# HISTOIRE

## DES VAVDOIS·

### 'VISEE EN TROIS PARTIES.

La premiere eſt de leur origine, pure croyance,&
perſecutions qu'ils ont ſouffert par toute l'Europe, par l'eſpace de plus de quatre cens cin-
quante ans.
La ſeconde contient l'Hiſtoire des VAVDOIS ap-
pellés ALBIGEOIS.
La troiſieſme eſt touchant la Doctrine & Diſcipli-
ne qu'ils ont eu commune entre eux, & la refutation de la Doctrine de leurs aduerſaires.

Le tout fidelement recueilli des Autheurs nommés
és pages ſuiuantes.

PAR IEAN PAVL PERRIN, LIONNOIS.

A GENEVE,
Pour Pierre & Iaques Chouët.

cIɔ, Iɔi. xix.

3. HISTOIRE DES VAUDOIS APPELÉS ALBIGEOIS
Page de titre de l'« Histoire des Vaudois » du pasteur Jean-Paul Perrin,
Genève 1619

**Plate 15**
The title page of Jean-Paul Perrin's *Histoire des Vaudois*, 1619 edition

# The Cathars and Occitan identity

For Simone Weil, though, the linear connection between the 'Albigenses' and the Protestants was more a demonstration of the continuity of the spirit of independence of Languedoc than a specific doctrinal similarity. More seductive was what has been termed the 'romantic historiography' of the Occitan past, writing which flourished best in the post-Revolutionary world of the early nineteenth century in which anti-clerical and regional loyalties often coincided, while at the same time the existence of a wider reading public increased the potential impact of these ideas. In some ways the ground had been prepared by Voltaire who, untroubled by any impulse to research, found the subject an ideal vehicle for demonstrating the evils of clerical fanaticism and feudal oppression. Both Augustin Thierry in 1820 and Simonde de Sismondi in 1823 built on this to lay the foundations of the pervasive myth of a Languedoc of civilised refinement in which the Albigensians, harbingers of free thought, were able to blossom.[28] Sismondi's influence was felt beyond France. By 1826 parts of volumes 6 and 7 of his *Histoire des Français* had been extracted and translated into English as a separate volume entitled *History of the Crusades against the Albigensians in the Thirteenth Century*, complete with an aggressively anti-papal introduction by the translator. Some flavour of Sismondi's message can be gained from the following extract:[29]

> To turn back the march of civilization, to obliterate the traces of a mighty progress of the human mind, it was not sufficient to sacrifice, for an example, some thousands of victims: the nation must be destroyed; all who participated in the development of thought and science must perish, and none must be spared but the lowest rustics, whose intelligence is scarcely superior to the beasts whose labours they share. Such was the object of the abbot Arnold, and he did not deceive himself as to the means of accomplishing it.[29]

This perception of thirteenth-century Languedoc, however, really began to solidify between the 1830s and the 1870s. Although late on the scene in comparison with the Catholic polemicists, whose view of the Cathars had

---

28  See C.-O. Carbonell, 'D'Augustin Thierry à Napoléon Peyrat: Un demi-siècle d'occultation (1820–1870)', in *CF* 14 (1979), p.144, and Martel, 'Les Cathares et les historiens', pp.427–9, 431–6.

29  J. C. L. Simonde de Sismondi, *History of the Crusades against the Albigenses in the Thirteenth Century* (London, 1826) (reprint New York, 1973) (trans. from parts of vols 6 and 7 of the author's *Histoire des Français*, publ. 1823 and 1826 respectively), quotation p.44.

been formed by the chronicle of Peter of Les Vaux-de-Cernay, these writers took inspiration from the other great narrative of the crusade, the second part of the *Chanson de la croisade albigeoise*, written in Occitan by a man whose bitter view of Simon of Montfort has since become clichéd by repetition in the form of his ironic obituary on the count's death in 1218.[30] Referring to his epitaph in the church of St Nazaire in Carcassonne, where he was buried, he describes how it says

> that he is a saint and martyr who shall breathe again and shall in wondrous joy inherit and flourish, shall wear a crown and be seated in the kingdom. And I have heard it said that this must be so – if by killing men and shedding blood, by damning souls and causing deaths, by trusting evil counsels, by setting fires, destroying men, dishonouring *paratge*, seizing lands and encouraging pride, by kindling evil and quenching good, by killing women and slaughtering children, a man can in this world win Jesus Christ, certainly Count Simon wears a crown and shines in heaven above.[31]

Beginning with the former *intendant*, Antoine Quatresoux de Parctelaine, in 1833, and culminating in the books of the liberal Protestants, Jean Bernard Mary-Lafon, librarian at Montauban, and Napoléon Peyrat, pastor of the Reformed Church of Saint-Germain-en-Laye, who published in 1842–45 and 1870–72 respectively, they created an image of the Albigensian Crusade as a papal attack upon a cultivated and blameless people, in which Raymond VI was a hero who stood up to the blind fanaticism of Simon of Montfort. A particularly striking example of the genre was Amédée Gouët's representation which appeared within his *Histoire nationale de France*, published in 1865. Gouët was a professional writer who, although he had read many of the sources, did not feel overly restricted by them when drawing his conclusions. His diatribes against the Catholic clergy are especially violent: Peter of Castelnau was a fanatic 'who had searched for a long time to find an occasion for a quarrel'; Arnald Amalric was 'a type of moral monster . . . the hideous model for whom it would be difficult to find among the most bloodthirsty evil-doers of humanity'; the fathers at the Lateran Council of 1215 were typical of 'the odious and infamous barbarity of the prelates of this epoch'. 'What man', he says, 'indeed, would not recoil with horror, with disgust, from a religion capable of adopting attitudes of this kind?' It is a view which, as Philippe Martel shows, owes its 'paternity' to Voltaire. The crusade therefore was the destruction of a civilisation by barbarians.

---

30  The *Chanson* had not been completely forgotten between the sixteenth and the eighteenth centuries, but its message appealed strongly to nineteenth-century romantics. See M. Zerner-Chardavoine, *La Croisade albigeoise* (Paris, 1979), pp.222–4.

31  *Chanson*, vol. 3, laisse 208, pp.226–9; trans. Shirley, p.176.

The French historian, Charles-Olivier Carbonell, calls Gouët, with some exaggeration, the 'theoretician of genocide'.[32]

Much of this writing concentrated upon the northern conquest, but Napoléon Peyrat focused much more on those he perceived to be the key figures in the south, lords like Raymond VII and Roger Bernard II, Cathar bishops like Guilhabert of Castres and Bertrand Marty, and troubadours like Piere Cardinal and Guillem Figueras. Once the seminal work of Charles Schmidt, professor of Practical Theology at the Protestant seminary at Strasbourg, had appeared in 1849, it was no longer feasible to imagine that the Waldensians and the Cathars were indistinguishable or, indeed, that the latter had any connection with Protestantism.[33] Neither Mary-Lafon nor Peyrat were comfortable with this undeniable fact, for it opened the way for counter-attacks from the Right and from Catholic historians who depicted the Cathars as an anti-social force intent on the destruction of the family, tolerated in a Languedoc not so much refined as frivolous and immoral.[34] Nevertheless, their ideas were in keeping with contemporary intellectual attitudes in the south; in 1854 the Félibrige movement had been founded to encourage the use of the Occitan language and, at the same time, the rediscovery of troubadour poetry offered powerful confirmation of the quality of the culture which had been suppressed.[35] The Cathars and their supporters, then, could still be presented as victims of 'the ferocious northern hordes' and, in a grandiloquent epilogue, Peyrat established the fall of Montségur as the potent symbol of the crushing of the Cathar world which it still is today.[36] Peyrat's claim that *la terre romane* (meaning the lands

---

32   A. Gouët, *Les Temps Féodaux d'aprés les documents originaux* (*Histoire nationale de France*, vol. 2) (Brussels, 1865), pp.337, 340, 366. See Martel, 'Les Cathares et les historiens', p.438, and Carbonell, 'D'Augustin Thierry à Napoléon Peyrat', p.150.

33   On Schmidt's work, see Y. Dossat, 'Un Initiateur: Charles Schmidt', in *CF* 14 (1979), pp.163–84, and B. Hamilton, 'The legacy of Charles Schmidt to the study of Christian dualism', *Journal of Medieval History* 24 (1998), pp.191–214.

34   See A. Roach, 'Occitania past and present: southern consciousness in medieval and modern French politics', *History Workshop Journal* 43 (1997), pp.12–13, and P. Martel, 'Qui n'a pas son albigeois? Le souvenir de la Croisade et ses utilisations politiques', in *CEI*, pp.319–21.

35   See Roach, 'Occitania past and present', p.11, and Carbonell, 'D'Augustin Thierry à Napoléon Peyrat', pp.149–55. For the wider context, see T. Zeldin, *France, 1848–1945*, vol. 2, *Intellect, Taste and Anxiety* (Oxford, 1977), pp.43–54.

36   N. Peyrat, *Histoire des Albigeois. Les Albigeois et l'Inquisition*, vol. 1 (Paris, 1870), p.7 ('hordes féroces'), vol. 2 (1870), pp.1–100 (Montségur), vol. 3 (1872), pp.411–66 (epilogue). For modern examples, see F. Niel, *Albigeois et Cathares* (Paris, 1955) and Z. Oldenbourg, *Massacre at Montségur. A History of the Albigensian Crusade*, trans. P. Green (London, 1961) (originally, *Le bûcher de Montségur*, 1959). The fall of Montségur is the culmination of Niel's little book (which appeared in the Que sais-je? series). For him it was 'a fatal blow to Occitan Catharism', since it was not just another fortress, but a temple of the cult, see esp. pp.113–15. See also M. Roquebert, 'Napoléon Peyrat, le trésor et le nouveau Montségur', in *CEI*, pp.345–73.

**Plate 16**
Montségur. It was rebuilt in the second half of the thirteenth century

south of the Loire) had been a centre of 'religious liberty and the freedom of the human spirit against Roman theocracy' established the myth which so appealed to Simone Weil.[37] For Peyrat the story of the Albigensian war was 'the Iliad of the Pyrenean peoples', an image irresistible to the Graecophile Weil for whom, in the *Chanson de la croisade albigeoise*, Troy becomes Toulouse.[38]

This interpretation of France's medieval past had never been unchallenged, especially from Catholic writers in the seventeenth and eighteenth centuries and later, in the nineteenth century, from the Right. The rise of Nazism had forced Simone Weil to consider the historical processes which had led to the dire situation of France in the early 1940s; in the historian Pierre Belperron it had a similar effect but produced a quite different reaction. Belperron castigated those who promoted what he saw as a sentimental attitude to the past. In the preface to his work, *La Croisade contre les Albigeois et l'union du Languedoc à la France (1209–49)*, published in 1942, he claimed that partisan passion had transformed the Albigensian wars – quite unexceptional in the annals of warfare – into expeditions intent upon pillage and cruelty. 'The Church, the feudality and the Capetian monarchy had, by iron and fire crushed the democratic, liberal and tolerant civilisation' which was supposed to be flowering in the Midi. While he accepted that such feelings were understandable in their original context, he believed that it was inadmissible 'to have willingly maintained the error despite the discoveries of historical science, and to have presented it as an absolute and obligatory truth'. He deplored the fact that 'pseudo-histories' such as that of Napoléon Peyrat still remained 'the breviary of too many Occitans', even though Peyrat was not always writing in good faith, and 'his errors were not always involuntary'. Worst of all was the recent work of Otto Rahn, where 'all that concerns the crusade is marked by ignorance and bad faith' and it was principally in reaction to *le méchant livre* that he had undertaken the present study. This had a lesson for his own time; indeed, he admitted that the 'disasters which have overwhelmed our country were not without influence on our judgements'. There were, he said, striking analogies between the Languedoc of 1209 and the France of 1939, for the same material and moral causes had produced the same effects. In order to accomplish the task facing it, today's France ought to draw on past examples of 'virility and energy'. France in the thirteenth century was 'the torch of the world', the political, intellectual, and architectural leader. Now was not the time for 'the subtleties and refinements of the court of the Raymonds', but that of 'these knights of the Ile-de-France, of

---

37  Peyrat, *Histoire des Albigeois*, vol. 1, p.1.
38  Ibid., pp.2, 16 (Iliad theme). Weil's comparison with Troy, 'Medieval Epic Poem', p.35.

Normandy and of Champagne, who for their honour and their faith, knew how to struggle, to suffer, and to die'.[39]

Belperron's view was powerfully influenced by the events of 1940; there had been a similar reaction against what some saw as self-indulgent regionalism in the wake of the defeat by Prussia in 1871. Peyrat had found a way around this, claiming that the existence in his day of an 'indivisible' nation was a consequence of the triumph of the Revolution which had moulded 'the two Frances' together: 'the monarchical North has given unity, the democratic Midi has furnished liberty'.[40] Peyrat's instincts may well have been correct, for popular support for this image of Languedoc's past has not been easy to stimulate. Neither appeals to the past during the great crisis of southern viticulture in 1907, nor more recent attempts to present touristic development as a form of northern exploitation seem to have found any great resonance among most of the population of the Midi.[41]

During the 1970s regionalist movements again became fashionable, not only in France but across Europe as a whole, once more encouraging a romantic view of the Languedoc. One manifestation of this was a 1976 recording of thirteenth-century troubadour poetry, including extracts from the work of Peire Cardenal, Guillem Augier Novella, Guillem Figueiras, Pierre Bremon Ricas Novas, Tomier and Palazi, and Bernart Sicart Marjevals, as well as elements from both parts of the *Chanson de la croisade albigeoise*. This was the work of the Occitan singer, Claude Marti, and the Studio der Frühen Musik led by Thomas Binkley, later director of early music at Indiana University. Echoing Simone Weil, it was presented under the evocative title of *L'Agonie du Languedoc*. According to Thomas Binkley's sleeve notes: 'The revitalization of this ancient language today makes this unusual combination possible; the texts are all original thirteenth-century poems, yet when Claude Marti is singing these texts he is thinking of today's Languedoc, striving

---

39  P. Belperron, *La Croisade contre les Albigeois et l'union du Languedoc à la France, 1209–1249* (Paris, 1942), preface, pp.i–xvii, and conclusion, pp.447–56. Belperron's remark that, initially, Montfort attempted 'une sage politique de collaboration' with the local nobility (p.449) has often led him to be described as a *pétainiste*, see Martel, 'Qui n'a pas son albigeois?', pp.341–2. Not surprisingly, Belperron is among those who deny that Arnald Amalric ever said, 'Kill them all . . .' Not unreasonably, he finds it strange that anyone should stop to ask such a question in the middle of such a *mêlée*, pp.165–6, and n.3.

40  Peyrat, *Histoire des Albigeois*, vol. 3, pp.455–6.

41  For the crisis of 1907, see Zerner-Chardavoine, *La Croisade albigeoise*, pp.235–7, and for tourism, see Roach, 'Occitania past and present', pp.17–18. This does not mean, though, that the spirit of Southern independence is completely dead. In February 1996, the possessions of Dr Pierre Salette of Ax-les-Termes were auctioned in order to pay for an outstanding tax bill. Dr Salette claimed that an edict of Count Roger of Foix in 1241 exempted the people of Ax from paying tax. The French Finance Ministry informed him that any such privilege had been annulled, *The Times*, 21 February 1996.

once again after seven centuries, for its deserved cultural independence, which was lost in this Albigensian Crusade.' The result is a very attractive recording, but the key to the spirit behind it can be seen in the last part of the sentence, for the notes are firmly in the tradition of Napoléon Peyrat. Although the texts are original, no music has survived, but 'it is not the musical style, it is the anger, despair and helplessness of the ravaging of Languedoc, the frustration of a people subjected to a cultural starvation economy that unites the pieces on this recording; magnificent poetry which has outlived that forgotten war, the Albigensian Crusade.' The crusade itself was epitomised by the cry of 'Kill them all, . . .', and conducted with cruelty and terror by Simon of Montfort. It was followed by the intimidation of the Inquisition, aimed especially at the poets, whose work was characterised by their bitter anti-clericalism and anti-papalism. The conflict is seen mainly in political terms which had relevance to the 1970s rather than in relation to religious issues. Indeed, the Cathars are described simply as 'a harmless, ascetic Paulician sect'.[42] But like its predecessors, the *occitaniste* movement of the 1970s lacked depth; by 1977 it had lost most of its impetus. The decentralisation and encouragement of regional languages which took place after 1981 was largely the result of governmental action rather than local protest. As has been pointed out by Alain Touraine, the two major elements in the movement – the cultural-historical and the economic – do not seem compatible, as one looks to a past which does not evoke the kind of response the militants might hope for, while the other thinks in terms of future regional economic development. Perhaps only in the promotion of tourism do the two elements achieve synthesis.[43]

Indeed, the major legacy of these ideas in the last generation seems to have been what Charles-Olivier Carbonell has called the *vulgarisation* of the subject, as expressed in television, advertising, and tourism.[44] The

---

42  *L'Agonie du Languedoc*, by Claude Marti and the Studio der Frühen Musik. Reflexe. Stationen Europäischer Musik. EMI Electrola GmbH (Köln, 1976) (IC063–30 132).

43  See A. Touraine, 'Sociological interaction and the internal dynamics of the Occitanist movement', in E. A. Tiryakion and R. Rogowski, eds, *New Nationalisms of the Developed West* (London and Boston, MA, 1985), pp.157–75. This, however, is hardly a new discovery, for it was as much a problem in the era of the Félibrige in the mid-nineteenth century, as in the second half of the twentieth. See Zeldin, *France, 1848–1945*, vol. 2, *Intellect, Taste and Anxiety*, p.50, where he compares the Provençal and Catalan regional movements.

44  C.-O. Carbonell, 'Vulgarisation et récupération: le catharisme à travers les mass-media', in *CF* 14 (1979), pp.361–80. This is not an exclusively French phenomenon. An article by Suzanne Lowry headed 'Haunted by the Inquisition', published in the *Weekend Telegraph* Travel Section, 22 February 1997, drew the area to the attention of potential British tourists. True to form, the crusade and the Inquisition 'remain among the worst atrocities in the history of the Catholic Church and of France'. At Béziers a soldier (rather than Arnald Amalric) is given the line, 'Kill them all . . .'.

**Plate 17**
'Cathar' wine and 'bonhomme' adhesive labels

**Plate 18**

Commemorative stone on the Esplanade du Plo, Jardin de l'Evêché, at the site of the castle of Lavaur. 'A Lavaur, le peuple occitan perdit son independance mais dans sept siècles le laurier reverdira.'

224

Hautes-Corbières have become *le pays cathare*, covered with the ubiquitous brown signs of the heritage industry, pointing to castles where, in return for clearing the thistles and improving the road access, the authorities now impose pay desks and piped music. Various towns have seized the opportunity to present their credentials. Lavaur is perhaps the most striking with its commemorative stone on the Esplanade du Plo, site of the former castle. Here, where Aimery of Montréal was hanged and his sister flung down a well, the laurel is evoked as the crown of the martyrs. Today, therefore, everybody can be a Cathar.[45] The most prolific form of this exploitation of Catharism has been in the creation of a whole genre of historical detective works, in which the authors claim to have uncovered 'mysteries' hidden from our ancestors for centuries, although it is worth remembering that Péladan's Grail fantasy is little more than a hundred years old.[46] Christiane Roy, in an introduction to a French edition of Otto Rahn's *Kreuzzuge gegen den Graal*, which appeared in 1964, claimed that his originality 'is to have made a synthesis of elements apparently without links'.[47] He has certainly not lacked successors. These are ideally suited to a world in which affluence has done nothing to undermine superstition and credulity, and where the Cathar Grail of Montségur can quite naturally join the Turin Shroud and the neo-Templars in a sacred triumvirate of the occult.

---

45  Sometimes, because of reincarnation, literally so. See A. Guirdham, *The Great Heresy* (Jersey, 1977), esp. pp.35–7, 56–7, 60, 67, 73–7, 90, 151. Dr Guirdham was a consultant psychiatrist. For his account of the experiences of his patient, see *The Cathars and Reincarnation. The Record of Past Life in 13th century France* (London 1970) (trans. C. Brelet, *Les Cathares et la réincarnation* (Paris, 1971)).

46  See L. Albaret, 'Les Publications contemporaines à thème cathare: délire, ésotérico-commercial et imaginaire catharophile', in *CEI*, pp.377–97, esp. pp.380–1, on the recipe for success in today's competitive book market. The scale of this is immense. Albaret found more than 200 books of this type published between 1970 and 1990 (p.384).

47  This comment was, seemingly, meant as praise. Rahn, *La Croisade contre le Graal*, p.19.

# FURTHER READING

## Sources

A choice of sources for the study of the origins of Catharism does in itself prejudge the question. Potential sources therefore (depending upon one's point of view) can be found in HH, which is a comprehensive collection, clearly introduced and skilfully annotated. Most important is the treatise of Cosmas the Priest, which is the basic account of tenth-century Bulgarian dualism, and the two complementary descriptions of dualism in Constantinople in the reign of Alexius I (1081–1118) by his daughter, Anna Comnena, and the monk, Euthymius Zigabenus. Most historians accept that the first signs of a heretical revival in Latin Christendom can be seen in the early eleventh century, although there is sharp disagreement as to whether the dissent shown is connected with Bulgaria or Constantinople, or is independent of outside influence. Further disagreement centres upon whether any of these heresies is recognisably dualist and, if so, whether this bears any relationship to the Cathars in the second half of the twelfth century. Much of the controversy stems from the methodology adopted to tackle the problems presented by the chronicles, letters, and synodal reports upon which historians depend for their evidence in this period. The reader has the opportunity to make up his or her mind, however, for almost all the relevant material can be found in English translation in R. I. Moore, trans., *The Birth of Popular Heresy* (Documents of Medieval History, 1) (London, 1975), pp.8–24, and WE, nos 1–6, pp.71–93, each with helpful introductions.

The earliest accounts of the existence of dualist heresy in the West about which there is general agreement are those found in the letter of the Premonstratensian, Eberwin of Steinfeld to Bernard of Clairvaux (1143/44) and the treatise of Eckbert, Cistercian Abbot of Schönau (1163), the Latin texts of which are in *PL*, vols 182 and 195 respectively. Eckbert's presentation has been re-edited with an introduction by R. J. Harrison, *Eckbert of Schönau's 'Sermones contra Katharos' (Volumes I and II)* (Ann Arbor, MI, 1990). There is a translation of Eberwin's letter in WE, no. 15, pp.126–32, and partial translations of the writings of both Eberwin and Eckbert in Moore, *The Birth of Popular Heresy*, pp.74–8, 88–94. For most (although not all) historians the next key stage in the spread of heresy in Languedoc is the holding of the Council of St Félix-de-Caraman, variously ascribed to 1167 or 1174–77, again because of disagreement about the significance and authenticity of the three main documents from which its existence is extrapolated. These are a brief account of the council, an extract from the sermon of *papa* Nicetas at the council, and a record of the agreement made about the boundaries of the new Cathar dioceses. The texts are printed in the articles by Antoine Dondaine, 'Les Actes du Concile Albigeois de Saint-Félix de Caraman. Essai de critique d'authenticité d'un document médiéval', in *Miscellanea Giovanni Mercati*, vol. 5 (Studi e testi, 125) (Città del Vaticano, 1946), pp.324–55, and Bernard Hamilton, 'The Cathar Council of Saint-Félix reconsidered', *Archivum Fratrum Praedicatorum* 48 (1978), pp.52–3, where, in common with the great majority of historians, they are accepted as genuine. Even so, the possibility that they were forged, either in the seventeenth or even in the thirteenth century, remains. During this period there was also a series of public debates between Catholic clerics and alleged heretics, most of which are referred to in the main narratives of the Albigensian Crusades described below, although the great confrontation at Lombers in 1165 was recorded by a scribe present for that purpose, *Acta concilii Lumbariensis*, in *RHG*, vol. 14, pp.431–4, trans. WE, no. 28, pp.189–94.

The crusades themselves are described by four authors who, between them, offer a variety of viewpoints: Peter of Les Vaux-de-Cernay (PVC), the fervent pro-crusader, William of Tudela (WT), pro-Catholic but full of sorrow rather than hatred, his pro-southern continuator (*Chanson*), a passionate advocate of Languedocian culture and rights, and William of Puylaurens (WP), a southerner who was employed by both Count Raymond VII of Toulouse and Fulk, Bishop of Toulouse, and was able to write with the benefit of a perspective developed over more than thirty years. A fairly conventional survey of these witnesses can be found in Yves Dossat, 'La Croisade vue par les chroniqueurs', *CF* 4 (1969), pp.221–59, which should be used in conjunction with the introductions to the various editions and translations. Both Pope Innocent III and his legates wrote many letters on the issues of the day, although there is no comprehensive collection of these: most can be found in *PL*, vols 214–17, or in C. Devic and J. Vaissète, eds, *Histoire générale de Languedoc*, ed. A. Molinier, vol. 8 (Toulouse, 1879) (reprint Osnabruck, 1973). A new edition of Innocent III's letters is in progress, ed. O. Hageneder et al., *Die Register Innocenz' III*, 2 vols (Cologne, 1965, Rome, 1979). Devic and Vaissète have a wealth of material which includes the charters of many southern lords, as well the treaties and conciliar decrees relevant to Languedoc. The decrees of the major Lateran councils are published in N. J. Tanner, ed., *Decrees of the Ecumenical Councils*, vol. 1, *Nicaea I to Lateran V* (London, 1990), with parallel Latin and English texts.

From the 1230s the inquisitors were responsible for the creation of a rich body of records, mostly in the form of sentences and depositions made by those who appeared before them. The majority of the surviving thirteenth-century depositions can be found in the *Fonds Doat*, vols 21–7, in the Bibliothèque Nationale, Paris, a collection of copies made under the supervision of Jean de Doat, a royal councillor and president of the Chambre de Navarre, in 1669, and in *Manuscrit 609*, originally of the Bibliothèque Municipale, Toulouse, now kept at the Institut de recherches des textes, Paris, which contains the remains of the massive inquiry conducted by Bernard of Caux and John of Saint-Pierre in the Lauragais in 1245–46. Various parts of these documents have been printed, notably by Jean Duvernoy, ed. and trans., *Le Dossier de Montségur. Interrogatoires d'inquisition (1242–1247)* (Toulouse, 1997), which is a French translation of selected depositions, and by Célestin Douais, ed., *Documents pour servir à l'histoire de l'Inquisition dans le Languedoc*, vol. 2 (Société de l'histoire de France) (Paris, 1900), who has edited the depositions associated with the case of Peter Garcias (1247), pp.90–114, extracted from Doat, vol. 22. There is a partial English translation of the Garcias testimony by Walter Wakefield, *Heresy, Crusade and Inquisition in Southern France, 1100–1250* (London, 1974), pp.242–9. Douais also edited the register of the *greffier* of the Inquisition of Carcassonne (1250–57), pp.115–301, which derives from the Bibliothèque municipale, Clermont-Ferrand, *Manuscrit 160*.

The history of Catharism in Languedoc in the later thirteenth and early fourteenth centuries can be reconstructed from the depositions edited and translated into French by Annette Pales-Gobilliard, *L'Inquisiteur Geoffrey d'Ablis et les Cathares du Comté de Foix (1308–9)* (Paris, 1984), and by Duvernoy in the register of James Fournier, Bishop of Pamiers, edited in 3 vols in 1965 (*RF*), and translated by him in a separate publication, also in 3 vols (Paris, 1977–78). In combination with the sentences of Bernard Gui (1307–21), published by Philipp van Limborch, *Historia inquisitionis* (Amsterdam, 1692), partially translated into English by Samuel Maitland, *Facts and Documents Illustrative of the History, Doctrine and Rites of the Ancient Albigensians and Waldensians* (London, 1832), it is possible to build up a detailed picture of the situation at this time, particularly in rural society. Georgine Davis's *The Inquisition at Albi 1299–1300. Text of Register and Analysis* (New York, 1948), gives a view of late Catharism in an urban setting, apparently unconnected to the revival orchestrated by the Autier group in the Pyrenees. A useful modern summary of the main sources of depositions, together with references to published editions can be found in Anne Brenon's *Le Vrai Visage du Catharisme*, 2nd edn (Portet-sur-Garonne, 1995), pp.334–5. Handled with appropriate critical care – for it is acknowledged that the inquisitors' concerns are not those of today's social historians and anthropologists – the depositions can yield valuable information on religious beliefs, the familial links, and the social grouping of the southerners, as well as tantalising glimpses of the everyday life of the local population.

The first manual of inquisitorial procedure was written by Friar Ferrier in 1244, published in Latin by A. Tardif, 'Document pour l'histoire du *processus per inquisitionem* et de *l'inquisitio heretice pravitatis*', *Nouvelle revue historique du droit français et étranger* 7 (1883), pp.669–78, and in English translation by Wakefield, *Heresy, Crusade and Inquisition*, pp.250–8. More famous and comprehensive is that of Bernard Gui, apparently completed in 1324, *Manuel de l'Inquisiteur*, ed. and trans. G. Mollat, 2 vols (Paris, 1926–27), partially translated in WE, no. 55, pp.379–86. These manuals are particularly valuable in showing the framework within which the depositions were produced. In addition, William Pelhisson's account of the experiences of inquisitors in the 1230s, although in many ways self-serving, gives a unique insight into the context of both the depositions and the manuals. The Latin text with a French translation has been published by Duvernoy (Pelhisson), and there is an English translation by Wakefield, *Heresy, Crusade and Inquisition*, pp.207–36.

The easiest way to gain access to the complex writings on Cathar belief and organisation is through the fine collection in WE, the use of which is facilitated by detailed notes. A new edition would be useful in order to take account of the extensive scholarship of the last thirty years but, despite a publication date of 1969, it remains an indispensable collection. The range of texts translated is remarkable, although it should be made clear that sometimes the material is extracted and, ultimately, the reader must return to the original materials, all of which are fully referenced. The two earliest works of the Cathars which, as might be expected, were of Bogomil origin, are the dialogue known as *The Secret Supper* or *The Book of St John*, and the reconstruction of the visible and invisible worlds in *The Vision of Isaiah*, both of which were in circulation in the West before 1200, the latter probably a generation earlier (WE, nos 56(A)(B), pp.447–65). Whereas the first text is an explanation of moderate dualism, the *Vision* seems to have been used by all literate Cathars. However, in the thirteenth century, textual survival is heavily biased towards versions of absolute dualism, that of Languedoc represented by the treatise contained in Durand of Huesca's refutation, the *Liber contra Manicheos*, probably produced between 1218 and 1222 (WE, no. 58, pp.494–510), and that of Lombardy in the highly polemical *Book of the Two Principles* of *c.* 1240 (WE, no. 59, pp.511–91), by a follower of John of Lugio. The key Cathar ceremony, the *consolamentum*, is set down in Latin (1235–50) and in Occitan (second half of the thirteenth century) versions, of which the Occitan is the fuller (WE, nos 57(A)(B), pp.465–94). The two texts known as *La Gleisa de Dio*, which describe the state of the Cathar Church, and the *Glosa Pater*, which is a commentary on the Lord's Prayer, seem to suggest a late form of syncretic belief, in which Catharism still had enough life left in it to play a part (WE, nos 60(A)(B), pp.592–630). Anne Brenon has dated these to the second half of the fourteenth century ('Syncrétisme hérétique dans les refuges Alpins?', *Heresis* 7 (1986), pp.5–23).

Cathar commentaries usually take the form of anti-Cathar polemic, often constructed in the prevailing scholastic mode. Some of these were written by former Cathars: the Milanese, Bonacursus (between 1176 and 1190) (WE, no. 25, pp.170–3), the anonymous author of the *De heresi catharorum* (between 1200 and 1214) (WE, no. 23, pp.159–67), and the Dominican, Rainier Sacconi (1250) (WE, no. 51, pp.329–46). Others were produced by Catholic writers, both clerical and lay. These included those by the Cistercians, Alan of Lille (around 1200) (WE, no. 35, pp.214–20) and Peter of Les Vaux-de-Cernay (*c.* 1213) (PVC, vol. 1, paras 10–19, pp.10–20), the Dominicans, Moneta of Cremona (early 1240s) (WE, no. 50, pp. 307–29), Anselm of Alessandria (1266–67) (WE, no. 54, pp.361–73), and Bernard Gui (1323–24) (WE, no. 55, pp.379–86), and the Franciscan, James Capelli (*c.* 1240) (WE, no. 49, pp.301–6) (although his authorship of the *Summa contra haereticos*, usually ascribed to him, remains in dispute). A layman, the Piacenzan, Salvo Burci (1235) (WE, no. 45(B), pp.269–74), and two former Waldensians, one of whom was possibly Ermengaud of Béziers (writing between 1208 and 1213) (WE, no. 37, pp.230–5) and Durand of Huesca (who wrote at least three works between *c.* 1190 and *c.* 1220) (see, for example, his *Liber Antiheresis*, analysed by C. Thouzellier, *Catharisme et Valdéisme en Languedoc*, 2nd edn (Louvain and Paris, 1969), pp.60–79), also wrote denunciations of the heresy from their own perspectives.

# General

The historiography of the Cathars is complex and, at times, bewildering. No two historians agree about even the main lines of their early history, although there is perhaps a greater degree of consensus about the causes of their decline. For these reasons I have tried to incorporate these debates both within the text and the footnotes, rather than attempting to summarise them in this appendix. As might be expected, most secondary writing is by French historians, many of them closely associated with Languedoc and its universities and institutes. I have, however, also tried to reflect the important work accomplished in the USA, Germany, and England, particularly on the origins of the heresy and on the development of inquisitorial activity in the thirteenth century.

Seven authors offer their own distinctive overviews. Arno Borst, *Die Katharer* (Stuttgart, 1953), remains fundamental, despite its age. It is systematic and clear, setting out the sources, beliefs, organisation, and history of the Cathars in a manner which effectively draws together the great progress made in research on the subject in the first half of the twentieth century. The four volumes by Elie Griffe (*Les Débuts de l'aventure cathare en Languedoc (1140–90)* (Paris, 1969); *Le Languedoc Cathare de 1190 à 1210* (Paris, 1971); *Le Languedoc Cathare au temps de la Croisade (1209–1229)* (Paris, 1973); *Le Languedoc Cathare et l'Inquisition (1229–1329)* (Paris, 1980)) are equally thorough, although his approach is more in the nature of a chronological narrative than that of Borst, and the fourth volume is more sketchy than the first three. However, given the ever-changing situation of the Cathars, this format has its advantages. Although sometimes criticised for its pro-Catholic stance (he was a canon of the Church), Griffe's work remains one of the best ways to achieve a grasp of the main outlines of this period. Jean Duvernoy's two volumes (*Le Catharisme*, vol. 1, *La Religion des Cathares* (Toulouse, 1976), and *Le Catharisme*, vol. 2, *L'Histoire des Cathares* (Toulouse, 1979)) reflect the considered views of a historian whose deep knowledge of the inquisitorial sources in particular enables him to reveal much more about the lives of the Cathars themselves than can be found in Borst and Griffe, although his often distinctive opinions on controversial matters such as the Council of St Félix-de-Caraman, should not be regarded as the last word on the subject. The books also include important reviews of the sources. More compact is Anne Brenon's *Le Vrai Visage du Catharisme*, 2nd edn (Portet-sur-Garonne, 1995), which incorporates much of the recent research, including Duvernoy's. Like everything in this field, however, not all her conclusions are beyond dispute.

Finally there are three general surveys in English. The oldest of these is Walter Wakefield's *Heresy, Crusade and Inquisition in Southern France, 1100–1250* (London, 1974). This is a lucid and concise distillation of the author's immense expertise on this subject and is undoubtedly the best starting-point for the English-speaking reader. Its modest approach belies the amount of useful information it contains and, as a consequence, its importance has often been underestimated. In addition, it contains six valuable appendices of key documents in English translation. The second of these is Michael Costen's *The Cathars and the Albigensian Crusade* (Manchester, 1997), which carefully delineates the context as well as the course of the crusade, taking particular care to analyse Languedocian society. The most recent study is Malcolm Lambert's *The Cathars* (Oxford, 1998). This is the only book in English exclusively devoted to this subject, despite the many references made to them in other historical literature. It is a wide-ranging work, covering the history of the Cathars in Italy, Germany, France, the Low Countries, and the Balkans, as well as southern France. It reflects the author's strength in eastern European history and is a useful antidote to the Francocentric approach of the bulk of the literature on the subject, since it gives full credit to recent work in German and Italian. Although Lambert does not provide a separate analytical bibliography, there is a useful running commentary on the nature of the sources and on the value of the vast but uneven secondary literature in the footnotes. Further bibliography can be obtained from Carl Berkhout and Jeffrey Burton Russell, *Medieval Heresies. A Bibliography, 1900–1979* (Toronto, 1981), and Daniel Walther, 'A survey of recent research on the Albigensian Cathari', *Church History* 34 (1965), pp.146–77, which can be used with M.-H. Vicaire's 'Le Catharisme: un religion (1935–1976)', in *CF* 14 (1979), pp.381–409. The subject remains dynamic: the best way to keep abreast of new research is to consult the journal *Heresis*, published by the Centre d'Etudes Cathares/René Nelli at Carcassonne. The Centre was established in 1981 and holds conferences, the results of which are published (for example, *CEI*), and maintains an important library of relevant books and microfilms.

# Chapter 1: The Spread of Catharism

It is evident historians will never agree about the origins of Catharism, for the sources are exiguous, enigmatic, or remote from the actual events, either mentally or geographically, and occasionally all three, so that they will simply not permit definitive conclusions. However, a sense of the nature of the debate and the issues raised can be found in the two different positions taken by Robert Moore and Bernard Hamilton. The most eloquent expressions of their respective views can be seen in Moore's *The Origins of European Dissent*, new edn (Oxford, 1985), and Hamilton's 'Wisdom from the East', in *Heresy and Literacy, 1000–1530*, edited by Peter Biller and Anne Hudson (Cambridge, 1994), pp.38–60. Both are original and subtle in their approach to the sources, but ultimately owe their perceptions to the ground-breaking research of Father Antoine Dondaine in the 1930s, 1940s, and 1950s. In 1939, Dondaine set out the state of knowledge in the light of his new discoveries, 'Nouvelles sources de l'histoire doctrinale du néo-manichéisme au moyen âge', *Revue des sciences philosophiques et théologiques* 28 (1939), pp.465–88, while in a later article, 'L'Origine de hérésie médiévale: à propos d'un livre récent', *Rivista di Storia della Chiesa in Italia* 6 (1952), pp.47–78, he declared his own position on the question of the early history of the Cathars.

Historians once felt that they were on surer ground in determining long-term influences upon Catharism, which they linked to a continuous dualistic tradition. This is reflected in the post-war publications of Steven

Runciman, *The Medieval Manichee* (Cambridge, 1947), Dimitri Obolensky, *The Bogomils* (Cambridge, 1948), and Hans Söderberg, *La Religion des Cathares* (Uppsala, 1949). All three books are now quite dated, but Obolensky's study remains valuable for its solid analysis of the various beliefs which might have influenced the Bogomils and, in turn, the Cathars. There is a modern synthesis of these problems by Yuri Stoyanov, *The Hidden Tradition in Europe* (Harmondsworth, 1994). A concise critique of the 'continuity' theses can be found in Ylva Hagman, 'Les Historiens des religions et les constructions des ésotéristes', in *CEI*, pp.131–43. Earlier work is summarised by Jeffrey Burton Russell, 'Interpretations of the origins of medieval heresy', *Medieval Studies* 25 (1963), pp.25–53.

# Chapter 2: The Cathars and Languedocian Society

At present there is no single volume which offers a general survey of the social, economic, political, and cultural context of the Cathar world of Languedoc. Thanks to the work of John Mundy, the best-known city is Toulouse. He has recently brought to a close a series of penetrative works of social history which build on his fundamental study, *Liberty and Political Power in Toulouse, 1100–1230* (New York, 1954). These include not only his books, *The Repression of Catharism in Toulouse. The Royal Diploma of 1279* (Toronto, 1985), *Men and Women at Toulouse in the Age of the Cathars* (Toronto, 1990), and *Society and Government at Toulouse in the Age of the Cathars* (Toronto, 1997), but also a lengthy and justly well-known article, 'Charity and social work in Toulouse, 1100–1250', *Traditio* 22 (1966), pp.203–88.

Two other historians, Walter Wakefield and Jean Duvernoy, basing themselves on inquisitorial records, have published many articles examining the histories of individual families, of villages, and social customs, which cumulatively provide an in-depth portrait of this society. Representative of Wakefield's work are 'The family of Niort in the Albigensian Crusade and before the Inquisition', *Names* 18 (1970), pp.97–117, 286–303, and 'Heretics and inquisitors: the case of Le Mas-Saintes-Puelles', *Catholic Historical Review* 69 (1983), pp.209–26. An example of Duvernoy's research on this theme can be seen in 'Les Albigeois dans la vie sociale et économique de leur temps', *Annales de l'Institut d'Etudes occitanes, Actes du colloque de Toulouse, années 1962–3* (Toulouse, 1964), pp.64–72. The three articles by Yves Dossat on the nobility, society, and the clergy, on the eve of the Albigensian Crusade (in the *Revue du Tarn* 9 (1943), pp.75–90, and the *Revue du Languedoc* 1 (1944), pp.66–87, 263–78), although published in 1944, are still valuable, even though he can only provide a snapshot within the length available. A later version of his approach can be found in 'Les Cathares d'après les documents de l'Inquisition', in *CF* 3 (1968), pp.71–104. Although basically a narrative, Michel Roquebert's five-volume study of the whole Cathar period in Languedoc contains a mass of material relevant to the social history of the thirteenth century and early fourteenth centuries. These have been published over a period of twenty-eight years, between 1970 and 1998. They are *L'Epopée cathare*, vol. 1, *1198–1212: L'Invasion* (Toulouse, 1970); vol. 2, *1213–16: La Depossession* (Toulouse, 1977); vol. 3, *1216–1229: Le Lys et la croix* (Toulouse, 1986); vol. 4, *1230–1249: Mourir à Montségur* (Toulouse, 1994); and *Les Cathares. De la chute de Montségur aux derniers bûchers (1244–1329)* (Paris, 1998). Moreover, these volumes have invaluable appendices identifying and mapping the geography of Catharism and demonstrating the familial links which underpinned the heresy through genealogical tables. A similar diagrammatic representation of orthodox monasticism in the region, both Benedictine and Cistercian, can be found in Philippe Wolff's *Documents de l'histoire du Languedoc* (Toulouse, 1969). As always, it remains difficult to find out much about the attitudes of 'the man in the street'; however, a new analysis of the contents of the depositions contained in the great inquiry of 1245–46 recorded in *Manuscrit 609* by Mark Pegg, *The Corruption of Angels: The Great Inquisition of 1245–1246* (Princeton, NJ, 2001), offers some intriguing insights into the minds of those obliged to face the tribunal of Bernard of Caux and John of Saint-Pierre.

Several historians have sought to define the role of women both in society as a whole and in Catharism in particular, beginning with the challenging Marxist interpretation of Gottfried Koch, *Frauenfrage und Ketzertum im Mittelalter* (Berlin, 1962). As this book shows, many historians approach this subject with their own preformed agenda, a situation which has led to some odd interpretations of the figures extracted by Richard Abels and Ellen Harrison, 'The participation of women in Languedocian Catharism', *Medieval Studies* 41 (1979), pp.215–51, based on analysis of inquisitorial records. The most recent overall study, which contains many sympathetic portraits of the experiences of individual women during the Cathar era is that of Anne Brenon, *Les Femmes Cathares* (Paris, 1992), in many ways a better book than her more impressionistic *Le Vrai Visage*. A literary historian with a sensitive appreciation of the relevance of the more obviously 'historical' sources is Linda Paterson. This can be seen most effectively in her book, *The World of the Troubadours* (Cambridge, 1994). As the title suggests, this is not a book about the Cathars (who receive relatively little direct attention in it), but it does present a detailed picture of contemporary mores of great utility to anyone interested in the nature of medieval Languedocian society.

# Chapter 3: The Cathar Church

Inevitably, perceptions of Cathar belief are closely related to opinions about their origins, but there are three analyses of increasing detail which offer a representative selection of ideas on the subject. These are Bernard Hamilton, 'The Cathars and Christian perfection', in P. Biller and R. B. Dobson, eds, *The Medieval Church: Universities, Heresy and the Religious Life* (Woodbridge, 1999), pp.5–23, the first volume of Duvernoy's synthesis, *Le Catharisme: La Religion des Cathares*, and Gerhard Rottenwöhrer, *Die Katharismus*, 2 vols in 4 parts (Bad Honnef, 1982). As nothing substantial has been discovered since Dondaine's time which can materially alter the balance of the evidence, Borst's (see above, General) analysis, pp.143–222, is still basic. These interpretations are mostly based on Cathar and Catholic writing, but Pegg's *Corruption of Angels* (see above, Chapter 2) offers a rather different approach, concentrating instead on popular belief.

The organisation of the Cathar Church is less controversial, although here too there are differences of opinion. Dondaine's work is again fundamental, especially 'Les Actes du Concile Albigeois de Saint-Félix de Caraman', pp.344–51 (see above, Sources), and 'La Hiérarchie cathare en Italie', *Archivum Fratrum Praedicatorum* 19 (1949), pp.280–312; 20 (1950), pp.234–324. Duvernoy's second volume includes tables of known Cathar bishops, Elder and Younger Sons, and deacons, in Languedoc (appendice II).

# Chapter 4: The Catholic Reaction

The story of the Albigensian Crusades is, in many ways, a familiar one, although there is still space for a modern narrative in English. There are two good, concise treatments by Austin Evans in K. M. Setton, R. Wolfe, and H. Hazard, eds, *A History of the Crusades*, vol. 2 (Philadelphia, PA, 1962), pp.277–324, and by Bernard Hamilton (Historical Association, 1974). At the other end of the scale is Roquebert's blow-by-blow account (see above, Chapter 2). Between these are Joseph Strayer (New York, 1971) and Jonathan Sumption (London, 1979), both useful for military events rather than Catharism as such. Strayer's book is best read in the light of Fréderic Cheyette's quietly critical review in *Speculum* 48 (1973), pp.411–15. Philippe Wolff's 'film' in *Documents de l'histoire du Languedoc* (see above, Chapter 2), helps to clarify the complicated movements of the crusader armies back and forth across the region. All studies of Pope Innocent III devote space to his policies on heresy, as in Hélène Tillmann, trans. W. Sax (Amsterdam, 1980;

originally 1954) and Jane Sayers (London, 1993). Albert Shannon's *The Popes and Heresy in the Thirteenth Century* (Villanova, PA, 1949) complements the more specific studies of Innocent III. More specialist is Raymonde Foreville, 'Innocent III et la Croisade des Albigeois', in *CF* 4 (1969), pp.184–217. Frederick Russell's *The Just War in the Middle Ages* (Cambridge, 1975) is the best introduction to the ideas behind the prosecution of warfare of this kind. Yves Dossat brings together the basic information on Simon of Montfort in *CF* 4 (1969), pp.281–302.

# Chapter 5: The Decline of Catharism

Not all historians judge the inquisitors to have been instrumental in pre-cipitating the decline of Catharism, but most would concede them a role to a greater or lesser extent. Two useful treatments of the medieval Inquisi-tion are by Albert Shannon (reprint Collegeville, MN, 1991) and Bernard Hamilton (London, 1981). At the other extreme is Jean Guiraud's sprawling *Histoire de l'Inquisition au moyen âge*, 2 vols (Paris, 1935–38), which is packed with detail drawn from the depositions of a wide range of witnesses. Yves Dossat's *Les Crises de l'Inquisition toulousaine en XIIIe siècle (1233–1273)* (Bordeaux, 1959) is essentially a study of the inquisitors and their vicissitudes during this period. James Given's *Inquisition and Medieval Society. Power, Discipline and Resistance in Languedoc* (Ithaca, NY and London, 1997) stresses the methods used by the inquisitors to bring pressure to bear on communities and individuals and shows the results achieved by their often innovative approaches.

As some historians argue, too much attention can be paid to the in-quisitorial role. Other methods, including the reform of the parish clergy, polemical and intellectual refutation, and preaching were used, as well as military force and administrative power, while the changes in the economic climate helped reconcile at least some of the populace to the new regime. Grasp of contemporary intellectual concerns and approaches and military activity are helpful here, even when the emphasis is not especially on attitudes towards the Cathars. The overall context of developments in thirteenth-century France is provided by Elizabeth Hallam, *Capetian France, 987–1328* (London, 1980).

# Chapter 6: The Last Cathars

Much of the fascinating story of the last Cathars in Languedoc can be reconstructed from witnesses brought before the inquisitors, most particularly in the depositions published by Pales-Gobilliard and Duvernoy (see above, Sources). One historian – Emmanuel Le Roy Ladurie – made brilliant use of Fournier's register to reconstruct the lives of a largely peasant community in one village, that of Montaillou, high on the Sault plateau above the spa town of Ax (trans. as *Montaillou. Cathars and Catholics in a French Village, 1294–1324* (London, 1978)). Criticism of his methodology notwithstanding (see especially Leonard Boyle, 'Montaillou revisited: *Mentalité* and methodology', in J. Raftis, ed., *Pathways to Medieval Peasants* (Toronto, 1981), pp.119–40), Ladurie's approach shows the potential value these materials have for the social historian, even though his study was not primarily concerned with Catharism as such. More directly relevant are Duvernoy's 'Pierre Autier', *Cahiers d'Etudes Cathares* 47 (1970), pp.9–49, and the last chapter of Lambert's *The Cathars*, where he convincingly justifies devoting so much space to such a limited and short-term revival. Both Duvernoy and Lambert build on the earlier research of Vidal ('Les Derniers ministres de l'albigéisme en Languedoc' and 'Doctrine et morale des derniers ministres albigeois', *Revue des Questions historiques* 79 (1906), pp.57–107, 86 (1909), pp.5–48, respectively), although neither share his pessimistic view that this represented a 'degeneration' of Catharism.

# Chapter 7: Cathars after Catharism

Charles Schmidt's *Histoire et doctrine de la secte des Cathares en Albigeois*, 2 vols (Paris and Geneva, 1848–49) marks the beginning of modern scholarship on the subject. As Hamilton's analysis shows ('The legacy of Charles Schmidt to the study of Christian dualism', *Journal of Medieval History* 24 (1998), pp.191–214), it has stood up remarkably well to the immense weight of more recent work pressing down upon it. The historiographical tradition is very fully covered in vol. 14 of *CF* (1979), which ranges from late medieval and sixteenth-century attitudes through the beginnings of scientific research to the commercial exploitation of the subject, or its 'vulgarisation' as Charles-Olivier Carbonell expresses it. The articles in this volume are complemented by M. Zerner-Chardavoine, *La Croisade albigeoise* (Paris, 1979), pp.217–49, where there is a collection of chronologically arranged extracts of writing from the sixteenth century onwards under the title 'L'Enjeu de l'histoire'. This historiography is so rich and complex, it has given rise to a considerable literature of its own: examples are Suzanne Nelli's *Montségur. Mythe et histoire* (Monaco, 1996), and Pilar Jimenez-Sanchez, 'La vision médiévale du catharisme chez les historiens des années 1950: un néo-manichéisme', in *CEI*, pp.65–96.

Finally, the Cathars have given rise to a whole variety of more or less eccentric viewpoints. Some of the books which have resulted are plainly based on their publishers' belief that invented 'mysteries' are more saleable than 'real history', but others are moulded largely by the authors' own personal philosophies, often formed before they had encountered the history of the Cathars. The most outstanding of the latter is clearly the philosopher, Simone Weil, but two others – Denis de Rougement and Arthur Guirdham – illustrate the varied forms these can take. Denis de Rougement saw the influence of the Cathars as pernicious. In his *Passion and Society* (originally published in 1940, but greatly revised in its 1956 English edition), his overriding thesis was what he called the 'inescapable conflict between passion and marriage'. He saw marriage as the basis of the social structure, yet undermined by a relentlessly rising divorce rate. He claimed that the Cathars, with what he perceived as their essentially negative view of marriage, bore a large measure of responsibility for this situation. For him there were close affinities between the troubadours of Languedoc and the Cathars (although he was careful not to 'oversimplify' by claiming that troubadour poems were a 'kind of secret language of Catharism'), for their ideas, both fed by eastern sources, the one by Manichaean thought, the other by Arab poetry, merged in combined opposition to marriage. In that sense, for him the modern breakdown of marriage had arisen because of the 'struggle between two religious traditions'. Arthur Guirdham, a retired English psychiatrist, represents the opposite extreme, identifying with the Cathars so completely that he believed that he had been contacted by the thirteenth-century heretics, who revealed to him aspects of their thought and activity previously unrecorded, the most important of which was their role as doctors and healers, based on a form of homeopathic medicine. 'It was made clear to me that the purpose behind the dissemination of knowledge of Catharism was to resist, as far as is in our power, the engulfing tide of materialism' (*The Great Heresy* (Jersey, 1977), p.37). Indeed, as a consequence of information gained from a patient during the 1960s he came to realise that both she and he had, in a previous existence, been Cathars in the first half of the thirteenth century (*The Cathars and Reincarnation* (London, 1970)). It was information from these 'discarnate' sources which persuaded him that, although the documentary evidence is not conclusive, the Cathars infiltrated the Order of the Temple after the fall of Montségur, and that the Templars were 'beyond doubt Dualists' (*The Great Heresy*, p.90). In the sense that he had lived before in the Cathar past, he saw himself as 'a convinced Cathar'.

# REFERENCES

## Sources

*Acta concilii Lumbariensis*, in *RHG*, vol. 14, pp.431–4. Trans. WE, no. 28, pp.189–94.

*Acta synodi Atrebatensi a Gerardo Cameracensi*, in P. Fredericq, ed., *Corpus documentorum inquisitionis haereticae pravitatis Neerlandicae*, vol. 1 (Ghent, 1899), pp.2–5. Trans. WE, no. 4, pp.82–6.

*Actus pontificum Cenomannis in urbe degentium*, ed. G. Busson and A. Ledru (Archives historiques du Maine, 2) (Le Mans, 1901), pp.407–15, 437–38. Trans. WE, no. 11, pp.107–15.

Adhemar of Chabannes, *Chronique*, ed. J. Chavanon (Collection de textes pour servir à l'étude et à l'enseignement de l'histoire, 20) (Paris, 1897). Trans. WE, no. 2, pp.73–4.

*L'Agonie du Languedoc*, by Claude Marti and the Studio der Frühen Musik. Reflexe. Stationen Europäischer Musik. EMI Electrola GmbH (Köln, 1976) (IC063–30 132).

Alan of Lille, *De fide catholica*, in *PL*, vol. 210. Partial trans. WE, no. 35, pp.214–20.

Anna Comnena, *Alexiad*, trans. E. Sewter (Harmondsworth, 1969). Greek text with French trans., Anne Comnène, *Alexiade (Règne de l'Empereur Alexis I Comnène 1081–1118)*, 3 vols (Collection Byzantine publiée sous le patronage de l'Association Guillaume Budé), 2nd edn (Paris, 1967).

Anselm of Alessandria, *Tractatus de haereticis*, in A. Dondaine, 'La Hiérarchie cathare en Italie, II', *Archivum Fratrum Praedicatorum* 20 (1950), pp.308–24. Trans. WE, no. 24, pp.167–70; no. 54, pp.361–73.

Avril, J., ed., *Les Statuts Synodales Français du XIIIe siècle*, vol. 4. *Les Statuts Synodaux de l'Ancienne Province de Reims (Cambrai, Arras, Noyon, Soissons et Tournai)* (Collection de Documents inédits sur l'histoire de France, Section d'Histoire Médiévale et de Philologie, vol. 23) (Paris, 1995).

Bernard of Clairvaux, *Epistolae*, in J. Leclercq and H. Rochais, eds, *S. Bernardi Opera*, vol. 8 (Rome, 1977), pp.125–7. Trans. WE, no. 14(A), pp.122–4, and B. S. James, *The Letters of St Bernard of Clairvaux* (reprint Stroud, 1998), pp.387–91.

Bernard Gui, *Manuel de l'Inquisiteur*, ed. and trans. G. Mollat, 2 vols (Paris, 1926–27). Trans. WE, no. 55, pp.379–86.

Bonacursus. *Manifestatio haeresis catharorum quam fecit Bonacursus*, in WE, no. 25, pp.170–3.

Bozoky, E., ed., *Le Livre secret des cathares: Interrogatio Iohannis*, édition critique, traduction, commentaire (Paris, 1980). Trans. WE, no. 56(B), pp.458–65.

Caesarius of Heisterbach, *Dialogus Miraculorum*, ed. J. Strange, vol. 1 (Cologne, Bonn, and Brussels, 1851).

*La Chanson de la croisade contre les Albigeois*, ed. and trans. E. Martin-Chabot, 3 vols (Les Classiques de l'Histoire de France au Moyen Age) (Paris, 1931, 1957, 1961). English trans. J. Shirley, *The Song of the Cathar Wars. A History of the Albigensian Crusade. William of Tudela and an Anonymous Successor* (Aldershot, 1996).

Charles, R. H., ed., *The Ascension of Isaiah, Translated from the Ethiopic Version, Which Together with the New Greek Fragment, the Latin Versions and the Latin Translation of the Slavonic, Is Here Published in Full* (London, 1900), pp.98–139. Trans. WE, no. 56(A), pp.447–58.

Clédat, L., ed., *Le Nouveau Testament traduit au XIIIe siècle en langue provençale, suivi d'un rituel cathare* (Paris, 1887). Trans. WE, no. 57(B), pp.483–94.

Cosmas the Priest. *Le Traité contre les Bogomiles de Cosmas le Prêtre*, ed. and trans. H.-C. Puech and A. Vaillant (Paris, 1945).

Davis, G. W., *The Inquisition at Albi, 1299–1300. Text of Register and Analysis* (New York, 1948) (reprint 1974).

*De heresi catharorum in Lombardia*, in A. Dondaine, 'La Hiérarchie cathare en Italie', I, *Archivum Fratrum Praedicatorum* 19 (1949), pp.306–12. Trans. WE, no. 23, pp.159–67.

Delaville Le Roux, J., ed., *Cartulaire général de l'Ordre des Hospitaliers de Saint-Jean de Jérusalem, 1100–1310*, vols 1 and 2 (Paris, 1894).

Denifle, H., ed., *Chartularium Universitatis Parisiensis*, vol. 1 (Paris, 1899) (reprint Brussels, 1964).

Dennis, G. T., ed. and trans., *Three Byzantine Military Treatises* (Washington, DC, 1985).

Devic, C. and J. Vaissète, eds, *Histoire générale de Languedoc*, ed. A. Molinier, vol. 8 (Toulouse, 1879) (reprint Osnabruck, 1973).

Doat. Paris, Bibliothèque Nationale, *Fonds Doat*, vols 21–7.

Doellinger, J. J. I. von, *Beiträge zur Sektengeschichte des Mittelalters*, vol. 2 (Munich, 1890).

Domairon, L., ed., 'Role des hérétiques de la ville de Béziers à l'époque du désastre de 1209', *Cabinet historique* 9 (1863), pp.95–103.

Dondaine, A., *Un Traité néo-manichéen du XIIIe siècle: Le Liber du duobus principiis, suivi d'un fragment de rituel cathare* (Rome, 1939).

Dondaine, A., 'Durand de Huesca et la polémique anti-cathare', *Archivum Fratrum Praedicatorum* 29 (1959), pp.268–71. Trans. WE, no. 37, pp.230–5.

Douais, C., ed., *Documents pour servir à l'histoire de l'Inquisition dans le Languedoc* (Société de l'Histoire de France), 2 vols (Paris, 1900).

Duvernoy, J., ed., *Le Registre d'inquisition de Jacques Fournier, évêque de Pamiers (1318–1325)*, 3 vols (Toulouse, 1965). Trans. J. Duvernoy, 3 vols (Paris, 1977–78).

Duvernoy, J., ed. and trans., *Le Dossier de Montségur. Interrogatoires d'inquisition (1242–1247)* (Toulouse, 1997).

Eberwin of Steinfeld, *Epistola ad S. Bernardum*, in *PL*, vol. 182. Trans. WE, no. 15, pp.126–32.

Eckbert of Schönau, *Sermones contra haereticos*, in *PL*, vol. 195, pp.11–102. Partial trans. R. I. Moore, *The Birth of Popular Heresy* (Documents of Medieval History, 1) (London, 1975), pp.88–94.

*Eckbert of Schönau's 'Sermones contra Kataros'*, vol. 1, ed. R. J. Harrison (Ann Arbor, MI, 1990), pp.1–373.

*Enquête de Bernard de Caux et Jean de Saint-Pierre en Lauragais (1244–1245)*, Toulouse, Bibliothèque Municipale, Manuscrit 609 (now in Institut de Recherches des Textes, Paris).

*Epistola ecclesiae Leodiensis ad Lucum papam II*, in E. Martène and V. Durand, eds, *Veterum scriptorum et monumentorum historicum, dogmaticarum, moralium amplissima collectio*, vol. 1 (Paris, 1724), pp.776–8. Trans. WE, no. 17, pp.139–41.

*Epistolae Domni Henrici Claraevallensis quodam Abbatis postmodum Episcopi Albanensis*, in *PL*, vol. 204.

Euthymius of the Periblepton, *Letter from Constantinople to his native land, identifying the heresies of the most godless and profane heretics, the Phundagiagitae, or as they are also called, the Bogomils*, in HH, no. 19, pp.142–66. Greek text in G. Ficker, *Die Phundagiagiten* (Leipzig, 1908), pp.3–86.

*Euthymius Zigabenus' Dogmatic Panoply against the Bogomils*, in HH, no. 25, pp.180–207. Greek text in J. P. Migne., ed., *Patrologia Cursus Completus, Series Graeca*, vol. 130, cols 1289–1331.

Fearns, J., ed., *Ketzer und Ketzerbekämpfung im Hochmittelalter* (Historische Texte, Mittelalter, 8) (Göttingen, 1968).

Geoffrey of Auxerre, *Sancti Bernardi Abbatis Clarae-Vallensis Vita et res gestae libris septem comprehensae: Liber tertius auctore Gaufrido monacho*, in *PL*, vol. 185. Trans. WE, no. 14(B), pp.125–6.

Geoffrey of Vigeois, *Ex Chronico Coenobitae Monasterii S. Martialis Lemovicensis ac Prioris Vosiensis Coenobii*, in *RHG*, vol. 12.

Gervase of Canterbury, *The Historical Works of Gervase of Canterbury*, vol. 1, in *The Chronicles of the Reigns of Stephen, Henry II and Richard I*, ed. W. Stubbs, (Rolls Series, 73) (London, 1879).

Guibert de Nogent, *Histoire de sa vie (1053–1124)*, ed. G. Bourgin (Collection de textes pour servir à l'étude et à l'enseignement de l'histoire, 9) (Paris, 1907). Trans. WE, no. 9, pp.101–4.

Guillaume Pelhisson, *Chronique de Guillaume Pelhisson (1229–1244), suivie du récit des troubles d'Albi (1234)*, ed. and trans. J. Duvernoy (Paris, 1994). English trans. W. L. Wakefield, *Heresy, Crusade and Inquisition in Southern France, 1100–1250* (London, 1974), Appendix 3, pp.207–36.

Guillaume de Puylaurens, *Chronica Magistri Guillelmi de Podio Laurentii*, ed. and trans. J. Duvernoy (Paris, 1976).

Guillaume de Tyr, *Chronique*, ed. R. B. C. Huygens, vol. 1 (Corpus Christianorum. Continuatio Medievalis, 63) (Turnhout, 1986).

Hamilton, J. and B. Hamilton, ed. and trans., *Christian Dualist Heresies in the Byzantine World c. 650–c. 1450*, with the assistance of Y. Stoyanov (Manchester Medieval Sources) (Manchester, 1998).

*Herigeri et Anselmi Gesta episcoporum Leodiensium*, ed. R. Koepke, in *MGH Scriptores*, vol. 7, pp.226–8. Trans. WE, no. 6, pp.89–93.

Hugh Eteriano, *Treatise against the Bogomils of Constantinople (c. 1165–80)*, in HH, no. 36, pp.234–50.

Hugh of Poitiers, *Historia Vizeliacensis monasterii*, in *RHG*, vol. 12, pp.343–4. Trans. WE, no. 41, pp.248–9.

Ilarino da Milano, 'Il "Liber supra Stella" del piacentino Salvo Burci contro i Catari e altre correnti ereticali', *Aevum* 16 (1942), pp.272–319, 17 (1943), pp.90–146, 19 (1945), pp.281–341. Trans. WE, no. 45(B), pp.269–78.

*Innocentii III Registrorum sive Epistolarum*, in *PL*, vols 215, 216.

Jacobus de Voragine, *The Golden Legend. Readings on the Saints*, trans. W. G. Ryan vol. 1 (Princeton, NJ, 1993).

James, B. S., trans., *The Letters of St Bernard of Clairvaux* (reprint Stroud, 1998).

James Capelli, *Summa contra haereticos*, in D. Bazzocchi, ed., *La Eresia catara: appendice* (Bologna, 1920). Trans. WE, no. 49, pp.301–6.

*Landulphi senioris Mediolanensis historiae libri quatuor*, ed. A. Cutolo, in *RIS*, vol. 4, pt. 2 (Bologna, 1900), pp.67–9. Trans. WE, no. 5, pp.86–9.

*Le Liber du duobus principiis*, in A. Dondaine, ed., *Un Traité néo-manichéen du XIIIe siècle: Le Liber du duobus principiis, suivi d'un fragment de rituel cathare* (Rome, 1939), pp.81–147. Trans. WE, no. 59, pp.511–91.

Limborch, Philipp van, *Historia inquisitionis, cui subjungitur liber sententiarum inquisitionis Tholosanae ab anno Christi MCCCVII ad annum MCCCXIII* (Amsterdam, 1692).

Maitland, S. R., *Facts and Documents Illustrative of the History, Doctrine and Rites of the Ancient Albigensians and Waldensians* (London, 1832).

Manselli, R., 'Il monaco Enrico e la sua eresia', *Bullettino dell'Istituto storico italiano per il medio evo e Archivio Muratoriano* 65 (1953), pp.44–63. Trans. WE, no. 12, pp.115–17.

Mansi, J. D., ed., *Sacrorum conciliorum nova et amplissima collectio*, vol. 23 (Florence, Venice, and Paris, 1799).

Matthew Paris, *Chronica Majora*, ed. H. R. Luard, vol. 4 (Rolls Series, 57) (London, 1877). Trans. WE, no. 27, pp.186–7.

Moneta of Cremona, *Adversus Catharos et Valdenses libri quinque I (Descriptio fidei haereticorum)*, ed. T. A. Ricchini (Rome, 1743). Partial trans. WE, no. 50, pp.307–29.

Moore, R. I., trans., *The Birth of Popular Heresy* (Documents of Medieval History, 1) (London, 1975).

Pales-Gobilliard, A., *L'Inquisiteur Geoffrey d'Ablis et les Cathares du Comté de Foix (1308–9)*, texte ed., traduis, et annoté (Paris, 1984).

Pasquier, F., ed., *Cartulaire de Mirepoix*, vol. 1 (Paris, 1921).

Paul of Saint-Père de Chartres, *Vetus Aganon*, ed. B.-E.-C. Guérard, in *Cartulaire de l'abbaye de Saint-Père de Chartres* (Collection des Cartulaires de France, 1) (Paris, 1840). Trans. WE, no. 3(B), pp.76–81.

Peter of Les Vaux-de-Cernay, *Hystoria Albigensis*, ed. P. Guébin and E. Lyon, 3 vols (Paris, 1926, 1930, 1939). Trans. W. A. and M. D. Sibly, *The History of the Albigensian Crusade* (Woodbridge, 1998).

Peter the Venerable, *Epistola sive tractatus adversus petrobrusianos haereticos*, in *PL*, vol. 189, pp.719–24. Trans. WE, no. 13, pp.118–21.

Rainerius Sacconi, *Summa de Catharis et Pauperibus de Lugduno*, in A. Dondaine, *Un Traité néo-manichéen du XIIIe siècle: Le Liber du duobus principiis, suivi d'un fragment de rituel cathare* (Rome, 1939), pp.64–78. Trans. WE, no. 51, pp.329–46.

Riley-Smith, L. and J. Riley-Smith, trans., *The Crusades. Idea and Reality, 1095–1274* (Documents of Medieval History, 4) (London, 1981).

Ripoll, T., ed., *Bullarium ordinis fratrum praedicatorum*, vol. 1 (Rome, 1779).

*Rodulfi Glabri Historiarum libri quinque. The Five Books of the Histories*, ed. and trans., J. France (Oxford Medieval Texts) (Oxford, 1989).

Roger of Howden, *Chronica*, ed. W. Stubbs (Rolls Series, 51), vol. 2 (London, 1868).

*Sigiberti Gemblacensis chronographia: Continuatio Praemonstratensis*, ed. L. C. Bethmann, in *MGH Scriptores*, vol. 6, p.449. Trans. WE. no. 8(B), pp.100–1.

*Stephani Tornacensis Episcopi Epistolarum Pars Prima (1163–77)*, in *PL*, vol. 211.

Tangl, G., *Studien zum Register Innocenz' III* (Weimar, 1929).

Tanner, N. J., ed., *Decrees of the Ecumenical Councils*, vol. 1, *Nicaea I to Lateran V* (London, 1990).

Tardif, A., 'Document pour l'histoire du *processus per inquisitionem* et de l'*inquisitio heretice pravitatis*', *Nouvelle revue historique du droit français et étranger* 7 (1883), pp.669–78. Trans. W. L. Wakefield, *Heresy, Crusade and Inquisition in Southern France, 1100–1250* (London, 1974), Appendix 6, pp.250–8.

Teulet, A., ed., *Layettes du Trésor des Chartes*, vols 1 and 2 (Paris, 1863, 1866) (reprint 1977).

*Theophylact Lecapenus (933–56) writes to Tsar Peter of Bulgaria about Bogomils*, in HH, no. 10, pp.98–102. Greek text in I. Dujčev, 'L'epistola sui Bogomili del patriarca constantinopolitano Teofilatto', in *Melanges Eugène Tisserant*, vol. 2 (Studi e testi, 232) (Città del Vaticano, 1964), pp.88–91.

Thouzellier, C., *Un traité cathare inédit du début du XIIIe d'après le Liber contra Manicheos de Durand de Huesca* (Louvain, 1961). Trans. WE, no. 58, pp.494–510.

*Traiectenses Fridericum I archiepiscopum Coloniensem hortantus, quod ceperit Tanchelmum haereticum eiusque socios, Manassen et Everwacherum, ne eos dimittat*, in *Codex Udalrici*, ed. P. Jaffé, in *Monumenta Bambergensis* (Berlin, 1869) (reprint 1964), pp.296–300. Trans.WE, no. 8(A), pp.96–100.

Venckeleer, T., 'Un Recueil cathare. Le manuscrit A.6.10 de la "Collection Vaudoise" de Dublin, I: Une Apologie; II: Une glose sur le Pater', *Revue belge de philologie et d'histoire* 38 (1960), pp.820–31; 39 (1961), pp.762–85. Trans. WE, no. 60(A)(B), pp.592–630.

Wakefield, W. L. and Evans, A. P., trans., *Heresies of the High Middle Ages. Selected Sources* (New York and London, 1969).

Weil, Simone, 'Letter to Déodat Roché' and *The Need for Roots*, in G. Panichas, ed., *The Simone Weil Reader* (New York, 1977).

William of Newburgh, *Historia rerum anglicarum*, ed. R. Howlett, in *Chronicles of
  the Reigns of Stephen, Henry II, and Richard I* (Rolls Series, 82) (London, 1884),
  pp.131–4. Trans. WE, no. 40, pp.245–7.
William of Tudela. See *La Chanson de la croisade contre les Albigeois*.
Wolff, P., ed., *Documents de l'histoire du Languedoc* (Toulouse, 1969).
Zerner-Chardavoine, M., *La Croisade albigeoise* (Paris, 1979).

# Secondary works

Abels, R. and E. Harrison, 'The participation of women in Languedocian
  Catharism', *Medieval Studies* 41 (1979), pp.215–51.
Albaret, L., 'Les Publications contemporaines à thème cathare: délire, ésotérico-
  commercial et imaginaire catharophile', in *CEI*, pp.377–97.
Angebert, J.-M., *The Occult and the Third Reich. The Mystical Origins of Nazism and the
  Search for the Holy Grail* (New York, 1974) (trans. L. A. M. Sumberg from *Hitler
  et la tradition cathare*, 1971).
Angold, M., *Church and Society in Byzantium under the Comneni, 1081–1261*
  (Cambridge, 1995).
Anguelou, D., *Le Bogomilisme en Bulgarie*, trans. L. Pétrova-Boinay (Toulouse,
  1972) (originally 1969).
Barber, M., 'Western attitudes to Frankish Greece in the thirteenth century',
  in B. Hamilton, B. Arbel, and D. Jacoby, eds, *Latins and Greeks in the Eastern
  Mediterranean after 1204* (London, 1989), pp.111–28.
Barber, M., 'Catharism and the Occitan nobility: the lordships of Cabaret,
  Minerve and Termes', in C. Harper-Bill and R. Harvey, eds, *The Ideals and
  Practice of Medieval Knighthood 3, Papers from the Fourth Strawberry Hill Conference,
  1988* (Woodbridge, 1990), pp.1–19.
Barber, M., *The New Knighthood. A History of the Order of the Temple* (Cambridge, 1994).
Barber, M., 'Moving Cathars: the Italian Connection in the thirteenth century',
  *Journal of Mediterranean Studies* (forthcoming).
Bedouelle, G., 'Les Albigeois témoins du véritable Evangile: l'Historiographie
  Protestante', in *CF* 14 (1979), pp.47–70.
Belperron, P., *La Croisade contre les Albigeois et l'union du Languedoc à la France, 1209–
  1249* (Paris, 1942) (rev. reprint Paris, 1967).
Berkhout, C. T. and J. B. Russell, *Medieval Heresies. A Bibliography, 1900–1979*
  (Pontifical Institute of Medieval Studies, Subsidia Medievalia, 15) (Toronto,
  1981).
Berlioz, J. and J.-C. Hélas, eds, *Catharisme: l'édifice imaginaire. Actes du 7e colloque
  du Centre d'Études Cathares/René Nelli, Carcassonne, 29 août–2 septembre 1994*
  (Carcassonne, 1998).
Bernadac, C., *Le Mystère de Otto Rahn (Le Graal et Montségur). Du catharisme au
  Nazisme* (Paris, 1978) (re-edited as *Montségur et le Graal – le mystère Otto Rahn*
  (Paris, 1994)).

Bertand, M., *Le Soleil des Cathares. Montségur, Citadel du Graal* (Paris, 1982).

Biget, J.-G., 'Mythographie du Catharisme (1870–1960)', in *CF* 14 (1979), pp.271–342.

Biget, J.-G., 'L'extinction du catharisme urbain: les points chauds de la répression', in *CF* 20 (1985), pp.305–40.

Biller, P., 'The Cathars of Languedoc and written materials', in P. Biller and A. Hudson, eds, *Heresy and Literacy, 1000–1530* (Cambridge, 1994), pp.61–82.

Bisson, T., *The Medieval Crown of Aragon. A Short History* (Oxford, 1986).

Boffito, G., 'Gli Eretici di Cuneo', *Bullettino Storico-Bibliografico Subalpino* 1 (1985), pp.324–33.

Borst, A., *Die Katharer* (Schriften der Monumenta Germaniae historica) (Stuttgart, 1953).

Boyle, L. E., 'Montaillou revisited: *Mentalité* and methodology', in J. Raftis, ed., *Pathways to Medieval Peasants* (Toronto, 1981), pp.119–40.

Brenon, A., 'Syncrétisme hérétique dans les refuges Alpins? Un Livre cathare parmi les recueils vaudois de la fin du moyen âge: Le Manuscrit 269 de Dublin', *Heresis* 7 (1986), pp.5–23.

Brenon, A., *Les Femmes Cathares* (Paris, 1992).

Brenon, A., 'La Lettre d'Evervin de Steinfeld à Bernard de Clairvaux de 1143: un document essentiel et méconnu', *Heresis* 25 (1995), pp.7–28.

Brenon, A., *Le Vrai Visage du Catharisme*, 2nd edn (Portet-sur-Garonne, 1995).

Brown, P., *Augustine of Hippo. A Biography* (Berkeley, CA and London, 1967).

Bullough, V. and C. Campbell, 'Female longevity and diet in the Middle Ages', *Speculum* 55 (1980), pp.317–25.

Carbonell, C.-O., 'D'Augustin Thierry à Napoléon Peyrat: Un demi-siècle d'occultation (1820–1870)', in *CF* 14 (1979), pp.143–62.

Carbonell, C.-O., 'Vulgarisation et récupération: le catharisme à travers les mass-media', in *CF* 14 (1979), pp.361–80.

Cazenave, A., 'Les Cathares en Catalogne et Sabarthès d'après les registres de l'Inquisition: La Hiérarchie cathare en Sabarthès après Montségur', *Bulletin philologique et historique* (1969), pp.387–436.

Cheyette, F. L., review of J. Strayer, *The Albigensian Crusades*, *Speculum* 48 (1973), pp.411–15.

Cheyette, F. L., 'The castles of the Trencavels: a preliminary aerial survey', in W. C. Jordan, R. McNab and T. F. Ruiz, eds, *Order and Innovation in the Middle Ages. Essays in Honor of Joseph R. Strayer* (Princeton, NJ, 1976), pp.255–72.

Chrysostomides, J., 'A Byzantine historian: Anna Comnena', in D. O. Morgan, ed., *Medieval Historical Writing in the Christian and Islamic Worlds* (London, 1982), pp.30–46.

Clasen, C.-P., 'Medieval heresies in the Reformation', *Church History* 32 (1963), pp.392–414.

Clément, P. A., *Les chemins à travers les âges en Cevennes et Bas Languedoc* (Montpellier, 1984).

Costen, M., *The Cathars and the Albigensian Crusade* (Manchester, 1997).

Coulson, C., 'Fortress policy in Capetian tradition and Angevin practice: aspects of the conquest of Normandy by Philip II', in R. A. Brown, ed., *Anglo-Norman Studies VI, Proceedings of the Battle Conference 1983* (Woodbridge, 1984), pp.13–38.

Coulton, C. G., *The Death Penalty for Heresy from 1184 to 1917* (London, 1924).

Darricau, R., 'De L'histoire theologienne à la grande érudition: Bossuet (XVIe–XVIIIes)', in *CF* 14 (1979), pp.85–118.

Delaruelle, E., 'Saint Louis devant les Cathares', in *Septième Centenaire de la Mort de Saint Louis. Actes des Colloques de Royaumont et de Paris (21–27 mai 1970)* (Paris, 1976), pp.273–80.

Dognon, P., *Les Institutions politiques et administratives du pays de Languedoc du XIIIe siècle aux guerres de religion* (Toulouse, 1895).

Dondaine, A., 'Nouvelles sources de l'histoire doctrinale du néo-manichéisme au moyen âge', *Revue des sciences philosophiques et théologiques* 28 (1939), pp.465–88.

Dondaine, A., 'Les Actes du Concile Albigeois de Saint-Félix de Caraman. Essai de critique d'authenticité d'un document médiéval', in *Miscellanea Giovanni Mercati*, vol. 5 (Studi e testi, 125) (Città del Vaticano, 1946), pp.324–55.

Dondaine, A., 'La Hiérarchie cathare en Italie, I: Le "De heresi catharorum in Lombardia"; II: Le "Tractatus de hereticis" d'Anselme d'Alexandrie, O.P.; III: Catalogue de la hiérarchie cathare d'Italie', *Archivum Fratrum Praedicatorum* 19 (1949), pp.280–312; 20 (1950), pp.234–324.

Dondaine, A., 'L'Origine de l'hérésie médiévale: à propos d'un livre récent', *Rivista di Storia della Chiesa in Italia* 6 (1952), pp.47–78.

Dondaine, A., 'Saint Pierre Martyr', *Archivum Fratrum Praedicatorum* 23 (1953), pp.66–162.

Dossat, Y., 'Le Comté de Toulouse et la féodalité languedocienne à la veille de la croisade albigeoise', *Revue du Tarn* 9 (1943), pp.75–90.

Dossat, Y., 'La Société méridionale à la veille de la croisade des Albigeois', *Revue du Languedoc* 1 (1944), pp.66–87.

Dossat, Y., 'Le Clergé méridional à la veille de la croisade des Albigeois', *Revue du Languedoc* 1 (1944), pp.263–78.

Dossat, Y., 'La Crise de l'Inquisition toulousaine en 1235–1236 et l'expulsion des Dominicains', *Bulletin philologique et historique (jusqu'à 1715), années 1953 et 1954* (Paris, 1955), pp.391–8.

Dossat, Y., *Les Crises de l'Inquisition toulousaine en XIIIe siècle (1233–1273)* (Bordeaux, 1959).

Dossat, Y., 'Les Cathares après les documents de l'Inquisition', in *CF* 3 (1968), pp.71–104.

Dossat, Y., 'La Croisade vue par les chroniqueurs', *CF* 4 (1969), pp.221–59.

Dossat, Y., 'Simon de Montfort', in *CF* 4 (1969), pp.281–302.

Dossat, Y., 'Un Initiateur: Charles Schmidt', in *CF* 14 (1979), pp.163–84.

Dufour, J., *Les Évêques d'Albi, de Cahors et de Rodez des origines à la fin du XIIe siècle* (Mémoires et documents d'histoire médiévale et de la philologie) (Paris, 1989).

Dupré-Theseider, E., 'Le Catharisme languedocien et l'Italie', in *CF* 3 (1968), pp.299–316.

Dutton, C., *Aspects of the Institutional History of the Albigensian Crusades, 1198–1229* (PhD diss., Royal Holloway and Bedford New College, University of London, 1993).

Duvernoy, J., 'Les Albigeois dans la vie sociale et économique de leur temps', *Annales de l'Institut d'Etudes occitanes, Actes du colloque de Toulouse, années 1962–3* (Toulouse, 1964), pp.64–72.

Duvernoy, J., 'Pierre Autier', *Cahiers d'Etudes Cathares* 47 (1970), pp.9–49.

Duvernoy, J., *Le Catharisme*, vol. 1, *La Religion des Cathares* (Toulouse, 1976).

Duvernoy, J., *Le Catharisme*, vol. 2, *L'Histoire des Cathares* (Toulouse, 1979).

Duvernoy, J., 'Confirmation d'aveux devant les Inquisiteurs Ferrier et Pons Gary (Juillet–Août 1243)', *Hérésis* 1 (1983), pp.9–23.

Duvernoy, J., 'L'air de la calomnie', in *CEI*, pp.21–38.

Emery, R. W., *Heresy and Inquisition in Narbonne* (New York, 1941).

Evans, A. P., 'The Albigensian Crusade', in K. M. Setton, R. Wolfe and H. Hazard, eds, *A History of the Crusades*, vol. 2 (Philadelphia, PA, 1962), pp.277–324.

Fearns, J., 'Peter von Bruis und die religiöse Bewegung des 12. Jahrhunderts', *Archiv für Kulturgeschichte* 48 (1966), pp.311–35.

Fichtenau, H., *Heretics and Scholars in the High Middle Ages, 1000–1200*, trans. D. A. Kaiser (Philadelphia, PA, 1998) (originally Munich, 1992).

Foreville, R., 'Innocent III et la Croisade des Albigeois', in *CF* 4 (1969), pp.184–217.

Gilchrist, J., 'The Lord's war as the proving ground of faith: Pope Innocent III and the propagation of violence (1198–1216)', in M. Shatzmiller, ed., *Crusaders and Muslims in Twelfth-Century Syria* (Leiden, 1993), pp.65–83.

Gillingham, J., *The Angevin Empire* (London, 1984).

Given, J., 'The inquisitors of Languedoc and the medieval technology of power', *American Historical Review* 94 (1989), pp.336–59.

Given, J., 'A medieval inquisitor at work: Bernard Gui, 3 March 1308 to 19 June 1323', in S. K. Cohn, Jr. and S. A. Epstein, eds, *Portraits of Medieval and Renaissance Living. Essays in Memory of David Herlihy* (Ann Arbor, MI, 1996), pp.207–32.

Given, J., 'Social stress, social strain, and the inquisitors of Medieval Languedoc', in S. C. Waugh and P. D. Diehl, eds, *Christendom and its Discontents. Exclusion, Persecution, and Rebellion, 1000–1500* (Cambridge, 1996), pp.67–85.

Given, J., *Inquisition and Medieval Society. Power, Discipline and Resistance in Languedoc* (Ithaca, NY and London, 1997).

Gouët, A., *Les Temps Féodaux d'aprés les documents originaux* (Histoire nationale de France, vol. 2) (Brussels, 1865).

Griffe, E., *Les Débuts de l'aventure cathare en Languedoc (1140–90)* (Paris, 1969).

Griffe, E., *Le Languedoc Cathare de 1190 à 1210* (Paris, 1971).

Griffe, E., *Le Languedoc Cathare au temps de la Croisade (1209–1229)* (Paris, 1973).

Griffe, E., *Le Languedoc Cathare et l'Inquisition (1229–1329)* (Paris, 1980).

Guenée, B., *Between Church and State. The Lives of Four French Prelates in the Late Middle Ages*, trans. A. Goldhammer (Chicago, IL, 1991) (originally 1987).

Guiraud, J., *Histoire de l'Inquisition au moyen âge*, 2 vols (Paris, 1935–38).

Guirdham, A., *The Cathars and Reincarnation. The Record of Past Life in 13th century France* (London 1970) (French trans. C. Brelet, *Les cathares et la réincarnation* (Paris, 1971)).

Guirdham, A., *The Great Heresy* (Jersey, 1977).

Hagman, Y., 'Les Historiens des religions et les constructions des ésotéristes', in *CEI*, pp.131–43.

Hallam, E., *Capetian France, 987–1328* (London, 1980).

Hamilton, B., *The Albigensian Crusade* (Historical Association, 1974).

Hamilton, B., 'The origins of the dualist church of Drugunthia', *Eastern Churches Review* 6 (1974), pp.115–24.

Hamilton, B., 'The Cathar Council of Saint-Félix reconsidered', *Archivum Fratrum Praedicatorum* 48 (1978), pp.23–53.

Hamilton, B., *The Medieval Inquisition* (London, 1981).

Hamilton, B., *Religion in the Medieval West* (London, 1986).

Hamilton, B., 'The Cathars and the seven churches of Asia', in J. D. Howard-Johnston, ed., *Byzantium and the West c. 850–c. 1200. Proceedings of the XVIII Spring Symposium of Byzantine Studies, Oxford* (Amsterdam, 1988), pp.269–95.

Hamilton, B., 'Wisdom from the East', in P. Biller and A. Hudson, eds, *Heresy and Literacy, 1000–1530* (Cambridge, 1994), pp.38–60.

Hamilton, B., 'The legacy of Charles Schmidt to the study of Christian dualism', *Journal of Medieval History* 24 (1998), pp.191–214.

Hamilton, B., 'The Cathars and Christian perfection', in P. Biller and R. B. Dobson, eds, *The Medieval Church: Universities, Heresy and the Religious Life. Essays in Honour of Gordon Leff, Studies in Church History: Subsidia* 11 (Woodbridge, 1999), pp.5–23.

Harrison, R. J., *Eckbert of Schönau's 'Sermones contra Kataros'*, vol. 2 (Ann Arbor, MI, 1990), pp.374–693.

Hefele, C. J. and H. Leclercq, *Histoire des Conciles*, vols 5(i), 5(ii), 6(i) (Paris, 1912, 1913, 1914).

Hellman, J., *Simone Weil. An Introduction to Her Thought* (Waterloo, Ontario, 1982).

Herlihy, D., 'The generation in medieval history', *Viator* 5 (1974), pp.347–64.

Herlihy, D., 'Life expectancies for women in medieval society', in R. T. Morewedge, ed., *The Role of Women in the Middle Ages* (Albany, NY, 1975), pp.1–22.

Holt, J. C., 'The end of the Anglo-Norman realm', *Proceedings of the British Academy* 61 (1975), pp.223–65.

Jimenez-Sanchez, P., 'Relire la charte de Niquinta', *Heresis* 22 (1994), pp.1–27; 23 (1994), pp.1–28.

Jimenez-Sanchez, P., 'La vision médiévale du catharisme chez les historiens des années 1950: un néo-manichéisme', in *CEI*, pp.65–96.

Julien, L., 'Celui qui fut Déodat Roché', *Cahiers d'Etudes Cathares* 29 (1978), pp.3–12.

Keen, M., *Chivalry* (New Haven, CT and London, 1984).

Kelly, H. A., 'Inquisition and the prosecution of heresy: misconceptions and abuses', *Church History* 58 (1989), pp.439–51.

Kieckhefer, R., 'The office of inquisition and medieval heresy: the transition from personal to institutional jurisdiction', *Journal of Ecclesiastical History* 46 (1995), pp.36–61.

Koch, G., *Frauenfrage und Ketzertum im Mittelalter. Die Frauenbewegung im Rahmen des Katharismus und des Waldensertums und ihre sozialen Wurseln (12.–14. Jahrhundert)* (Forschungen zur Mittelalterlichen Geschichte, 9) (Berlin, 1962).

Kölmer, L., *Ad Capiendas Vulpes. Die Ketzerbekämpfung in Südfrankreich in der ersten Hälfte des 13. Jahrhunderts und die Ausbildung des Inquisitionverfahrens* (Deutches Historisches Institut in Paris, Historische Studien, 19) (Bonn, 1982).

Lambert, M. D., *Medieval Heresy. Popular Movements from the Gregorian Reform to the Reformation*, 2nd edn (Oxford, 1992).

Lambert, M. D., *The Cathars* (Oxford, 1998).

Langlois, G., 'La Formation de la seigneurie de Termes', *Heresis* 17 (1991), pp.51–72.

Lansing, C., *Power and Purity. Cathar Heresy in Medieval Italy* (Oxford, 1998).

Lea, H. C., *A History of the Inquisition in the Middle Ages*, vol. 2 (New York, 1889).

Le Roy Ladurie, E., *Montaillou. Cathars and Catholics in a French Village, 1294–1324*, trans. B. Bray (London, 1978) (originally Paris, 1975).

Livingstone, E., ed., *The Oxford Dictionary of the Christian Church*, 3rd edn (Oxford, 1997).

Lobrichen, G., 'The chiaroscuro of heresy: early eleventh-century Aquitaine as seen from Auxerre', in T. Head and R. Landes, eds, *The Peace of God. Social Violence and Religious Response in France around the Year 1000* (Ithaca, NY and London, 1992), pp.80–103, 347–50.

Loos, M., *Dualist Heresy in the Middle Ages* (Prague, 1974).

Luttrell, A., 'The earliest Hospitallers', in B. Z. Kedar, J. Riley-Smith and R. Hiestand, eds, *Montjoie. Studies in Crusade History in Honour of Hans Eberhard Mayer* (Aldershot, 1997), pp.37–54.

McLellan, D., *Utopian Pessimist. The Life and Thought of Simone Weil* (New York, 1990).

Madaule, J., *The Albigensian Crusade* (London, 1967).

Magnou-Nortier, E., 'Fidelité et féodalité méridionales d'après les serments de Fidelité, Xe–début XIIe siècles', in *Les structures sociales de l'Aquitaine, du Languedoc et de l'Espagne au premier âge féodal* (Paris, 1969), pp.115–42.

Manselli, R., 'Les "chrétiens" de Bosnie: le catharisme en Europe orientale', *Revue d'histoire ecclésiastique* 72 (1977), pp.600–14.

Manselli, R., 'Evangelisme et mythe dans la foi Cathare', *Heresis* 5 (1985), pp.5–17.

Markus, R. A., 'Saint Augustine's views on the "Just War"', in W. J. Shiels, ed., *The Church and War. Studies in Church History* 20 (1983), pp.1–13.

Martel, P., 'Naissance de l'Occitanie', in A. Armengaud and R. Lafont, eds, *Histoire d'Occitanie* (Paris, 1979), pp.139–255.

Martel, P., 'Les Cathares et les historiens', in R. Lafont and R. Pech, eds, *Les Cathares en Occitanie* (Paris, 1982), pp.403–77.

Martel, P., 'Qui n'a pas son albigeois? Le souvenir de la Croisade et ses utilisations politiques', in *CEI*, pp.309–42.

Meer, F. van der, ed., *Atlas de l'Ordre Cistercien* (Paris and Brussels, 1965).

Molinier, C., *L'Inquisition dans le Midi de la France au XIIIe et au XIVe siècle* (Paris, 1880) (reprint 1974).

Moore, R. I., *The Origins of European Dissent*, new edn (Oxford, 1985) (originally 1977).

Morghen, R., *Medievo Cristiano* (Bari, 1951).

Morghen, R., 'Il Cosidetto neo-manicheismo occidentale del secolo XI', in *Convegno di Scienze Morali Storiche e Filologiche* (Rome, 1957), pp.84–104.

Morghen, R., 'Problèmes sur l'origine de l'hérésie au moyen âge', *Revue historique* 336 (1966), pp.1–16.

Mundy, J. H., *Liberty and Political Power in Toulouse, 1100–1230* (New York, 1954).

Mundy, J. H., 'Charity and social work in Toulouse, 1100–1250', *Traditio* 22 (1966), pp.203–88.

Mundy, J. H., 'Village, town and city in the region of Toulouse', in J. Raftis, ed., *Pathways to Medieval Peasants* (Toronto, 1981), pp.141–90.

Mundy, J. H., 'Urban society and culture: Toulouse and its region', in R. L. Benson and G. Constable, eds, *Renaissance and Renewal in the Twelfth Century* (Oxford, 1982), pp.229–47.

Mundy, J. H., *The Repression of Catharism at Toulouse. The Royal Diploma of 1279* (Studies and Texts, 74) (Toronto, 1985).

Mundy, J. H., *Men and Women at Toulouse in the Age of the Cathars* (Studies and Texts, 101) (Toronto, 1990).

Mundy, J. H., *Society and Government at Toulouse in the Age of the Cathars* (Studies and Texts, 129) (Toronto, 1997).

Nelli, S., 'L'Évêque Cathare, Guilhabert de Castres', *Heresis* 4 (1985), pp.11–24.

Nelli, S., *Montségur. Mythe et histoire* (Monaco, 1996).

Nelson, J. L., 'Religion in *"Histoire Totale"*: some recent works on medieval heresy and popular religion', *Religion* 10 (1980), pp.61–85.

Niel, F., *Albigeois et Cathares* (Que sais-je?) (Paris, 1955).

Niel, F., *Montségur. Temple et Forteresse des Cathares d'Occitanie* (Grenoble, 1967).

Obolensky, D., *The Bogomils* (Cambridge, 1948).

Obolensky, D., 'Papa Nicetas: a Byzantine dualist in the land of the Cathars', in *Okeanos: Essays Presented to Igor Sevčenko* (Harvard Ukrainian Studies, 7) (1983), pp.489–500.

O'Brien, J., 'Jews and Cathari in medieval France', *Comparative Studies in Society and History* 10 (1968), pp.215–20.

Oldenbourg, Z., *Massacre at Montségur. A History of the Albigensian Crusade*, trans. P. Green (London, 1961) (originally, *Le bûcher de Montségur*, 1959).

Painter, S., *William Marshal* (Baltimore, MD, 1933).

Paolini, L., 'Italian Catharism and written culture', in P. Biller and A. Hudson, eds, *Heresy and Literacy, 1000–1530* (Cambridge, 1994), pp.83–103.

Paterson, L., *The World of the Troubadours* (Cambridge, 1994).

Peal, A., 'Olivier de Termes and the Occitan nobility', *Reading Medieval Studies* 12 (1986), pp.109–29.

Pegg, M. G., *The Corruption of Angels: The Great Inquisition of 1245–46* (Ph.D diss., Princeton University, NJ, 1997).

Pegg, M. G., *The Corruption of Angels: The Great Inquisition of 1245–1246* (Princeton, NJ, 2001).

Peyrat, N., *Histoire des Albigeois. Les Albigeois et l'Inquisition*, 3 vols (Paris, 1870–72).

Poupin, R. 'De metempsycose en réincarnation ou la transmigration des âmes des temps cathares à nos jours', in *CEI*, pp.145–64.

Rahn, O., *Kreuzzug gegen den Gral* (Freiburg im Breisgau, 1933) (reprint 1985). Trans. R. Pitrou, *La Croisade contre le Graal (Grandeur et chute des Albigeois)*, new edn, C. Roy, preface R. Nelli (Paris, 1974).

Rahn, O., *Luzifers Hofgesind. Eine Reise zu Europas guten Geistern* (Leipzig and Berlin, 1937). Trans. R. Nelli, *La Cour de Lucifer. Les Cathares Gardiens du Graal* (Paris, 1974).

Renouard, Y., 'Les voies de communication entre la France et le Piémont au moyen âge', *Bullettino Storico-Bibliografico Subalpino* 61 (1963), pp.233–56.

Roach, A., 'The Cathar economy', *Reading Medieval Studies* 12 (1986), pp.51–71.

Roach, A., 'The Relationship of the Italian and Southern French Cathars, 1170–1320', (DPhil diss., Wolfson College, Oxford, 1989).

Roach, A., 'Occitania past and present: southern consciousness in medieval and modern French politics', *History Workshop Journal* 43 (1997), pp.1–22.

Roquebert, M., *L'Épopée cathare*, vol. 1, *1198–1212: L'Invasion* (Toulouse, 1970).

Roquebert, M., *L'Épopée cathare*, vol. 2, *1213–16: La Depossession* (Toulouse, 1977).

Roquebert, M., 'Le Catharisme comme tradition dans la "familia" languedocienne', in *CF* 20 (1985), pp.221–42.

Roquebert, M., *L'Épopée cathare*, vol. 3, *1216–1229: Le Lys et la croix* (Toulouse, 1986).

Roquebert, M., *L'Épopée cathare*, vol. 4, *1230–1249: Mourir à Montségur* (Toulouse, 1994).

Roquebert, M., *Les Cathares et le Graal* (Toulouse, 1994).

Roquebert, M., 'Napoléon Peyrat, le trésor et le nouveau Montségur', in *CEI*, pp.345–73.

Roquebert, M., *Les Cathares. De la chute de Montségur aux derniers bûchers (1244–1329)* (Paris, 1998).

Rottenwöhrer, G., *Die Katharismus*, 2 vols (Bad Honnef, 1982).

Rougemont, D. de, *Passion and Society*, 2nd edn, trans. M. Begion (London, 1956) (originally 1940).

Runciman, S., *The Medieval Manichee. A Study of Christian Dualist Theory* (Cambridge, 1955) (originally 1947).

Russell, F. H., *The Just War in the Middle Ages* (Cambridge, 1975).

Russell, J. B., 'Interpretations of the origins of medieval heresy', *Medieval Studies* 25 (1963), pp.25–53.

Russell, J. C., *Medieval Regions and Their Cities* (Newton Abbot, 1972).

Sanjek, F., 'L'Initiation Cathare dans l'Occident médiéval', *Heresis* 5 (1985), pp.19–27.

Sayers, J., *Innocent III: Leader of Europe, 1198–1216* (London, 1993).

Schmidt, C., *Histoire et doctrine de la secte des Cathares en Albigeois*, 2 vols (Paris and Geneva, 1848–49) (reprint with new introduction by J. Duvernoy, Bayonne, 1983).

Šemkov, G., 'Le Contexte socio-économique du Catharisme au Mas-Saintes-Puelles dans la première moitié du 13e siècle', *Heresis* 2 (1984), pp.35–53.

Shannon, A. C., *The Popes and Heresy in the Thirteenth Century* (Villanova, PA, 1949).

Shannon, A. C., *The Medieval Inquisition* (reprint Collegeville, MN, 1991).

Sharenkoff, V. N., *A Study of Manichaeism in Bulgaria* (New York, 1927).

Siberry, E., *Criticism of Crusading, 1095–1274* (Oxford, 1985).

Simonde de Sismondi, J. C. L., *History of the Crusades against the Albigenses in the Thirteenth Century* (London, 1826) (reprint New York, 1973) (trans. from parts of vols 6 and 7 of the author's *Histoire des Français*, publ. 1823 and 1826 respectively).

Söderberg, M., *La Religion des Cathares. Etude sur le Gnosticisme de la basse antiquité et du moyen âge* (Uppsala, 1949).

Stoyanov, Y. P., *The Hidden Tradition in Europe* (Harmondsworth, 1994).

Strayer, J., *The Albigensian Crusades* (New York, 1971).

Sumption, J., *The Albigensian Crusade* (London, 1978).

Thouzellier, C., 'Hérésie et croisade au XIIe siècle', *Revue d'Histoire Ecclésiastique* 49 (1954), pp.855–72.

Thouzellier, C., *Catharisme et Valdéisme en Languedoc à la fin du XIIe siècle et au début du XIIIe siècle*, 2nd edn (Louvain and Paris, 1969).

Tillmann, H., *Innocent III*, trans. W. Sax (Amsterdam, 1980) (originally 1954).

Touraine, A., 'Sociological interaction and the internal dynamics of the Occitanist movement', in E. A. Tiryakion and R. Rogowski, eds, *New Nationalisms of the Developed West* (London and Boston, MA, 1985), pp.157–75.

Ullmann, W., 'The significance of Innocent III's decretal "Vergentis"', in *Études d'histoire du droit canonique dédiées à Gabriel Le Bras* (Paris, 1965), pp.729–41.

Vicaire, M.-H., 'Les Albigeois ancêtres des protestants: assimilations catholiques', in *CF* 14 (1979), pp.23–46.

Vicaire, M.-H., 'Le Catharisme: un religion (1935–1976)', in *CF* 14 (1979), pp.381–409.

Vidal, J.-M., *Un Inquisiteur jugé par ses "victimes": Jean Galand et les Carcassonais, 1285–1286* (Paris, 1903).

Vidal, J.-M., 'Les Derniers ministres de l'albigéisme en Languedoc', *Revue des Questions historiques* 79 (1906), pp.57–107.

Vidal, J.-M., 'Doctrine et morale des derniers ministres albigeois', *Revue des Questions historiques* 85 (1909), pp.357–409; 86 (1909), pp.5–48.

Vidal, J.-M., 'Esclarmonde de Foix', *Revue de Gascogne* 11 (1911), pp.53–79.

Viguier, M.-C., 'Otto Rahn entre Wolfram von Eschenbach et les néo-Nazis', in *CEI*, pp.165–89.

Wakefield, W. L., 'The family of Niort in the Albigensian Crusade and before the Inquisition', *Names. The Journal of the American Name Society* 18 (1970), pp.97–117, 286–303 (and revised version, privately circulated in typescript, 1989).

Wakefield, W. L., 'Friar Ferrier, Inquisition at Caunes, and escapes from prison at Carcassonne', *Catholic Historical Review* 58 (1972), pp.220–37.

Wakefield, W. L., 'Some unorthodox popular ideas of the thirteenth century', *Medievalia et Humanistica* 4 (1973), pp.25–35.

Wakefield, W. L., *Heresy, Crusade and Inquisition in Southern France, 1100–1250* (London, 1974).

Wakefield, W. L., 'Heretics and inquisitors: the case of Le Mas-Saintes-Puelles', *Catholic Historical Review* 69 (1983), pp.209–26.

Wakefield, W. L., 'Burial of heretics in the Middle Ages', *Heresis* 5 (1985), pp.29–32.

Wakefield, W. L., 'Friar Ferrier, Inquisitor', *Heresis* 7 (1986), pp.33–41.

Walther, D., 'A survey of recent research on the Albigensian Cathari', *Church History* 34 (1965), pp.146–77.

Walther, D., 'Were the Albigenses and Waldenses forerunners of the Reformation?' *Andrews University Seminary Studies* 6 (1968), pp.178–202.

Weil, Simone, *Selected Essays, 1934–43*, trans. R. Rees (Oxford, 1962).

Weil, Simone, *Gateway to God*, ed. D. Raper (London, 1974).

Wolff, P., 'Rôle de l'essor économique dans les ralliement social et religieux', in *CF* 20 (1985), pp.243–55.

Zambon, F., 'Le Catharisme et les mythes du Graal', in *CEI*, pp.215–43.

Zeldin, T., *France, 1848–1945*, vol. 2, *Intellect, Taste and Anxiety* (Oxford, 1977).

# Table 1   The Albigensian Crusades: chronology

| | | |
|---|---|---|
| 1208 | 14 January | Murder of Peter of Castelnau, papal legate |
| | 28 March | Arnald Amalric, Abbot of Cîteaux, appointed leader of crusade |
| 1209 | 18 June | Reconciliation of Raymond VI of Toulouse |
| | 22 June | Raymond VI takes the cross |
| | Late June | Crusaders assemble at Lyon |
| | 22 July | Sack of Béziers by the crusaders |
| | 1 August | Crusaders reach Carcassonne |
| | 15 August | Surrender of Carcassonne |
| | Late August | Montfort chosen as Viscount of Béziers and Carcassonne |
| | 10 November | Death of Raymond Roger Trencavel |
| 1210 | Early June–22 July | Siege and capture of Minerve by the crusaders |
| | July–22 November | Siege and capture of Termes by the crusaders |
| 1211 | 22 January | Conference at Narbonne between Peter of Aragon, Raymond VI, Montfort, and the papal legates |
| | 6 February | Excommunication of Raymond VI at the Council of Montpellier |
| | March | Submission of Cabaret to Montfort |
| | 1 April–3 May | Siege and capture of Lavaur by the crusaders |
| | April | Massacre of crusaders at Montgey (near Puylaurens) by Raymond Roger, Count of Foix |
| | May | Puylaurens submits to Montfort. Siege and capture of Les Cassès |
| | 17–29 June | Montfort besieges Toulouse, but gives up |
| | September | Defeat of the count of Foix by the crusaders at St-Martin-Lalande |
| | September | Count of Toulouse fails to take Castelnaudary |
| 1212 | 12 March | Arnald Amalric becomes Archbishop of Narbonne |
| | April | Siege and capture of Hautpoul by the crusaders |
| | 20–21 May | Montfort captures St Antonin |
| | 3 June–26 July | Siege and capture of Penne d'Agenais by the crusaders |
| | 14 August– 8 September | Siege and capture of Moissac by the crusaders |
| | 1 December | Statutes of Pamiers |
| 1213 | Mid-January | Council of Lavaur, attended by Peter of Aragon, Montfort, and the legates |
| | 15 January | Innocent III instructs Montfort to return territories of counts of Foix, Comminges, and Gaston de Béarn |
| | 21 May | Innocent III revokes bulls of January |
| | 12 September | Battle of Muret |

| 1214 | February | Capture and hanging of Count Baldwin |
| | 28 June–18 August | Siege and capture of Casseneuil by the crusaders |
| | Early November | Fall of Sévérac to Montfort |
| 1215 | January | Council of Montpellier recommends that Montfort be invested with the county of Toulouse |
| | April–June | First expedition of Louis of France |
| | November | Fourth Lateran Council |
| | 30 November | Innocent III confirms Montfort as lord of Toulousan lands |
| 1216 | 8 March | Toulousans promise homage to Montfort |
| | April | Simon of Montfort in Melun and Paris |
| | June–August | Siege and capture of Beaucaire by Raymond, son of Raymond VI |
| | 16 July | Death of Innocent III |
| | September | Montfort establishes control over Toulouse |
| 1217 | 6 February–25 March | Siege and capture of Montgrenier by the crusaders |
| | 13 September | Raymond VI enters Toulouse. French confined to Narbonnais castle |
| 1218 | 25 June | Simon of Montfort killed at the siege of Toulouse |
| | 25 July | Crusaders depart from Toulouse |
| | Winter | Battle of Baziège. Young Raymond defeats the crusaders |
| 1219 | June | Second expedition of Louis of France. Fall of Marmande |
| | 16 June–1 August | Failure of Louis's siege of Toulouse |
| 1221 | February | Capture of Montréal by the forces of young Raymond |
| 1222 | August | Death of Raymond VI, Count of Toulouse |
| 1223 | March | Death of Raymond Roger, Count of Foix |
| | 14 July | Death of Philip II, King of France |
| | Summer | Truce between Raymond VII and Amaury of Montfort |
| 1224 | January | Raymond VII enters Carcassonne |
| 1225 | 30 November–December | Council of Bourges rejects claims of Raymond VII |
| 1226 | June–September | Crusade of Louis VIII |
| | 10 June–9 September | Siege of Avignon by Louis VIII |
| | September | Submission of the Marquisate of Provence, most of Languedoc east of Toulouse, the Gévaudan, Rouergue, and much of Quercy to Louis VIII |
| | 8 November | Death of Louis VIII, King of France |
| 1227 | Summer | Siege and capture of Labécède by royal forces |
| 1228 | Summer | Destruction of the land around Toulouse by Humbert of Beaujeu |
| 1229 | 12 April | Peace of Paris |

## Table 2 The Albigensian Crusades: Simon of Montfort's campaigns

| Siege/Battle | Date | Result | Heretics | Source |
|---|---|---|---|---|
| Preixan (Aude) | September 1209 | | | PVC, 120 |
| Puisserguier (Hérault) | November 1209 | | | PVC, 126 |
| Montlaur (Haute-Garonne) | March 1210 | | | PVC, 141 |
| Bram (Aude) | March 1210 | | Before 1209 | PVC, 142; Roquebert, 526 |
| Alaric (Aude) | c. 18 April 1210 | | | PVC, 145 |
| Foix (Ariège) | April 1210 | Fails | | PVC, 147 |
| Bellegarde (Aude) | May 1210 | | | PVC, 150 |
| Minerve (Hérault) | Early June–22 July 1210 | | Before 1209; 140 *perfecti* burnt; 3 women reconciled; all other inhabitants renounce heresy | PVC, 151–7; WT, 49; Roquebert, 531 |
| Termes (Aude) | Late July–22 November 1210 | | | PVC, 168–89; WT, 56–7 |
| Puivert (Aude) | 23–26 November 1210 | | Before 1209 | PVC, 192; Roquebert, 533 |
| Lavaur (Tarn) | 1 April–3 May 1211 | | Before 1209; 300–400 heretics burnt; 80 knights hanged | PVC, 214–16, 222–7; WT, 67–8, 71; WP, XVI; Roquebert, 530 |
| Les Cassès (Aude) | May 1211 | | Before 1209; 50–60 *perfecti* burnt | PVC, 233, 392; WP, XVII; Roquebert, 527 |
| Montferrand (Aude) | May 1211 | | | PVC, 235 |
| Toulouse (Haute-Garonne) | 17–29 June 1211 | Fails | Before 1209 | PVC, 239–43; WT, 80–3; Roquebert, 536 |
| Caylus (Tarn-et-Garonne) | July 1211 | | | PVC, 247 |
| Unidentified, near Pamiers (Ariège) | July 1211 | | | PVC, 250 |
| Castelnaudary (Aude) | September 1211 | | Before 1209 | PVC, 253–76; Mem. 1209; Roquebert, 527 |
| Saint-Martin-Lalande (Aude) (B) | September 1211 | | Before 1209 | PVC, 270–3; WT, 94–103; WP, XVIII; Mem. 1209; Roquebert, 534 |
| La Pomarède (Aude) | December 1211 | | | PVC, 288 |
| Les Touelles (Tarn) | January 1212 | | | PVC, 291 |

| Place | Date | Result | Before 1209 | References |
|---|---|---|---|---|
| Cahuzac (Tarn) | January 1212 | | Before 1209 | PVC, 292; Mem. 1209; Roquebert, 526 |
| Saint-Marcel (Tarn) | Late February–23 March 1212 | Fails | Before 1209 | PVC, 294–6; WT, 113; Mem. 1209; Roquebert, 534 |
| Hautpoul (Tarn) | 8–12 April 1212 | | | PVC, 301–4 |
| Saint-Antonin (Tarn-et-Garonne) | 20–21 May 1212 | | | PVC, 314–16 |
| Penne d'Agenais (Lot-et-Garonne) | 3 June–25 July 1212 | | | PVC, 321–33; WT, 114–15 |
| Biron (Dordogne) | July 1212 | | | PVC, 337; WT, 116 |
| Moissac (Tarn-et-Garonne) | 14 August–8 September 1212 | | | PVC, 340–53; WT, 117–24 |
| Muret (Haute-Garonne) (B) | 12 September 1213 | | | PVC, 448–83; AC, 140–1; WP, XXI |
| Le Mas d'Agenais (Lot-et-Garonne) | 13–16 April 1214 | Fails | | PVC, 505 |
| Morlhon (Aveyron) | Early summer 1214 | | | PVC, 513 |
| Marmande (Lot-et-Garonne) | Early summer 1214 | | | PVC, 518 |
| Casseneuil (Lot-et-Garonne) | 28 June–19 August 1214 | | | PVC, 519–27 |
| Sévérac-le-Château (Aveyron) | October–early November 1214 | | | PVC, 538–41 |
| Castelnaud (Lot-et-Garonne) | Late summer 1215 | | | PVC, 569 |
| Beaucaire (Gard) | 6 June–24 August 1216 | Fails | | PVC, 579–84; AC, 156–71; WP, XXVI |
| Toulouse (Haute-Garonne) | November 1216 | | | PVC, 585–7; AC, 171–9; WP, XXVII |
| Lourdes (Hautes-Pyrénées) | 6 November 1216 | Fails | | AC, 180 |
| Montgrenier (Ariège) | 6 February–25 March 1217 | | | PVC, 589–90; AC, 180 |
| Posquières (Gard) | Mid-summer 1217 | | | PVC, 594; AC, 180 |
| Bernis (Gard) | Mid-summer 1217 | | | PVC, 594; AC, 180 |
| Port St Saturnin (Vaucluse) | Mid-July 1217 | | | PVC, 595 |
| Crest (Drôme) | September 1217 | Settlement | | PVC, 598–9; AC, 180 |
| Toulouse (Haute-Garonne) | 1 October 1217–25 July 1218 (Montfort killed 25 June) | Fails | | PVC, 600–14; AC, 187–207; WP, XXVIII |

AC    Anonymous continuator of the *Chanson*

Mem. 1209    Memorandum of 1209, in *Cartulaire du Maguelonne*, vol. 2, ed. J. Roquette and A. Villemagne (Montpellier, 1913), no. CCC, pp.59–60.

PVC    Peter of Les Vaux-de-Cernay

WP    William of Puylaurens

WT    William of Tudela

Before 1209    M. Roquebert, *L'Épopée cathare*, vol. 1, *1198–1212: L'Invasion* (Toulouse, 1970), Appendice, pp.525–37.

# Table 3   The Autier revival: chronology

| | | |
|---|---|---|
| 1234 | | Peter and Raymond Autier named as Cathars |
| 1295 | | Bernard Saisset becomes first bishop of Pamiers |
| 1296 | | Peter and William Autier, brothers, leave for Lombardy |
| 1299 | | The Autier brothers return to Ax from Lombardy |
| *c.* 1299 | | The Autiers console Prades Tavernier |
| 1299 or 1300 | | Peter Autier goes to Toulouse |
| 1300 | | The Autiers are denounced to the Dominicans in Pamiers by William Déjean, a beguin, but escape after a warning. William Déjean later murdered by two believers |
| 1301 | | Peter and William console James, Peter's son, and Pons Bayle of Ax |
| 1302 | March | Peter Autier consoles Roger Bernard III, Count of Foix, on his death-bed |
| | | Peter Autier goes to Cahors to hereticate two believers |
| *c.* 1303 | | Geoffrey of Ablis becomes Inquisitor at Carcassonne |
| 1303–5 | | Extensive coverage of the Lauragais, and the valleys of the Agout and the Tarn by Peter Autier |
| 1305 | | Peter Autier at Toulouse, where he holds a meeting of believers at the church of Sainte-Croix |
| | 8 September | James Autier and Prades Tavernier betrayed and imprisoned at Carcassonne, but they escape |
| | Christmas | Believers from Arques reconciled by Pope Clement V at Lyons |
| 1306 | All Saints | Peter Autier consoles Peter Sanche, former *nuntius* |
| 1307 | 16 January | Bernard Gui becomes Inquisitor at Toulouse |
| 1308 | September | All the adult population of Montaillou taken to Carcassonne to depose about the Autiers |
| | 29 September–18 May 1309 | Peter Autier and Peter Sanche forced to hide for eight months because of the pressure of the Inquisition |
| 1309 | Spring | Capture of William Belibaste and Philip of Alairac. Imprisoned at Carcassonne, but escape soon after, and flee to Catalonia |
| | | Peter Autier consoles Sanche Mercadier |

| | | |
|---|---|---|
| | 23 May | Inquisition goes to the farm of Bertrand Salas, near Verlhac-Tescon (south-west of Montauban), where Peter Autier and Peter Sanche have been hiding, but they have gone |
| | May–end August | Peter Autier hiding at Beaupuy, the home of the Maurel brothers |
| | 10 August | Bernard Gui issues mandate for the arrest of Peter Autier, Peter Sanche, and Sanche Mercadier |
| | Early September | Peter Autier delivered to Inquisition by betrayal of Peter of Luzenac. Taken to Toulouse and then Carcassonne |
| | Late December | Most of the rest of the group arrested William Autier burnt to death |
| 1310 | 9 April | Peter Autier burnt to death |
| 1314 | | Death of the *bonhomme*, Raymond of Toulouse |
| *c.* 1315 | | William Belibaste settles at Morella in Valencia |
| 1317 | 19 March | James Fournier becomes bishop of Pamiers |
| 1318 | | Beginning of the Fournier investigations Arnold Sicre makes contact with William Belibaste |
| 1320 | Early | Arnold Sicre goes to James Fournier at Pamiers and receives commission from him to bring back William Belibaste |
| | Christmas | William Belibaste agrees to travel to the Palhars to see Alazais, aunt of Arnold Sicre |
| 1321 | Mid-Lent | Capture of William Belibaste at Tirvia (west of Andorra) |
| | Spring | William Belibaste burnt to death at Villerouge-Termènes (south of Carcassonne) |
| 1322 | 13 January | Arnold Sicre exonerated of all blame for association with heretics |
| 1324 | 12 August | Peter and John Maury sentenced to perpetual prison |

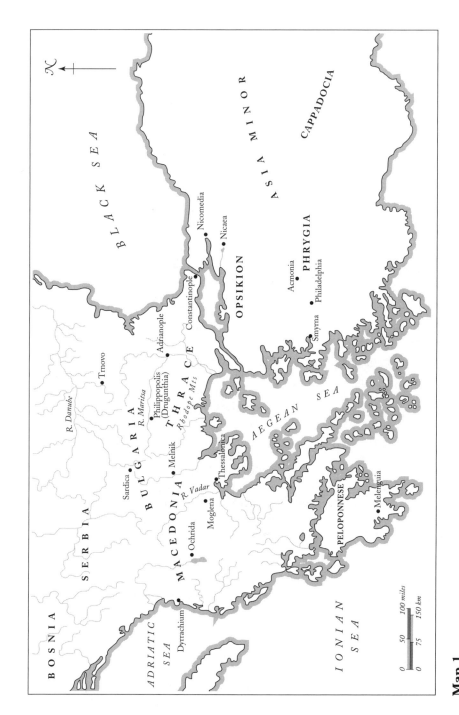

**Map 1**
The Bogomils in the Byzantine Empire

260

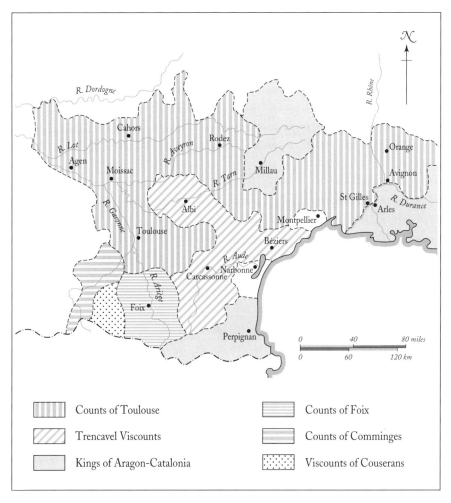

**Map 2**
The political structure of Languedoc before the Albigensian Crusades

Counts of Toulouse

Trencavel Viscounts

Kings of Aragon-Catalonia

Counts of Foix

Counts of Comminges

Viscounts of Couserans

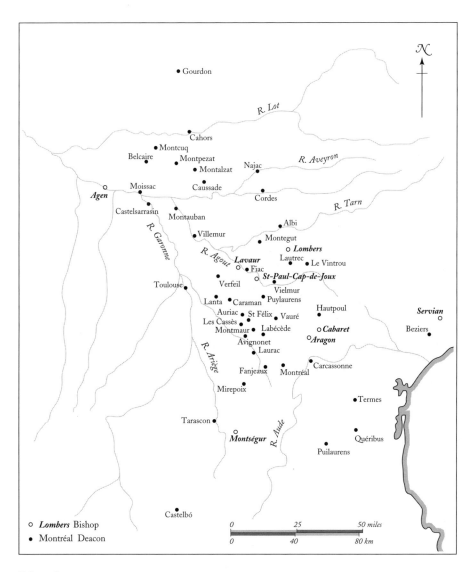

Gourdon

R. Lot

Cahors
Montcuq
Belcaire • Montpezat
Montalzat
Najac
R. Aveyron

Moissac
Agen
Caussade
Cordes
R. Tarn

Castelsarrasin
Montauban
Villemur
Albi
Montegut
R. Garonne
R. Agout
Lombers
Lavaur
Lautrec • Le Vintrou
Fiac
St-Paul-Cap-de-Joux
Toulouse
Verfeil
Vielmur
Lanta • Caraman Puylaurens
Auriac • St Félix • Vauré
Hautpoul
Servian
Les Cassès
Montmaur • Labécède
Cabaret
Beziers
Avignonet
Aragon
R. Ariège
Laurac
Fanjeaux • Montréal
Carcassonne
Mirepoix
Termes
Tarascon
R. Aude
Quéribus
Montségur
Puilaurens

Castelbó

○ *Lombers* Bishop
• Montréal Deacon

0          25          50 miles
0        40        80 km

# Map 3

The geography of Catharism in Languedoc

These represent the known sites during the thirteenth century and were therefore not all operating simultaneously

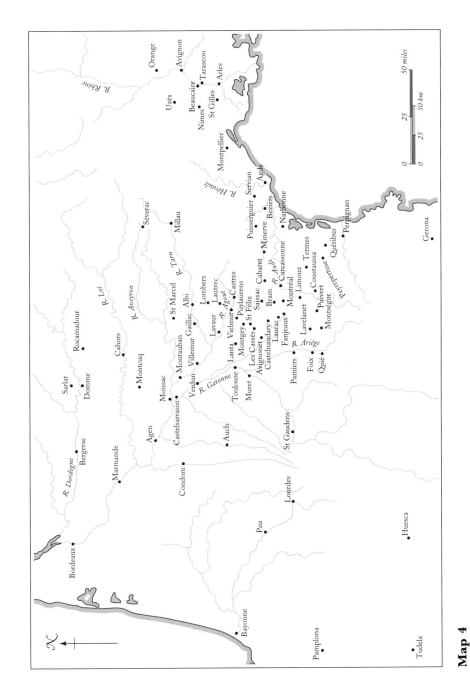

**Map 4**
Territories affected by the Albigensian Crusades

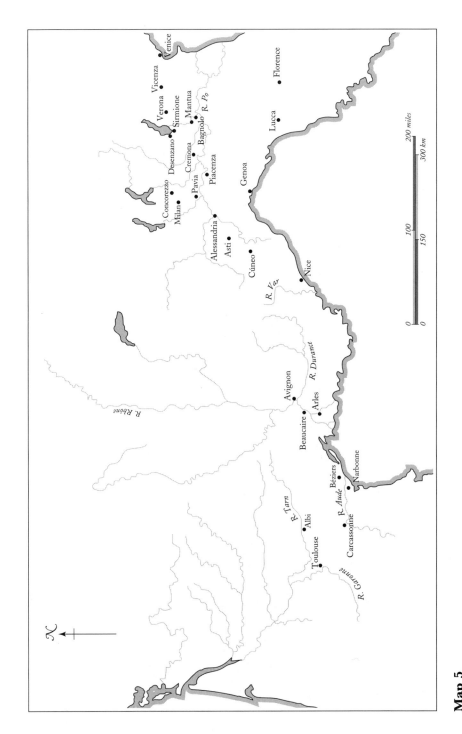

**Map 5**

The Italian connection: the links between Languedoc and Lombardy in the thirteenth century

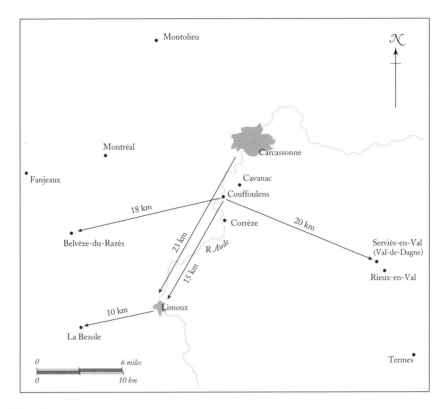

**Map 6**

The milieu of the Cathar Bonhomme, Bernard Acier of Couffoulens, 1241–59

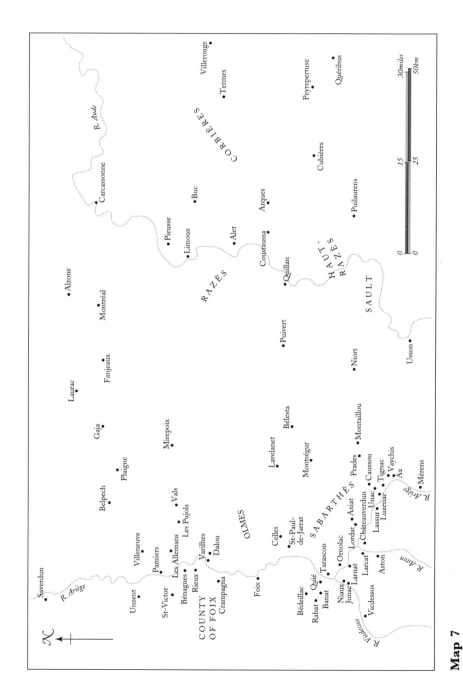

**Map 7**

The world of the Autier revival, 1299–1321

# INDEX

Acmonia, diocese, 19
Acqui, 195
*Ad Abolendam*, papal bull (1184), 115
Adelaide, wife of Roger II of Trencavel,
   39–40, 49, 50
Adelbert of Uzès, Bishop of Nîmes
   (1141–80), 60
Adhemar of Chabannes, chronicler, 29
Adriatic, 116
Agde, Catholic diocese, 50
Agen, 66, 142
   Cathar diocese, 21, 27, 28n., 59, 72, 74,
     135
   Catholic diocese, 59, 142
   *consuls*, 67
Agenais, 40, 45, 130, 134, 169
*L'Agonie du Languedoc*, recording, 221
Agout, river, 38, 40, 142, 181
Aguilar, 160, 164
Aigrefeuille, 153
Aillon, 181
Aimery, lord of Montréal, 35–8, 41–2, 56,
   159, 225
Aix, archbishopric, 107
Alan of Lille, theologian and poet, 95
Alan of Roucy, crusader, 135, 160
Alashehr, *see* Philadelphia
Alazais, sister of Sibylla den Balle, 199
Alazais of Vernaux, 200–1
Albanenses, 88–9
Albi, 46, 49, 66–7, 88, 113, 118, 124, 140,
   142, 148, 151, 190–2, 195
   Cathar diocese, 21, 27, 59, 71–2, 135,
     165, 190
   cathedral of St Cecilia, 192
   Catholic diocese, 49, 59, 142, 148, 169
   *consuls*, 67, 191–2, 195
   Hospitaller commandery, 61
Albigensian Crusades (1209–29), 4, 6,
   34, 40n., 41, 46, 53, 63, 70, 94, 96,
   107–11, 113, 120–40, 146, 174,
   205–6, 208, 211, 217–18, 220–2

Albigeois, 6, 35, 43, 114, 134, 190
Aldricus of Bando, 32
Alessandria, 166
Alexander III, pope (1159–81), 60, 112,
   113
Alexander IV, pope (1254–61), 175,
   190
Alexander, Abbot of Cîteaux, 49, 71
Alexiopolis, 17
Alexius I Comnenus, Byzantine emperor
   (1081–1118), 17–21
Alfonso II, King of Aragon and Count of
   Barcelona (1162–96), 46
Alfonso-Jordan, Count of Toulouse
   (1105–48), 31, 45, 50, 112
Alice of Montmorency, wife of Simon of
   Montfort, 39, 123
allods, 55
Alphonse of Poitiers, Count of Toulouse
   (1249–71), 68, 99, 141–2, 174–5
Alps, 45, 166, 167, 201–2
Alzalais, Cathar *perfecta*, 41
Amanianus of Grisinhac, Archbishop of
   Auch (1226–42), 121
Amaury of Montfort (d.1241), 123, 134,
   139, 142
Amiel of Perles, Cathar *perfectus*, 104n.
Anatolia, 9
Andorra, 199
Andreas Cholert, royal seneschal, 153
Andreas of Prades, *see* Prades Tavernier
Angebert, Jean-Michel, *Hitler et la tradition
   cathare* (trans. *The Occult and the Third
   Reich*), 210
Angelarius, missionary to Bulgaria, 15
angels, 1, 7–8, 13, 18, 84, 87, 90–1
Angevin rulers, 37, 45
Angold, Michael, historian, 20
Anguelou, Dimitur, historian, 16
animals, 90, 91n., 98
Anjou, 109
Anna Comnena, *The Alexiad*, 17–21, 83

INDEX

Cosmas the Priest, *Treatise against the Bogomils*, 12–17, 19, 23, 25, 26, 30n., 70, 80
Coterelli, 57
Coudens, 153
Couffoulens, 171–2
Couserans, 73
  Catholic diocese, 59
Coustaussa, 104, 159, 184, 196
creation, 1, 7, 10, 18–19, 83–4, 86, 89–90, 98, 100
*credentes*, 1, 23–4, 115, 166–7, 173, 182, 187, 197–201
Cremona, 73, 168n.
Cubières, 198
Cumans, 17
Cúneo, 32, 166–8, 180
*Cupientes*, statute (1229), 144
Cyril, St, missionary to the Slavs (d.819), 15

Dalmatia, 116
  Cathar diocese, 20
deacons, Cathar, 1, 40, 74–5, 135, 173n., 190
debates
  between Cathars and Catholics, 35, 36, 49, 119
  between Cathars and Waldensians, 35
*De heresi catharorum*, anonymous Lombard treatise, 7, 8n., 21–2, 33, 73–4, 81
Delaruelle, Etienne, historian, 158
demons, 10
Desenzano, Cathar diocese, 73, 86, 88, 165
Desiderius, Elder Son of the Cathar Church of Concorezzo, 86
Devil, the, 2, 7, 8, 13–14, 18–19, 34, 44, 83, 84–5, 87, 90, 96–8, 100–1, 104
Diego, Bishop of Osma (1201–7), 6, 9, 35, 36, 88, 119–20
dioceses
  Cathar, 1, 7–8n., 20, 21–2, 27, 28n., 59, 71–4, 104, 115, 142, 165
  Catholic, 49, 59–60, 68, 142
Domairon, Louis, historian, 65
Dominic Guzman, St (d.1221), 105, 110, 119
Dominic, companion of Peter of Verona, 168
Dominicans, 101, 146–9, 152, 154, 168, 169, 174, 177, 180, 196
Domme, 130
donatist heresy, 22, 31, 81
Dondaine, Antoine, historian, 7n., 22–3

Dordogne, 130, 132, 134
Dragovitsa, 20, 73
  *see also* Drugunthia
Drugunthia, Bogomil diocese, 8n., 20, 21–2, 28, 71, 73, 74
dualism, 69, 74, 201, 211
  mitigated or moderate, 2, 7–9, 7–8n., 15, 20, 71, 73, 80, 81, 83–5, 86–8, 103, 142, 202
  absolute, 2, 7–8n., 9, 10, 20, 71, 73, 81, 86–93, 96, 103, 142, 202
*ductores, see nuntii*
Dun, Cathar house, 52
Durand, Bishop of Albi (1228–54), 158
Durand of Huesca (d.c.1237), 96n.
  *Liber contra Manicheos*, 88–91
Durand of St Ybars, Vicar of Toulouse, 153
Dutton, Claire, historian, 135
Duvernoy, Jean, historian, 8n., 69n., 103, 158

Eaunes, abbey, 159
Eberwin, Premonstratensian Prior of Steinfeld (near Cologne), 23–4, 25
Eckbert, Abbot of Schönau, *Sermones contra Catharos*, 25–6, 28, 76
Eco, Umberto, philologist and novelist, 211
Edessa, 10
Egypt, 206
  crusade of Louis IX (1248–50), 164
Eleanor of Aragon, wife of Raymond VI, Count of Toulouse, 54
Elijah, 85
Elizabeth of Schönau, St, 28
Elne, 72, 155
  Catholic diocese, 59
Embrun, archbishopric, 107
Emma of Provence, wife of William III, Count of Toulouse, 45
endogamy, 69n.
*endura*, 103–4, 188, 204
Enoch, 84
Ermengaud of Béziers, Waldensian, 88n., 96n.
Esclarmonda of Foix, sister of Raymond Roger, Count of Foix, Cathar *perfecta*, 51–2, 138, 208–9
Esclarmonda, wife of William of Niort, 35, 38
Esshaura of Larcat, 177
Eucharist, 13, 14, 23–5, 26, 29, 30, 31, 112
Eugenius III, pope (1145–53), 112

271